D0687388

The Economies of Southeast Asia,
Second Edition

The Economies of Southeast Asia, Second Edition

Before and After the Crisis

Jose L. Tongzon

*Associate Professor, Department of Economics,
National University of Singapore, Singapore*

Edward Elgar
Cheltenham, UK • Northampton, MA, USA

Published by
Edward Elgar Publishing Limited
Glensanda House
Montpellier Parade
Cheltenham
Glos GL50 1UA
UK

Edward Elgar Publishing, Inc.
136 West Street
Suite 202
Northampton
Massachusetts 01060
USA

A catalogue record for this book
is available from the British Library

Library of Congress Cataloguing in Publication Data

Tongzon, Jose L., 1951–
  The economies of Southeast Asia: before and after the crisis/
  Jose L. Tongzon. – 2nd ed.
    p. cm.
  Includes bibliographical references and index.
    1. Asia, Southeastern—Economic conditions. 2. Asia, Southeastern—
  Economic integration. I. Title.
HC441. T663 2002
330.959—dc21   2002022846

ISBN   1 84064 318 8 (cased)
       1 84064 952 6 (paperback)

Typeset by Cambrian Typesetters, Frimley, Surrey
Printed and bound in Great Britain by Biddles Ltd, *www.biddles.co.uk*

Contents

Figures

Tables

Preface and acknowledgements

Since the first edition of my book, *The Economies of Southeast Asia: the Growth and Development of ASEAN Economies* (1998), was published, major economic developments affecting the countries of Southeast Asia have unfolded. The Asian economic crisis in particular, which hit the region in 1997 and 1998, has had significant economic implications for these countries so that another edition is required to incorporate this event and its aftermath.

The new title for this book, *The Economies of Southeast Asia: Before and After the Crisis*, is appropriate because it attempts to analyse the economic development experiences of the member countries of the Association of Southeast Asian Nations (ASEAN) in the context of ASEAN economic cooperation before and after the 1997 crisis. Apart from the traditional issues of concern to ASEAN such as domestic capital development, environmental implications of continued industrialization and prospects for and challenges of an ASEAN Free Trade Area (AFTA), this book will also analyse the economic implications of China's accession to the World Trade Organization (WTO) for the ASEAN countries, their growth prospects in the aftermath of the crisis and other challenges facing ASEAN as an institution.

Some words of gratitude and acknowledgements are expressed to all the people and institutions who in one way or another have helped me in the process of completing this new edition. In particular, I wish to thank the ASEAN Secretariat for providing me with access to their trade data on the individual member countries, the National University of Singapore for the computer and library resources made available in writing this new edition, and all those who have read the first edition of this book whose constructive comments have encouraged me to write its second edition.

Last, but not least, I would like to extend my sincerest thanks to all those who have provided me with moral support and the inspiration to complete this second edition, especially my wife, whose understanding has lightened the burden of writing this manuscript, my lovable and sweet daughter, who has brought joy and meaning into my life and of course my dear parents, who have given me life and without whose love and guidance I would not have been where I am.

Overview

Throughout the second half of the 1980s and the entire decade of the 1990s we have witnessed a spectacular economic performance by most of the founding members of the Association of Southeast Asian Nations (ASEAN), only to be interrupted by an economic crisis which severely gripped the Southeast Asian region in the years 1997 and 1998.[1] For instance, for the period of 1987 to 1992 the growth rates of the ASEAN5 (Indonesia, Malaysia, the Philippines, Singapore and Thailand) had averaged 7.3 percent. This average growth rate was well above that posted by the developed market economies (2.8 percent) as a group, above that achieved by North America (2.5 percent) and generally above the world growth rate (2.2 percent).

As a result of their high growth rates, their standards of living, as measured by their per capita incomes and other quality of life indicators, have vastly improved. Over the same pre-crisis period the per capita income of the ASEAN5 countries grew on average by 5.1 percent, although the individual country experiences varied with Thailand posting a remarkable growth of 8.3 percent, followed by Singapore (6.4 percent). The Philippines, because of its numerous economic and political problems in the 1980s, only managed to grow in per capita terms by less than 1 percent during the same period. But overall they have graduated from the ranks of low-income countries, as classified by the World Bank, to the ranks of middle- and in some cases upper-middle-income countries. Singapore in particular has enjoyed the highest per capita income among the five ASEAN countries and subsequently attained the advanced developing country status by 1996. Malaysia was well on its way to becoming one, while Indonesia and Thailand were deemed to be on the threshold of significant economic transformation, and the Philippines was well on its way to a robust economic recovery. Accompanying this spectacular growth was a significant structural change, poverty alleviation and improved level of income distribution. Their success story has become a model to emulate for many developing countries so that their development experiences have been the subject of many studies.

The Asian economic crisis, which started in July 1997, has put a brake on the momentum of ASEAN economic progress, and has created some doubt about the soundness of their development strategies. In 1997 and 1998, their growth rates had either substantially declined or had become negative. As a result, their standards of living deteriorated. Poverty incidence, which was significantly reduced before the crisis, has again become a significant problem particularly for the hardest-hit economies of Thailand, Indonesia and Malaysia. However, the years 1999 and 2000 remarkably saw some signs of economic recovery for the region.[2]

What did these countries do to achieve this remarkable growth and economic development? What factors accounted for their differences in economic development experiences? Explaining their economic growth and development has been the subject of many empirical studies. All these studies pointed to a number of factors such as high saving rates, massive inflow of foreign capital, export-oriented industrialization policies, political and economic stability and others. How are these factors interrelated? What were the underlying factors behind their economic success?

To what extent was this economic success attributable to ASEAN economic cooperation? If so, what kind of cooperation? This issue on ASEAN cooperation requires a formal analysis in the light of many years of attempts to forge regional cooperation among the ASEAN countries. It has been argued that, although intra-ASEAN trade has not been particularly significant, there has been peace and security in the ASEAN region largely due to the growing mutual trust, understanding and cooperative efforts of these countries. This socio-political environment has allowed the market forces to work effectively and, with the export-oriented development strategies adopted, has contributed to the spectacular economic performances of these countries. Despite their varied stages of economic development and differences in development priorities, they were successful in forging economic cooperation not only in various productive sectors but also in their dealings with their traditional trading partners. By developing common positions and a united stance in their negotiations with the US, Japan, the European Union (EU), Australia and other developing countries on matters of market access, investments and security, they have strengthened their bargaining power and have made the ASEAN countries a significant force in international fora.

After many years of substantial economic progress, how did the 1997 Asian crisis come about? What economic and social implications did the crisis have for the ASEAN economies? In the midst of a rapidly changing international environment, what future challenges and opportunities are they likely to face? Will the ASEAN cooperation and solidarity evolve into a higher level? What opportunities and challenges do the admission of the transitional economies of Vietnam, Laos, Myanmar and Cambodia into ASEAN present? How can the ASEAN countries achieve sustainable growth and development?

This book attempts to answer all these questions while tracing the economic development experiences of the ASEAN countries in the context of their economic development aspirations. Due to insufficient data on Brunei, and the transitional economies of Vietnam, Laos, Myanmar and Cambodia, the focus is on the five original members of ASEAN (ASEAN5). However, an attempt is made to give the most comprehensive coverage, as data availability permits.

As a useful background to the formation of this regional grouping, it first explains the evolution of the regional cooperation in Southeast Asia and ASEAN's institutional structure in Chapter 1. Then, it proceeds with a review of the structural changes occurring in the ASEAN economies during the period of high economic growth in Chapter 2. After a general assessment of their remarkable economic success, in Chapter 3 it examines the extent to which their economic development experiences have been attributable to ASEAN cooperation. Four major sectors are selected for more detailed analysis: trade, manufacturing, agriculture, and services. Chapter 4 takes a closer look at sub-regional cooperation within ASEAN in the form of economic growth triangles. Chapter 5 discusses in detail the role of government in ASEAN. Chapter 6 examines ASEAN external economic relations, particularly with their major export markets of the US, Japan and the European Union, and their newly emerging markets of China and Vietnam in bilateral contexts. Chapter 7 evaluates the implications of other regional trading arrangements (RTAs) for ASEAN. Chapter 8 looks at the issue of regionalism as an approach to achieving global free trade and the role of the World Trade Organization. Chapter 9 examines further the role of foreign investments in ASEAN economic development. Chapter 10 re-examines the causes and impacts of the Asian crisis. Chapter 11 evaluates the prospects and future of ASEAN economic cooperation. Chapter 12 explores the economic and political implications of the admission of Vietnam, Laos, Myanmar and Cambodia into ASEAN and AFTA. Chapter 13 looks at the role of domestic capital in ASEAN economic growth and explores the impact of growth on their environment and the various measures to deal with it. Chapter 14 explores the economic implications of China's accession to the World Trade Organization (WTO), and Chapter 15 evaluates the economic recovery and long-run growth prospects of the ASEAN countries.

NOTES

1. ASEAN now encompasses all countries of Southeast Asia consisting of Indonesia, Malaysia, the Philippines, Singapore, Thailand, Brunei (which has joined the grouping since 1984), Vietnam, Laos, Myanmar and Cambodia, the most recent member, which joined the grouping in 1999.
    The spectacular growth of ASEAN is part of the overall phenomenal rise of the East Asian economies. Today, the nominal share of East Asia in world output is comparable with North

America and Europe (EU-15), when in 1980 its nominal share was only about half of North America or Europe (*The Straits Times*, 9 October 1996, p. 38).

2. Indonesia, which faces the most difficult challenge in getting its economy into a sustainable path of economic recovery due mainly to its enormous problem of political and social instability, was predicting a growth rate of 4 percent for the year 2000 (*The Straits Times*, 19 January 2000, p. 63).

PART ONE

ASEAN Economic Development and
Cooperation Before the Crisis

1. Evolution of ASEAN cooperation and institutional structure

On 8 August, 1967 in Bangkok, the Association of Southeast Asian Nations (ASEAN) was born. Its formation, however, and the level of commitment it requires of its members did not occur without any difficulties. It went through a painful process of transcending differences (differences in linguistic, religious, historical and economic backgrounds) and of working towards compromises. Reflecting the evolution of ASEAN cooperation is its concomitant institutional structure. Its present institutional machinery is a product, to a large extent, of the ASEAN determination to enhance ASEAN political and economic cooperation, reflecting its changing vision and objectives. Since 1967 it has gone through some modifications in an attempt to provide an institutional environment supportive of greater ASEAN cooperation.

1.1 PRE-ASEAN ORGANIZATIONS

Before the formation of the Association of Southeast Asian Nations (ASEAN) in 1967, there were few attempts at developing forms of regional cooperation in response to certain political and economic events. These pre-ASEAN organizations have a pronounced bearing on ASEAN's formation and development.

1.1.1 SEATO (1954–77)

The Southeast Asian Treaty Organization (SEATO) emerged out of a conference in Manila in 1954 which was held shortly after the Geneva Conference on Indochina following the victory of the Viet Minh over the French colonizers. Initiated by the US and dominated by Western powers (only the Philippines and Thailand were full members from Southeast Asia), this was part of the worldwide US-led system of anti-communist military alliances or security arrangements. SEATO elicited criticisms not only from the Soviet Union and China, but also from the non-communist countries of Southeast Asia including Indonesia. With the military withdrawal of the US military forces from Vietnam, SEATO came to an end in 1977.

1.1.2   ASPAC (1966–73)

Organized in 1966 at the initiative of South Korea, the Asian and Pacific Council (ASPAC) was another major example of a multi-regional organization designed to bring together most of the leading non-communist nations of the Western Pacific to deal with external threats and to provide a framework for more widespread cooperation. Only four of its members were Southeast Asian states – Malaysia, the Philippines, South Vietnam and Thailand. Indonesia refused to join. This was dissolved in 1973.

1.1.3   ASA (30.07.61–16.09.63)

As a first attempt by countries of Southeast Asia to form a regional cooperation, the Association of Southeast Asia (ASA) was formed on 30 July, 1961 at the instigation of the former Prime Minister of Malaya, Tunku Abdul Rahman in 1959, with very limited membership (that was composed of Malaya, the Philippines and Thailand) and a set of economic objectives (that is to promote cooperation in economic and cultural areas). This was later dissolved on 16 September, 1963 with the formation of the Federation of Malaysia comprising Malaya, Sabah, Sarawak and Singapore. The Philippines, which had a longstanding claim on Sabah, did not recognize the enlarged Federation. Further, it did not get any support from Indonesia under the regime of the late President Sukarno who was against the formation of the Federation of Malaysia.

1.1.4   MAPHILINDO (31.07.63–16.09.63)

As a rival organization to ASA, this organization, consisting of Malaya, the Philippines and Indonesia, was established at a Conference held in Manila on 31 July, 1963 to promote cooperation in economic, military, cultural and social fields and primarily designed for the welfare of the MELAYU region in Southeast Asia. This was shortlived (more than a month old) when the Federation of Malaysia came into being. Neither the Philippines nor Indonesia recognized the new Federation. Sukarno soon launched a guerilla war against Malaysia which led to a bitter and sometimes bloody confrontation. This lasted until Sukarno's fall in 1967. It did not get support from non-Malay members of the region as it was perceived to be for the promotion of the Melayu region.

   Thus, the early attempts failed due to nationalism, lack of mutual trust and regional identity, territorial claims and conflicting perceptions of the regional political order.

1.2 FORMATION OF ASEAN

The formation of ASEAN was officially opened at the signing of the Bangkok Declaration on 8 August, 1967 by the five countries of Indonesia, Malaysia, the Philippines, Singapore and Thailand. Brunei joined the grouping later, in 1984. Political and economic considerations have influenced these countries to form a regional cooperation. All the signatory countries saw the need to foster their economic development and promote regional security in the face of a growing communist threat in Southeast Asia, precipitated by the fall of IndoChina to communism and the declared intention of the West to withdraw their military forces from the region. Their common objectives could be best achieved through mutual cooperation in the economic, social and cultural areas.

1.2.1 Overcoming Obstacles

A number of obstacles were in the way of the formation of ASEAN and during the initial stages of development of the ASEAN cooperation. These countries have had diverse colonial traditions and influences. The American colonization of the Philippines and the Dutch colonization of Indonesia have produced legal and political systems in their respective economies quite diverse from those in Malaysia and Singapore which were colonized by the British. Only Thailand was not colonized by a foreign power. Further, their pre-independence and post-independence problems such as ethnic pluralism, communist insurgency and irredentism (for example, the Philippine claim on Sabah) have called for nationalism rather than regionalism.

There are also different economic priorities arising from their different stages of economic development and differences in factor endowments. Singapore was striving for full employment, and due to its small domestic market has been pursuing an export-oriented strategy with heavy reliance on foreign investments since its separation from the Federation of Malaysia. The other ASEAN countries, particularly Indonesia, the Philippines and Thailand, were slow in adopting an export-oriented strategy due to their relatively large domestic markets and inefficient agricultural sector.

Despite these obstacles, there were common grounds for a regional cooperation. First, there was a realization that regional cooperation would confer economic benefits on member countries. Second, they have realized that a common bargaining position and unified stance in their negotiations with the outside countries would make them a significant force in the international sphere, and thus enable them to influence the outcome of multilateral negotiations. Third, the threat of growing protectionism and regionalization, as manifested in the formation of regional economic trade blocs and diminishing flows of capital to the developing countries, has made them more committed to regional cooperation. Fourth, from the political perspective the growing threat of communism, vulnerability to external powers and the need for physical security have bound the ASEAN countries under one group. Fifth, there was geographical proximity and the importance of maritime trade. Sixth, the existence of quasi-authoritarian regimes and similarities in approach to development have facilitated cooperation and coordination.

1.3   ASEAN INSTITUTIONAL STRUCTURE (1967–76)

During the first ten years of ASEAN existence (1967–76), the ASEAN organizational structure was based on the Bangkok Declaration of 1967 where the highest decision-making body was the *Annual Meeting of Foreign Ministers* which met on a rotational basis in each of the ASEAN capitals. This grouping was responsible for policy formulation, coordination of activities and reviewing of recommendations from lower-level committees (see Figure 1.1).

The ongoing work of the Association between ministerial meetings was conducted by the *Standing Committee*, comprising the Foreign Minister of the host country as chairman and the resident ambassadors of the other four ASEAN countries in that country. The seat of this committee, which was also on a rotational basis, conformed with the site of the next Annual Ministerial Meeting. This committee met several times a year and its Annual Report was submitted to the meeting of Foreign Ministers for adoption. It also reviewed recommendations from other lower-level committees before they were submitted for ministerial consideration.

The Standing Committee was an overseer of the three *Special Committees* created to handle the external relations of ASEAN. These were the *Special Coordinating Committee of ASEAN Nations* (SCCAN) created in 1972 to coordinate links with the European Community. This was reinforced by the establishment of the *Joint Study Group* in 1975 charged with the task of examining the substance and mechanism of cooperation between the two regional organizations. The other two committees handling external relations and coming under the purview of the Standing Committee were the *ASEAN Brussels Committee* (ABC) and the *ASEAN Geneva Committee*, made up of ASEAN representatives in Brussels and Geneva, respectively.

Preserving an element of continuity was a more permanent group of officials who were involved in the actual supervision of ASEAN's activities and the preparatory work of the Standing Committee including the screening of recommendations submitted by the various permanent and *ad hoc* committees. This group of officials were the Secretaries-General of the five ASEAN National Secretariats.

Source: ASEAN Secretariat (1978, pp. 17–20).

Figure 1.1   Organization of ASEAN, 1967

One important group that was invisible within the formal institutional structure of ASEAN was the *Senior Officials Meeting*. This committee of senior Foreign Ministry Officials (at Permanent Secretary level or its equivalent) was established by the ASEAN Ministerial Meeting in 1971 to discuss the implementation of the Zone of Peace, Freedom and Neutrality (ZOPFAN), and has now become a regular forum for intra-ASEAN political consultation.

There were 11 *permanent committees* of officials and experts in the pre-Bali summit years which worked on a range of ASEAN programmes with their respective sites in brackets: Civil Air Transportation (Singapore), Communications Air Traffic (Malaysia), Food and Agriculture (Indonesia), Shipping (Thailand), Commerce and Industry (the Philippines), Finance (Malaysia), Mass Media (Malaysia), Tourism (Indonesia), Land Transport and Telecommunications (Malaysia), Science and Technology (Indonesia), and Socio-Cultural Activities (the Philippines).

There were several *special* and *ad hoc committees*, which reported directly to the Standing Committee. In addition to the three previously mentioned special committees, the following were created to deal with special issues: Special Committee on ASEAN Central Banks and Monetary Authorities, Special Committee on ASEAN Secretariat, ASEAN Coordinating Committee for Reconstruction and Rehabilitation of Indo-China States, Senior Officials on Synthetic Rubber, Senior Officials on Sugar, and Senior Trade Officials on Multilateral Trade Negotiations.

1.4   INSTITUTIONAL STRUCTURE BEFORE 1992

The changing orientation of the organization and the need for an expanded ASEAN cooperation led to attempts at reorganization of the ASEAN structure (see Figure 1.2). The pre-1992 ASEAN structure is derived mainly from the major restructuring endorsed at the time of the 1976 Bali summit meeting of ASEAN Heads of Government. Three changes were introduced in the ASEAN institutional structure in the 1976 Bali summit: first, two blocs of ministerial meetings were introduced in addition to the Foreign Ministers Meeting: the *Economic Ministers Meeting* (AEM), and the bloc of *Other ASEAN Ministers* (OAM), a general rubric which covers separate meetings of ASEAN Ministers of Labour, Social Welfare, Education, Information, Health, Environment, Energy, Science and Technology; second, the permanent and *ad hoc* committees of the pre-Bali period were regrouped into five economic and three non-economic committees; thirdly, the establishment of an *ASEAN Secretariat* based in Jakarta and headed by its own Secretary General.

The *ASEAN Economic Ministers* were charged with the task of accelerating economic cooperation, and met annually to review various areas of economic cooperation and to consider the reports and recommendations. Among the ASEAN projects and areas of cooperation were the ASEAN Industrial Projects (AIP), Industrial Joint Venture Schemes (AIJV), Industrial Complementation Schemes (AIC) and the Preferential Trading Arrangements (PTA). The ASEAN Economic Ministers were serviced by *Senior Economic Officials Meeting* (SEOM).

The *Annual Meeting of ASEAN Foreign Ministers* (AMM) formulated policy guidelines and coordinated all ASEAN activities. It also provided for the convening of the *ASEAN Heads of Government Meeting*, 'as and when necessary' to give overall directions to ASEAN. The Bali Conference was the first ASEAN Heads of Government Meeting or Summit (1976), followed by the second Summit in 1977. It took 10 years before the Third Summit was held (1987). The fourth Summit was in 1992, and the fifth Summit was held in December, 1995.

The five economic committees, serviced by the *interim technical secretariat* were: Committee on Trade and Tourism (COTT) based in Singapore,

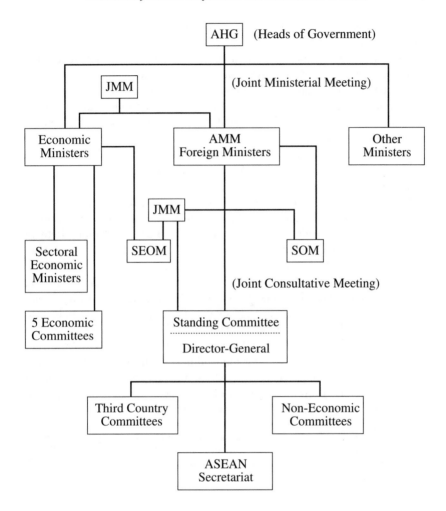

Source: Chng (1992, p. 92).

Figure 1.2   Pre-1992 ASEAN organizational structure

Committee on Industry, Minerals and Energy (COIME) based in the Philippines, Committee on Finance and Banking (COFAB) based in Thailand, Committee on Food, Agriculture and Forestry (COFAF) based in Indonesia, and Committee on Transport and Communications (COTAC) based in Malaysia. The 1992 ASEAN Summit in Singapore decided to dissolve these five economic committees and all their subsidiary bodies and committees.

Their work and activities have been taken over by the Senior Economic Officials Meeting (SEOM).

The three non-economic committees were: Committee on Science and Technology (COST), Committee on Social Development (COSD) and Committee on Culture and Information (COCI). These committees reported to the Standing Committee. There were also committees set up to deal with the dialogue partners such the ASEAN–Australia, ASEAN–Canada, ASEAN–New Zealand, ASEAN–EC, ASEAN–Japan and ASEAN–US.

Two multilateral groupings have been set up to deal with political and economic issues affecting the ASEAN as well the non-ASEAN countries: the *ASEAN Regional Forum* (ARF) and the *Asia–Pacific Economic Cooperation* (APEC). With the ultimate objective of enhancing political stability and security in the Asia–Pacific region, the ASEAN Regional Forum includes countries such as Australia, Canada, South Korea, China, the European Union, Vietnam and Laos and major superpowers such as the US, Japan and Russia. Quite recently, India and Myanmar were admitted into the Forum. The APEC consists of the six ASEAN countries, US, Canada, Japan, South Korea, Australia, New Zealand, China, Papua New Guinea, Taiwan, Hong Kong, Mexico and Chile. Peru, Russia and Vietnam were later officially admitted to APEC in 1998. The overlapping membership of these two forums underlines the growing economic, political and security linkages which ASEAN wants to expand beyond Southeast Asia. This motivation arises from the realization that a sustainable economic progress in the ASEAN region crucially depends upon cooperative efforts from the countries of the Asia–Pacific. As the Singapore Foreign Affairs Minister Professor Jayakumar put it,

> while ASEAN can continue to play an instrumental role in forging predictability, it can not do so alone. The need for stability in the region is not just an ASEAN or even Asian concern. An unstable Asia–Pacific will have wide global repercussions.[1]

1.5   EXISTING INSTITUTIONAL STRUCTURE

The basic features of the pre-1992 ASEAN institutional structure are retained in the current structure, except for some reforms introduced since 1992 to streamline its organization, reduce the overlapping of functions and to make it more supportive of the ASEAN organization's new vision and objectives, as follows. First, the institutionalization of the *ASEAN Heads of Government* meeting, the ASEAN Summit. In 1992 the Fourth ASEAN Summit in Singapore decided that the ASEAN Heads of Government would meet formally every three years and informally at least once in between to lay down directions and initiatives for ASEAN activities. Second, the establishment of the AFTA Council to supervise, coordinate and review the implementation of the Common Effective Preferential Tariff (CEPT) scheme for ASEAN Free Trade Area (AFTA). Third, the five economic committees were dissolved after 1992 and their functions taken over by the Senior Economic Officials Meeting.[2] Fourth, the ASEAN Secretariat's role has recently been strengthened to support the Summit's initiatives. The Protocol Amending the Agreement on the Establishment of the ASEAN Secretariat, signed at the 25th Annual Ministers Meeting in Manila in 1992, vested the Secretariat with an expanded set of functions and responsibilities to initiate, advise, coordinate and implement ASEAN activities. The Secretariat has been expanded from three to five Bureaus – General Affairs, Economic Cooperation, Functional Cooperation, ASEAN Cooperation Unit and Dialogue Relations, and the AFTA Unit – the last one established to support the Secretariat's role in assisting the implementation of AFTA.

The current ASEAN institutional structure reflects to some extent the nature and objectives of ASEAN. With more emphasis given to economic cooperation since the Bali Summit of 1976 and to meet the need for expanded ASEAN cooperative activities, the introduction of a separate ASEAN Economic Ministers structure, the establishment of a central ASEAN Secretariat and other changes were added to the original institutional structure. However, despite its changes, ASEAN's institutional structure is still based on a loosely-structured decentralized committee system geared to political consultation and consensus building. A policy of consensus based on a constructive, cautious and confidence-building approach is reflected in the absence of a supranational body that demands an all-embracing commitment from the member countries.

SUGGESTIONS FOR FURTHER READING

For an historical account of previous attempts at regional cooperation and the evolution of ASEAN institutional structure, read Sandhu, et al. (eds) (1992, pp. xvii–xxii, 3–49, 50–82); and Saw Swee-Hock (1980, pp. 322–36). For more recent evaluations of ASEAN institutional structure and prospects, read Chng (1992, pp. 91–105) and Tan (1996, pp. 4–22).

NOTES

1. Taken from *The Straits Times*, 9 August 1994, p. 23.
2. The 1992 ASEAN Summit in Singapore decided to dissolve the five Economic Committees on Food, Agriculture and Forestry (COFAF), Finance and Banking (COFAB), Industry, Minerals and Energy (COIME), Transport and Communications (COTAC), and Trade and

Tourism (COTT) and all their subsidiary bodies and committees. The work and activities of the five defunct economic committees and their subsidiary bodies have been taken over by the Senior Economic Officials Meeting (SEOM). SEOM reports to the AEM which meets at least once a year.

The AEM oversees and provides policy guidance in the implementation of economic cooperation programmes and activities. The policy decisions of the Ministers are carried out, implemented and monitored by the SEOM, which is required to meet at least four times a year. In carrying out its functions and responsibilities, SEOM is supported by the strengthened ASEAN Secretariat which assists, among others, in coordinating, monitoring and implementing economic cooperation activities.

2. ASEAN economic development: an overview

Economic development in the current literature refers to a consistent rise in real per capita income accompanied by structural transformation, poverty alleviation and improved distribution of income. It is, therefore, more than just about economic growth. There are other equally important aspects to economic development such as high life expectancy, better educated workforce, quality of housing and health care, lower incidence of poverty and so on. It is, therefore, a multidimensional process involving physical and social transformation with the fruits of economic growth being widely shared.

This chapter attempts to explain the economic development performance of the ASEAN group of countries before the 1997 crisis, focussing on the ASEAN5 (particularly the remarkable economic success achieved by Indonesia, Malaysia, Singapore and Thailand and the economic recovery of the Philippines) in the early 1990s.[1] Despite the two serious crises (1985 and 1997), the past two decades had witnessed a remarkable economic progress achieved by the ASEAN4 economies (ASEAN5 minus the Philippines) so that these countries were often dubbed as 'new Asian tigers'. Before doing so, however, it is useful to present, first, an overview of the ASEAN6 economies (that is, the ASEAN5 and Brunei) in terms of their common characteristics, economic strengths and weaknesses.

2.1 OVERVIEW OF THE ASEAN6 ECONOMIES

2.1.1 Common Characteristics

The ASEAN6 economies are highly diverse economically and socially (that is in terms of size, historical background, resource endowments, stages of economic development, and culture). However, they have a number of common economic characteristics that can define ASEAN as an economic region. First, although the extent of government intervention varies among the ASEAN economies, they are all market-based economies. Second, they are all export-oriented with a high degree of export dependence. Third, they have common economic aspirations with a lot of emphasis placed on economic growth as they had generally a long history of underdevelopment, poverty and high unemployment. Fourth, except for Brunei and Singapore, their economies are dualistic where more than 50 percent of their population lives in the agricultural and rural sector. These commonalities have bound them together in their pursuit of greater economic development and improvement of the life of their respective constituents.

2.1.2 Economic Strengths and Weaknesses

The ASEAN economies differ in terms of economic strengths and weaknesses. Brunei has enjoyed political stability and is blessed with abundant oil and gas resources free from the problems associated with high population density and urban congestion. But Brunei, having the smallest population size and the second highest per capita income in ASEAN, relies heavily on its oil and natural gas reserves for export revenue. Although these resources have provided Brunei with high and consistent flow of income for many years, they are exhaustible. Once these depletable resources run out, the economy will have to face a very uncertain future. Diversification of its economy with reduced dependence on the two products has long been recognized as the only long-term path to a sustainable development. However, the diversification policy has so far been unsuccessful. The volume of investments in the manufacturing sector has been inadequate due to high operating costs, shortage of skilled and unskilled labour, very limited domestic market and inadequate support services sector.[2]

Indonesia is rich in agricultural and mineral resources, not to mention its abundant supply of human resources. Due to its large domestic market, relatively low-cost labour and political stability under the Suharto regime, Indonesia had for some time been attracting foreign and domestic investments into its manufacturing sector, resulting in a more diversified economy. There are, however, weaknesses and potential sources of problems if not handled effectively. Its level of bureaucratic efficiency and quality of rural infrastructure are still inferior to some of its ASEAN neighbours such as Singapore and Malaysia. Moreover, political stability after Suharto has remained unresolved. Although Indonesia had successfully and peacefully conducted parliamentary and presidential elections, the current political leadership faces internal rivalry, a growing threat from secession movements in Aceh and Papua (Irian Jaya), ethnic tensions such as between the *Dayaks* and the *Malduras* and religious conflicts in the Maluku islands and other parts of Indonesia. While the current President needs the military to re-establish peace and order in these troubled islands, there is at the same time a growing public outcry for bringing to justice the military leaders responsible for the recent carnage in East Timor.

Malaysia is also well endowed with mineral and agricultural resources, without problems associated with high population density.[3] It has good infrastructure in the urban as well as in the rural sector. It has enjoyed political and economic stability under the political leadership of Mahathir. There is a transparent smooth mechanism for a transfer of political power in Malaysia.[4] However, currently Malaysia is facing unskilled and skilled labour shortage. Malaysia's short-term solution to this labour shortage has so far been to import foreign labour. Apart from its negative social implications, it does not provide a long-term solution. Malaysia has experienced infrastructural bottlenecks and a large current account deficit mainly due to its excessive imports of shipping and insurance services.[5] There is also some doubt expressed by some quarters over the future political stability in Malaysia after Mahathir. Opposition against Mahathir, precipitated by the sacking of Anwar and his eventual imprisonment, is growing, which could become a potential threat to Malaysia's political stability.

The Philippines is well endowed with natural and human resources (an area of 300 080 square km and a population of 70 million, as of May, 1995) and had shown some signs of economic recovery before the 1997 crisis, resulting from greater confidence in its economic and political future, as manifested in the increased inflow of foreign capital.[6] However, the sustainability of its economic recovery and its long-term future would greatly depend on how successfully it can resolve its long-standing problems of inadequate infrastructure, bureaucratic inefficiency, high rates of underemployment and unemployment and social instability.[7] The political and social uncertainties created by the long-standing unresolved Mindanao conflicts and pro-Estrada loyalists trying to jeopardize the current administration's plan to prosecute ex-President Estrada on charges of economic plunder, betrayal of public trust and violation of the constitution, have eroded investors' confidence and further stimulated capital flight. Unless these political and social crises are resolved, the Philippines will face an uncertain future.

Singapore's economic strength is based on its superior infrastructure, efficient bureaucracy, political stability and sound macroeconomic fundamentals. But, due to its limited domestic market, high labour and land costs and lack of natural resources including water, Singapore constantly has to depend on foreign trade. It is, therefore, highly vulnerable to changes in external conditions.

Thailand is well endowed with agricultural resources and abundant labour. It has an area of 514 000 square km and a population of 60.25 million, as of May, 1995. Thailand's high growth rate has been largely driven by exports of labour-intensive manufactures such as textiles, footwear and labour-intensive segments of electronics and a significant inflow of foreign direct investment. But its urban-biased development policy has resulted in poor infrastructure in the rural areas and greater economic opportunities in the urban sector, contributing to greater income inequality. Thailand has a persistent current account problem due to its heavy dependence on oil imports. It is now trying to move up the production ladder from highly labour-intensive manufacturing to more capital-intensive and technology-intensive ones as it faces increasing competition from the low-wage newly-emerging economies of India, China and Vietnam.[8] But its effort to restructure its industry is hampered by the shortage of skilled labour.[9] Its urban traffic congestion problem has further constrained its ability to move ahead.

2.2   ECONOMIC PERFORMANCE OF THE ASEAN5

A remarkable record of consistently high economic growth for the ASEAN countries in the three decades before the 1997 crisis is well-known.[10] The group's four 'growth economies' (that is, Singapore, Malaysia, Thailand and Indonesia) had consistently outperformed most other regions, particularly in the 1980s and first half of 1990s. On the other hand, the Philippines showed a remarkable recovery after 1992. Table 2.1 illustrates this economic dynamism after their mid-1980s recession until the crisis years of 1997 and 1998. The pre-crisis growth rates of the ASEAN5 had averaged around 7 percent, well

Table 2.1   ASEAN real GDP growth (%)

ASEAN10	87–92	1993	1994	1995	1996	1997	1998
Brunei	1.2	0.5	1.8	2.0	2.8	2.5	–
Indonesia	6.3	6.5	7.4	7.3	7.8	4.6	–13.7
Malaysia	8.3	8.3	8.5	9.6	8.2	7.5	–6.2
Philippines	3.2	2.2	4.3	5.0	5.5	5.1	0.3
Singapore	8.4	10.1	10.1	8.9	7.0	7.8	1.2
Thailand	10.1	8.2	8.5	8.5	6.7	–0.4	–7.7
Cambodia	7.0	4.1	4.0	7.6	6.5	2.0	0.0
Laos	5.3	5.2	8.0	6.7	6.9	7.2	–
Myanmar	4.6	6.9	6.8	7.7	6.0	5.0	0.6
Vietnam	6.5	8.1	8.8	9.5	9.3	9.2	5.8

Notes
–: not available; the average growth rates for the period 1987–92 for Cambodia, Laos and Myanmar are based on 1991–92 data only while for Vietnam it was based on 1990–1992 data.

Sources: Asian Development Bank, *Asian Development Outlook* (1993); *Asiaweek*, 12 January 1996, pp. 46–7; US-ASEAN Business Council,<www.us-asean.org/index.html>

above that posted by the developed market economies (around 3 percent) and significantly above the world average growth rate (around 2 percent). Despite the economic recession in the late 1980s, they continued to post high growth rates so that most analysts at that time were fairly optimistic that this dynamism would continue into the rest of the 1990s.

High economic growth rates experienced by the ASEAN countries were accompanied by significant improvements in the quality of life, as measured by such standard indicators as infant mortality, literacy rates and life expectancy. As illustrated in Tables 2.2a and 2.2b, the ASEAN6 (that is Brunei, Indonesia, Malaysia, the Philippines, Singapore and Thailand) had performed better in improving life expectancy, infant mortality and literacy than the South Asian economies and the Southeast Asian transitional economies (SATEs). There was a strong positive correlation between per capita income and quality of life indicators, except in the case of the Philippines with respect to literacy rates. Singapore, which had the highest per capita income in nominal as well as in purchasing power parity (PPP) terms, also had the longest life expectancy, lowest mortality rate, highest calorie intake and literacy rate (excluding the Philippines and Thailand). However, the correlation was not very close.

Table 2.2a   ASEAN major development indicators, 1996

ASEAN-10	Per capita GNP, Nominal (US$)	Per capita GDP (PPP)	Life expectancy 1996	Life expectancy 1990	Infant mortality (per 1000)	Literacy rate (%)	Calorie intake (ave per person/ day)
Brunei	20 000	20 589	74	–	8	89.2	2 837
Indonesia	780	3 388	63	62	60	84.4	2 750
Malaysia	3 530	8 763	72	70	12	89.3	2 884
Philippines	1 010	2 660	67	64	40	93.5	2 452
Singapore	22 520	21 493	76	74	5	91.6	3 198
Thailand	2 315	6 816	69	69	26	93.8	2 443
Vietnam	220	1 263	67	–	34	88.6	2 250
Myanmar	890	676	59	61	79	81.5	2 598
Laos	325	2 071	52	–	94	83.9	2 630
Cambodia	215	1 266	52	–	110	37.8	2 021

Note: –: not available.

Source: *Asiaweek*, 19 January 1996, p. 60.

Table 2.2b   Major development indicators: selected countries, 1996

Countries	Per capita GNP, nominal (US$)	Per capita GDP (PPP)	Life expectancy 1996	Life expectancy 1990	Infant mortality (per 1000)	Literacy rate (%)	Calorie intake (ave per person/ day)
South Asia							
Bangladesh	245	1 350	56	52	90	36.6	2 100
India	335	1 280	61	59	75	52.1	2 243
Nepal	180	1 165	54	52	84	27.0	2 246
Pakistan	465	2 235	62	56	88	35.0	2 377
Developed							
US	26 620	25 900	77		8	95.5	3 671
Japan	36 315	21 350	80		4	100.0	2 956
Australia	19 100	19 007	78		7	99.5	3 216
Canada	18 900	21 268	78		6	99.0	3 482
France	25 860	19 774	77		6	98.8	3 465
Germany	24 905	20 165	76		6	100.0	3 522

Source: *Asiaweek*, 12 July 1996, p. 53; *Asiaweek*, 19 January 1996, p. 60; World Bank (1992, pp. 218–19, 274–75).

Vietnam, which had the lowest per capita income among the ASEAN7 countries (that is, Brunei, Indonesia, Malaysia, the Philippines, Singapore, Thailand and Vietnam), had performed better than Indonesia and the Philippines in terms of infant mortality rates, and better than Indonesia in terms of life expectancy. Compared to the selected developed countries, it is quite clear that Singapore had performed better in terms of per capita income than any other country except the US and Japan, and in terms of infant mortality except Japan, as Table 2.2b shows.

2.3   STRUCTURAL CHANGES IN ASEAN5

2.3.1   Transformation from Low-income to Middle and Upper-middle income

Reflecting this rapid growth, the rate of improvement in living standards had been significant for the ASEAN5 countries. As Table 2.3 below shows, although their standards of living, as measured by their per capita income,

Table 2.3   ASEAN's per capita GNP for selected years

	Population (1994) (million)	Per capita GNP (US$)			
		1985	1992	1994	1995[d]
Brunei	0.285	15 878	14 276[a]	15 918	20 589
Indonesia	190.00	400	570	888	3 388
Malaysia	19.25[c]	1 848	2 320	3 495[b]	8 763
Philippines	65.65	575	730	1 010	2 660
Singapore	2.70	7 160	13 057	20 380	21 493
Thailand	60.00	710	1 420	–	6 816

Notes:
[a]based on available 1990 data. [b]based on Malaysia's 1993 population count. [c]based on 1993 population count. [d]in terms of per capita GDP (PPP). –: not available.

Sources: IMF, *International Financial Statistics* (various issues); Singapore's Department of Statistics, *Economic Survey of Singapore* (1995); Brunei Statistics Division, Ministry of Finance, *Brunei Darussalam Key Indicators 1994*.

differed considerably, the ASEAN5 countries consistently enjoyed an increasing living standard during the period. They have graduated from the ranks of low-income countries, as classified by the World Bank, to the ranks of middle and in some cases upper-middle-income countries. Singapore in particular has the highest per capita income amongst ASEAN.

The World Bank has classified Indonesia, the Philippines and Thailand as lower-middle income; Malaysia as upper-middle income; Brunei as high income, and Singapore as an advanced developing country since 1996. The Philippines, due to political crisis and power shortage in the early 1990s, did not perform well, as expected. However, since 1993 the Philippine economy showed some signs of economic recovery. It posted a growth rate of 4–6 percent before the 1997 crisis, much higher than the growth rates it experienced in the 1980s.

2.3.2   Diminishing Role of Agriculture and Growing Importance of Manufacturing and Service Sectors

Although primary exports still account for a significant proportion of total exports for most ASEAN countries, the share of manufactured exports has been increasing distinctly, as a result of their deliberate policy to diversify their exports and to reduce their dependence on the exports of agricultural and mining products. As can be gleaned from Table 2.4, in 1970 the share of manufactures in total merchandise exports was marginal, ranging from 1.2 percent

*Table 2.4   Shares of manufactures (SITC 5–8) in total merchandise
export (%)*

	1970	1980	1990	1993
Japan	92.5	94.5	95.9	95.8
Hong Kong	95.7	91.1	91.8	93.5
Korea, S.	76.5	89.5	93.5	93.1
Taiwan	75.8	87.9	92.5	92.9[a]
Brunei	0.1	n.a.	12.6	2.4[a]
Indonesia	1.2	2.3	35.5	53.1
Malaysia	6.5	18.8	54.2	69.7
Philippines	7.5	21.1	39.0	41.6
Singapore	27.5	43.1	71.7	78.5
Thailand	4.7	25.2	63.1	71.1

Note: [a]Based on 1992 data since 1993 data are not yet available at the time of writing.

Source: UNCTAD, *Handbook of International Trade and Development Statistics*, Table 4.1
(1994).

to 7.5 percent among the ASEAN4 (Indonesia, Malaysia, Philippines and
Thailand). This was largely due to their reliance on their natural resource
endowments. But since 1980 the share of manufactured exports has started to
rise.[11]

2.4   EXPLAINING ECONOMIC GROWTH IN ASEAN5 COUNTRIES

There was a strong correlation between per capita income and other standard
indicators of the quality of life in the ASEAN economies, as shown in the
previous section. Their remarkable economic growth largely contributed to the
achievement of other equally important development objectives. For this
reason, explaining ASEAN economic growth is crucial to understanding
ASEAN economic development experience.

Explaining the growth performances of the ASEAN5 countries has been the
subject of many empirical studies.[12] However, not one of the explanations is
totally satisfactory because not one explanation by itself has covered all the
facets of the phenomenon in a logical and consistent framework. The spectacular growth of the ASEAN countries can only be explained to a certain extent
by traditional economic growth theories which consider capital accumulation

and technological improvements as sources of economic growth. Apart from these, other important factors have also accounted for their economic success such as their openness, high quality of government intervention, high degree of political stability, pragmatic economic policies and social values.

In this section an attempt is made to explain the phenomenon in a consistent, logical and comprehensive framework. To do this, a new analytical framework proposed by Lim (1996) is appropriate. This is a four-step backtracking analytical approach which: (i) identifies the sources of output growth; (ii) identifies the factors behind these sources; (iii) identifies the economic policies adopted to produce the factors and ensure their efficient use; and (iv) examines the social values that facilitate the introduction of such economic policies.

2.4.1 Sources of Output Growth

To identify the sources of output growth of the ASEAN5 countries and quantify the contribution of each of these to the measured growth rate of output requires the use of the production function framework. This framework is based on the theory of the firm. If a production function can be written for a firm, so one can also be done for the economy as a whole. The output of the economy is thus a function of the factor inputs available for the economy as a whole and the technology prevailing:

$$Q = f(L, N, K, T)$$

where Q is aggregate output, and L, N, and K the total supply of labour, land and capital, respectively, and T is the prevailing technology. All are expressed over a period of time.

The above aggregate production function shows that there are three broad sources of economic growth: first is input accumulation; second is increasing returns to scale and third is technological progress which increases the productivity of the productive inputs.

2.4.1.1 Prominence of capital accumulation

Tongzon and Loh (1995) attempted to identify the influences of these sources of growth on four ASEAN countries, namely Indonesia, Malaysia, the Philippines and Thailand by fitting unconstrained production functions to their individual annual data on output, labour and capital for the period 1962–91. In addition, possible influences of trade liberalization and investment in human capital were taken into account in light of the current debate between endogenous and exogenous theories of economic development and controversy on the influence of trade liberalization on economic growth.

These countries were chosen because they had initially adopted an import-substitution strategy in their industrialization efforts and have subsequently undergone various stages of trade liberalization. Singapore has always pursued an export-oriented industrialization strategy since its political separation from the Federation of Malaysia largely due to its small domestic market. Brunei is left out in this study due to insufficient data.

The production function estimated for these four individual ASEAN countries is written in log form as:

$$Y_t = b_0 + b_1 L_t + b_2 K_t + b_3 E_t + b_4 X_t + \sum_{i=1}^{x} b_5 D_i + \sum_{j=1}^{y} b_6 D_{j,k} X_t$$

where

Y = growth in real GDP per capita (net of exports);
L = labour force growth;
K = gross fixed capital accumulation growth;
E = educational expenditure growth;
X = growth of real exports;
D_i = intercept dummy variable for each liberalization period;
$D_{j,k}$ = slope or interaction dummy variables.

The dependent variable (Y) is netted out of exports to remove the simultaneity problem between exports and GDP since exports is a component of domestic output. By using per capita GDP, effects of population growth on GDP growth are factored out of consideration. This variable is deflated by its corresponding consumer price indexes due to the unavailability of data for GDP deflators for the entire period of study.

Labour (L) and capital (K) are measured by the number of persons in the labour force and gross capital expenditure, respectively. Real exports (X) are obtained by deflating nominal exports by the corresponding export price indexes. Investment in human capital is proxied by expenditures on education (E) by the respective four ASEAN governments.

Trade liberalization effects are represented by the dummy variables. The intercept dummy (D_i) is supposed to capture the externality effect which leads to an improvement in total factor productivity. The slope dummy $(D_{j,k})$ is supposed to capture the productivity differential effect of trade liberalization that will alter the sensitivity of one of the parameters of the model, in this case exports.

The empirical results show the lack of significant effect trade liberalization has on all four of the ASEAN countries. However, the most salient feature of the results is the high significance of the capital variable (K) in all the four countries (except for Thailand where K is significant at the 10 percent level), although the labour force variable did not come out statistically significant. This suggests that capital accumulation has played the most significant role in the output growth of these four countries.

The above finding about capital is consistent with previous studies for other developing countries. In Maddison's (1970) study of 22 developing countries (including the Philippines, Malaya and Thailand) for the 1950–65 period, capital accumulation was the most important source of output growth for all countries covered. For most countries, additions to the effective labour force came next with technical progress a very distant third.

The same conclusion was reached in the widely circulated study by the World Bank (1993b). Using cross-country data and regression analysis, the World Bank in its report on *The East Asian Miracle: Economic Growth and Public Policy* found that the rapid growth of the four fastest-growing ASEAN economies (Thailand, Singapore, Malaysia and Indonesia) was primarily driven by the rapid capital accumulation both in human and physical terms. The role of technological progress was found to have a secondary role. The above findings were further confirmed by Abimanyu (1995) for Indonesia, Kawai (1994) for Malaysia, Austria and Martin (1995) for the Philippines, and Limskul (1995) for Thailand.

Studies to quantify the relative influences of the sources of output growth for Singapore have also supported the prominence of capital accumulation. Tsao's study (1986), which examined the period 1966–80 for Singapore using the growth accounting framework, found no role for technological progress (TFP) growth, a marginal role for labour force and a very important role for capital accumulation, behind Singapore's high growth rates in its early years of industrialization. Young (1992, 1994a) also produced the same results for the period 1970–90.

Young's studies generated some debate and further work on explaining output growth in Singapore. In addition to informal reactions, three technical papers attempted to challenge the findings of Young. One was by Toh and Low (1994) whose estimates implied a virtually zero contribution of technological progress (TPF growth) over the entire period 1971–92, but whose estimates for the specific period 1982–92 registered some positive contribution (contributing either 0.51 or 1.87 percentage points to the observed 7 percent output growth after 1981) of technological progress.

The other paper by Wong and Gan (1994) accounted for Singapore's output growth in manufacturing in the 1980s. They examined the role of technological progress (TFP growth) in 27 manufacturing industries in the 1980s and found that from 1981 to 1990 overall TFP growth contributed 24 percent of the observed 6.7 percent average growth in gross manufacturing output. However, going by industry for the entire decade of the 1980s, the results showed 16 industries with negative TFP growth offset by positive growth in 11 industries. After 1986 TFP growth was negative in 12 industries offset by large positive estimates in a few sectors.

The most recent paper on explaining ASEAN growth by Rao and Lee (1995) broke up the time period into three sub-periods: 1966–73, 1976–84 and 1986–94, and adjusted the labour input for hours and changing educational composition. Using the growth accounting framework, they estimated a TFP growth of 1.3 percent for 1966–73, 0.6 percent for 1976–84 and 2.6 percent for 1986–94. The 2.6 percent growth in TFP implied that technological progress alone accounted for 30 percent of output for 1986–94. Structural shifts in manufacturing from less efficient to more efficient sectors were considered a major factor.

The three studies have come up with different estimates of the relative contributions of the sources of growth due to differences in data used and assumptions, but all found a positive role of technological progress in Singapore's output growth particularly from the second half of the 1980s. Further, they have not ruled out the prominence of capital accumulation in Singapore's output growth.

2.4.1.2   Sustained increase in exports

Another major source of output growth for the ASEAN5 countries is their sustained increase in exports. There is a link between economic growth and export growth, as supported by a number of cross-sectional empirical studies (see, for example, Michalopolous and Jay, 1973; Michaely, 1977; Balassa, 1978, 1985; Tyler, 1981; Feder, 1983; Kavoussi, 1984; Esfahani, 1991 and the World Bank, 1993b). The link is both direct and indirect. Since exports are a component of national output in a national accounting sense, an increase in exports means an increase in GDP, assuming no offsetting fall in any one of the other components.

The indirect link is through the impact on productivity. Productivity increases due to the resource allocation effect, externalities and greater import capacity. The resource allocation effect refers to the greater capacity utilization driven by the external markets and to the more rapid shift of resources from low productive sectors to high productive sectors. Externalities include the economies of scale associated with a larger market and better access to information and technology. Exports also increase their capacity to import the required capital for industrialization and economic development.

The finding of no positive impact of trade liberalization on growth by Tongzon and Loh (1995) is consistent with previous time-series studies, for example, Greenaway and Sapsford (1994), Greenaway (1993) and Jung and Marshall (1985). It, however, contradicts the findings based on cross-sectional studies. This result could be due to two possible factors: first, the approach adopted in dealing with the problem of double-counting was to net out the export element from the output growth variable. Thus, the regression analysis was run for the non-export GDP against a set of explanatory variables. It is highly possible that the effects of trade liberalization have not yet been reflected in the non-export GDP variable for the period of study (1962–91). Second, the effects of trade liberalization are more subtle and complicated than those captured by the econometric model. In particular, the dummy variable technique could not fully quantify the effects of trade liberalization. The interaction with other policy variables and the role of other non-quantifiable factors are likely to be more important. This casts doubt on the sufficiency of the production function framework to deal with other non-quantifiable factors such as the indirect effects of export growth on output growth.

2.4.2   Factors Behind the Sources

In the previous section it was argued that to have a consistent increase in national output requires a sustained increase in exports. This section will describe the factors behind the sustained increase in exports experienced by ASEAN5 countries before the crisis.

2.4.2.1   Diversification of exports

The ASEAN5 export expansion was largely a result of their success to diversify their export base and markets. Their export diversification consisted of enlarging their primary export base, promoting manufactures and shifting their emphasis from labour-intensive manufactures to capital-intensive ones at a later stage of industrialization.[13]

As mentioned in Section 2.3.2, since 1980 the reliance by ASEAN4 resource-rich countries (that is Indonesia, Malaysia, the Philippines and Thailand) on primary exports has declined. Since the 1980s they have also diversified their primary commodity exports to include other primary products such as liquefied natural gas, palm oil, wood, marine products and copper in addition to oil, natural rubber and tin (in the case of Indonesia and Malaysia), and fruits, corn, coffee, tapioca, cassava, cacao, natural fibres and marine products (in the case of the Philippines and Thailand) in addition to sugar, copra, coconut oil and rice.

Singapore and Malaysia in particular started with exporting labour-intensive manufactures and later on shifted their emphasis on capital-intensive manufactures as their comparative advantage in labour-intensive production diminished.[14] Singapore was pursuing with remarkable success an export-oriented labour-intensive industrialization since its separation from the Federation of Malaysia in 1965. But since the 1970s Singapore has begun to experience an increasingly tight domestic labour market and a threat of competition from lower-wage competing countries. By 1979 a restructuring programme, together with a 'high wage' policy and fiscal incentives for research and development, were introduced to promote capital-intensive, skill-intensive and higher value-added exports of goods and services (Peebles and Wilson, 1996, p. 168).

Malaysia started to emphasize capital-intensive and technology-intensive exports in its Seventh Malaysian Plan (1996–2000) after experiencing a short-age of labour constraint for the last five years. The adoption of an export-oriented labour-intensive industrialization strategy by Malaysia since 1970 was so successful that more than 50 percent of Malaysia's total manufactured exports were accounted for by its labour-intensive electronics, clothing and textile industries in the early 1980s (Osman-Rani, 1985, p.22). After the reces-sion of the mid-1980s its labour-intensive exports continued to perform well in the late 1980s. However, due to labour constraints aggravated by infra-structure bottlenecks in the early 1990s, Malaysia saw the need to make the policy shift towards higher value-added exports.

Market diversification to reduce their dependence on the markets of the US and Western Europe has also helped the ASEAN5 countries maintain their strong export growth, particularly in the late 1980s when the Western markets experienced a prolonged recession. This issue will be discussed further in Chapter 6.

2.4.2.2   Rapid expansion of foreign direct investment (FDI)

One important contributing factor behind the strong capital accumulation as a prime source of ASEAN output growth is the massive inflow of foreign capital in the form of export-oriented and manufacturing-based foreign direct investments, especially from Japan and the newly industrialized Asian countries of Taiwan, South Korea and Hong Kong.[15] Table 2.5a shows the respective shares of the ASEAN5 countries in overall foreign direct invest-ment inflows to developing countries over the 1983–95 period based on the UNCTAD data. Malaysia and Singapore's shares were consistently increas-ing until 1992 after which a decline in their shares was noticeable. Thailand experienced a declining share from 1991 while the Philippines, which had the lowest share, started to attract more FDI from 1993. No evident pattern can be seen from Indonesia's shares. The general deceleration in the inflow of FDI into ASEAN in the 1990s can be seen from Table 2.5b, partly due to the emerging competition from China. The importance of FDI to Malaysia and Singapore cannot be overemphasized in the context of their massive capital requirements for a sustainable growth and export orientation due to their limited domestic markets. By bringing in capital, technology, export market linkages, managerial skills and an in-built capacity to respond to changes in comparative advantage, foreign direct investment has been an

Table 2.5a   Foreign direct investment inflows to developing countries: ASEAN shares (US$ million)

	1983–88	1989	1990	1991	1992	1993	1994	1995
Developing countries	19 757	28 622	34 689	40 889	54 750	73 350	84 441	99 670
Indonesia	341	682	1 093	1 482	1 777	2 004	3 000	4 500
	(1.7)	(2.4)	(3.6)	(3.6)	(3.3)	(2.7)	(3.6)	(4.5)
Malaysia	731	1 668	2 332	3 998	5 183	5 206	4 500	5 800
	(3.7)	(5.8)	(6.7)	(9.8)	(9.5)	(7.1)	(5.3)	(5.8)
Philippines	249	563	530	544	228	763	1 500	1 500
	(1.3)	(2.0)	(1.5)	(1.3)	(0.4)	(1.0)	(1.8)	(1.5)
Singapore	1 947	2 887	5 575	4 888	6 730	6 829	7 900	5 302
	(9.9)	(10.1)	(16.1)	(12.0)	(12.3)	(9.3)	(9.4)	(5.3)
Thailand	439	1 775	2 444	2 014	2 116	1 715	2 700	2 300
	(2.2)	(6.2)	(7.1)	(4.9)	(3.9)	(2.3)	(3.2)	(2.3)

Note: Figures in brackets are percentage shares.

Source: UNCTAD, *World Investment Report 1995*. Transnational Corporations & Competitiveness Annex Table 1 (1995); *World Investment Report 1996*. Investment, Trade and International Policy Arrangements, Annex Table 1 (1996).

Table 2.5b   Foreign direct investment inflows to developing countries: China and the ASEAN5 countries (1987–98) (US$ million)

	1987–92 (Annual Ave)	1993	1994	1995	1996	1997	1998
China	4 652	27 515	33 787	35 849	40 180	44 236	45 460
% Share	**13.2**	**34.9**	**33.4**	**33.8**	**29.7**	**25.6**	**27.4**
Indonesia	999	2 004	2 109	4 346	6 194	4 673	–356
% Share	**2.8**	**2.5**	**2.1**	**4.1**	**4.6**	**2.7**	
Malaysia	2 387	5 006	4 342	4 178	5 078	5 106	3 727
% Share	**6.8**	**6.4**	**4.3**	**3.9**	**3.8**	**3.0**	**2.2**
Philippines	518	1 238	1 591	1 478	1 517	1 222	1 713
% Share	**1.5**	**1.6**	**1.6**	**1.4**	**1.1**	**0.71**	**1.0**
Singapore	3 674	4 686	8 550	7 206	7 884	9 710	7 218
% Share	**10.4**	**6.0**	**8.5**	**6.8**	**5.8**	**5.6**	**4.3**
Thailand	1 656	1 805	1 364	2 068	2 336	3 733	6 969
% Share	**4.7**	**2.3**	**1.3**	**2.0**	**1.7**	**2.2**	**4.2**
ASEAN5	9 234	14 739	17 956	19 276	23 009	24 444	19 271
% Share	**26.1**	**18.7**	**17.7**	**18.1**	**17.0**	**14.2**	**11.6**
Developing Countries	35 326	78 813	101 196	106 224	135 343	172 533	165 936
World	173 530	219 421	253 506	328 862	358 869	464 341	643 879

Source: UNCTAD, *World Investment Report 1999*. Annex Table B.1.

important catalyst in their sustained rapid growth and industrial development. To a lesser extent, but still significant, foreign direct investment has also been behind the economic performance of Indonesia and Thailand.

2.4.3   Economic policies

2.4.3.1   Foreign direct investment

The ASEAN5 countries, with the exception of the Philippines, had attracted a significant amount of foreign direct investment particularly during the 1987–92 period. A number of push factors were responsible for this significant inflow including the appreciation of the yen since the 1985 Plaza Accord, rising costs of labour in Japan and other newly industrializing countries, increasing lack of security in Taiwan and the 1997 reversion of Hong Kong to China (Lee, 1990).

In terms of the pull factors, three major factors had made ASEAN attractive to foreign investors: stable macroeconomic environment, liberal economic regimes, and secure competitive rates of return on investments.[16]

(a) Stable macroeconomic environment   Economic and political stability rank high in the list of factors influencing portfolio decisions of capital-exporting countries. On these counts the ASEAN5 countries had done well, although individually their performances varied.[17] As suggested by the indicators of long-term economic stability in Table 2.6, from 1987 onward (when FDI inflows accelerated) all the ASEAN5 countries had achieved lower inflation, reduced their debt–service ratios and accumulated more international reserves, but individually had recorded differently on these indicators. They had improved their current account balance, with the exception of Thailand, and maintained relatively stable exchange rates, with the exception of the Philippines and Indonesia.[18] These country differences must have accounted for their different performances in attracting foreign investments.

Generally, continuity in political leadership played an important role in maintaining political stability in all the ASEAN5 countries but the Philippines. Frequent changes in Thailand's political leadership is well-known, but the unifying presence and public admiration for Thailand's king have given Thailand some sense of continuity and stability in leadership. Thus, frequent changes in political leadership have been stabilized by the presence of Thailand's well-respected royalty which has enjoyed the support of all Thais, including the opposing political parties. Although their political systems were often criticized for being autocratic and undemocratic, the ruling parties continued to enjoy popular public support based on their remarkable record of economic performance.

Table 2.6 *ASEAN indicators of macroeconomic stability*

	Indonesia		Malaysia		Philippines		Singapore		Thailand		Vietnam	
	1980–86	1987–96	1980–86	1987–96	1980–86	1987–96	1980–86	1987–96	1980–86	1987–96	1980–86	1987–96
Inflation rate	10.4	8.3	4.4	3.7	18.0	8.7	3.4	2.8	6.7	5.1	211.9	44.4
Current account balance[a]	−4.0	−3.3	−7.0	−5.7	−3.7	−2.8	−3.6	12.6	−4.2	−6.7	−17.6	−7.9
Debt–service ratio[b]	28.1	26.9	21.2	7.7	36.0	19.5	2.0	0.57	27.5	14.5	–	17.2
International reserves[c]	5.6	2.8	6.2	8.6	0.30	0.25	25.3	39.3	2.0	4.1	–	–
Exchange rate[d]	892.67	2209.7	2.36	2.54	12.97	25.65	2.15	1.49	23.63	23.60	–	9560

Notes:
[a]As a percentage of Gross Domestic Product.
[b]Total debt service as a percentage of exports of goods and services, except for Vietnam where it is a percentage of its GDP. Due to datta limitation, the years 1993 and 1994 are not covered for the ASEAN countries, except for Vietnam.
[c]Quoted in millions of SDRs as a proportion of their respective gross national product quoted in national currency units. Except for Malaysia and Singapore, all the GNPs are in billions of their national currencies.
[d]With respect to the US dollar.

Source: Asian Development Bank, *Asian Development Outlook* (various issues); International Monetary Fund, *International Financial Statistics* (various issues); World Bank, *World Debt Tables* 1992/93.

(b) Liberal economic regimes   All of the ASEAN5 countries have embraced a free-market philosophy. Although in their initial years of political independence the respective ASEAN governments had intervened in the markets by regulation and direct participation in some sectors, over time they have gradually dismantled regulatory controls and deregulated particularly the financial and trade sectors of their economies.

Virtually all foreign exchange markets in ASEAN were liberalized, except for a few remaining restrictions. In Thailand, for example, commercial banks were subject to limits on their net foreign exchange positions. Public sector borrowings were subject to an annual ceiling set in line with the government policy on public debt management. Because of international reputation and credit rating, only top companies in Thailand had direct access to foreign funds. Residents were not allowed to hold foreign exchange-denominated deposits, except for exporters. Certain outbound investment such as property and portfolio investment continued to require approval from the authorities. Despite these limitations, the financial markets in ASEAN exhibited many characteristics common to those of a highly open economy. The most important is that domestic interest rates were increasingly influenced by foreign interest rates (Nijathaworn, 1993).

The Philippines, which used to have the most protected banking sector, opened up its banking system to more foreign competition by admitting more foreign banks into the country.

(c) Competitive rates of return on investment   The ASEAN5 countries have deliberately enticed foreign investments by offering a guarantee scheme and elaborate tax incentives.[19] It is guaranteed that assets will not be appropriated and earnings can be repatriated. There is a guarantee against competition from new state enterprises, state monopolization, competing imports by government agencies and price controls, permission to own land and to bring in foreign technicians. Tax exemptions on imported capital goods, raw materials and on income from companies granted a pioneer status are a common feature of their tax incentive scheme. They have allowed, however, different periods of tax relief, different rates of deduction from taxable corporate income with respect to depreciation allowance during the relief period, and company expenses. They also have different foreign equity guidelines (a maximum of 95 percent in the case of Indonesia), although they all allow for 100 percent foreign ownership in areas where no local partners can be found, in export-oriented projects and designated investment promotional zones. In the case of Thailand, for example, up to 100 percent foreign ownership is allowed for export-oriented projects and a maximum of 49 percent is permitted for industries supplying mainly the domestic market. Bureaucratic procedures and tariff systems have been simplified as part of the overall trade reform.

(d) Quality of government intervention It is beyond any doubt that the government sector has played a significant role in ASEAN's remarkable growth and structural change. But it should be pointed out that the high quality of government intervention, rather than quantity, has been the factor behind ASEAN5's economic success story. A good example was the contrasting development approach adopted by Singapore and Thailand. The Singapore government has been by far more interventionist than Thailand's, but both economies were highly successful.[20]

It is argued that not only were their bureaucracies less corrupt than those in other developing countries, but they were also effective in raising productivity, in generating employment and developing their human resources. In addition, they supplied the necessary infrastructures, physical as well as legal, for the efficient conduct of free enterprise.

2.4.3.2 Policies on exports
The ASEAN countries have successfully promoted their manufactured exports by shifting from an import-substituting (IS) to an export-oriented (EOI) industrialization strategy.

The ASEAN5 countries, with the exception of Singapore, from the time they obtained their political independence, had adopted an import-substitution strategy for the development of their manufacturing industry.[21] This strategy was designed to save on foreign exchange and to reduce their reliance on their previous colonial masters for imports of manufactures. However, this approach resulted instead in foreign exchange crisis, deterioration in their external trade position and inefficient manufacturing sector.[22] The accelerated industrialization plan through import substitution required heavy importation of capital, technology and industrial materials under a highly capital-intensive Western technology. It meant provision of protection for their import-substituting industries sheltering from foreign competition to the detriment of their export-oriented primary sector. Further, the limited size of their modern sector ran counter to the economies of scale principle, and the protection afforded to the import-substituting industries encouraged inefficiency in the absence of foreign competition.

On the other hand, their traditional primary exports (their major source of foreign exchange at that time) had experienced secular deterioration in terms of trade and instability due to the vagaries of the weather, low income and price elasticities for these commodities. Further, the import–substitution policies encouraged the maintenance of overvalued currencies and a consequent discrimination against traditional and potential new exports.

Hence, due to the failure of their import-substitution policies, the ASEAN (particularly Indonesia, Malaysia, the Philippines and Thailand) countries have shifted to an export-oriented industrialization strategy from the 1980s.[23] Apart from the success stories of their Asian neighbours which had earlier adopted an outward-looking strategy, this shift was necessary for other reasons: for Indonesia this was considered a means of offsetting the anticipated slowdown in oil exports and of generating more employment opportunities for its large pool of labour;[24] the Malaysian government recognized the importance of the manufactured exports in light of its depleting tin reserves and uncertain long-term prospects for its natural rubber exports; the Philippines expected a substantial reduction in dependence on primary exports, significant increases in foreign exchange earnings and expansion of employment opportunities; and for Thailand this export promotion was part of its overall industrial development programme. Measures to promote both manufactured exports and to assist its import-substituting industries were adopted as early as 1972.

It is now a well-known fact that their export-oriented policies have partly been responsible for the significant growth of their manufacturing sector and thus contributed to the rapid expansion and diversification of their exports (see, for example, Abimanyu, 1995; Limskul, 1995; Tham Siew Yean, 1995; World Bank, 1993b).

The rapid growth of their manufactured exports has made their export–GDP ratios grow. Reflecting their different degrees of export orientation and openness, the performance of their manufactured exports (as indicated by their export–GDP ratios) has varied within ASEAN. Indonesia, who has had the least outward-looking (most inward-looking) policy, has the lowest export–GDP ratio among ASEAN, whereas Malaysia and Singapore, who are the most outward-looking (least inward-looking) of them, have the highest ratios. Singapore has, since its political separation from Malaysia, been the most outward-looking with almost all its items being import duty-free, and it is no surprise that it has the highest export–GDP ratio. Malaysia's overall simple average tariff rate is quite low, and effective protection rates for manufactured goods are also low (Naya and Imada, 1990). Malaysia has had few non-tariff trade restrictions. The Philippines and Thailand, which are intermediate cases, have resorted to non-tariff barriers with fairly high nominal tariff rates for manufactures. Effective rates of protection are also relatively high, particularly for capital-intensive import-competing industries.

2.4.4   The Role of Social Values

The economic policies required to bring about the factors responsible for output growth are not easy to implement because they involve a great deal of sacrifice on present consumption and often are politically unpalatable. The ASEAN5 countries, particularly the high performing ones, were able to implement the required economic policies due to their competent and honest bureaucracy and appropriate social values.

The role of social values in economic development has been recognized in a number of studies such as Weber (1904), Rostow (1952), Lewis (1955), McClelland (1961), Inkeles and Smith (1974), and Triandis (1971, 1973). Although some of these studies are not without their limitations, they do bring out the point that social values can impinge on economic growth.

The values of hard work, diligence, loyalty and reverence for education are some of the values that can facilitate the implementation of the required economic policies. In the case of the ASEAN countries, their varied economic performance in terms of savings and fiscal prudence can be partly explained by their social values of hard work and diligence. Loyalty increases labour productivity and the reverence for education reinforces the willingness to acquire education and skills, formally or on the job.

2.5   POVERTY AND INCOME DISTRIBUTION

Except for some government efforts to assist indigenous groups, the ASEAN countries have emphasized the importance of promoting economic growth, rather than income redistribution.[25] It is, therefore, interesting to consider the poverty and distribution implications of their economic growth experience.

2.5.1   Poverty

The acid test for economic development is not just the economic growth numbers, but equally important is also whether human lives are improving and whether the fight against poverty is achieving success. Measuring poverty incidence and its trend for the purpose of inter-country comparison is fraught with conceptual and statistical difficulties. Data availability dictates the use of headcount indexes representing the proportion of the population that falls below (but ignoring how far below) a given poverty line.[26] The choice of the poverty line itself is necessarily subjective. The most commonly used definition of poverty line pertains to the *income level sufficient to purchase a certain amount of calorie intake per person.*[27]

The World Bank (1993b), Balisacan (1996) and Wolfensohn (1996) revealed that all ASEAN5 countries reduced poverty incidence for the periods under consideration, as dictated by data availability. Their estimates of poverty incidence are shown in Table 2.7. It is likely that poverty alleviation in these countries was partly attributable to the rapid economic growth. Bautista (1992, pp. 11–16) has shown that there is a systematic relationship between poverty incidence and economic growth. Rapid output growth accompanied by growth in productivity and wages have led to more employment opportunities for the unemployed and low skilled, and increased overall per capita income. Other

Table 2.7   Changes in poverty incidence

	Year	% of population below the poverty line First year	Last year
Indonesia	1972–90	58	15
Malaysia	1973–90	37	10
Philippines	1971–97*	49	32
Singapore	1972–82	31	10
Thailand	1962–86	59	26

Notes: These years are chosen based on data availability.

Sources: World Bank (1993b); Balisacan (1996, p. 448); Wolfensohn (1996); *<http://www.nscb.gov.ph>.

factors include their success in slowing down population growth, improvements in agricultural productivity resulting from the adoption of modern technology and the provision of welfare-enhancing public goods such as subsidies to education, housing and healthcare.

Singapore had the lowest poverty incidence with only 10 percent of the population living in poverty by 1982. This trend continued into the 1980s so that for Singapore absolute poverty is now an issue of the past. The other remarkable achievements were made by Indonesia and Malaysia. The Indonesian and Malaysian fight against poverty had been so successful that in 1990 the percentage of their people living in absolute poverty dropped to 15 percent and 10 percent, respectively (Wolfensohn, 1996).

2.5.2   Poverty in the Philippines

Although poverty alleviation was achieved between 1971 and 1997, the Philippines had the highest poverty incidence in ASEAN. Bautista (1992, p. 15) attributed this to the 15 percent decline in per capita income that accompanied the adoption of stabilization measures prescribed by the International Monetary Fund in 1984–85.

However, there were other long-standing structural factors behind the severe poverty incidence in the Philippines compared to other ASEAN countries. Balisacan (1996) attributed this to its historically feudal system with one of the highest tenancy rates in Asia, lack of off-farm job opportunities and to the failure of the land reform programmes.

The Philippines has a very large agricultural sector where land ownership is highly concentrated, especially in areas dominated by sugar. The landless agricultural workers (the poorest of the poor) are unskilled and less educated and thus face little prospect of obtaining employment in the industrial sector. The lack of off-farm employment opportunities in the rural sector has locked them in poverty.

Various attempts have been made to institute land reform virtually throughout the entire Philippine post-colonial history. The objective of the land reform before 1986 was basically to abolish share tenancy in lands primarily devoted to rice and corn and to transfer to tenants the ownership of the land which they were tilling with the exemptions given to less than seven hectares of tenanted rice and corn lands. The exclusion of farms and plantations planted to export crops meant that the scope of the programme missed the larger source of land inequality. The impact was further eroded by misdeclarations by many landowners, conversion of rice and corn lands into residential enclaves, or planting crops not covered by the land reform programme, evicting tenants and replacing them with hired workers (Otsuka, 1991) and by the exclusion of landless agricultural workers (Balisacan, 1996, p. 489).[28]

The new land reform programme during the Aquino government, dubbed as the Comprehensive Agrarian Reform Program (CARP), has included all agricultural lands and gone beyond tenancy arrangements to also include other alternative production arrangements such as production or profit-sharing, labour administration and distribution of shares of stock. The progress of this ambitious programme, however, has been very slow due to strong political opposition, administrative weakness and financial constraints (Hayami et al. 1990).

The Green Revolution, which resulted in greater agricultural productivity through the introduction of high-yielding varieties, mechanization and input subsidies, have favoured the large farm owners and reduced the demand for labour in the early implementation of the Green Revolution.

The Philippine government's pricing policies and over-valued currencies, resulting from industrial protection, have indirectly discriminated against the agricultural sector. The Philippines, like Indonesia, has had programmes to stabilize prices, especially for rice, which is a sensitive political issue. Through the operation of marketing authorities, explicit export taxes and direct price controls, producer prices of many farm products are suppressed to the detriment of the poor rural workers. Low agricultural prices have penalized landless workers via the reduced demand for their labour. This is especially true for the landless sugar workers where the food-price effect is marginal. High levels of protection for the manufacturing sector are biased against the primary export sector.

The agricultural sector in the Philippines has been less productive than its urban counterpart due to inadequate rural infrastructure (such as irrigation, electricity, transport and credit) and due to the lack of work incentives. Since a number of farmers are tenants, the lack of land ownership has produced uncertainties.

2.5.3 Income Distribution

This issue may not present a problem as serious as poverty for some policy makers, but it has been argued that the extent of poverty depends on the country's per capita income and the degree of inequality. Thus, for a given per capita income, it is most likely that the higher the degree of inequality, the higher is the level of poverty incidence. Maintaining fairly equitable income distribution is also beneficial as it could lead to increased national productivity, more foreign exchange available to purchase capital, increased national spending on wage goods and other necessities and social stability. It is, therefore, important that we now consider the degree of income inequality in the ASEAN5 countries before the crisis.

2.5.3.1 Measures of income inequality

Income inequality can be measured in many ways. Here the Gini ratio, an index of income inequality representing the Lorenz curve, is used mainly due to easy inter-country comparison and data availability. Using this measure, Table 2.8 describes their relative performances in this area for selected years.

2.5.3.2 Declining levels of income inequality

Based on the available data, all ASEAN countries experienced declining levels of income inequality, except for Thailand. Krongkaew (1994) attributed the fall in inequality in Indonesia to the following factors: improvements in the real earnings for most workers in lower-income groups resulting from the

Table 2.8   ASEAN income inequality for selected years (Gini ratios)

	1976	1984	1987	1990	1993
Indonesia	0.34	0.33	0.32	–	0.34
Malaysia	–	0.48	0.45	–	–
Philippines	0.48	0.45	0.45	–	–
Singapore	0.44	0.47	0.46	0.43	–
Thailand	0.43	0.50	0.48	0.50	–

Note: -: not available.

Sources: Krongkaew (1994); Oshima (1993), pp. 201–202.

strong pace and pattern of economic growth; reduced burden of adjustment during the adjustment period 1983–88 on the agricultural sector resulting from the exchange rate depreciation, agricultural pricing policies and some diversification from rice to profitable non-rice crops; and a surge in the non-oil exports and the maintenance of public consumption particularly with respect to human resource development.

The 1971 launching of the New Economic Policy (NEP) in the Second Malaysian Plan 1971–75 after the racial riots of 1969 was the key factor that reduced the level of inequality in Malaysia. In an effort to raise the income of the poor Malays (most of whom live in the agricultural sector), several rural development programmes were launched including the land rehabilitation programme, irrigation and land distribution schemes. The increase in educational attainment among the Malays relative to other ethnic groups has resulted from universal primary education and highly subsidized tertiary education. Higher education brought greater employment opportunities and higher income, reducing the ethnic income gap and thus improving income equality. The shift to labour-intensive industrialization policy with the dispersal of industries in the rural sector by way of export zones and industrial states, and the rapid expansion of the public sector in the 1970s and early 1980s benefited the poor. Finally, the asset ownership restructuring in favour of the Malays has reduced the concentration of wealth among the non-Malays.

The declining level of income inequality in the Philippines from 0.48 in 1976 to 0.45 in 1984 and 1987 is not surprising. If the data are accurate, the following factors could have explained this declining trend. Although the land reform programme was fraught with deficiencies, it was, however, a partial success particularly in the conversion of tenancy to leasehold arrangements, and the protection of tenants' rights against unlawful eviction by landlords has boosted the tenants' sense of security, resulting in greater productivity. The benefits of the Green Revolution which used to be concentrated among the large farms have gradually benefited the small farmers. The increased farm incomes resulting from the adoption of the new technology expanded the demands for non-farm goods and services and generated off-farm employment opportunities.[29]

Singapore's strong economic growth with the achievement of full employment and the expansion of employment opportunities in the manufacturing and services sectors were mainly responsible for its declining income inequality during the period under consideration. The government's policy of granting substantial subsidies to education, housing and health care has also contributed to this trend.

Thailand's poor performance in this area was unstable. The commercialization of agriculture in the 1960s and 1970s had benefited only large farms near Bangkok and large rivers, but had not affected most farms away from the cities and large rivers. With agricultural prices falling and unemployment rising in the first half of the 1980s, income inequality rose to 0.50 in 1984 from 0.43 in 1976. With prices improving and unemployment falling, the Gini ratio fell slightly to 0.48 in 1987. But income inequality rose again to 0.50 in 1990. The main feature underlying the Thai trend is the strong concentration of industrial activities and services in Bangkok. The emphasis has been on industrial development promotion favouring capital-intensive activities.

One can discern some general trends in the pattern of income distribution for the ASEAN5 countries. There is a tendency for income inequality, with the exception of Singapore, to rise to a peak and then fall much earlier in the development stage than it is in the West, which is not consistent with Kuznets' hypothesis. Agriculture has led the way, in contrast to the industrial revolution in the West. The ASEAN5 experiences have provided further evidence that the neglect of agricultural development enables economic development to proceed without any long-term stability. The experiences of the Philippines and Thailand which had initially focussed on industrial development to the neglect of agriculture could attest to this.

2.6   CONCLUSION

Inter-country differences in poverty and income inequality reduction are largely due to the differences in economic policies pursued, differences in history, style of economic development and differences in the extent and quality of government intervention. Countries whose governments are more involved in providing welfare-enhancing public goods such as subsidized education, health care, housing and sanitation and implement them more effectively are better off. With the partial exception of the Philippines and Malaysia, ASEAN5's food crop economy is not historically characterized by marked inequalities in the distribution of landholdings and wealth. Since agrarian holdings were invariably the precursor of large commercial–industrial empires and political power, the initial conditions in most of ASEAN5 have favoured relatively even distribution of income. Pro-urban policies of development have resulted in rural poverty and greater income inequality.

Rapid growth in ASEAN5, except for Thailand, has not prevented the achievement of a more egalitarian income distribution and a wider participation of the poor in that growth. The foregoing discussion has shown that rapid economic growth can be accompanied by a rapid progress in various aspects of social development. This economic development experience is not consistent with the Kuznets' hypothesis which says that during the initial stages of economic development income inequality gets worse as economies grow. The ASEAN5 experience has also demonstrated that reduction in income inequality is not automatically achieved with rising economic growth. This is particularly true for Thailand. This means that effective appropriate policies are needed in order to distribute the fruits of economic growth more widely.

Redistribution from growth remains a challenge for all ASEAN countries today and in the future. In the process of promoting high growth, the equity aspect of development could easily be overlooked. Unless this is taken seriously, there is the danger that their economic growth may not be sustainable. Growth must not be pursued for its own sake. It is but a means to achieve a better quality of life. The social aspects of development (for example, poverty alleviation, respect for human rights, and the like) must be given equal importance in the overall economic planning, rather than just as a by-product of economic growth.

SUGGESTIONS FOR FURTHER READING

Lim, David (1996) is recommended for a systematic and rigorous examination of the growth experiences of the newly industrializing economies of East Asia, using his new analytical framework. For a comprehensive account of the East Asian miracle and of the role of capital accumulation (physical and human), read The World Bank (1993b). Perkins (1994) shows that there is no single model of East Asian development.

For a more detailed appraisal of poverty and income distribution in Indonesia, the Philippines and Thailand, read Krongkaew (1994) and Quibria (1996).

NOTES

1. Cambodia, Laos, Myanmar and Vietnam, due to their very recent membership of ASEAN, are not included in this discussion and will be treated separately. Brunei will be included only when data availability permits.
2. The government in Brunei still remains a major source of production, investment and employment, although its role has declined (Hashim, 1996).
3. Malaysia has an area of 329 758 square km and a population of 20.26 million, as of May, 1995.
4. Malaysia was classified as a very low-risk country for investments based on International Country Risk Guide (ICRG) Composite Index, with a high rating for its political and economic environment, higher than those obtained by the Philippines, Thailand and Indonesia (*International Country Risk Guide*, 1996).
5. Malaysia, together with Thailand and Indonesia, had larger foreign debts as a share of GDP than did Mexico in 1994. The forecast for Malaysia's current account deficit as a proportion of GDP in 1996 was almost 10 percent. As a rule of thumb, any deficit greater than 5 percent of GDP is dangerous (*The Straits Times*, 31 August 1996, p. 37).
6. The Asian Development Bank in its country economic review predicted that the Philippines is capable of growing at an annual rate of 6 to 7 percent over the next few years. Other economists were also optimistic about the Philippine economic future in the context of the

growing peace and political stability in the country (*The Straits Times*, 12 September 1996, p. 41).

7. Based on the International Country Risk Guide composite index, the Philippines was ranked 76th, well behind Singapore, Brunei, Malaysia, Thailand and Indonesia, as of May, 1996.

8. For example, footwear exports, which had been growing an average of 40 percent a year between 1992 and 1995 as Korean and Taiwan industry relocated factories to Thailand, experienced a decline by nearly half over 1995.

9. Thailand is short of trained engineers, in contrast to South Korea and Taiwan which have ten times as many per capita (*Asiaweek*, 4 October 1996, p. 27).

10. Rapid growth rates of Indonesia, Malaysia, Singapore and Thailand between 1960 and 1985 were observed and analysed by Naya (1987) and by Lee (1990) for the period 1971–89. Both studies attempted to explain the continued rapid growth of the ASEAN4 countries.

11. Singapore has experienced an increasing importance of manufactured exports since 1970. Due to its lack of natural resources, Singapore has been promoting the export of manufactures. In the 1970s they were largely labour-intensive exports until the economy was faced with labour cost constraints. Since the 1980s the policy has been to promote high value-added and capital-intensive exports in line with changing comparative advantage.

12. For example, the World Bank's *East Asian Miracle* (1993b), Lee (1990)and Naya (1987).

13. There has been a significant shift in the composition of ASEAN5 manufactured exports towards more capital-intensive products since the 1980s such as office and telecommunications equipment, computer parts, chemicals, electronic goods, semiconductors, consumer durables, machinery and equipment. As well as ASEAN5's policy of export diversification, the relocation of production and outsourcing of parts, components and intermediaries in the ASEAN5 countries by major companies from Japan and newly industrializing countries have contributed to this trend.

14. The ASEAN industrialization experience will be discussed further in Chapter 3.

15. High domestic savings rates experienced by the ASEAN5 countries, especially Singapore, Malaysia, Thailand and Indonesia, was also cited in the literature as a major factor behind the massive accumulation of capital. The following were their domestic savings rates in 1994: Indonesia (38.7 percent), Malaysia (35.6 percent), Philippines (15.4 percent), Singapore (51.3 percent) and Thailand (37.2 percent), (Asian Development Bank, 1995).

16. Other desirable pull factors are efficient and adequate infrastructure and relatively cheap but educated labour force (Chia, 1985, 1986, 1993).

17. In the 1970s to 1980s, the Philippines and Thailand underwent political instability which led to adverse effects on the inflow of FDI (Idem, 1974). For example, between 1982 and 1985 when there was political crisis and uncertainty engendered by the political assassination of Aquino, FDI from the US and Japan dropped from 10 to –82 US$million and from 62 to 21 US$million, respectively (Alburo, Bautista and Gochoco, 1992).

    In the period 1972–75, public discontent over the Japanese domination of the Thai economy caused the inflow of FDI from Japan to drop significantly from 707.7 million baht in 1973 to 423 million baht in 1975 (Chinwanno and Tambunlertchai, 1983).

18. The significant depreciation of the Philippine peso was largely due to the massive capital outflow engendered by economic and political instability starting from the political assassination of the late Benigno Aquino.

19. For a description of the various tax incentives offered in ASEAN for promotion of foreign investments, see Pussarangsri and Chamnivickorn (1995). This will be discussed in greater detail in Chapter 9.

20. It is quite evident from the smooth traffic flow in Singapore and the long traffic jams in Thailand that both governments have adopted different degrees of intervention.

21. Singapore, since its political separation from Malaysia in 1965, has discarded the import-substitution policy due to its small domestic market resulting from the associated collapse of the Malaysian common market proposal and the British military withdrawal. An import-substituting strategy is an attempt to replace imports, usually manufactured products, with domestic production and supply. The idea is to develop certain domestic industries by protecting them against foreign competition. It generally involves the cooperation of foreign firms behind the walls of protection.

22. Except for Indonesia and Malaysia, which were substantial oil producers, the ASEAN5 countries experienced deteriorating trade balances throughout the 1960s and 1970s. The IS strategy failed due to the limited domestic market and concentration of benefits among the few foreign firms and local partners, adoption of capital-intensive technology, overvalued currency and inefficient forward and backward linkages.

23. Indonesia was the last ASEAN5 country to adopt an export-oriented industrialization (EOI) strategy starting in 1986. Malaysia attempted to adopt EOI in the 1970s, but slipped into a second round of an import-substitution industrialization (ISI) strategy in the early 1980s due to Malaysia's heavy industrialization plans (Jomo, 1994). Thailand started to initiate an export-oriented scheme in the third plan (1972–76) and followed it up with further trade liberalization in the fifth plan (1982–86). But Thailand experienced a rising and persistent balance of payment deficit during the fifth plan so that the ISI was implemented together with EOI. Thailand's trade regime underwent a drastic change in the beginning of the 1990s (Pussarangsri and Chamnivickorn, 1995, p. 14).

24. Hence, special emphasis was initially given to small-scale and cottage industries.

25. The ASEAN5 countries do not have welfare assistance programmes to assist the poor and the underprivileged to an extent similar to the West. Nor do they have substantial measures to redistribute income in the form of high marginal tax rates.

26. Another problem is the lack of up-to-date data on poverty due to the lack of frequent income and expenditure surveys in the ASEAN countries.

27. Chenery (1979, p. 459) defined this poverty line as the income level accruing to the 46th percentile of the Indian population in 1975 – roughly equal to the total consumption expenditure needed to ensure a daily supply of 2150 calories per person.

28. Evidence of eviction is also provided by Ledesma (1982) and Mangahas (1985).

29. For a review of the literature on the adoption of the new rice technology in Asia, issues and empirical evidence on technology adoption, see Herdt and Capule (1983), Feder et al. (1985) and Balisacan (1989).

3. ASEAN development and economic cooperation

The previous chapter has provided an overview of the economic development experiences of individual ASEAN countries, focussing on its five founding members and highlighting the major sources and factors behind their varied economic performances.

This chapter will review the role and progress of ASEAN economic cooperation in four important sectors of ASEAN such as international trade, agriculture, manufacturing or industry and services. As discussed in Chapter 1, one major objective in the formation of ASEAN was to foster regional economic cooperation. Since 1976 this objective has grown in importance as economic development has become their main priority in view of, among other things, the increasing need to maintain their international competitiveness in the midst of growing international competition and sustain their pace of economic development in light of rising expectations.

There have been two types of economic cooperation in ASEAN: market sharing and resource pooling. These types of economic cooperation have developed since the Bali Summit of 1976. At this summit the ASEAN5 leaders signed a Declaration of ASEAN Concord which laid out a programme of action for regional cooperation in political, economic, social, cultural and security matters.

3.1 DEVELOPMENT AND COOPERATION IN INTERNATIONAL TRADE

The most important form of market-sharing cooperation envisaged in the Bali Summit was the establishment of preferential trading arrangements to promote intra-ASEAN trade. The agreement on ASEAN Preferential Trading Arrangements (PTA), signed in February 1977, was the first attempt by ASEAN member countries to promote a higher level of intra-ASEAN trade.

Five measures have been identified to achieve the objective of greater intra-ASEAN trade: exchange of tariff preferences; purchase finance support at preferential rates for selected products of ASEAN domestic origin; long-term

(3–5 years) quantity contracts for basic commodities such as fuels and agricultural products;[1] preference in procurement by government agencies; and liberalization of non-tariff barriers on a preferential basis.

3.1.1 Theory of Preferential Trading Arrangements (PTAs) and Intra-ASEAN Trade

The basic concepts of trade creation and diversion, as developed by Viner (1950), Meade (1955), Lipsey (1957, 1960) and other international economists, in their analysis of economic implications of a formation of a customs union provide a relevant framework for evaluating the role of ASEAN preferential trading arrangements in promoting intra-ASEAN trade. However, more relevant to the issue of trade preferences among developing countries are the work by Cooper and Massell (1965), Johnson (1965), Bhagwati (1968) and Krishna and Bhagwati (1994) which provide an economic justification for such trade preferences.[2]

The standard (Vinerian) theory of customs union stresses the short-run static effects of preferential trading arrangements. Under constant cost technology, perfect elasticity of substitution between alternative sources of supply, static market size and exclusion of the most efficient supplier from the customs union, the theory predicts two major consequences for the member country joining the preferential trading club: the welfare-enhancing trade creation effect (resulting from the replacement of the home country's high-cost industries by low-cost industries in the preferred country) and the welfare-reducing trade diversion effect (which results from the replacement of lowest cost non-preferred suppliers by preferred suppliers). The trade creation effects are caused by changes in both production and consumption – the replacement of the domestic by the preferred country's production (production effect) and the increased consumption of the preferred country's substitutes for the home country's goods (consumption effect). Thus, trade creation produces an economic gain of two types: savings on the real cost of goods previously produced domestically and now imported from the preferred country and gain in consumer surplus from a substitution of lower-cost for higher-cost means of satisfying economic needs. The overall impact for member countries, therefore, depends on the size of the trade creation and trade diversion effects.

The standard (Vinerian) theory can be modified and extended to allow for the fact that similar commodities from alternative sources are imperfect substitutes and that industries are subject to increasing costs. To illustrate the trade impact of preferential trading arrangements under assumptions of increasing costs and imperfect substitutability of products, refer to Figure 3.1. S_f represents the nonpreferred export supply curve before the imposition of trade barriers. S_f' represents the nonpreferred export supply curve inclusive of tariffs

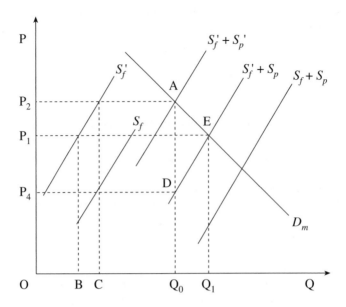

Figure 3.1   Trade effects of preferential trading arrangements

and price effects of other trade barriers. D_m represents the preference-granting country's import demand curve. $S'_f + S'_p$ represents the combined export supply curve of the non-preferred and preference-receiving countries inclusive of tariffs and other price-inflating trade barriers. $S'_f + S_p$ represents the combined supply curve after the trade preferences have been granted. As can be gleaned from the graph, the volume of exports from the nonpreferred country reduces from C to B, but unlike the perfect elasticity of substitution case, the trade preferences do not lead to a complete replacement of the nonpreferred imports with similar imports from the preferred country. Moreover, due to the increasing cost assumption, domestic prices fall only by less than the amount of trade preferences, and part of the reduction in prices is reaped by the preference-receiving country in terms of higher export prices. See Appendix 1 for estimation models based on Figure 3.1.

The above partial equilibrium model does not take into account the dynamic and long-run economic benefits associated with the growth of the internal market brought about by the reduction or removal of trade barriers. The enlargement of internal markets has important effects on productive efficiency within firms and on the rate of growth by way of its impact on the inducement to invest and the opportunities to exploit the economies of scale. Firms of member countries will be subject to more competition, and competition enforces efficiency and leads to greater specialization of production. In this process of interpenetration of markets, as producers can enjoy the savings arising from longer runs in production, consumers will benefit from lowered prices and improved quality of goods and services traded. But the greatest long-run implication is that more competition will lead to increasing average growth of member countries since the enlargement of markets creates special incentives for firms to invest their resources and efforts in the introduction of innovation and expansion.

The extent to which members and nonmembers can gain or lose by the establishment of PTAs will depend largely on the following factors: elasticities of domestic demand and supply, production patterns and costs, size and initial level of protection. A country is more likely to gain from trade creation, the more elastic the domestic demand and supply of goods which the member country is capable of producing. Further it is more likely to gain on its terms of trade with outside countries, the more inelastic is the foreign supply of imports relative to its domestic supply of exports. On the other hand, a country is also less likely to lose from trade diversion, the smaller are the initial differences in costs between the member and the outside countries.

For trade creation to dominate, the economies of the member countries must be competitive before the integration but potentially complementary after the integration because the possibility of relocation of resources will be greater.

The larger the economic area of the integration, the greater is the chance that the world's most efficient producer is a member, and hence all other members could enjoy the advantage of being able to buy from the most efficient producer.

The extent of an unfavourable redistributive effect on a member country is determined by the degree of preferential access it gives to the partner country in relation to the preferential access it receives from the latter. The greater the margin of preference the country gives the more it stands to lose. This means that when a country with a high degree of protection forms a preferential trading arrangement with a country with relatively open markets, the former may well be faced with a net welfare loss (Bhagwati, 1996).

3.1.2 ASEAN PTA and Intra-ASEAN Trade

Whether or not the ASEAN Preferential Trading Arrangements (PTA) was effective in promoting intra-ASEAN trade can be ascertained by investigating whether the value of intra-ASEAN trade as a proportion of ASEAN total trade has grown over time. In 1977, the year of signing the ASEAN PTA, intra-ASEAN trade as a proportion of total ASEAN trade was roughly 15 percent (Naya and Barretto, 1994, p. 3). This share increased considerably to about 20 percent in 1984 (when Brunei joined the grouping), but dropped in 1992 to about 18 percent. It then recovered in 1994 to slightly over 20 percent and remained roughly at the same level in 1995.

Based on this pattern one can say that intra-ASEAN trade cooperation via the PTA has not been a significant contributor to ASEAN trade growth. Although intra-ASEAN trade as a share of ASEAN's total trade increased generally in the 1980s and 1990s, the increase has not been persistent.

The ASEAN PTA clearly failed to increase the share of intra-ASEAN imports which dropped slightly from 20.8 percent (of total ASEAN imports) in 1984 to 19.0 percent in 1992 and which dropped again to 18.4 percent and 16.9 percent in 1994 and 1995, respectively. The trend in intra-ASEAN exports is slightly more encouraging. Its share dropped from 20.0 percent in 1984 to 16.5 percent in 1992, before it went up to 22.7 percent in 1994, and 22.8 percent in 1995.

Singapore–Malaysia–Indonesia trade continues to dominate intra-ASEAN trade. Four major trade flows, in order of magnitude, have dominated trade within ASEAN: Singapore's exports to Malaysia, Malaysia's exports to Singapore, Indonesia's exports to Singapore and Singapore's exports to Indonesia. To investigate further the importance of one ASEAN country in another ASEAN country's foreign trade, the trade intensity approach is adopted. The trade intensity indexes for each of the ASEAN6 countries are presented for selected years in Table 3.1. In 1977 when the ASEAN PTA was signed, the highest trade intensity indexes were between Singapore, Malaysia and Indonesia (Tan, 1996). The trade intensity index between Singapore and Brunei has also been quite high, but Brunei did not join ASEAN until 1984.

These flows (Singapore–Malaysia–Indonesia trade) accounted for 61 percent of all intra-ASEAN trade in 1992 (inclusive of Brunei).[3] In 1995 these flows accounted for 79 percent of all intra-ASEAN trade flows. The increase in trade flows between these three countries occurred together with increases in trade activity in Thailand, the Philippines and Brunei. Singapore remains the most important component of these trade flows, accounting for more than half of total intra-ASEAN trade in 1995 (see Table 3.2).

Trade between Malaysia and Thailand and between Malaysia and Indonesia has been relatively little, but since 1989 this trade has risen strongly, reflecting mainly the robust growth in exports (ESCAP, 1994) and growth in intra-industry trade.[4]

It is, however, interesting to note a diminishing importance of Singapore–Malaysia–Indonesia trade as reflected in their declining trade intensity indexes, particularly in the case of Malaysia's exports to Singapore, Indonesia's exports to Singapore and Singapore's exports to Indonesia between 1987 and 1995, as Table 3.1 shows.

Table 3.1 ASEAN trade intensity indexes: 1977, 1987, 1995

Countries		Brunei	Indonesia	Malaysia	Philippines	Singapore	Thailand
Brunei	1977		0.00	6.93	0.00	4.04	1.68
	1987		0.06	2.64	2.91	5.40	18.27
	1995		0.06	0.13	1.18	3.92	8.51
Indonesia	1977	0.00		0.45	2.91	9.45	0.08
	1987	0.37		1.05	2.89	16.09	1.26
	1995	1.57		1.67	2.30	1.75	0.97
Malaysia	1977	15.60	0.53		3.13	16.29	2.27
	1987	7.91	0.74		7.00	13.69	5.81
	1995	5.71	1.69		1.63	8.22	2.67
Philippines	1977	1.33	1.23	1.65		2.09	0.65
	1987	0.39	0.19	3.84		2.38	3.12
	1995	0.29	0.91	1.36		2.13	3.08
Singapore	1977	55.31	10.91	33.73	3.59		6.49
	1987	44.09	3.48	11.96	4.36		8.21
	1995	17.71	0.75	12.29	2.86		3.91
Thailand	1977	7.31	10.33	12.45	0.66	6.47	
	1987	5.27	1.21	0.60	1.29	7.18	
	1995	1.57	1.83	1.78	1.30	5.66	

Source: Tan (1996, Table 8.3); International Monetary Fund, *Direction of Trade Statistics Yearbook* (1996).

Table 3.2 Intra-ASEAN trade matrix, 1995 (%)

Countries	Brunei	Indonesia	Malaysia	Philippines	Singapore	Thailand	ASEAN
Brunei		2.2	12.9	0.60	71.2	13.1	44.9
Indonesia	0.70		31.3	10.0	36.5	21.5	8.4
Malaysia	0.90	6.6		3.4	74.2	14.9	21.9
Philippines	0.4	14.7	20.5		40.5	23.9	11.0
Singapore	2.7	4.1*	67.2	4.9		21.2	25.7
Thailand	1.8	7.5	24.3	5.1	61.3		15.1
Total							19.7

Notes: Columns 2–7 show trade of individual ASEAN countries as a proportion of total trade with ASEAN. Col. 8 shows intra-ASEAN trade as a proportion of total trade. *Singapore's trade with Indonesia is not reported, and has been estimated from Indonesia's trade with Singapore. 1994 figures are used as 1995 figures are unavailable.

Source: IMF, *Direction of Trade Statistics Yearbook* (1996).

48

3.1.3 The Declining Role of Petroleum in Intra-ASEAN Trade

Petroleum had predominated in intra-ASEAN trade in the last three decades, that is, the 1960s, 1970s and 1980s. In 1989 exports, for example, of mineral fuels accounted for about 23 percent of Malaysia's total exports, and about 20 percent of Singapore's total exports. However, since 1992 machinery and transport equipment have become the dominant items in intra-ASEAN trade. For example, in 1992 Malaysia's main exports to Singapore were manufactured products comprised mainly of telecom equipment, electronic component parts, electrical machinery, transport equipment and office equipment. Manufactures, together with mineral fuels (mainly crude petroleum) and food items, accounted for more than 90 percent of Malaysia's total exports to Singapore. The share of manufactures in total exports to Singapore rose dramatically and consistently from 45 percent in 1987 to 65 percent in 1990 and 74 percent in 1992. Malaysia's imports from Singapore are now dominated by manufactured goods (especially electrical machinery, electronic component parts, telecom equipment, chemicals, office equipment and metal products) and mineral fuels, with the shares of manufactures in total imports from Singapore rising from 58 percent in 1987 to 65 percent in 1990 and 75 percent in 1992 (ESCAP, 1994).

Until 1991 Malaysia's exports to Thailand were dominated by crude petroleum, but in 1992 exports of manufactured goods (mainly machinery and transport equipment) became Malaysia's leading export to Thailand.

3.1.4 Factors Hindering the Growth of Intra-ASEAN Trade

A number of factors could explain the insignificant role of ASEAN PTA in promoting intra-ASEAN trade. First, in the early phase of tariff liberalization, the voluntary and open-ended (no time frame) tariff reduction resulted in the offer of irrelevant items. For example, Thailand offered a 40–50 percent margin of preference for more than 100 log items, most of which other ASEAN countries could not produce, while the Philippines included snow ploughs in its list of preference items. Indonesia offered a 20 percent margin of preference to imports of pure-bred cows and day-old chicks for which the existing tariff rate was zero. Second, the product-by-product and consensus approach to tariff reduction was time consuming as each product had to be discussed and examined closely before tariff preferences could be agreed upon. Third, the across-the-board tariff reduction approach adopted in 1980 was undermined by the exclusion (sensitive) list provision. Since each member country decided its own list of sensitive items, the impact was minimized to the extent that the ASEAN countries made use of this rule. Further, most of the preference items were low-valued. For example, Thailand's 1978 trade statistics listed 1512 items of an import value below US$50 000. Of these only 813 or just under 54 percent were included in Thailand's list of preference items. Fourth, while there has been an attempt to reduce the tariff barriers, the non-tariff barriers have been largely ignored. Quotas, varied customs procedures and technical norms have been the most widely encountered barriers in intra-ASEAN trade. Finally, there has been a general trend within the region towards lower tariffs for goods imported from outside ASEAN. This has eroded any advantage gained in ASEAN tariff preferential agreement. Indonesia, as part of the economic restructuring programme advised by the World Bank, has reduced tariffs on some 94 products to 5 percent from a range of 10–40 percent, and abolished import duties on 59 products. The Philippines and Thailand have been moving in the same direction. Malaysia's tariff rates on average are low, and Singapore's trade regime is virtually free (Ooi, 1987, p. 59).

Underlying the poor performance of ASEAN PTA are the structural problems inherent in the ASEAN economies. (a) Different stages of economic development: these countries have different levels of development, structure and pace of industrialization which have led to different national policies and priorities. Indonesia, Thailand and the Philippines, with relatively less efficient export sectors and with sizeable domestic markets, tend to be inward-looking, while Singapore and Malaysia, with limited domestic markets and relatively more efficient export sectors, tend to be outward-looking. (b) Dependence on extra-ASEAN trade: Northeast Asia is the most important trading partner for Brunei and Malaysia while the USA is the most important trading partner for the Philippines, Singapore and Thailand; Japan is Indonesia's most important trading partner. (c) Competitive rather than complementary economies: similar factor endowments in their early stages of economic development have made the ASEAN economies less complementary relative to their major trading partners. These have made them more competitive and thus made it difficult to arrive at agreements that result in mutually beneficial trade.

Due to the above structural problems, the growth of intra-ASEAN trade has not been as remarkable as the growth of total ASEAN trade. However, it should be recognized that ASEAN economic cooperation, particularly in formulating a common stance and forming a united bloc in dealing with their extra-regional trading partners, has significantly contributed to enhancing their clout and bargaining power in international trade negotiations and other fora, especially on matters of market access for their exports.

3.1.5   Conclusion

The ASEAN Preferential Trading Arrangements (PTA) has been the main instrument of intra-ASEAN trade cooperation to enhance greater intra-ASEAN trade. However, it has contributed only marginally to the promotion of intra-ASEAN trade due to factors including their conflict of interests resulting from their different stages of economic development, weak complementarities and their dependence on extra-ASEAN trade.

3.2 INDUSTRIALIZATION AND INDUSTRIAL COOPERATION

The preceding chapter has outlined the rationale for the switch from an import-substituting industrialization (ISI) strategy to an export-oriented one (EOI) in ASEAN. It has argued that this switch was one major factor behind the ASEAN economic success. This section will discuss in more detail the ASEAN industrial development experiences under an export-oriented industrialization strategy. Under this strategy, they have achieved a significant economic transformation, as reflected in the increasing importance of manufactured products in their national output. But it must be noted that the adoption has been a matter of emphasis, rather than a mutually exclusive one, in terms of government policy and outcome. The ASEAN experience with industrialization is generally best described as an emphasis on an import-substituting industrialization (ISI) in the initial stages, particularly in the 1960s and the 1970s, and a gradual shift towards an export-oriented industrialization (EOI) since the 1980s.

3.2.1 ASEAN Experience with Export-Oriented Industrialization Policy

Growth performance and industrialization are intricately related in ASEAN, where manufacturing has emerged as an engine of growth and bellwether of the state of the economy. Thus, for instance, manufacturing growth of 13.3 percent per annum in Singapore from 1965 to 1980 led to an average GDP growth of 10.4 percent, but when manufacturing growth fell to 2.2 percent per annum from 1980 to 1986, Singapore's average GDP growth fell to only 5.3 percent (Chng, 1991).

Industrialization has been seen by the ASEAN countries as the key to economic independence and progress ever since they attained their political independence. Hence, though varying in degrees and duration, they have embarked on a programme of industrialization.

The Philippines was the first ASEAN country to embark on industrialization in the early 1950s, followed by Malaysia in the late 1950s, Singapore and Thailand in the early 1960s, and Indonesia in the late 1960s. Though late starters, Brunei and the transitional economies of ASEAN are also intensifying their efforts to diversify their economies through industrialization. For Brunei its over-reliance on oil and gas makes it imperative to industrialize. A break from central planning and the adoption of a market-based economic system was necessary for former centrally-planned economies' complete integration with the world economy.

Indonesia

Prior to 1986 Indonesia's industrialization strategy was generally inward-looking due to its enormous natural resources and large domestic market. As pointed out earlier, there were liberalization attempts in the late 1960s in terms of tariff reduction, removal of import licensing and foreign exchange controls, but from 1974 to 1985 there was a general reversal to the economic nationalism of the early 1960s with the re-introduction of protection and regulations aided by the windfall gains in oil exports, especially from the 1973 and 1979 oil price hikes.

The oil crisis in 1986 with a resultant BOP deficit and foreign debt crisis had prompted Indonesia to re-embark on trade liberalization. Tax reforms, export incentives and subsidies were introduced to boost its non-oil exports.

Malaysia

The launching of the Second Malaysian Plan in 1979 marked the start of Malaysia's adoption of an export-oriented industrialization strategy. The strategy was more of an increase in assistance to exports, rather than a substantial reduction in protection levels. Malaysia, compared to other ASEAN countries, had traditionally low protection levels. The import-substitution policy in Malaysia only resulted in low protection levels due to the perception that the protectionist policy would only benefit the Chinese industrialists to the detriment of the rural indigenous population.

Philippines

The enactment of the Export Incentives Act of 1970, followed by devaluation of the peso, marked the Philippine adoption of an export-oriented approach to industrialization. The Act involved the provision of subsidies and tax exemptions to companies exporting more than 50 percent of their production. The establishment of export processing zones, such as the Bataan Export Processing Zone, depreciation of the peso and simplification of its tariff structure were other instruments used to boost its manufacturing exports in the 1970s.

However, the unfavourable external conditions, aggravated by political instability, led to an exchange rate crisis which prompted the Philippine government to re-impose quantitative restrictions and foreign exchange rationing during the first half of the 1980s. It was only in 1985 that there was a final reversal of policy towards export orientation.

Thailand

Thailand adopted the EOI strategy with the launching of its Third Plan (1972–76) and its Investment Promotion Act of 1971. This was followed by a series of currency devaluations in 1984 and 1986 as part of its export promotion drive in response to its foreign debt crisis.

3.2.2 Results of EOI strategy

One prominent consequence of the ASEAN export promotion policy is the industrial transformation from being producers and exporters of low value-added primary products to those of high value-added manufactures. The rapid growth of their manufactured exports since the 1970s has led to a restructuring of their manufacturing sector towards higher value-added production, as Table 3.3 shows.

In all the ASEAN5 countries, as shown in Table 3.3, the share of machinery in total manufacturing output increased substantially during the period, especially for Malaysia, Singapore and Thailand. In all cases the share of food declined significantly. With the exception of Indonesia, the share of other industries dropped substantially as the ASEAN countries shifted away from predominantly extractive activities to more capital- and technology-intensive production.

Malaysia's major manufactured products for exports are mainly electronic components and electrical appliances. Thailand's major manufactured products are textiles and clothing, electronics and processed food while Indonesia's are textiles and clothing, footwear and processed wood products. However, the fast-growing sectors are electrical appliances, telecom equipment, electronic components and processed food. Singapore's main manufactures are electronic products, computers, hard disk drives and printers.

However, Brunei and the Philippines did not experience the kind of industrial transformation experienced by the abovementioned ASEAN countries. Brunei's economy is still very much dependent on oil and natural gas, although its dependence is declining. In 1990, for example, oil and gas accounted for more than 60 percent of Brunei's GDP, down from its 88 percent share in Brunei's GDP in 1974. This was of course accompanied by an increasing share of the non-oil sector from 12 percent in 1974 to 40 percent in 1991 (31 percent in 1993). A greater part of this increase, however, was due to increases in government sector activities which registered a percentage share of about 22 percent in 1991 (30 percent in 1993) from only 4 percent in 1974. This is not a commendable structural transformation simply because it did not bring about the desired impact of its diversification drive.[5]

In the case of the Philippines, manufactured exports are small in absolute value and its manufacturing value-added is dominated by food processing industries.

Table 3.3   ASEAN structure of manufacturing (% of manufacturing value added)

	Indonesia		Malaysia		Philippines		Singapore		Thailand	
	1970	1992	1970	1992	1970	1992	1970	1992	1970	1992
VA (million $)	994	27 854	500	–	1 665	12 811	379	13 568	1 130	31 185
Food	65	23	26	10	39	37	12	4	23	16
Textile	14	16	3	6	8	13	5	3	14	16
Machinery	2	14	8	34	8	11	28	54	4	40
Chemicals	6	7	9	11	13	12	4	9	25	5
Others	13	40	54	39	32	27	51	30	34	23

Notes:
Food = Food, beverages and tobacco (ISIC division 31); Textile = textiles and clothing (Division 31); Machinery = machinery and transport equipment (major groups 382–4); Chemicals = chemicals (major groups 351 and 352); Other = wood and related products (division 33), paper and related products (division 34), petroleum and related products (major groups 353–6), basic metals and mineral products (divisions 36 and 37), fabricated metal products and professional goods (major groups 381 and 385), other industries (major group 390).
–: not available

Source: The World Bank, *World Development Report 1995*, Table 6.

3.2.3   Prospects and Challenges

The prospect for continued industrialization among the ASEAN5 countries largely depends on how they can successfully deal with the following problems and constraints:

Indonesia
As a latecomer in the EOI strategy, Indonesia has performed well in labour-intensive manufactures, but with the emergence of labour-surplus historically-planned economies such as China and Indo-China, Indonesia is most likely to face more competition in the textile and footwear industry.

Malaysia and Thailand
Their main problem is the shortage of skilled labour and available labour to work in the agricultural sector. In some parts of Malaysia and Thailand, the infrastructure is still not adequate to cope with the fast increasing demand. Malaysia is too dependent on electronic components and electrical appliances while Thailand is on exports of textiles and footwear.

Philippines
The presence of vested interests remains a major obstacle in the current government's deregulation and microeconomic reform. Further, the basic requirement of establishing law and order is still a slippery area and has been challenged from time to time. Inefficient infrastructure, bureaucracy and growing income inequality are other major constraints (*The Sunday Times*, 5 January 1997, p. 15).

Singapore
Although Singapore has the most superior infrastructure in Southeast Asia, it is increasingly plagued with rising wages and land costs due to its limited size and shortage of skilled labour.

3.2.4   ASEAN Industrial Cooperation

The individual ASEAN experiences with industrialization vary in terms of timing, emphasis and impact, although there are elements common to them. One common element is the ASEAN resolution that the industrialization and economic development of is members can be largely facilitated through industrial cooperation. There is also a common realization that a significant increase in intra-ASEAN trade can only occur if the supply side of the market is also increased. Thus, since 1976 three major schemes of ASEAN industrial cooperation, that is ASEAN Industrial Projects (AIP) Scheme, ASEAN Industrial

Complementation Scheme (AIC) and ASEAN Industrial Joint Venture (AIJV) Scheme, have been established to create a new industrial capacity jointly owned by member countries serving the regional market. Unlike the trade liberalization which raises apprehensions of uncontrolled trade flows and market disruption, industrial cooperation is linked to the creation of specific new production facilities giving rise to much more predictable trade flows.

3.2.4.1   Rationale for industrial cooperation

(a) Larger combined market and economies of scale   The various schemes are based on the concepts of resource pooling and market sharing. Most of the ASEAN countries have relatively small domestic markets because of their small population. But taken as a whole, ASEAN has a combined population of roughly 350 million (excluding Cambodia, Laos, Myanmar and Vietnam), larger than the US. Moreover, the ASEAN market is expected to increase and its per capita income to grow over the next two decades. Given such a large and expanding market, ASEAN can sustain high volume manufacturing industries which are not presently viable in any of the individual ASEAN countries. Regional projects require less investment and less labour per unit of output than similar national projects and can therefore operate at lower costs. And cooperation allows ASEAN countries not only to reduce, but also to share the capital costs of regional industrial projects and make the maximum use of their limited skilled manpower resources.

(b) Reorientation of traditional ties   Industrial cooperation enables the ASEAN countries to reorient their traditional ties, that all these countries except Thailand have, with their former colonial rulers. Due to their past colonial relationships, the ASEAN countries have been more closely integrated with the industrially advanced countries than within the region. The industrialization programmes of ASEAN are, therefore, designed to suit national rather than regional requirements. Industrial cooperation helps to disengage the traditional economic ties of the member countries and reintegrate them by redirecting economic activities towards the region.

(c) Specialization and enhancement of investment climate   Most importantly, industrial cooperation is expected to enable each ASEAN country to specialize in the manufacture of selected components. Given the present competitive environment, this may be the only strategy to ensure the development of certain large-scale industries such as motor vehicles and machinery. Such a strategy will not only help to increase intra-ASEAN trade but also enhance the overall investment climate in the region and induce more investors to invest in the ASEAN countries. Hence, industrial cooperation will

help ASEAN countries increase their industrial complementarity and promote regional trade in manufactured products.

In the long run, industrial cooperation can lead to coordinated industrial planning on a regional scale which will increase the industrialization potential of the region as a whole. The process of regional industrial cooperation and the region's industrial development can feed on each other and provide an impetus for further industrial growth in the region through the opening up of opportunities for the establishment of new industries to take advantage of the regionally-based division of labour.

3.2.4.2 ASEAN schemes of industrial cooperation: success or failure?

(a) ASEAN Industrial Projects (AIPs)   Proposed by the UN team in 1973 and officially adopted at the Bali Summit of 1976, these are large-scale joint industrial projects between ASEAN governments designed to utilize the raw materials of member countries and produce for the ASEAN market at preferential rates.

Four industrial projects were initially proposed to be located in the following ASEAN5 countries: urea projects in Indonesia and Malaysia; a natural soda ash project in Thailand; a superphosphate project in the Philippines; and a diesel engine project in Singapore. At the estimated cost of US$300–400 million each, 60 percent of the equity was to come from the host country and 10 percent each from the other four ASEAN countries. The private sector in each country was expected to take up about 40 percent of equity participation, while most of the infrastructure costs of these projects were to be financed through foreign loans.

In 1977 the Japanese government had announced it would provide US$1 billion in loans (Fukuda soft loan) to help finance the AIPs. This prompted proposals for a further set of AIPs to be considered including the manufacture of heavy-duty rubber tyres in Indonesia, machine tools in Malaysia, newsprint in the Philippines, television picture tubes in Singapore and potash in Thailand (Tan, 1996).

Limitations. The above proposals under the AIP scheme have met with very limited success. Only the urea projects in Indonesia and Malaysia out of the five proposals got off the ground. All the other ASEAN members had withdrawn from their original AIP projects. The following reasons explain the lack of progress in the AIP scheme:

1. Project identification. The most serious limitation with the AIPs was that they were conceived and announced rather hastily. Without the benefit of detailed feasibility studies, most of the proposed projects were subsequently found to be unprofitable due to high production costs found to be

much higher than originally thought. The cancellation of Thailand's soda ash project after it was found that a 500-kilometre railway had to be built to transport the raw materials to the plant, and that it needed to export more than half its output, is a good example. Projections of raw material and operating costs indicated that the plant would not be able to compete in world markets.

2. Project implementation. There were several weaknesses in the institutional and procedural framework. The need for a consensus in their decision making and need for the participation of all ASEAN countries in the AIPs made agreement difficult to achieve which resulted in the abandonment of some AIPs. Long delays in the implementation resulted in cost escalation, making some AIPs ultimately non-viable.

3. Project financing. Government-to-government projects were difficult to negotiate especially in financing the projects. Although the Japanese government had pledged a loan of US$1 billion towards the AIPs, other terms of the loan package were not specified at the time. There were long negotiations and delays when the Japanese government was approached to finance the scheme.

4. Lack of private sector participation in the identification, formulation, financing or implementation. It underestimated the role of small industry in ASEAN development. Also since they were large-scale, capital-intensive and high-risk investments due to the long gestation period, the AIP did not appeal to the private sector. Thus, it was left to the ASEAN governments and respective national agencies and corporations to participate in such projects. Of the five AIPs identified, only two (urea projects) have been implemented on a reduced scale.

5. Lack of commitments by member countries to market-sharing arrangements. The experience of the last two decades has demonstrated the unwillingness of ASEAN national governments to grant others – and therefore deny themselves – exclusive rights of production in specific areas even if these were part of an exchange arrangement. All of them had highly ambitious plans for their countries' industrial future, and for many ASEAN governments, receiving a specific AIP often seemed unequal to the apparent sacrifice of industrial ambitions in various areas. Thus, every government had tried to restrict as much as possible the scope of the AIPs hosted by other countries so as to give themselves the greatest freedom for future action, even to the point of rendering such projects non-viable. One good example was the proposal to locate a 200 hp diesel engine in Singapore. But Indonesia wanted the diesel engine project. After unsuccessful attempts to divide the project between the two countries according to the capacity of the diesel engines, Singapore abandoned it completely (Tan, 1996). Another good example was the Indonesian announcement of

its decision to proceed with a national soda ash plant in 1981 despite the apprehension of the other ASEAN countries, especially Thailand, that this would adversely affect the ASEAN soda ash.

6. Complexities and bureaucracy. Given the range of issues to be settled and complexities involved, the implementation of the AIP had not been facilitated by the decentralized ASEAN machinery. Matters had been negotiated and decisions arrived at through a series of meetings at different levels held at different time intervals. The procedures for receiving Japanese soft loans had been long drawn out. For example, in the case of Indonesia's ASEAN urea project, from the feasibility study to the final approval it took 20 months to complete. By the time the project was ready for launching, its cost had escalated by more than 30 percent (from the initial cost of US$300 million to US$400 million). At another level private sector cooperation, frustrated by ASEAN bureaucracy, was moving forward without ASEAN support.

(b) ASEAN industrial complementation (AIC) and brand-to-brand complementation (BBC) The AIC (established in 1981) is an improved version of the AIP after facing implementation difficulties. Under this scheme member countries are allocated complementary products in the specific industrial sectors for the production and preferential trade among themselves, that is the provision of tariff preferences of 50 percent and protection from competition up to three years by disallowing competing projects during this period.[6] By dividing different production stages of vertically integrated industries among themselves, the ASEAN countries hope to increase intra-ASEAN trade and investment and bring about competitive prices and product quality of international standard.

Based on resource pooling and market sharing, the scheme is to be participated in by at least four member countries, and the identification of appropriate products for inclusion in the scheme is to be done by the ASEAN Chambers of Commerce and Industry (CCI), as its key feature, subject to the approval of the ASEAN Committee of Industry, Minerals and Energy (COIME) and by the ASEAN Committee on Trade and Tourism (COTT) for tariff preferences. The ASEAN CCI is supposed to act as an official spokesman of the private sector and as a channel of communication between the government and the private sector for the purpose of industrial complementation (Chee and Jang-Won, 1988, p.53). This identification and consultation role of the ASEAN CCI is meant to bring out the much needed private sector initiative which was lacking in the AIP programme.

A number of AIC projects have been recommended to the government for consideration, but only one package, involving automobile parts and components, has been approved. This project has proven to be unsuccessful. Similar problems were encountered in the identification and implementation of the AIC projects. The long bureaucratic procedure adopted in the identification and implementation of an AIC project had produced a number of time-consuming extensive consultations, discussions and approvals. Another stumbling block in the area of industrial complementation has been the absence of established goals and guidelines shared by the interested private sector bodies and the respective ASEAN governments. Such shared goals could make negotiations regarding product choice, market access and investment funding less prone to bureaucratic delays. But there was too little private sector participation. The AIC guidelines in terms of planning and implementation were drawn up without private sector participation and have been described as inflexible and impractical by ASEAN businessmen. The exclusivity clause of three years provided in the AIC basic agreement did not offer sufficient incentives. Also, apart from the preferential tariffs, other forms of incentives and assistance were excluded. It did not allow a firm to have a full monopoly by specifying an unfavourable time limit for exclusive privileges of AIC products. The requirement that at least four ASEAN countries participate in an AIC project has made it difficult to identify projects. Existing avenues of AIC procedures did not facilitate easy identification or approval of projects. Even if it were easy to identify the projects, it would have been difficult to allocate them, especially those deemed desirable by most ASEAN countries. In the AIC scheme every country wanted to produce the high value-added rather than the low value-added component. Thus, the allocation of products to participating member countries has proven to be difficult. Further, the proliferation of different models and brands has led to a situation where a country imported a product of one brand from another member country without exporting to that country due to the mismatch of brands.

In view of the above, the AIC project for automotive components was not successful. With the exception of Singapore, all the other ASEAN countries have developed their own automobile industries with participation from multi-national automotive companies.

The BBC (established in 1988) is an offshoot of the AIC and is similarly concerned with the production and exchange of automotive parts and components to facilitate horizontal specialization in the production of these products in the region. But unlike the AIC, this scheme encourages automotive brand owners to exploit the economies of scale of production by exchanging approved automotive parts and components for specified automotive brands. There have been about 70 approved BBC projects implemented so far involving more than 10 automotive manufacturers (ASEAN Secretariat, 1995, p.14).

(c) ASEAN industrial joint venture (AIJV)   About the same time that the AIC scheme was announced, the ASEAN-CCI Council, which met in Jakarta at the

end of 1980, proposed a new scheme in response to the difficulties encountered in the AIP and AIC schemes. AIJVs are private sector equivalents of AIPs enjoying exclusivity and other privileges similar to the AIC projects, but with added elements of flexibility. They are not required to have total ASEAN ownership. In contrast to the AIP and AIC projects, investors are free to locate their projects in any participating countries to produce accredited AIJV products. They are open to non-ASEAN nationals, and ASEAN ownership can be waived as long as the ASEAN component is at least 51 percent. Any manufactured products involving investors from at least two ASEAN countries holding a combined 51 percent minimum equity would qualify for tariff preferences in all ASEAN countries. Tariff preferences on AIJV products apply to participating countries only for a four-year period (this exclusivity was subsequently waived). A margin of preferences at 90 percent based on the prevailing ASEAN PTA rate of the importing country is extended to approved AIJV products. While receiving AIJV preferences, they must also extend the same preferences. There is an emphasis on equity and market sharing, unlike AIC's reciprocity.

There are two types of AIJV projects: single AIJV – single product produced by two or more ASEAN countries, and complementary AIJV – for example machinery, textile, automobile. Most of the AIJV projects proposed in the early 1980s were large scale and involved heavy industry such as the manufacture of paper, tractors, ferro-alloys and so on. Of the 21 projects which have been proposed, very few have been implemented. Most of the AIJV projects have foreign equity participation and few are ASEAN-wide in their coverage (Tan, 1996, p. 154). As of 1995, 23 AIJV projects have been approved (ASEAN Secretariat, 1995, p.14).

Limitations. The AIJV projects have encountered bureaucratic delays in identification, formulation and approval. The time and bureaucracy involved in gaining the acceptance by governments of an AIJV in most cases far exceed the economic benefits obtainable after the acceptance within the scheme. For example, it took three years to win the ASEAN ministers' approval to launch the AIJV agreement.

Dumping actions by non-ASEAN suppliers have also eroded the tariff preferences provided under the scheme and some in the private sector have found the tariff preferences insufficient incentives. But the most serious problem has been the reluctance of member countries to participate in such joint ventures which could pose a threat to their own existing domestic industries.

3.2.5 Conclusion

In summary, although progress has been made to make the industrial cooperation schemes more attractive to the private sector by shifting away from the government-initiated AIPs to the more private sector-based AIJV and brand-to-brand complementation, the impact of the schemes on industrial development has been quite limited due to administrative and implementation problems and lack of private sector involvement.

Having realized the shortcomings of current industrial cooperation schemes, the ASEAN countries have been exploring ways to improve their effectiveness. First, at their informal meeting in Phuket last April, 1995 the ASEAN Economic Ministers agreed to scrap the brand-to-brand complementation and AIJV schemes, and to develop a more effective industrial cooperation scheme with the active participation of the ASEAN private sector. Secondly, at the Fifth ASEAN Summit in December 1995 held in Jakarta, the ASEAN Heads of Government approved the establishment of an ASEAN–CCI permanent secretariat at the ASEAN Secretariat in Jakarta.[7] Thirdly, the ASEAN Senior Economic Officials in Jakarta on 12 September, 1996 agreed to set in motion another investment liberalization scheme – ASEAN Industrial Cooperation Scheme (Aico) by November, 1996. The main privilege under Aico is that participating companies can enjoy preferential tariff rates of 0–5 percent immediately upon approval for the export of their products within the region, in addition to other non-tariff privileges a member country may accord.

3.3   DEVELOPMENT AND COOPERATION IN AGRICULTURE

This section describes the importance of agriculture to ASEAN; reviews the past developments in agriculture; the transformation and modernization of the food sector, largely under the impetus of the Green Revolution; and cooperative undertakings within ASEAN agriculture.

Although the importance of agriculture as a source of output to the ASEAN countries is diminishing, more than half of the ASEAN population still live in the rural sector and are engaged in agriculture. Agricultural development has, therefore, been given due importance by most of the ASEAN countries. But the ASEAN development experiences in this sector have been varied due to the differences in policies pursued and the different institutions existing in each country. Further, ASEAN cooperation in this sector has been highly technical and developmental in nature, rather than in terms of market sharing arrangements.

3.3.1   Importance of Agriculture

As can gleaned from Table 3.4, agriculture has been and still is an important sector in ASEAN. It is a major contributor to the GDP of the ASEAN

Table 3.4   ASEAN share of agriculture in GDP (%)

	1980	1985	1990	1993	1994	1995
Brunei	0.6	1.2	1.7	–	–	–
Indonesia	30.7	22.6	19.7	18.0	16.6	15.9
Malaysia	22.9	20.7	19.4	16.0	14.8	13.9
Philippines	25.6	29.2	26.9	22.7	22.3	21.5
Singapore	1.1	0.7	0.3	0.2	0.2	0.2
Thailand	20.6	19.6	14.2	12.2	11.1	10.9
Vietnam	50.0	47.2	37.5	28.8	27.7	–

Note: –: not available.

Sources: ADB, *Key Indicators of Developing Asian and Pacific Countries* (1991); *Asian Development Outlook* (1995/1996 and 1996/97).

countries, except for Brunei and the city-state Singapore, which have limited agricultural land. During the past decade 1980–90, the relative share of agriculture declined significantly, except in the Philippines, as a result of rapid industrialization: from 30.7 percent to 19.7 percent in Indonesia; 22.9 percent to 19.4 percent in Malaysia; 1.1 percent to 0.3 percent in Singapore and 20.6 percent to 14.2 percent in Thailand.[8] This trend continued into the early 1990s so that in 1995 agriculture's share was reduced for all ASEAN (minus Brunei). Although there has been a significant decline in the relative share of agriculture in the total GDP, agriculture still occupies a substantial portion of GDP in ASEAN and will continue to have profound socioeconomic implications.

Although the agricultural sector is the backward sector in the ASEAN economies (plagued with problems of high unemployment, underemployment and mass poverty, due to the rural population explosion and low productivity), the number of employed persons found in the agricultural sector is significant. No less than 45 percent of the employed persons in Indonesia, the Philippines, Thailand and Vietnam are found in the agricultural sector in 1995. Thus, it is the main provider of jobs in ASEAN. The share of agricultural employment in Singapore and Brunei has always been negligible as their economies are not agri-based, as Table 3.5 shows.[9] Except for Brunei and Singapore, ASEAN countries are net exporters of food, agriculture and forest products. They are major world exporters of natural rubber (Malaysia), palm oil (Indonesia and Malaysia), copra and coconut oil (the Philippines), and rice (Thailand and Vietnam). Other major agricultural products for each of the four ASEAN countries are: for Indonesia rubber, coffee, tea, tobacco, pepper; for Malaysia sawn logs and sawn timber; for the Philippines sugar, desiccated coconut and

Table 3.5 Number of persons employed by main industry (as % of total number of persons employed)

ASEAN Countries	Agriculture					Manufacturing					
	1970	1980	1990	1994	1995	1970	1980	1990	1994	1995
Brunei[a]	–	5.0	2.0	–	–	–	4.0	8.8	–	–
Indonesia[b]	64.0	56.0	55.9	50.8	–	7.0	9.1	10.1	11.4	–
Malaysia[c]	18.0	37.2	26.0	19.9	18.9	13.0	15.5	19.9	24.7	25.5
Philippines	54.0	51.4	45.2	44.7	44.5	12.0	11.0	9.7	10.3	9.8
Singapore	4.0	1.6	0.4	0.3	0.2	22.0	30.1	28.4	25.7	24.0
Thailand[d]	79.0	70.8	64.0	56.7*	–	4.0	7.9	10.2	12.3*	–
Vietnam	–	69.9	71.6	72.5*	68.9	–	10.7	11.2	10.7*	12.1

Notes:

–: not available; *figures for 1993 as 1994 data are unavailable.

[a]Only figures for 1981 and 1991 are available.

[b]Figures for 1970 are based on 1971 figures.

[c]Figures for 1970 are based on 1974 figures. The 1974 figures are for Peninsular Malaysia only.

[d]Figures for 1970 are based on 1971 figures.

Sources: ASEAN *Statistical Yearbook on Food, Agriculture and Forestry, 1980–90;* ADB, *Key Indicators of Developing Asian and Pacific Countries* (1995, 1996); Brunei Ministry of Finance, *Brunei Darussalam Statistical Yearbook* (1993).

lumber and for Thailand corn, cassava, sugar, molasses and rubber. Agricultural exports represent a substantial source of foreign exchange earnings for most ASEAN countries and are thus crucial to their economic growth and stability.

Agriculture has also proven to be a potent engine of growth for the whole economy. In the case of the Philippines, for example, in the 1980s GDP growth had averaged –0.02 percent while agriculture posted a positive growth.

3.3.2   ASEAN Agricultural Performance

The ASEAN agricultural sector is basically made up of two subsectors: the large landholding subsector which produces cash crops mainly for export markets and the relatively small landholding subsector which produces mainly rice and corn for domestic consumption and domestic markets.

This dualistic nature has posed as a serious obstacle to achieving a balanced growth and agricultural integration within ASEAN. But despite this, the ASEAN countries on the whole have achieved a significant agricultural progress in terms of increased productivity and reduced income inequality in the rural sector through the effective implementation of appropriate policies and technological improvements.

The most significant development in ASEAN agriculture has been the successful transformation and modernization of their food sector, largely under the impetus of the Green Revolution, that is the introduction and diffusion of modern high-yielding varieties (HYVs) of rice. In the past, expansion of the land area had been the main source of agricultural output growth, but since the 1970s increase in productivity has become the major source of growth, aided by the expansion of rural infrastructure and introduction of new technology, closing the gaps in rice productivity between ASEAN and other East Asian countries.[10] By 1975, 62 percent of the rice area in the Philippines was planted with the modern varieties, 41 percent in Indonesia, 36 percent in Malaysia, but only 7 percent in Thailand.[11]

The most notable success stories are Indonesia (which had been the largest world rice importer due its large population and partly as a result of the neglect of agricultural development under Sukarno) and Malaysia (which had traditionally been a net food importer as cash crops dominated their agricultural sector). There has been a creditable growth in rice production over the 1980s, but in the past the growth in domestic demand had outpaced the growth in domestic production.[12] The same thing was true with corn. The Philippines has gone through a number of food production programmes since the mid-1970s, but has remained as one of the region's biggest food importers until quite recently. Among the ASEAN countries, Thailand seems to be the only consistent rice exporter.

Green Revolution

The basis of the ASEAN Green Revolution is a biological and chemical innovation involving the use of high yielding varieties of miracle rice, fertilizers, insecticides, pesticides, rodenticides, herbicides and fungicides. It also requires mechanical innovation, for example mechanical farming, requiring heavy capital investment and new pattern of farm management and cultivation technology and water control.

Although there are direct costs and indirect costs such as environmental degradation due to rapid use of fertilizers and multiple cropping-induced erosion, there are substantial benefits including increased rice production, increase in efficiency (measured by output per unit of input), diversification of agricultural commodities (multiple cropping concept), provision of additional rural employment, increased income at an individual level and the generation of foreign exchange with spillover effects into other economic sectors (forward/backward linkages).[13]

The overall pattern of agricultural development progress in the ASEAN4 since the adoption of the new production technology has been uneven, however, partly due to their differences in capacity to absorb and diffuse improved technology and partly due to their different institutional responses (Wong, 1979, p. 96). Their varied experiences with the Green Revolution is a good reminder that institutions do play a significant role and that productivity increases depend not just on the strength of technological innovations but also on the favourable interaction of the technological change with the institutional environment.

Quality of institutional environment

Institutional environment refers to a country's legal, political and regulatory framework. Indicators often used to measure the quality of the institutional environment are security of land ownership or use, policy environment (right policies and stable/credible government) and bureaucratic quality.

Security of land ownership

The principal consequence of an inadequate institutional environment is insecure land rights. In the context of ASEAN agriculture, these land rights refer to the right of a farmer to the land, to the revenue streams generated by the land, and to any other contractual obligations due to a farmer. These rights are more secure to the extent that political and legal institutions inhibit unilateral private and public decisions that reassign land rights. Well-defined and transparent laws on land ownership and use are examples of an institution that protects individuals from violation of their land rights. Differences in structure of land ownership and in the legal protection of the rights of tenants have given rise to the differences in the agricultural performance among the ASEAN countries. There is a strong link between the benefits of technological progress and secured tenure of land ownership or use. This explains Thailand's more notable performance in agricultural productivity compared to the Philippines where land redistribution under the land reform programme failed. Such land reform is essential in the Philippine context where land ownership is highly skewed. Without effective protection of the tenants' rights or guaranteed investment, land use will be unsecured and thus farmers tend to refrain from investment in new agricultural technology.

Policy environment
Appropriate policies conducive to the adoption of a new technology, accompanied by a stable and credible government are necessary. Credit policy is the most important component of these policies. ASEAN agriculture consists of a large proportion of small-scale farmers who usually are short of capital and have difficulty in access to credit financing. Since costly inputs like machineries, fertilizers and pesticides are necessary complements for the adoption of high-yielding varieties (HYVs), small-scale farmers are unlikely to benefit from the use of the HYV seeds if they could not finance the purchase of these inputs. Therefore, credit policies that favour only large-scale farmers and fail to cater to the needs and abilities of the small-scale farmers will hinder the adoption of new technological methods by small-scale farmers.

Policies that emphasize industrialization without equal attention to agricultural development have also acted as barriers to the balanced distribution of the benefits of the Green Revolution. This over-emphasis on urban development has led to inadequate provision of required infrastructure (such as irrigation, harvest facilities, transport, electrification, agricultural research and extension of services) critical to the generation and diffusion of technology in the agricultural sector.

Inadequate funds allocated for the rural sector have also contributed to the low literacy rate in the ASEAN rural areas, preventing the farmers from being receptive to new technological methods and to the transfer of relevant skills and knowledge for the proper application and management of new technology. Except for Malaysia, the ASEAN countries had embarked on urban-biased development strategies in the 1960s and 1970s, leading to significant income disparity between the urban and rural sectors. In contrast, Malaysia's impressive record of agricultural performance in productivity and poverty alleviation in the rural sector were largely due to its less urban-biased policies. Consequently, more resources have been channelled to the agricultural sector in terms of infrastructure provision and subsidies.

Stable and credible government
Governments perceived to be unstable and without credibility create an uncertain atmosphere which is not conducive to agricultural investment in

new technological methods. This is because the returns from such a heavy investment are substantially affected by changes in taxing and subsidising policies.

The less notable performances of Indonesia in the 1960s, and the Philippines in the 1970s and early 1980s could be largely attributed to their political instability resulting in frequent changes in policy and creating an atmosphere of uncertainty for investment in agricultural technology.[14]

Quality of bureaucracy

Policies and projects are only successful if they can be implemented and managed effectively, and the effective implementation of policies and management of projects hinges on the efficiency of bureaucracy. Bureaucratic efficiency is particularly important in the management of an irrigation system. Since success of cropping depends on the adequate and timely supply of water, proper maintenance and operation of an irrigation system is crucial. Hence, bureaucratic inefficiency, which prevents a proper operation and maintenance of an irrigation system, would hinder a broad-based adoption of new cultivation technology.

3.3.3   ASEAN Economic Cooperation in Agriculture

As an important sector in ASEAN, cooperation in agriculture has been numerous. But all the cooperative undertakings in agriculture have so far been technical and developmental in nature. The Committee on Food, Agriculture and Forestry (COFAF) is responsible for the identification and implementation of cooperative undertakings in the agricultural sector. Formed in March 1977, it undertakes the following tasks: (a) to coordinate, review and prepare studies on the prospects of the agricultural sector; (b) to develop efficient methods for the exchange of information on agriculture; (c) to identify areas for cooperation; (d) to maintain close ties with related committees in ASEAN and with other related organizations inside and outside the region; and (e) to report its progress to the ASEAN Economic Ministers (AEM).

Between 1978 and 1988 COFAF had identified 46 cooperative projects – 7 in food, 10 in agriculture, 15 in forestry, 8 in livestock and 6 in fisheries. By 1985, 13 of them were ongoing, 4 completed and 29 not yet implemented. The largest number of projects were located in the Philippines followed by Malaysia, Thailand and Indonesia in descending order. The majority of the fundings for these projects came from sources outside the region. And only a few projects were pursued on a long-term basis. One of them was the ASEAN Food Security Project which established in 1979 an ASEAN Emergency Rice Reserve to be contributed to by each of the member countries. The objective was to create a stockpile of 50 000 tonnes of rice to meet shortfalls in domestic supply. This is currently being reviewed for the purpose of creating a more dynamic food security arrangement to enhance intra-ASEAN trade and promote food production under the principle of comparative advantage. Others included the Food Handling and the Seed Technology project.

ASEAN cooperation in agriculture has also been fostered in their dealings with the developed countries on matters of market access for their primary exports, better terms of trade, stabilization of export earnings and other non-sensitive areas of cooperation.

3.3.4 Obstacles to Trade Liberalization for Agriculture

The type of ASEAN cooperation in agriculture has been technical in nature aimed at increasing production and guaranteeing supply, rather than at market sharing. Despite the perceived benefits of integrating agriculture, progress in this area has been slow because of the following reasons:

(i) Political priorities (for example national security). The first and foremost justification for trade restrictions in agriculture is the need to safeguard national security. Any country with an agricultural capacity tends rather to be self-sufficient or to hedge and diversify sources of imports especially of food supplies. Although specialization under free trade could lead to efficient allocation of resources, it could also lead to dependency which is politically risky. This fear was vindicated in 1973 when a rise in the price of Thai rice created some problems in countries importing heavily from Thailand. Agriculture is protected by almost all countries for other political reasons such as to improve the balance of payments and redistribute income in favour of farm groups in the context of high unemployment and inefficiency in the agricultural sector.

(ii) Structural and technological dualism in agriculture. Another obstacle is the inherent structural and technological dualism of ASEAN agriculture, with its small-landholding subsector producing primarily food (rice) and feed grains (corn) and the large-scale landholders producing cash crops (for example sugar, bananas, rubber) mostly for export. In the event that complete liberalization takes place, the small-scale subsector could be left behind while increased competition propels the latter to greater efficiency and productivity, thereby exacerbating income disparity and social problems. Thus, trade liberalization may hurt the agro-industries and the livelihood of small farmers. This partly explains the exclusion of rice from immediate tariff reduction under the ASEAN Free Trade Area's (AFTA) Common Effective Preferential Tariff (CEPT) scheme.[15]

(iii)   Competition rather than complementarity. Another problem is the highly competitive nature of agricultural products produced by the ASEAN countries. Due to similarity in factor endowments and climatic conditions, they have produced similar agricultural products. Under integration there will clearly be losers, and thus the public support for intra-regional trade in agriculture is weak.

(iv)   Inadequate infrastructure. Transportation and telecommunication networks within the region are relatively costly and inefficient. ASEAN infrastructure networks have been set up to serve the domestic markets and their traditional extra-regional trading partners like Japan, the US and European Union (EU). This lack of regional orientation is a significant obstacle to trade expansion as the costly and inefficient port and other related transport facilities hinder the trading of agricultural products which are relatively bulky and low-valued.[16]

Other minor obstacles include ASEAN countries' lack of first-hand experience in agricultural cooperation relative to other areas like the joint service and industrial projects. Thus, ASEAN is uncertain as to which is the best approach and what effects would result. Moreover, some ASEAN countries do not have the capacity to liberalize trade significantly and yet protect farmers from price fluctuations and more efficient regional suppliers.

3.3.5   Prospects for Agricultural Integration

Given the political sensitivity and low degree of complementarity of agriculture in ASEAN, the type of economic cooperation could only be in terms of resource pooling, rather than market sharing. Trade liberalization can also occur in commodities of a less politically sensitive nature, and in new products that will not affect the original level of employment.

However, the long-term prospect for a complete agricultural integration in ASEAN is far from bleak. Agriculture is already included in the proposed ASEAN Free Trade Area, except for a few obstacles. Most of the above problems have partly been resolved, and thus the ASEAN governments need to merely encourage and consolidate more joint ventures in agriculture and agri-processing to increase productivity and to ensure a constant and stable source of primary commodities and to be selective in its inclusion of the various agricultural products in the integration programme.

Laudable proposals attempted at previous AFTA council meetings are ambitious yet brave and commendable. Under the proposed Common Effective Preferential Tariff (CEPT) scheme, all ASEAN members are expected to cut tariff rates on most agricultural products by 0–5 percent by the year 2002. Given the strong competition posed by China, India and other regional groupings, ASEAN must respond quickly so as not to be left behind. The CEPT scheme is a move in the right and much needed direction. In view of the trends to explore more ways of speeding up liberalization, and noting how the other regions were removing tariffs swiftly, the complete integration of agriculture in ASEAN should not be long. This can be seen in reports from Thailand claiming to be a strong advocate for free trade in agriculture, wanting as much access to other markets as possible and in the Brunei Sultan's persistent call to speed up the trade liberalization process. Thus, the tricky question to ask is how to cut the number of items in the sensitive list, which are shielded from tariff reduction under the CEPT scheme, because of the perceived strategic and security value to the member countries. Some products which are considered sensitive – such as rice, maize and soya bean – are excluded from tariff reduction until the year 2010, instead of the proposed 2002, the target date for trimming tariffs to 0–5 percent. However, with much confidence, this would probably be resolved in due time, through greater flexibility and sensitivity of the ASEAN member countries towards one another.

3.3.6 Conclusion

The ASEAN cooperation in agriculture has been successful so far in areas that only require the pooling of resources to guarantee food supply and improve production as well as in their external economic relations to gain more market access and better terms of trade. To the extent that agricultural development implies food security and improved productivity, the ASEAN cooperative undertakings, most notably the ASEAN Food Security Reserve Project and the Seed Technology project, have played a significant role in ASEAN agricultural development.

3.4 DEVELOPMENT AND COOPERATION IN SERVICES

Another important feature of ASEAN economic development has been the rapid growth of their services sector since the 1960s. In 1994 the services sector contributed roughly 40 percent to 62 percent of Gross Domestic Product (GDP) in ASEAN countries, as Table 3.6 shows, and consistent with the normal pattern of economic development, its share has grown over time. It is now the largest contributor to national output in the ASEAN countries, with the exception of Indonesia and Malaysia. Singapore has the largest and most developed services sector as a proportion of GDP, its activity accounting for 62 percent of its GDP in 1994.

ASEAN cooperation in this sector has been instrumental in the sector's rapid growth, although its contribution has not been as spectacular. ASEAN

Table 3.6　ASEAN share of services in GDP (%)*

	1970	1980	1993	1994	1995
Brunei	–	12.4	43.8	–	–
		(73.8)	(37.3)		
Indonesia	37.0	34.3	40.3	39.8	41.9
	(28.0)	(41.3)	(42.1)	(43.6)	(42.2)
Malaysia	–	41.3	40.0	39.8	39.0
		(35.8)	(44.2)	(45.4)	(47.1)
Philippines	38.1	36.0	42.9	42.8	43.0
	(33.7)	(40.5)	(34.4)	(34.8)	(35.5)
Singapore	61.4	60.0	63.3	62.4	57.1
	(36.4)	(38.8)	(36.5)	(37.4)	(42.7)
Thailand	44.1	49.7	46.9	46.8	46.9
	(25.7)	(30.1)	(40.9)	(42.1)	(42.2)
Vietnam	–	31.0	–	42.4	38.4
		(26.3)		(25.3)	(27.7)

Notes:　*Figures in brackets are shares of industry in GDP; –: not available.

Sources:　ADB, *Asian Development Outlook* (1994,1995, 1996 and 1997); Brunei Ministry of Finance, *Brunei Darussalam Statistical Yearbook* (1993).

cooperation in the services sector has been technical in nature and the ASEAN countries have been reluctant to expand their scope of cooperation in trade (trade liberalization) to the services sector. There has, however, recently been an attempt to include the trade in services for trade liberalization within ASEAN. In the last ASEAN Economic Ministers Meeting held in Brunei, September 1995 (*The Straits Times*, 9 September, 1995), the ASEAN officials accepted in principle an ASEAN Framework Agreement on Services which was signed at the ASEAN Summit in December 1995. They have identified seven priority areas in the services sector for specific negotiations for market concessions: financial services, tourism, construction, air and maritime transport, tele-communications and business services.

This part of the chapter will highlight some of the key characteristics of the services sector in ASEAN and then outline the role of ASEAN cooperation in each of the specific subsectors: banking and finance, transport and tourism.

3.4.1　Key Features

Since the 1980s one has seen a rapid technological revolution in ASEAN in almost all services activities. Moreover, considerable variety exists between services sectors of the ASEAN countries, reflecting different stages of economic development, resource endowments and economic orientation. As already shown in Table 3.6, Singapore has the most developed services sector which provides most of the country's output and employment.

Significant variation also exists within their services sector. In finance, for example, the services range from those of the rural moneylenders to those from multinational banks; road transport can also range from modern intercity buses to trishaws.

Moreover, in this sector their respective governments have played a key economic role, both as a direct source of employment and indirectly through expenditure programmes designed to improve the quality of physical and social infrastructure. In Singapore the big banks such as the Development Bank of Singapore (DBS) and Post Office Savings Bank (POSBank) are government banks. In Indonesia and Malaysia, banks have been set up not only for economic objectives but also for political reasons.

Finally, there is the internationalization of services. Services were traditionally regarded as non-tradables, an ancillary to the goods sector and rarely traded across national borders. However, reduced barriers to international commerce, increasing personal mobility, and revolution in transport and telecommunications have internationalized the services industries. Banking, professional and personal services, insurance, tourism, data processing and construction services are increasingly traded within and beyond the region.

3.4.2 Subsectors

The rapid growth of the services sectors in ASEAN is to a large extent reflective of the strong performance of the following subsectors: financial services, transport and tourism.

3.4.2.1 Financial services

The financial subsector has grown and evolved into a more sophisticated financial system due to technological innovation, the rise of non-traditional modes of service production and delivery, growth of the real sector, greater internationalization, deregulation and greater mobility of financial resources within the region.

Based on standard microeconomic theories, deregulation and greater mobility of financial resources can lead to an efficient allocation of savings and real capital, and increase the supply of savings by increasing the rate of return and eliminating the non-price disincentives to savings. These allow individual asset holders to diversify their portfolio investments and enjoy a higher risk–return trade-off. They can also broaden and deepen the financial markets and increase liquidity in secondary markets, lower the cost of borrowing and improve the matching between the borrowers and lenders.[17]

The role of government was crucial in the ASEAN's financial development by establishing a favourable macroeconomic environment in terms of low inflation. The stable environments of Malaysia, Singapore and Thailand were particularly important in instilling confidence in holding cash and quasi-money holdings; on the other hand, the less predictable environment of Indonesia and the Philippines had once hindered financial development. Further, their respective governments have taken the lead in deregulating their financial sector. Prior to the 1980s, Indonesia and the Philippines had the most heavily regulated formal banking sectors. They later recognized the self-defeating nature of financial regulation, and in the 1980s started deregulating their financial sector.

They have also directly participated in the financial sector through ownership of banks. Bank ownership has been part of a deliberate strategy of economic development in Singapore and in the more regulated environments of Indonesia and the Philippines. In Indonesia and Malaysia state-owned banks have been a key instrument of ethnic redistribution and promotion of indigenous businesses. But over time there has been a trend towards privatization, and the share of state-owned banks in the total financial sector has shrunk, or has grown slower compared to their private competitors.

3.4.2.2   Transport
All major forms of transport have expanded quickly due to the ASEAN governments' massive infrastructure programmes, reduction in costs of transport due to technological advancements in air travel and light commercial transport, simplification of government regulations and rising incomes leading to more personal mobility and demand for transport services.

3.4.2.3   Tourism
Tourism is an important ASEAN foreign exchange earner, ranking highly with major manufactured exports such as textiles. It has expanded quickly due to the deregulation and simplification of immigration requirements, rising income and competitive exchange rate regimes, decline in the real cost of international travel and effective promotional efforts.

Apart from being a major foreign exchange earner, tourism is important to the ASEAN countries because the ASEAN region has now become one of the fastest growing tourist destinations in the world. Although tourism has made different contributions to individual ASEAN members, intra-ASEAN tourism has become an important and growing fraction of total ASEAN tourism.

3.4.3   ASEAN financial cooperation

The ASEAN cooperation in the area of financial services has contributed to the growth and development of their financial sector by fostering greater mobility of financial resources within the region through the standardization and harmonization of rules and regulations governing the banking and financial practises in ASEAN and the reduction of the 'ability and willingness barriers' to financial integration.[18] Among ASEAN's notable achievements are the ASEAN Swap Arrangement to assist member countries bridge temporary international liquidity problems in times of crisis and the increased use of ASEAN currencies in the settlement of intra-ASEAN trade in recent years.

3.4.3.1   Government

On the governmental level, the Committee of Finance and Banking (COFAB), established in 1976, is in charge of exploring and monitoring the possible area of financial cooperation. The major activity of COFAB is to supervise the meetings of ASEAN insurance commissioners, tax administrators and ASEAN working groups on customs matters. The major accomplishments of COFAB include the agreement on the need for bilateral investment guarantees and avoidance of double taxation and acting as a vehicle for ASEAN-Third party dialogue in financial matters.

COFAB is responsible for the creation of the ASEAN swap facility (1977). The ASEAN swap arrangement is intended for short-term liquidity crises. The fund was US$100 million in 1977 and US$200 million in 1979 which members can borrow in times of short-term liquidity crisis. The borrowing limit was up to US$ 80 million repayable in three months, renewable once for three months. In 1983, four swap transactions took place. At this time Benigno Aquino was assassinated causing a large outflow of capital from the Philippines.

3.4.3.2   Private sector

On the private sector level, there is the creation of the ASEAN Bankers Association (1976). Membership consists of member countries' banking industry associations. There are three components of the ASEAN Bankers Association: conference (ASEAN Banking Conference), council (ASEAN Banking Council) and secretariat. ASEAN Banking Conference's major accomplishments include the formulation of policy for coordination of the ASEAN cooperation among ASEAN bankers, financing of agriculture and agro-based industries, and banking education and cooperation in investment, trade and finance. The ASEAN Banking Council's major accomplishment is the establishment of AFC (ASEAN Financial Corporation). As a joint venture among the private banks of the ASEAN member countries, it is intended as a vehicle for the pooling of resources required to finance regional development projects. Its specific objectives are to promote industrial development, intraregional trade, financial cooperation and mobilization of financial resources.

A number of proposals were proposed in the late 1970s and early 1980s such as the setting up of an ASEAN Trading and Investment Corporation (ATIC) and an ASEAN Bankers Acceptance (ABC), but were not successful due to the lack of interest and financial non-viability.

3.4.4   Prospects for ASEAN Financial Integration

It is evident from the previous section that ASEAN financial cooperation has played an important and supportive role in the growth and development of their financial sector and in facilitating trade and investment in the region. ASEAN financial cooperation, however, is only one of the many factors responsible for the rapid growth of their financial sector. Individual countries' uncoordinated policies of deregulation, stable macroeconomic environment and growth of their real sector have also played a very important role.

The prospect for greater ASEAN financial cooperation depends on how the ASEAN countries can influence the following factors or determinants affecting the level of financial integration: (i) Comparative levels of financial development. Domestic financial development is a prerequisite for international financial integration; Singapore is the most financially developed among ASEAN. (ii) Level of intra-ASEAN banking linkages. The ASEAN Finance Corporation and ASEAN Banking Council are formal links between ASEAN banking industries. (iii) Level of real economic integration. Intra-ASEAN trade and other forms of economic cooperation lay the essential groundwork for financial integration. As real economic linkages increase, the demand for financial cooperation will increase. (iv) Degree of foreign exchange/capital controls. (v) Exchange rate variability which relies on the adoption of a common unit of account and the strength of the existing forward markets. (vi) Tax treatment neutrality. (vii) Comparative regulatory policies for domestic financial institutions, particularly in relation to the asset and liability structure of banks. (viii) Conformity/nonconformity with acceptable commercial standards. Noncompliance with certain regulations may form a barrier to financial integration if significant loss of confidence results. Financial crises or scandals can undermine both the domestic and international financial systems.

3.4.5   ASEAN Cooperation in Transport

Cooperation in the area of transport falls under the supervision of the Committee on Transportation and Communications (COTAC). Working to implement and follow up on the decisions of COTAC are subcommittees. Based on the Integrated Work Programme on Transport and Communications (IWPTC) 1982–86, COTAC has identified 59 cooperative projects (mostly in the maritime sector), but only 8 had been completed by the end of 1986. Many were withdrawn or deferred and included in the IWPTC 1987–91. Of the 90 projects included, only 20 were completed by the end of 1991. Completion of a project, however, in many cases just meant that the data gathering and technical part of the study had been realized. Nothing happened in terms of closer regional cooperation in the movement of goods and people. Overall, despite the priority accorded to regional cooperation in transport, the record has not been impressive.[19]

It has been argued that the lack of progress in regional cooperation in transport could be attributed to the following: absence of a coherent set of objectives; national priorities superseding regional priorities; lack of regional character in the projects identified aggravated by the lack of expertise on the part of the COTAC members; and over-reliance on external sources for project funding.[20]

3.4.6   ASEAN Cooperation in Tourism

The ASEAN Cooperation in Tourism is under the jurisdiction of the Committee of Trade and Tourism (COTT) which has established a Subcommittee on Tourism (SCOT) to deal with tourism matters. Much of the progress in this area is highly concentrated in certain operational areas such as marketing, promotion and research, with little private sector involvement. It has taken the form of establishing: (i) the ASEAN Tourism Information Centre to coordinate and manage marketing programmes and projects approved by SCOT, liaise with other world and regional tourism bodies and the private sector, and conduct public relations and other activities related to the promotion of ASEAN travel; (ii) ASEAN Tourism Fora, annually organised and funded by ASEAN NTOs, to bring together ASEAN sellers and buyers from government and private sectors. Efforts to get the ASEAN private sector to assume a greater role have not been successful; (iii) ASEAN Promotional Chapters which are promotional arms in major tourist markets, staffed by government personnel and collective representation to project the 'ASEAN Image'; (iv) ASEAN Travel Films and Brochures which are combined resources to produce a travel film, 'ASEAN Mosaic' and 'ASEAN Welcome' brochure; (v) Research and Manpower Training to foster exchange of information and training of personnel; (vi) Third Party Technical Assistance and Dialogue which are tourism market studies funded by UNDP, ASEAN–EU Cooperation and ASEAN–NZ Cooperation; and (vii) ASEAN Circle and Promotional Fares providing inexpensive travel within ASEAN.

3.4.7   Obstacles to Tourism Cooperation

Despite the significant progress in ASEAN cooperation in the field of tourism, there is still great scope for improvement, such as addressing the following problems: (a) Lack of a unified tourism promotion plan and cooperation in developing the ASEAN region as a common destination, rather than as different tourist sites. Although ASEAN cooperation has been strong in this area, additional refinements are required to make the region a more attractive and appealing destination. (b) Lack of cooperation in planning and research. This is probably the most difficult, but most important, task because it requires ASEAN cooperation in identifying the region's strengths and weaknesses, and in formulating short-term and long-term plans to take advantage of anticipated tourism opportunities. (c) Travel barriers. The governments of Indonesia, the Philippines and Thailand have imposed travel taxes on departing nationals. (d) Inadequate private sector involvement. The ASEAN NTOs can provide the institutional framework for cooperation, but it is only the private sector which can implement the plans. More frequent and intensive consultations among the representatives of the national airlines and shipping and rail services should take place to provide an integrated logistical support package for tourists in the region.

3.5   CONCLUSION

ASEAN cooperation has been partly responsible for the rapid growth and development of their financial services and tourism subsectors. In the case of financial services, ASEAN cooperation has played a significant role by fostering greater mobility of financial resources, by harmonizing the rules and regulations governing the banking and financial practices in ASEAN and by promoting an exchange of information between their private sectors and government counterparts. With respect to tourism, they have been successful in undertaking cooperative efforts in the area of marketing and promotion. Unlike the financial services and tourism, the growth and development of the transport subsector could not have been partly attributable to ASEAN cooperation due to many factors including the presence of strong national interests.

SUGGESTIONS FOR FURTHER READING

For a good historical background of ASEAN cooperation in trade, Meyanathan and Haron (1987), Ooi(1987), Tan (1987) and Rieger (1985) are recommended. Chng (1991) and Chee Peng Lim (1987) are recommended for a comparative study of the industrialization experience of the ASEAN countries.

For a good coverage of ASEAN agricultural development, see Chiew (1987), Cabanilla (1988, pp. 55–68), and Wong (1979, Chapter 4). For good background reading and evaluation of ASEAN cooperation in transport, see

Naidu (1988, pp. 191–204) and Navaratnam (1987, pp. 357–69). On ASEAN cooperation in financial services, read Schulze (1988, pp. 157–88) and on ASEAN cooperation in tourism, read Wong (1987, 372–93) and Puntasen (1988, pp. 205–27). For a more updated coverage of ASEAN economic cooperation, refer to ASEAN Secretariat (1997).

NOTES

1. Commodities sold under these contracts enjoy preferential duties and priority supply in times of worldwide shortage. In 1977 an emergency sharing scheme for petroleum was drawn up. Singapore, Malaysia and Indonesia were given priority over non-ASEAN countries for Thailand's exports of rice in times of shortage.
2. The establishment of preferential trading arrangements represents the first stage in the process of achieving a complete economic integration of ASEAN economies.
3. Until 1992 Malaysia was Singapore's third largest trading partner. In 1994 it overtook the US as Singapore's top trading partner (*The Straits Times*, 16 August, 1996, p. 46).
4. The increasing importance of intra-industry trade is due to the globalization strategies of the multinational companies (MNCs) which undertake the various stages of production across its affiliates in different countries to achieve greater functional specialization and exploit the benefits of comparative advantage.
5. A major objective of the diversification drive is to maximize the role of the private sector in propelling the economy in terms of output turnover and employment creation. For details, see Hashim (1996, pp. 123–4).
6. The virtual guarantee of monopoly power under this exclusivity as well as its small domestic market were the reasons for Singapore's decision not to participate in the AIC scheme on automotive parts.
7. The ASEAN–CCI Secretariat is meant to help foster greater communication and linkages between the policy-making bodies and the private sector, and thus make the private sector closely involved from the early stages of ASEAN economic policy formulation. This has been operational since July 1996. Further, consultations between high-level private sector representatives and ASEAN Economic Ministers are held every year.
8. However, during the Philippine economic crisis of the 1980s, agriculture posted positive growth rates while all the other sectors experienced negative growth (Esmara, 1988, p. 56).
9. Vietnam is probably the most agricultural economy in ASEAN, but due to its special case, is not included in the analysis.
10. In the 1960s rice productivity in Japan was twice that in Malaysia, three times that in Indonesia and Thailand, and four times that in the Philippines.
11. Thailand was slowest to adopt the modern HYVs since it did not run out of arable lands until the 1970s, reinforced by a buoyant export market and world food crisis. In addition, it has been reported that Thailand is well known for its fragrant Thai rice which is preferred to the miracle rice (of HYVs).
12. Indonesia achieved self-sufficiency in rice in 1985. A heavily managed and generously funded programme of subsidies and extension services overcame bureaucratic inertia, droughts and pests. The Philippines had been a net importer of rice until 1994.
13. This was partly discussed in Chapter 2. For a more detailed discussion of benefits and other issues on new rice technology adoption, Feder et al. (1988) is recommended.
14. The Sukarno era and the early years of Suharto regime were politically unstable while the Marcos regime in the 1970s and early 1980s was marred by political and social crisis.
15. This issue will be discussed in more detail later in another chapter.
16. A comparative study on ASEAN ports' efficiency by Tongzon and Ganesalingam (1994) has revealed that except for Singapore, and to a certain extent Malaysia, all other ASEAN ports' efficiency levels are below international standards.

17. There are also costs in terms of the loss of exchange rate flexibility and loss of domestic monetary autonomy.

18. Schulze (1988) classifies obstacles to financial integration in terms of 'ability and willingness barriers'. 'Ability barriers' include capital and foreign exchange controls, government regulations of banks and other financial institutions, government expenditure and official reserves policy. 'Willingness barriers' include fiscal policy, unstable exchange rates, higher cost of acquiring information and greater risks resulting from poor information.

19. ASEAN's collaborative efforts in this field can be grouped into the areas of shipping and ports, land transportaton, civil aviation and related services. ASEAN cooperation in this sector has been enhanced by the launching of the Plan of Action in Transport and Communications (1994–96) to develop multi-modal transport and trade facilitation and to harmonize road transport laws and regulations. This will promote trade, investment and industrial linkages, thus further integrating the ASEAN economies (ASEAN Secretariat, 1995).

20. The deregulation of the transport sector in ASEAN are individual members' unilateral actions, rather than joint and cooperative efforts.

4. Sub-regional economic cooperation

Perhaps another significant development in the area of ASEAN economic cooperation is the emergence of economic growth triangles (GTs). This development is part of the overall emergence of several subregional economic cooperation zones in Asia since the 1980s (see Figure 4.1 for other subregional development zones in Asia). Min and Myo (1993) define growth triangles as transnational economic zones spread over large but defined, geographically proximate areas covering three or more countries where differences in factor endowments are exploited to promote external trade and investment.[1] Since growth triangles are increasingly becoming an important form of ASEAN economic cooperation, this chapter will examine the rationale for their emergence, their costs and potential benefits, lessons for successful and sustainable growth triangles and how they can facilitate the achievement of a regionwide economic cooperation under ASEAN.

To date, in Southeast Asia SIJORI (consisting of Singapore, Johore of Malaysia, Indonesia's Riau Province of Batam and Bintan, covering 20 000 sq km) is the oldest, having been operational since 1989. It has successfully integrated Singapore's technology and infrastructure with cheap land and labour offered by Johore and the Riau islands, giving rise to proposals for growth areas in other parts of the region (see Figure 4.2).

Three more GTs are in the making: (i) Northern Triangle or IMTGT (comprising North Sumatra of Indonesia, Northern Peninsular Malaysia, and Southern Thailand, covering 180 000 sq km of land), has passed the feasibility study stage, and the recent intergovernmental and joint business council meetings on this GT have led to agreements on a range of issues and identified a menu of possible projects and initiatives. Some projects are already in operation. (ii) East ASEAN Growth Area – EAGA (comprising Mindanao of the Philippines, Kalimantan and Sulawesi of Indonesia, Sarawak, Sabah and Labuan of Malaysia and Brunei, covering an area of 695 000 sq km) aims to take advantage of Brunei's capital, Indonesia and Malaysia's rich natural resources and Mindanao's agricultural output and manpower. (iii) Greater Mekong Economic Sub-region (comprising Cambodia, Laos, Myanmar, Thailand, Vietnam and Yunnan, China), is now on its second phase. The Asian Development Bank (ADB) has played a

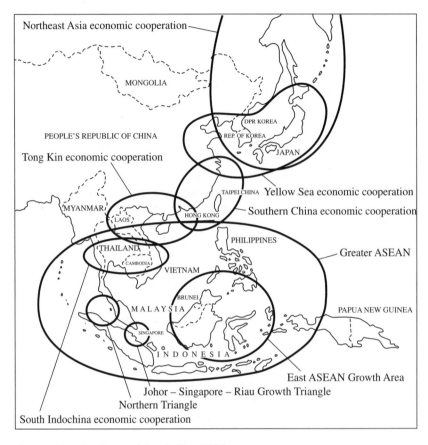

Northeast Asia economic cooperation

MONGOLIA

PEOPLE'S REPUBLIC OF CHINA

Tong Kin economic cooperation

DPR KOREA

REP. OF KOREA

JAPAN

MYANMAR

LAOS

HONG KONG

TAIPEI CHINA Yellow Sea economic cooperation

Southern China economic cooperation

THAILAND

CAMBODIA

VIETNAM

PHILIPPINES

Greater ASEAN

BRUNEI

MALAYSIA

SINGAPORE

PAPUA NEW GUINEA

I N D O N E S I A

East ASEAN Growth Area

Johor – Singapore – Riau Growth Triangle

Northern Triangle

South Indochina economic cooperation

Source: Based on Perry and Grundy-Warr (1996).

Figure 4.1   Subregional development zones in Asia

central role here as facilitator through a regional technical assistance programme (RETA).

The sectors covered for sub-regional cooperation comprise infrastructure, energy, trade, industry, investment, tourism, human resource development, environment and telecommunications.

The success of the SIJORI growth triangle has provided some lessons for the newly emerging growth triangles in the Southeast Asian region. The SIJORI experience has shown the key factors for a successful and sustainable growth triangle and the problems and costs likely to be encountered.

Source: Ghaffar (1996, p. 8).

Figure 4.2   The Indonesian–Malaysia–Singapore growth triangle

4.1   THE EMERGENCE OF GROWTH TRIANGLES

Political and economic factors have explained the emergence of these sub-regional economic zones. The end of the Cold War has left a super-power vacuum in the region. To prevent any nation from filling this super-power vacuum, regional states want to strengthen relationships with each other. Growth triangles are thus seen as apolitical power-balancing mechanisms which can build up trust and mutual understanding among the Asian states.

There is an increasing awareness that bilateral and sub-regional cooperation is an imperative to cope with increasing international competitive pressure. This will allow them to exploit the complementarity of factor endowments and proximity for their mutual benefit. The best example is the establishment of SIJORI. Singapore's economy has expanded rapidly, resulting in higher labour and land costs and thus in the erosion of its international competitiveness in many labour-intensive and land-intensive activities. The establishment of the SIJORI has allowed multinational and local industries to redistribute their labour-intensive operations to the lower-cost Batam.[2] The geographical proximity of Singapore to Johore and Riau islands also help minimize travel and transport costs, making production and distribution more efficient and competitive. Batam is linked to Singapore by a 30–40 minute ferry ride and Johore to Singapore by a short causeway. On the other hand, for Johore and Riau, Singapore's investments have provided employment opportunities and other spillover effects into other industries. Apart from its capital and managerial resources, Singapore has provided Batam and Johore with a modern and efficient transportation and telecommunication network and financial infrastructure to support their business operations.

Growth triangles are also seen as a protection against protectionist trends without committing prematurely to the all-or-nothing venture of setting up formal trading blocs of their own. The formation of the North American Free Trade Area (NAFTA) and consolidation of the European Common Market into the Economic Union (EU) and the slow progress made in the multilateral and regional trade liberalization have made GTs an alternative way of promoting cooperation in the region that are more flexible, less bureaucratic (more activity and project-specific) and more cost-effective than the larger and formal trade blocs of their own.

4.2   POTENTIAL BENEFITS

Recent developments in growth theory have emphasized the fact that economic growth is highly concentrated in its location. Under conditions of openness and liberal government policies rapid growth in recent decades has occurred in clusters. Once economic growth in a certain area or region starts to take hold, it quickly spreads to neighbouring locations and transforms the whole region. This is true both within and across national boundaries. The most notable example of the former is the industrial belt of the United States with a concentration in a small part of the northeast and eastern part of the Midwest. An example of the latter is the manufacturing triangle of continental Europe, containing the Ruhr, Northern France and Belgium. A similar concentration exists in many other industrialized and newly industrialized Asian countries. In Japan growth is concentrated around Tokyo and Osaka, in Thailand around Bangkok and in the Philippines around Manila. One major benefit, therefore, from the economic growth triangles is that it allows the policymakers to focus its developmental efforts in economically depressed and peripheral areas of the country.

Since growth triangles are activity specific and project driven, compared with more formal and larger regional arrangements, they incur lesser political and economic complexities and related risks, but yield tangible benefits more quickly and with less uncertainty which can be subsequently applied to the rest of the economy. Flexible, low-cost, fast-track, uncomplicated and well-focussed, they can be started quickly with little fuss. They require no changes in national concepts of sovereignty, administration or national preferences. They do not engage national prestige completely because they require no elaborate political commitments to neighbouring states. They offer the benefits of regional integration without great loss of economic sovereignty. They expand access to key factor inputs and to new markets beyond national boundaries. Each participating state benefits from static gains (increased production and consumption) and dynamic gains (transformation of the economy).

Growth triangles provide a way of addressing their national priorities and concerns in the context of intense global competition. For the capital-rich partners they are a way of sustaining the competitiveness of their exports despite rising wages and increasing shortages of land and labour. For capital-poor but labour-surplus countries they are a means of speeding up economic development, creating jobs and importing technology. They are an easily organized way of protecting themselves against adverse global economic environment (trade blocs in developed countries), without committing prematurely to the all-or-nothing venture of setting up formal trade blocs of their own.

4.3 COSTS AND POTENTIAL PROBLEMS

Although there are certainly potential economic benefits to be derived from establishing a GT, there are also costs and potential problems which constitute challenges to GTs. There are *direct costs* involved in the provision of infrastructure and energy; *indirect costs* in the form of subsidies, concessions, exemptions from tariff and custom duties and other incentives to attract investors; and *political costs*. Governments involved in GTs could be perceived by their constituents as favouring one portion of their country involved in the GT. These could bring about questions about the concentration of government resources to the 'favoured' GT province, the widening of the income inequality gap and other political issues.[3] There are also *negative externalities* such as environmental degradation, social and ethnic problems such as overpopulation, rising cost of living and prostitution, illegal immigration and labour exploitation.

Other costs include *policy adjustment and harmonization costs*. With economic linkage–globalization, states need to adjust domestic policies and programmes to cope with the demanding dynamism of sub-regional cooperation as well as to maximize benefits derived therefrom. From the perspective of the more developed country in the GT, the key issue is 'hollowing out' of industrial capacity. The building of complementarity among the economies of GTs can only be achieved through the enhanced mobility of labour. However, this may conflict with one's national priority and policy. For example, with respect to the mobility of labour, there is a concern that with the availability of cheap labour from other member countries, industries in the labour-shortage country may be encouraged to postpone the decision to restructure into high-skill and high-technology ones. This concern is reinforced by considerations of the social cost of importing labour. This policy may have to be altered somewhat if greater integration within a GT is considered to be a desirable option.

In the long run, relocation of labour-intensive segments of the industries to the labour-surplus economies may be an optimal solution, but such relocation is not always possible and is limited only to certain industries such as electronics and automobile parts. In addition, many multinationals prefer to relocate not only certain parts or segments of their industries, but also encourage the suppliers of other ancillary equipment to move with them to an adjoining location. Therefore, an attempt to relocate labour-intensive industries could in some degree run the risk of 'hollowing out' the more developed member of the GT.

For the lesser-developed members, the question is one of creating employment opportunities for its growing labour force and acquiring and improving the technological base. In the case of the Philippines, the millions of dollars overseas contract workers (OCWs) have brought into the formal and informal sectors of the Philippine economy have not only alleviated its unemployment problem, but have also been a major source of capital for its development process.[4] If not for the steady outflow of millions of Filipinos to the overseas labour market the unemployment situation would have been worse. Between 1975 and 1994 the percentage increases in OCW deployment averaged at 18.9 percent or 364 254 employed individuals annually, while unemployment growth averaged at 9.1 percent. Apart from the unemployment alleviation, OCW remittances have also been a major source of capital. While FDI as a proportion of the country's GNP declined to below 1 percent for the 1978–87 period before finally recovering in 1988, growing slightly more than one percent between 1989 and 1992, OCW remittances as a proportion of GNP has consistently increased, averaging 4 percent of GNP between 1989 and 1992. It is, therefore, necessary for the members to develop a policy of more systematic and liberal movement of labour within their GT.

There is an old issue of the distribution of gains. Uneven distribution of benefits among member states in a GT could arouse suspicion of exploitative relationships. The SIJORI provides such an example. Some segments of the Indonesian and Malaysian public are of the view that Singapore gains most from the SIJORI partnership. In its early years of implementation, there was some fear in Malaysia that the growth triangle could turn Johore into a 'backyard' of Singapore and Batam (*The Straits Times*, 20 October 1990, p. 23). Jakarta was reportedly sensitive to the fact that Singapore, which occupies only 3 percent of the land area within SIJORI accounts for about 50 percent of its population and 90 percent of its income (*Time*, 17 January 1994, p. 27). There is, therefore, a need to ensure that benefits derived from GTs are spread to all member states and that regional income inequality is not heightened.

This problem is likely to get worse as competition between Johore and Singapore is growing due largely to growing industrialization in Johore. Johore's recent expression of the possibility of stemming the outflow of labour to Singapore and turning down Singapore's request for more water indicate this growing competition. The upgrading and expansion of port facilities in Johore may also help divert Malaysia's shipping and container traffic from Singapore.

4.4 GROWTH TRIANGLES AND ASEAN

Former President Suharto of Indonesia and Singaporean Prime Minister Goh Chok Tong made another milestone in Singapore–Indonesia economic relations by embarking on a new marine and industrial complex in Karimun island, after successful joint ventures in Batam and Bintan (*The Straits Times*, 18 March 1997, p. 20). Located about 40km southwest of Singapore, this 1 050ha complex has facilities for ship repairs, shipbuilding and engineering fabrication works.

Both leaders agreed to increase their level of economic cooperation without involving other ASEAN countries. Do growth triangles conflict or dilute ASEAN solidarity? GTs can actually facilitate and complement the region-wide ASEAN cooperation in the following ways:

4.4.1 Building Blocks

Growth triangles can be perceived as building blocks for economic cooperation in the region. They are complementary, rather than alternatives for the regionwide economic cooperation as long as the ultimate objective remains strengthening the region for foreign investment and opportunities which could reinforce and expand ASEAN cooperation. Member countries could gain confidence and trust in each other, with economic growth as the common goal and binding force. They would then strengthen internal ties among ASEAN states and eventually lead to greater regional economic and political cooperation.

4.4.2   Testing ground

Growth triangles can serve the role of 'reality tests' for selected dimensions or assumptions of AFTA. They can be instrumental in moving them from national comparative advantage to regional competitive advantage. Since GTs are activity-specific, they encourage specific linkages of complementary activities across borders and help promote intra-ASEAN integration and may sharpen and even accelerate certain elements of AFTA's implementation.

4.4.3   National Integration and Linkage with the Rest of Southeast Asia

Growth triangles could also be a means by which the region's economic dynamism could be spread to the lagging parts of the region. Involving economically lagging parts or countries in GTs could spur their domestic growth which will ultimately contribute to the economic robustness of the region as a whole.

Sub-regional cooperation can provide a pragmatic and effective mechanism for linking the more developed members of ASEAN to the rest of Southeast Asia as in the case of the Greater Mekong Sub-region. This is especially significant to ASEAN as an institution, in that the participating countries of this particular sub-region include economies in transition not only domestically but also in their relationship with the region, as new members of ASEAN (Abonyi, 1994).

4.4.4   Economization of politics

The economizaton of politics is the key to ASEAN success. Regional cooperation was achieved by playing down political and security issues. As long as they are not seen as rival entities but are committed to liberal principles, GTs can provide a venue through which the member states can focus on similarities such as mutual economic gains. In GTs the strong presence of private sector involvement will help hasten the speed of trade liberalization in the region.

4.5 KEY FACTORS FOR SUCCESSFUL AND SUSTAINABLE GTS

What lessons, if any, can one derive from the success of the SIJORI for other future growth triangles? As discussed in the preceding section, the main economic aim of SIJORI is to combine the comparative advantages of Singapore, Johore and Riau to attract investment in the manufacturing and services sectors and develop an integrated tourist sector. Has SIJORI achieved this objective?

If we go by the statistics for Johore, it was reported in 1995 that investments in Johore associated with the GT have already reached M$15 billion since the inception of SIJORI (*The Straits Times*, 4 August 1995). For the first six months of 1995 M$1.7 billion in investment capital had been poured in Johore. For the period 1989–94 almost half of the 1 028 projects approved by Malaysia's Ministry of Industry, Trade and Investment emanated from Singapore, while more than half of Singaporean manufacturing project investments were located in Johore (Myo Thant, 1998, p. 5).

To facilitate continued capital flows, Johore embarked upon massive infrastructure projects including a second land link to Singapore, a new port, enhanced water and gas supply to Singapore and expansion of industrial and recreational developments which would increase its integration with Singapore. All these, together with the establishment of a science park in Johore and immigration 'smart cards' for investors, are expected to make Johore the second largest industrial centre in Malaysia after the Klang Valley.

The SIJORI has also kickstarted development in Riau with industrial estates, mega resorts, agribusiness and heavy industrial projects, and has established Riau as a new centre of FDI in Indonesia after Jakarta and West Java. Singapore's involvement is exemplified in Batam Industrial Park (BIP), a joint venture between Singapore GLCs (primarily Singapore Technologies Industrial Corporation and Jurong Environmental Engineering) and Indonesia's conglomerates, which employed in 1994 32 000 employees and $600 million worth of exports.

The most dramatic changes have occurred in Batam island where the population increased by almost 60 percent, exports increased from $151 million to almost $1 400 million and tourist arrivals from 579 000 to over 870 000 for the period 1990–94 (Myo Thant, 1998). Despite the recent economic crisis and Indonesia's current political and social problems, Batam remains an attractive place for investments particularly for Singaporean investors operating in labour-intensive industries. At the same time, the Indonesian government continues to improve security and stability in Batam and other areas near Singapore. The newly opened Heshe-Kabil cluster consisting of more than 30 garment manufacturing and supporting plants and expected to employ at least

15 000 workers, is just one of the three new projects in Batam. Singaporean interests control nearly 70 percent of the nearly 400 foreign-owned projects in Batam (*The Sunday Times*, 25 February 2001, p. 18).

The rapid development of SIJORI has reinforced Singapore's role as a regional hub, facilitated industrial restructuring and provided greater security of access to resources such as land, labour, water and recreational facilities.

Can the SIJORI's success be replicated in other emerging growth triangles in the region? It should be pointed out that the circumstances surrounding SIJORI differ from other GTs in the region. First, SIJORI has only three components or legs. The IMTGT has a larger number of states, made up of territories without a clear lead player, although Penang has been recognized for its central location and its more advanced economic and communication status. As they are supposedly equal players, there appear problems of coordination and in identifying major areas of cooperation. Although that may eventually contribute to the developmental goals of the region, it may also become unmanageable, leading to mini growth zones within the larger IMT growth triangle. EAGA is not merely a triangle but a polygon. The entire sub-region constitutes a vast geographical spread covering vast land and sea areas, comprising several diverse entities. Currently, the centre of the polygon's activities seems to be concentrating on the economically vibrant and externally linked areas around Labuan, Brunei, Northern Sarawak, Sabah and Southern Mindanao. The mere physical distance would make communication links a burden. Second, political instability in certain localities in EAGA may raise doubts among prospective investors.

Whether or not the success of SIJORI can be replicated in other emerging GTs would depend on whether or not they are able to meet the following requirements:

4.5.1 Geographical Proximity

This is one of the most compelling factors for capital, labour, trade and investment flows among the member states. Similar language and cultural background which can prevail in geographically proximate areas are conducive to close business relationships in GTs. But geographical distance can be overcome by establishing adequate communication links or by capitalizing on certain links between two members. IMTGT and EAGA seem to fulfil this requirement.[5]

4.5.2 Economic Complementarity and Infrastructure

This is not only a justification but also an important factor for a successful GT. Different stages of economic development and factor endowments can provide an impetus for sub-regional cooperation to achieve an international competitive edge. With cooperation, productive factors such as capital and labour will be more mobile so as to produce goods to be exported outside the sub-region. Infrastructure is a prerequisite for transforming geographical proximity into economic complementarity. Legal and physical infrastructure can facilitate the flows of resources between member states.

There is some economic complementarity among the member states of IMTGT and EAGA with the active involvement of Penang as a source of industrial know-how and capital for the former, and of Brunei as a source of capital for the latter, but infrastructure in Penang may still be inadequate and Brunei does not have well-developed industrial, communication and financial services sectors.

4.5.3 Political Commitment and Private Sector Participation

Strong political commitment at the highest level and the will to adjust national policies to effectively participate in the GTs is another key factor. Government policies must encourage the necessary participation of the private sector since the role of the private sector is crucial in determining whether economic linkages actually take place. The government must assure investors of the reduced political risks involved in the sub-regional cooperation.

GTs to be successful must be market-driven with the private sector playing a crucial role. There are problems when the private sector is not yet fully developed. Lack of managerial capabilities and a less developed financial sector can also constrain the potential benefits of greater complementarities and markets offered by GTs.

Although both IMTGT and EAGA have enjoyed political support at the national level, they seem to be weak in relation to other requirements to attract the private sector such as adequate infrastructure, accessible markets, support services, and stable social and political climate.

4.5.4 Presence of a Catalyst

The state must take the lead in proposing and establishing the GT, or a third party like a multilateral institution must act as a catalyst to facilitate the consultative process in forming the GT. But the entrepreneurial function of identifying market opportunities is best left to the private sector. To achieve quick results requires a lead player that sets the agenda for the triangle. In the case of IMTGT and EAGA there is no clear lead player, although Penang and Brunei have been recognized for their central location and relatively advanced economic and communication status.

4.6   CONCLUSION

Growth triangles are a key indicator of the economic dynamism and growing economic cooperation in the region. They have both positive and negative implications on the domestic, intra- and interregional scenes in the economic and political arena. Generally, the GTs are confidence-building and security-enhancing mechanisms. They are instrumental in promoting harmonious relations in the region and in addressing both regional and domestic concerns. Nonetheless, there are challenges to be addressed such as economic and political costs involved in setting up and sustaining the GT, policy adjustment and harmonization, negative externalities, distribution of benefits among member countries and the apprehension that involvement in GTs might diffuse ASEAN solidarity. These challenges can be addressed by concerted efforts of participating governments, third party institutions and the private sector.

The SIJORI experience has provided some valuable lessons for other emerging GTs in the region. The different circumstances facing the emerging GTs will make their tasks more difficult to achieve. Their success in forging a sustainable sub-regional cooperation would depend to a large extent on their ability to surmount the constraints facing them and on how they can fulfil such requirements as economic complementarity, adequate infrastructure, political commitment and strong private sector participation, and the presence of a lead player which can set the agenda for the sub-regional consultative and planning process.

SUGGESTIONS FOR FURTHER READING

For conceptual issues and operation problems of growth triangles, read Min and Myo (1993); for a wide-ranging collection of papers on growth triangles, Lee (ed.)(1991), Toh and Low (eds) (1993) and Myo and Min (eds) (1996) are recommended.

NOTES

1. Growth triangles (GTs) are distinguished from regional groupings in that they are government-initiated but business-propelled and are based on sub-regional cooperation.
2. The minimum wage for Batam is 510 000 rupiah (S$97) a month, high by Indonesian standards, but still attractive to foreign investors (*The Sunday Times*, 25 February 2001, p. 18).
3. A major source of concern for the Malaysian authorities with respect to SIJORI is the accentuation of regional inequalities both within Johore as well as between Johore and other states. The concentration of industrial activities in Johore in the context of SIJORI is seen to have contributed to the polarization of economic growth in Malaysia. The heavy concentration of industrial estates in Johore Bahru is also seen to have aggravated income inequality within Johore.

4. Based on the statistics available from the Philippine Department of Labour and Employment, the Philippine unemployment rate moved up to 10.4 percent (for the first half of 1995) from 9.9 percent in 1994.

5. Distances are further eased with the establishment of six direct shipping routes between the island of Mindanao and neighbouring Southeast Asian cities in the fledgling East ASEAN Growth Area (EAGA). The six routes are: Zamboanga-Labuan island in Malaysia serviced by 18 vessels; Zamboanga-Sandakan in East Malaysia serviced by one vessel; General Santos City-Bitung port in Manado of Indonesia serviced by two ships; Davao-Bitung serviced by one ship; Zamboanga-Bitung serviced by one ship; and Cotabato-Labuan serviced by one ship. However, poor port infrastructure and facilities remain a road block to increasing trade (*The Business Times Shipping Times*, 6 January 1997, p. 1).

5. The role of government in ASEAN

As discussed in the preceding chapters, the adoption of appropriate economic policies has been a major factor responsible for the significant inflow of foreign direct investment (FDI) and high savings rates experienced by most of the ASEAN countries. In particular, their respective governments have played a critical role by formulating and implementing policies that help them achieve macroeconomic and political stability, a liberal export-oriented economic regime and competitive rates of return for investment. Thus, it can be argued that the differences in development performance among the ASEAN countries could be largely explained by their differences in the nature and quality of government intervention.

Their respective governments have intervened not only on a macro level but also on a micro level.[1] On the microeconomic level, ASEAN governments have intervened by direct and indirect ownership of certain industries, by providing different types of assistance to the private sector and by implementing policies aimed at reducing poverty and income inequality. But the extent and form of microeconomic intervention have varied among the ASEAN countries. This chapter examines the extent and nature of microeconomic intervention in ASEAN and how this type of government intervention has affected their economic development.

5.1 EXTENT AND NATURE OF GOVERNMENT INTERVENTION

There is a general consensus that one of the major factors behind the economic performance of the newly industrializing countries and the ASEAN group of countries has been the role played by their respective governments particularly in the maintenance of law and order, and in the formulation and implementation of policies to achieve macroeconomic stability (World Bank, 1993b). The role of government and good governance in creating and maintaining political stability, required for effective and efficient implementation of appropriate and usually harsh policies, is quite indisputable.[2]

However, there is still some controversy over whether or not state-owned enterprises (SOEs) have played a positive role in the economic development of the ASEAN countries. Another controversy is whether or not strategic trade policy or industry intervention has played a critical role in ASEAN economic success (Pomfret, 1994).

World Bank (1993b, p. 293) produced a hierarchy of microeconomic interventionism in eight high-performing Asian economies. Singapore among the ASEAN5 was ranked the most interventionist, followed by Indonesia and Malaysia. Thailand and the Philippines were not listed, presumably because they were the least interventionist. With its extensive ownership in diversified industries, ranging from housing, transport, shipbuilding to tourism and lotteries to country club operations, the Singapore government has been acknowledged as the most important entrepreneur in the Singapore economy (Lim Chong Ya, 1991, p. 207).

5.1.1   State Enterprises (SOEs)

Although virtually all ASEAN countries have already embarked on privatization, state or public enterprises still remain a significant economic force in their economies. This is one of the most extensively analysed and debated forms of government intervention in the region (Hill, 1994). Their rationale, organization, performance and contribution to economy vary significantly across ASEAN countries (Ng and Wagner, 1991; Ng and Toh, 1992; Mohamed, 1994; Pangestu, 1996). Singapore stands out from the rest of the ASEAN countries in terms of performance and economic contribution. Apart from Singapore, state enterprises in other ASEAN countries have generally performed poorly based on economic criteria for a number of reasons: lack of clear objectives and delineation of functions between state enterprises, some degree of ambiguity on criteria for selecting programmes and projects, inefficient management, lack of transparency and accountability, high gearing ratios, high input costs, inadequate technology and political patronage. In some cases, poor commercial performances have contributed negatively to national fiscal positions (like the Philippine case in the 1970s and Malaysia in the early 1980s). Thus, since the 1980s there has been an increasing trend towards privatization of state enterprises in the ASEAN countries to improve their fiscal position and to improve national efficiency and international competitiveness.

Singapore
The Singapore government has been seen to take a paternalistic role, nurturing and guiding the nation towards the desired goal of economic development. Direct and indirect ownership through state enterprises is, therefore, viewed as the principal means of directing the allocation of its scarce resources. Specifically, the Singapore government's intervention through state enterprises

is based on the standard market failure arguments such as the provision of public goods, reduction of income inequality, poverty alleviation and management of externalities and natural monopolies or oligopolies. In addition, even in areas where there is no market failure, the government intervenes to promote basic industries, build public infrastructure, correct entrepreneurial inadequacies and to invest in areas where the private sector is unwilling to bear the risks (Lim Chong Ya, 1991, p. 206).

There are generally two types of state enterprise in Singapore: the government-linked companies (GLCs) and statutory boards. The former operate along business lines like other private sector companies, but they are either directly or indirectly owned or controlled by the government holding companies (namely Temasek, Sheng-Li and Ministry of National Development). GLCs are operated like private enterprises and are not given special privileges or concealed subsidies. GLCs that are well-known in Singapore for their outstanding successes include the Singapore International Airlines (SIA) and the Development Bank of Singapore (DBS).

The statutory boards are autonomous organizations set up by the government for specific functions, such as for public housing, laid down by legislation. They are separate entities from the civil service system, but are placed under the jurisdiction of the relevant ministries. Examples of statutory boards are the Housing Development Board, Port of Singapore Authority (recently renamed as Maritime and Port Authority with the corporatization of the port of Singapore in 1997), Jurong Town Council and Sembawang. These state enterprises are not intended to replace the private sector, except in special cases. These special cases occur when the private sector has clearly failed to provide proper services. But the state enterprises are not given special privileges or subsidies, and must be competitive with the private sector (Goh Keng Swee, 1977). The government's emphasis has been on performance rather than on ownership *per se*. The state enterprises are required to achieve commercial performance consistent with acceptable financial norms, unless there is an explicit social objective. Clear and unambiguous objectives are assigned to them with commercial autonomy.

The Singaporean experience represents a unique example of how state-owned enterprises (SOEs) can become an effective tool for promoting economic development. They have not imposed any financial burden on the budget but have in fact contributed to the overall budget surpluses.[3] Alten (1995) pointed out that in 1986 the ten top earning statutory boards made profits more than twice as much as the combined earnings of the ten most profitable companies listed on the Singapore stock exchange. Carling (1995) has also noted that in the last three fiscal years statutory boards' contributions to the budget averaged 2.8 percent of total budget revenue while subsidies from the budget to statutory boards averaged only 1 percent of total budget revenue.

Likewise, Singapore's GLCs have performed well with higher average sales and average profits per company than foreign MNCs or the local private sector (*The Sunday Times*, 23 August 1992). The state enterprises have created forward and backward linkages since the initial period of Singapore's economic take-off by transmitting growth to other sectors of the economy. Other contributions include capital formation, employment, value-added and technological development.

However, there has been increasing concern among the private local entrepreneurs over the growing involvement of state enterprises in areas viewed as the private sector's domain such as commercial banking and housing. They argued that the state enterprises are not only competing with the private sector with unfair advantages, but are also 'crowding out' the private sector so that they have inhibited the development of local private entrepreneurship. Because of this pressure, and to improve the stake of Singaporeans in the economy, the Singapore government in 1987 formed the Public Sector Divestment Committee to look into ways of divesting and/or privatizing state enterprises. The basic objective was to allow the private sector to play a larger role in the economy. The divestment programme started with the public floating of the Singapore Telecom shares, and more will be carried out in the future.

Despite the privatization drive, the SOEs in Singapore continue to be an important instrument of government microeconomic intervention. They have taken the lead in Singapore's regionalization strategy by developing industrial estates or parks in the region such as Indonesia, China, Vietnam and India, thus contributing to the development of an external wing for the economy. On the domestic front, they have also been involved in the continuous restructuring of the economy by venturing into technology-based manufacturing like wafer fabrication and aerospace industries.

Indonesia
Although Indonesia has embarked on a privatization drive since the mid-1980s after the slump in oil prices with an increasing recognition of the importance of the private sector, the absolute size of the state enterprise sector has changed little, if at all (Habir, 1990).

The strong presence of the state in the Indonesian economy is based on such market failure arguments as the provision of public goods, reduction of income inequality and poverty alleviation (Pangestu, 1996). In addition, there is the political argument based on the perceived need to counteract the private sector dominated by Chinese Indonesian business groups and foreign investors.[4] A large state enterprise sector is seen as a desirable counterweight to non-*pribumi* dominance of the economy. Thus, ownership issues in the state enterprise sector in Indonesia have historically been related to the question of 'who controls what' (Habir, 1990). Another argument is to give priority to certain strategic industries aimed at transforming Indonesia into an advanced industrial country. The strategic industries identified are the ten state enterprises which were to be supervised by the Strategic Industry Board (BPIS, Badan Pengelola Industri Strategis).[5] Most of all, there is Article 33 of the Indonesian Constitution which is usually interpreted to mean that economic activities concerned with the daily life of the people should be controlled by the government through state enterprises.[6]

Based on the above arguments, it is not surprising to see that the utilities sector is 100 percent government owned. The Indonesian government also owns 50 percent of shares in the oil and gas sector as well as in the transport and communications sector. The role of state-owned enterprises is also dominant in the financial sector in which 65 percent of the shares is government owned (Hill, 1992). It is also somewhat prevalent in the manufacturing sector accounting for around 24 percent. The role of the state in the agricultural sector, however, has not been through direct ownership, except for the plantation sector comprising a combination of nationalized plantations and those set up under subsidized credit programmes. Government intervention has been in the form of subsidizing inputs and programmes to increase food production. The commitment to achieving rice self-sufficiency after the 1971 drought led to massive investments in supporting infrastructure and services, subsidies for fertilizers and a strong central direction for farmers to plant rice. As pointed out previously, this type of government intervention together with the adoption of the high yielding varieties of rice under the Green Revolution has made Indonesia self-sufficient in rice by 1985. The overall state ownership in the economy is slightly under one third (Pangestu, 1996).

SOEs in Indonesia are divided into three broad categories: (a) Perjan which are enterprises responsible for the provision of public services, attached to the ministerial department and financed out of government budget; (b) Perum which comprises enterprises concerned with profits as well as public services and expected to generate sufficient income and (c) Persero which are limited liability companies whose shares are owned wholly or partly by the Ministry of Finance on behalf of the government and expected to operate as profit-oriented ventures. Theoretically, government intervention would have differed across categories, but no difference in government control has been observed as many Persero continued to receive government subsidies and were regulated to support government policies.

An absence of commercial autonomy, unclear economic objectives and political patronage have characterized the Indonesian experience with state enterprises (Hill, 1994).[7] Consequently, only a small portion of these state entities have recorded an acceptable rate of return on investments while most incurred losses with 37 percent and 30 percent recorded in 1985 and 1986, respectively. The SOEs in Indonesia have been the target of economic reforms during the post oil-boom period, but there is little evidence that the presence of the state has diminished.

Malaysia

Microeconomic intervention in the form of SOEs in Malaysia has manifested itself in three main forms: the establishment of new companies with the government as the sole owner; the setting up of joint-venture companies with private entrepreneurs as part owners; and the buying of a proportion of the publicly-traded shares of existing companies (Mohamed, 1994, p. 240).

These SOEs are considered to have a more explicit political objective. From 1970 to 1990 the economic priority was to reduce poverty and ethnic income inequalities in Malaysia. This economic thrust was reinforced by the political pressure to promote *bumiputra* (indigenous Malay) interests and thus reduce the economic dominance of the nonindigenous people (mainly the Chinese) in Malaysia (Jomo, 1994). In the 1970s and early 1980s the Malaysian government was probably the most active promoter of the interest of the poor in ASEAN through various policy options. From 1956 to 1990 the share of social services had got the highest priority in Malaysia's plans, with the exception of the Second and Fifth Malaysia Plans (Huq, 1994, p. 152).[8]

The introduction of New Economic Policy (NEP) after the racial riot of 1969 marked a shift in the Malaysian government's role from a passive facilitator to a proactive structuralist one. This shift occurred out of the realization that any effort to alter income distribution must undertake structural changes in terms of redistribution of productive assets. This realization was vindicated by Snodgrass (1980) who found that the former *laissez faire* approach pursued by the Malaysian government in the 1960s could neither accelerate growth from the macroeconomic perspective nor improve the economic well-being of the mainly rural populace from the microeconomic standpoint. Thus, since then, the policymakers of the time have pursued a growth strategy that also takes care of the redistribution of corporate assets along with other expenditure benefits in favour of the underprivileged.

Consequently, the size of its state enterprise sector grew substantially especially in the 1970s and early 1980s as the state took on a proactive role by participating directly in commercial and industrial activities and acting as a trustee through the various trust agencies to help increase the *Bumiputra*'s share of corporate equity. This assertive role of the state saw the ratio of public sector expenditure rise from 29.2 percent in 1970 to a peak of 58.4 percent in 1981 (Ariff, 1994b, p. 177). Compared with other ASEAN member countries, central government expenditure per capita in Malaysia in 1980 was nearly ten times that of Indonesia, five times that of the Philippines and three times that of Thailand (Chee and Navaratnam, 1992, p. 369). However, the economic performance of its state enterprise sector was largely disappointing, as reflected in their low rates of return recorded by all sectors with the exception of the extractive industry. Shaikh (1992) noted that the combined rate of return for all SOEs, excluding the extractive industry, was negative in 1986. Chee and Navaratnam (1992) estimated the external debt for 525 government companies at M$14.9 billion and the total accumulated losses for non-financial SOEs at over M$2.3 billion in 1987. But, despite their inefficiencies, they were often shielded from being liquidated or closed down because of their social structuring function. It should be pointed out that the SOEs have played an important role in the social restructuring process. Through SOEs, poverty incidence was reduced significantly to about 17 percent in 1987, and the *Bumiputra*'s share in corporate assets increased from 1.5 percent in 1969 to 19.4 percent in 1988 (Jomo, 1991). It can be argued that by reducing income inequality and poverty incidence in Malaysia, the SOEs have eased the social tensions that could have led to political and social instability and thus have indirectly contributed to Malaysia's economic development.

Its state enterprise sector started to diminish in importance in the 1990s as Malaysia continued to embark on a privatization programme. This policy reversal is aimed at relieving the financial and administrative burden of the government in maintaining its investments in infrastructure and a network of services, promoting competition, efficiency and productivity of the services, stimulating private entrepreneurship and investment. This helped reduce the size of the public sector and contributed towards meeting the objectives of the NEP, especially as *Bumiputra* entrepreneurship and presence have improved and are, therefore, capable of taking a share of the privatized services (Jomo, 1994, p. 271). Various arguments against privatization in Malaysia have also been advanced, but one thing is unequivocally clear, that is, in many instances, especially in public utilities, the government has maintained effective control despite changes in ownership.

Brunei

The involvement of the Brunein government in oil and gas exploration and the dominance of oil and gas production and employment in the Brunein economy, as mentioned in Chapter 2, indicate the significant role played by the Brunei government in its economic development. As we saw in Chapter 2, Brunei is a special case with its over-reliance on these two sectors.

Thailand

Table 5.1 shows government expenditures in the ASEAN states as proportion of their respective GDPs in the 1970s and most of the 1980s. Thailand, compared to the other ASEAN economies, has been relatively non-interventionist, as indicated by its low level of government expenditure as a proportion

Table 5.1 Government expenditure as a proportion of GDP (%)

ASEAN	Average 1971–80	1981	1982	1983	1984	1985	1986	1987	1988
Indonesia	20.9	25.8	24.1	24.8	22.3	24.1	22.8	23.5	22.5
Malaysia	30.2	46.6	44.5	39.9	35.0	34.6	38.0	30.1	29.8
Philippines	12.4	15.4	14.8	13.2	11.6	12.8	14.9	17.4	16.7
Singapore	25.9	33.0	30.8	33.1	34.4	45.7	43.3	45.5	34.7
Thailand	16.4	17.6	19.1	18.4	18.7	19.7	18.7	17.2	15.4

Source: Asian Development Bank, *Asian Development Outlook* (1989).

of GDP relative to the other ASEAN members. Its low levels of government intervention coupled with high levels of growth rates suggest that quality, rather than quantity, of government intervention matters.

Although the size of the government in Thailand has been small and has not assumed a leading role in steering the course of its economic development, its involvement in the economy is quite encompassing. By the end of 1987, these enterprises, which are engaged in almost all sectors of the Thai economy, employed a total of about 257 556 employees which was about half the total number employed in the civil service (Ingavata, 1989).

The state enterprises in Thailand have performed relatively well compared to Malaysia, Indonesia and the Philippines, based on financial profitability criterion. However, despite their profitability, they have relied heavily on foreign borrowings due to insufficient internally generated funds. By 1985 the total outstanding foreign debt of all state enterprises was about US$5 billion – about half of Thailand's public sector foreign debt (Ingavata, 1989). This factor largely accounted for the privatization drive initiated by the then Prime Minister of Thailand Prem Tinsulanond in 1986.

Philippines
The Philippines had a small state enterprise sector inherited from the American colonial regime. Such enterprises proliferated during the Marcos era as several 'crony' corporations had become more than extensions of the state apparatus. SOEs increased from 44 in 1966 to 246 in 1985 (Godinez, 1989, p. 261). Since the Aquino administration several of these have been removed from the state sector.

5.1.2   Strategic Trade Policy (Industry Intervention) vs. Neutral Trade Policy

Among the successful ASEAN economies, Singapore, Indonesia and Malaysia are probably the most interventionist in terms of strategic industry intervention by providing fiscal incentives and subsidies to certain industries.[9] The Singapore government has consistently intervened by providing investment incentives to those favoured industries. Those strategic industries, identified as crucial for Indonesia's economic transformation into an industrialized economy, are granted the exclusive right of operation, preferential access to funds and immunity against bankruptcy (Pangestu, 1996). Indonesia and Malaysia's agricultural sectors, as referred to in the preceding section, have also been accorded a 'strategic' status. Malaysia's policy of developing its automobile, iron and steel, petrochemicals and cement industries under its Heavy Industrialization programme is another example of a strategic trade policy intervention.

That this type of intervention (based on strategic trade policy) has played a critical role in NIEs economic success was first proposed by Johnson (1982). Later, more economists restated this view by saying that a key feature of Japan's development strategy was the targeting of industries on the basis of their perceived potential for economic growth and technological change. Amsden (1989) has argued that similar policies were crucial to South Korea's rapid growth beginning in the 1960s. Wade (1990) has documented the role of interventionist policies in Taiwan's rapid development. Beason and Weinstein (1993) tested the hypothesis that Japanese industrial policy tools (that is, cheap credit, net transfers, tariff protection and tax relief) favoured high growth or increasing returns to scale sectors or enhanced productivity growth. They found that these were directed disproportionally in favour of two sectors, textiles and mining, which had poor growth records, and that there is no evidence that they had any impact on productivity. This hypothesis is difficult to test because the industrial policy in successful economies appears success-ful if judged by aggregate growth performance; there is no doubt that Japan and South Korea adopted an intervention-based strategic trade policy and no doubt these countries have been economically successful (Pomfret, 1994, p.5).

The counterargument to the interventionist view is that the NIEs have inter-vened to neutralize distortions and that the key to their economic success is their policies which match their import barriers with export subsidies and thus create neutral regimes which do not discriminate between industries (Balassa, 1991). In cases where policymakers picked the winners, they were only repli-cating what market mechanisms would have achieved anyway. According to this view, the role of their respective governments was to provide a stable macroeconomic environment conducive to international competition free from distortionary policies, rather than to promote specific industries. Thus, their governments have allowed their economies to do what comes naturally (Riedel, 1988). The recent study by the World Bank (1993b) was in support of this view. It argued that microeconomic interventionism could not explain the economic success of the NIEs. Pomfret (1994) investigated this issue further by correlating the World Bank-based hierarchy of microeconomic interven-tionism in eight high-performing Asian economies (Japan, South Korea, Singapore, Taiwan, Hong Kong, Indonesia, Malaysia and Thailand) with the order of long-term growth performance of these countries, and found that while all these countries enjoyed rapid growth those whose governments tried to direct resources to strategic activities may have performed less well than they would had their policymakers sat on their hands (Pomfret, 1994, p. 9).[10]

There are other theoretical and empirical studies which support the view that neutral policies, rather than microeconomic interventionist policies, were responsible for the success of the ASEAN4 economies (that is Indonesia, Malaysia, Singapore and Thailand). Theoretically, Romer (1994) pointed to the crucial importance of making the fixed cost of introducing new goods or activities as low as possible, and Riedel (1988) characterized economic success based on doing what comes naturally. According to these models, those governments that succeeded in removing the obstacles that inflate the costs of doing business and in enabling firms to specialize according to their comparative advantage, have successful economies.

Empirical studies (for example, Edwards, 1992) on determinants of growth are inconclusive, but among the consistently significant variables in econometric studies are measures of openness. Although these results are often cited in support of the case for export-led growth, they also support the case for the trade–growth relationship (Levine and Renelt, 1992). Literature surveys have criticized the empirical and conceptual shortcomings of many of these studies and the conditional nature of the trade–growth relationship (Edwards, 1993, p. 1389; Levine and Renelt, 1992). Nevertheless, the presumption remains from the recurring positive correlation between openness measures and growth and from the earlier generation of cross-country trade and development case studies that openness is conducive to growth (Pomfret, 1994, p. 14).

The Malaysian, Indonesian and Singaporean experiences with strategic trade intervention provide further empirical evidence on how strategic industry intervention can affect economic development. The protectionist measures adopted by the Malaysian government under its Heavy Industrialization programme to shield the selected heavy industries from international competition have led to higher production costs and consumer prices. For example, in the cement industry a surcharge of over 50 percent was imposed on imported cement to protect the domestic market.

The poor performance of the steel and cement industry coincided with the generally weak Malaysian economy in the early 1980s. Malaysia's automobile industry protection produced mixed results. In the first decade of its existence, the economic burden of the national car project, Proton, was estimated at M$1.6 billion (Jomo and Edwards, 1993, p. 32). Further, the problem of deepening technological dependence was evident due to Mitsubishi's reluctance to transfer its technology to Proton. However, with continuous protection from the state, Proton's market share steadily increased and has made some inroads into the international markets, particularly in the UK. It is, however, doubtful if Proton can compete with the more established foreign brands once government protection is removed.

Malaysia's strategic industry intervention manifested itself again in its Industrial Master Plans (IMP) which guide the country's industrialization efforts from 1985. The first IMP for the period 1985–95 has identified 12 priority sub-sectors comprising seven resource-based industries and five non-resource-based industries for industrial expansion. Malaysia's International Trade and Industry Report (1994) has observed that the state's industry targeting under the IMP has been relatively successful in contributing to Malaysia's economic development based on the following economic indicators: Malaysia's actual growth rate in 1985–92 was 6.7 percent, higher than the targeted growth rate of 6.4 percent; the annual average growth rate of manufacturing value-added was 12.6 percent exceeding the IMP target of 8.8 percent for the entire period; the export performance of all sub-sectors, with the exception of the palm oil, and iron and steel industries, exceeded the IMP targets; and manufactured exports as a percentage of total exports grew from 43.5 percent in 1986 to 69.0 percent in 1992.

The government of Indonesia has identified the following upstream industries for microeconomic intervention: iron and steel, synthetic fibres, cement, chemicals, fertilizers, motor vehicles' engines, aircraft, telecommunications, electronics and shipbuilding sectors. These sectors are considered to have high growth potential and important for a diversified and sustainable industrial development. Indonesia's industry intervention is different from Malaysia's in that its industry targeting is more directed towards its domestic market and employment creation, with little attention given to export promotion. This microeconomic intervention is, therefore, a deviation from Indonesia's overall economic orientation of export promotion and trade liberalization. This inward orientation has been fostered by adopting significant protective measures in the form of tariffs and quantitative restrictions.

Perhaps the most controversial sectors of industry intervention in terms of contribution to Indonesia's economic development are the state-run industries of iron and steel, motor vehicle and aeronautic engineering. The iron and steel industry has been the most controversial because its high capital intensity and limited employment-generating capacity render it inconsistent with its factor intensity. Thus, during the developmental stage the government policy had resulted in providing it with a high level of protection. But it is now considered as a success story of Indonesia's industry intervention. The Krakatau Steel company established in 1971 is a good case in point. This company was given virtual monopoly from 1980 to 1990 with full protection. The tariff protection was gradually lowered as the company was developed to a world-class standard. Now it can compete against the best steel producers in the world, and the tariff rate on imported steel products is now only at 5 percent (*The Sunday Times*, 31 March 1996, p. 4).

In contrast, the motor vehicle and components industry has remained inefficient and heavily dependent on government assistance and protection.[11] The decision to impose a 20 percent surcharge on imports of propylene (used in the manufacture of plastics) and the granting of tax incentives and tariff exemptions for a private firm and its South Korean counterpart involved in the development of a national car project are just some of the examples of government assistance given. In addition, its motor vehicle industry is highly fragmented with five main producers of motor cycles producing approximately 25 separate models and some 40 assemblers of passenger cars and commercial vehicles producing approximately 50 makes and 140 models, all in relatively small numbers, apart from an insufficient number of supporting (car components) producers. This implies that most producers are prevented from achieving the minimum efficient scale of production and are highly reliant on foreign imports of car components.

Similarly, Indonesia has also produced its first domestically designed and built commercial airplane which had its maiden flight in 1995. However, in spite of this achievement, this venture is likely to be inefficient. The Indonesian government has justified this investment on the grounds of technology acquisition and development, and a range of non-economic considerations such as national prestige (Hill, 1992, p. 217).

As pointed out previously, Singapore was ranked by the World Bank as the most interventionist among the ASEAN5 countries. The state has continually led the private sector to achieve the country's economic development by promoting industries with high growth potential and which are crucial to maintaining its international competitiveness. In the mid-1970s due to tight labour conditions, the state intervened by promoting higher value-added industries such as computers, electronic components, precision engineering and pharmaceuticals, and by offering them investment incentives. After the 1985 recession the Singapore government under its Strategic Economic Plan (1989) identified 14 industries for industrial clustering – commodity trading, shipping, precision engineering, electronics, information technology, petroleum and petrochemicals, construction, heavy engineering, finance, insurance, general supporting industries, tourism, international hub and domestic industries (Alten, 1995, pp. 128–9).

Since 1992 the Singapore has been actively promoting and facilitating the 'go-regional' drive to maintain Singapore's international competitiveness and thus sustain its economic development. Through regionalization Singapore would be able to tap the growth potential in the other parts of the region where it can relocate its labour-intensive operations.

Singapore's continued economic dynamism is highly attributable to the government's foresight and effective leadership in providing the guiding framework which has prepared the private sector for coping with the changing challenges of global competition.

5.2   CONCLUSION

The preceding discussion has shown that the nature, extent and effects on economic development of microeconomic intervention have varied significantly among the ASEAN countries. It has also demonstrated that the quality, rather than the extent, of microeconomic intervention in terms of state-owned enterprises has played the most critical role in ASEAN economic development experiences. ASEAN government intervention by way of direct and indirect ownership of certain enterprises has generally resulted in economic efficiency loss and lower growth, except for the Singapore case. Consequently, the observed trends towards deregulation and privatization of state enterprises in Indonesia, Malaysia, the Philippines and Thailand are designed mainly to improve their overall productivity and efficiency. The privatization drive by Singapore is largely the government's deliberate policy of allowing the private sector to be more directly involved in economic development and to increase the stakes of Singaporeans in their economy. It was announced by the Singapore government that the public floatation of Singapore Telecom shares was intended to allow more Singaporeans to own shares and thus distribute the fruits of economic growth more widely.

With respect to the link between strategic industry intervention and economic development, the evidence is also varied. Industry intervention has proven quite successful in Singapore, but only to a lesser extent in Malaysia and a very limited extent in Indonesia. The main factor explaining these differences is the general orientation of the government intervention. There seems to be a pattern that an export-oriented government intervention encourages firms to be efficient as they know they have to compete in the international market in the long run. A domestic market-oriented intervention encourages rent-seeking activities and inefficiency as the firms are shielded from foreign competition in the short term and longer term.

Further, there is no conclusive evidence from the experiences of the ASEAN countries that strategic industry intervention has been a significant factor behind their strong economic performance.

SUGGESTIONS FOR FURTHER READING

Ng and Wagner (1991) have a fairly comprehensive account of the rationale, organization, performance and economic contribution of ASEAN state enterprises, while Pomfret (1994) has surveyed the different viewpoints on the role of strategic industry intervention in the development of the highly successful East Asian economies.

NOTES

1. Government intervention on a micro level can take many forms. In this chapter it may be in the form of direct allocation of resources (via state enterprises) or in the form of indirect

allocation of resources to certain industries through targeted and subsidized credit to selected industries, low deposit rates and ceilings on borrowing rates, protection from import competition, subsidies to declining industries, establishment and financial support of government banks, development of export-marketing institutions and cooperative venture between the private and public sector.

2. Good governance is built on three interrelated principles: democratic accountability, long-term orientation and social justice.

3. Statutory boards are required to transfer 20 percent of their annual operating surplus to the government; this transfer is broadly equivalent in its impact to the imposition of a corporate income tax.

4. It is reported that, although ethnic Chinese Indonesians represent only 3 percent of the nearly 200 million population in Indonesia, they control about 70 percent of the Indonesian economy (*Asiaweek*, 24 January 1997, p. 23). The economic dominance of ethnic Chinese businessmen in ASEAN economies will be discussed again in Chapter 13.

5. The ten are PT IPTN (aircraft manufacturing), PT PAL Indonesia (shipbuilding), PT PINDAD (ammunition), Perum Dahana (explosives), PT Krakatau Steel, PT Barata Indonesia (machine working), PT Boma Bisma Indra (machine working), PT INKA (rail industry), PT Inti (telecommunications) and Unit Produksi Lembaga Elektronika Nasional Lembaga Ilmu Pengetauhan (electronics). For a more detailed discussion, see Habir (1990).

6. This philosophy reflects the influence of socialist traditions in Western Europe before World War II on the founding fathers of Indonesia (Pangestu, 1996).

7. Despite the financial crisis in the state oil company *Pertamina* in 1975–76, large investments were directed to oil refining, fertilizer, cement, aircraft and other sectors until the oil price slump forced a cancellation of these projects.

8. Social services include expenditure on health, education and other social welfare expenditures including transfers.

9. Intervention here refers to microeconomic policies aimed at directing resources to the production of specific goods or services.

10. Thailand is cited as a good example. Thailand recorded the highest per capita income growth rate between 1987 and 1992. Government has been an important factor, especially in the creation of macroeconomic stability in the 1980s and investment in primary education, but the government has not been interventionist at the microeconomic level. Policies to influence the sectoral and spatial distribution of activities pursued during the 1970s were abandoned later.

11. Okamoto and Sjoholm (1999) showed that all of the sub-sectors (assemblers, car body makers and parts suppliers) experienced a decline in labour productivity and total factor productivity between 1990 and 1995, while real wages of both production and non-production workers increased for the assemblers and the parts suppliers.

PART TWO

ASEAN External Economic Relations

6. ASEAN economic relations: the US, Japan, EU, China and Vietnam

As discussed in Chapter 2, the older members of ASEAN (ASEAN5 + Brunei) are not only market-oriented but have also adopted an export-oriented policy. The export-oriented industrialization policy of these countries has made their economic relations with developed and developing countries an important part of their overall economic development. This chapter will evaluate the ASEAN6 (ASEAN5 + Brunei) external economic relations particularly with the US, Japan and the European Union (EU), their major trading and investment partners, and two important newly emerging market economies in Asia, before the crisis.

6.1 DEVELOPED COUNTRIES

Although the ASEAN6 countries have expanded trading and investment links among themselves and with other Asian countries, as a group their trade and investments are still concentrated with developed countries. ASEAN6 economic relations with developed countries (the US, Japan and the EU) have essentially revolved around three major issues: (a) trade and market access; (b) foreign investments and technology; (c) foreign aid.

In the past the dominant issues were aid and development assistance in the era of 'non-reciprocity' in multilateral relations. Over time as the ASEAN6 countries continued to grow, the issues of trade, market access and investments based on reciprocity have increasingly been gaining prominence in ASEAN–developed countries' economic relations. The ASEAN6 countries continue to demand access to the markets of the industrialized countries for their manufactures in the context of rising nontariff barriers while the developed economies continually demand market access for their financial and other services, and for effective protection of intellectual property rights. The economic dynamism occurring in the Asian region especially before the 1997 crisis and the region's great market potentials have made ASEAN an important market for the developed countries. On the other hand, there is a growing misconception that strong economic growth in developing countries has occurred at the expense of the developed countries' prosperity, based on the belief that the inflow of goods from the developing countries has resulted in more job losses for their domestic industries. This has allegedly fuelled protectionist pressures in the developed countries by linking trade with labour standards and human rights.

6.1.1   United States

The United States has been the ASEAN6's largest export market and major source of foreign investment. Between 1980 and 1995 ASEAN6 exports to the US as a proportion of total ASEAN6 exports increased from 16.9 to 19.2 percent while the share of exports to Japan declined from 26.8 to 14.3 percent so that by 1995 the US had replaced Japan as ASEAN6's largest export market, as Table 6.1 shows. It is also an important source of imports for the ASEAN6 countries, accounting for about 14.1 percent of ASEAN6 imports in 1995.

The importance of the US as an export market varies between ASEAN6 countries. Table 6.2 shows that the Philippines has the highest proportion of exports to and imports from the US due to historical reasons while Brunei has the lowest proportion of exports to and imports from the US. The other ASEAN6 countries have proportions of their exports to the US in the range of 15.9 and 20.7 percent. On the import side, the US is not as prominent, although the share of the US in the individual ASEAN6 countries' imports is considerable, ranging from 5.9 to 18.4 percent. Over the same period 1980–95, the ASEAN6 countries have increased their trade surpluses with the US significantly, starting with US$1549.0 million surplus in 1980 and increasing to US$14118.0 million in 1995.

Table 6.1   ASEAN6 major trading partners (% of total)

Country	Exports		Imports	
	1980	1995	1980	1995
US	16.9	19.2	15.4	14.1
Japan	26.8	14.3	21.8	23.1
European Union	13.4	14.4	12.7	15.7
NEA NICs	5.3	12.7	3.4	12.5
ASEAN	16.7	22.4	13.3	17.3
Australia	2.2	1.8	3.1	2.4
Others	18.7	15.2	30.3	14.9
Total	100.0	100.0	100.0	100.0

Source: IMF, *Direction of Trade Statistics Yearbook* (various issues)

Table 6.2   Share of US in ASEAN6 total trade, 1995 (%)

ASEAN6 Countries	Share in ASEAN6 Exports	Share in ASEAN6 Imports
Brunei	1.7	5.9
Indonesia	15.9	9.1
Malaysia	20.7	12.7
Philippines	35.3	18.4
Singapore	18.2	15.0
Thailand	17.8	15.6

Source: IMF, *Direction of Trade Statistics Yearbook* (1996).

The significant US–ASEAN6 bilateral trade is largely due to a substantial inter-industry trade owing to strong economic complementarities. ASEAN6 countries are major exporters of such goods as petroleum, rubber, sugar, tin, textiles, garments and other labour-intensive products, and these items are imported by the US. Indonesia and Thailand have the highest proportion of exports to the US in the form of labour-intensive manufactures such as textiles, clothing and footwear. The US in turn exports capital-intensive, technically-intensive goods such as chemicals, electrical and nonelectrical goods, and these goods are in turn heavily imported by the ASEAN6 countries.

The US is also becoming an important destination of high value-added manufactured products from ASEAN6. Except for Brunei, the largest share of ASEAN6 exports to the US is made up of manufactured goods. Over the years, there has been a shift in ASEAN6 from exporting primary and labour-intensive manufactured goods to capital-intensive and higher value-added manufactured goods to the US. At least more than half of ASEAN6 total exports in the category of machinery and miscellaneous manufactures go to the US market. Singapore and Malaysia have the highest proportion of exports to the US made up of electronic components such as memory chips, transistors and integrated circuits, followed by Thailand.[1] A significant portion of ASEAN6–US bilateral trade is intra-industry due to the global strategy adopted by the US MNCs aimed at locating the various stages of production in different countries to exploit the differences in comparative advantage.

The US is the most significant source of FDI in the ASEAN6 region. The US direct investment in the ASEAN6 region has also doubled over the same period. This topic will be discussed in more detail in Chapter 9. Although the US is a very important trading partner to ASEAN6, the US is not as dependent on the ASEAN6 countries as the ASEAN6 countries are on the US. Even so, the US is seeking to expand its exports to the ASEAN region as it is a fast-growing market, and this would also help the US to overcome its trade deficit in the region.

One of the areas where the US wants to expand is in the exports of services to the ASEAN markets. In ASEAN6 several barriers to trade in the services sector currently exist, including leasing restrictions, motion picture limitations, limited foreign ownership of banking, advertising restrictions and preferential treatment of domestic transportation. The US too is not without its share of barriers in this sector, especially at the state level. The conflict between the US and ASEAN6 has generally been over the US legislative measures in areas such as patents, copyrights and intellectual property rights. The US has been pressuring developing countries including ASEAN to step up intellectual property rights protection efforts, and threatening retaliatory measures against those that fail to do so (for example the US/China dispute on piracy). The ASEAN6 countries have stepped up efforts, but the US has not been satisfied.

6.1.2   Japan

The declining importance of Japan as a market for ASEAN6 exports since 1980 was noted in Table 6.1, indicating a significant drop in the Japanese share of ASEAN6 total exports from a high 26.8 percent in 1980 to 14.3 percent in 1995. In 1980 Japan was ASEAN6's biggest export market. In contrast, Japan remains the largest source of ASEAN6 imports, accounting for 23.1 percent in 1995.

Table 6.3 shows that Japan is a very important export market for Brunei and Indonesia, accounting for 57.3 and 28.4 percent, respectively, of total ASEAN6 exports in 1995. This is because these countries are relatively

Table 6.3   Share of Japan in ASEAN6 total trade, 1995 (%)

ASEAN6 Countries	Share in ASEAN6 exports	Share in ASEAN6 imports
Brunei	57.3	4.1
Indonesia	28.4	26.8
Malaysia	12.7	20.5
Philippines	15.8	22.4
Singapore	7.8	21.1
Thailand	16.7	30.2

Source: IMF, *Direction of Trade Statistics Yearbook* (1996).

endowed with mineral resources which Japan needs. Japan is also important for Thailand and Philippine exports primarily because of Thailand's exports of crude materials and oils and fats, and of the Philippines' exports of crude materials and mineral fuels.

ASEAN6 imports from Japan are dominated by capital-intensive manufactures such as machinery. Japan is also a significant source of imports of capital-intensive manufactures for all ASEAN6 countries, as well as imports of chemicals and miscellaneous manufactures in all ASEAN6 countries, except Brunei. Thus, there is a symbiotic trade relationship between ASEAN6 and Japan. Japan relies on ASEAN6 for its supply of strategic raw materials and as a market for its industrial exports. ASEAN6, on the other hand, relies on Japan for its capital and technology.

The ASEAN6 countries as a group have had a balance of trade deficit with Japan. In 1995 this deficit amounted to US$31 134 million. On an individual country basis, only Indonesia and Brunei have enjoyed a positive trade balance with Japan due to the nature of their exports. The other four ASEAN countries have had negative trade balances because they import a great deal of manufactured products particularly in the form of machinery and manufactured goods from Japan, but Japan does not import as much in return.

It is likely that as intra-ASEAN trade continues to grow, there will be an increase in ASEAN6–Japan bilateral trade. Growing economic interdependence among Pacific basin countries is also likely to improve Japan–ASEAN6 trade relations. Further, Japan should continue to shift its exports to ASEAN due to ASEAN's growing industrialization and trade restrictions in the US and the EU.

Japan has always been an important source of foreign investment for ASEAN6 countries. By 1990 a third of total foreign direct investment in ASEAN6 was accounted for by Japanese foreign direct investment. Indonesia was the second largest recipient of Japanese foreign direct investment after the US, particularly in oil. Japanese investments in the Philippines have been mainly in copper, and in other ASEAN6 countries they have been mainly in manufacturing, particularly in textiles, iron and non-ferrous metals, chemicals, transport equipment and electrical machinery. Japanese investments are generally directed to obtain or produce components at low cost. There is also a strong link between parent companies and their overseas affiliates. The average size of investments is small, and usually takes the form of joint ventures with strong Japanese control. They are largely import-substituting investments and are located close to consuming centres.

ASEAN6 has traditionally been a priority region for Japanese economic assistance. About a third of total Japanese official assistance goes to ASEAN6. Indonesia and the Philippines are the main recipients in the form of technical assistance.

Table 6.4   Share of European Union in ASEAN6 total trade, 1995 (%)

ASEAN6 Countries	Share in ASEAN6 exports	Share in ASEAN6 imports
Brunei	9.1	22.0
Indonesia	16.2	20.4
Malaysia	14.2	15.2
Philippines	17.1	10.9
Singapore	13.4	13.3
Thailand	15.0	20.6

Source: IMF, Direction of Trade Statistics Yearbook (1996).

6.1.3   European Union (EU)

The European Union (formerly known as the European Economic Community) has been traditionally not as important a market for ASEAN6 exports as the US or Japan. Its share of total ASEAN6 exports was 13.4 percent in 1980, which only slightly increased to 14.4 percent in 1995. Considering that there are a number of countries comprising the EU, this share is indeed quite small compared to the US and Japanese shares. The EU shares in individual ASEAN6 countries' exports do not vary significantly, with Brunei having the lowest proportion of exports going to the EU (see Table 6.4).

The trade relationship between ASEAN6 and the EU is characterized by dependence rather than interdependence. The share of ASEAN6 in the EU total exports has been roughly less than 1 percent, quite marginal compared to the EU share in total ASEAN6 exports. For the ASEAN6 countries, except for Brunei, the EU is an important market particularly for their manufactured exports.

Unlike the US and Japan, the ASEAN6 countries export to the EU a substantial amount of primary products as well as manufactures. ASEAN6's major export items to the EU include timber, rubber and tin (mostly from Malaysia), tapioca and cassava (mostly from Thailand), palm oil (mostly from Malaysia), machinery (mostly from Singapore), basic manufactures and miscellaneous manufactures. ASEAN6 imports from the EU are predominantly manufactures and chemicals. Almost half are machinery and transport equipment.

The EU is ASEAN6's third largest source of foreign direct investment (FDI). But its share has been declining due to increasing Japanese and US shares. From 1982 to 1992 only 1 percent of the EU's cumulative FDI went to

East Asia, compared with 18 percent to the US (*The Straits Times*, 23 September 1995).

The declining share is due to the lack of encouragement from the national governments to invest in Asia, the absence of significant business links between business communities in the EU and in ASEAN, for example, the lack of a real European counterpart to the grouping of Chambers of Commerce of ASEAN as a whole. Also ASEAN did not rate high in Europe's range of interests.

The ASEAN6 countries have always considered the EU an important market for their exports in the context of their export-oriented and market diversification policies. This importance was demonstrated by the establishment of a Commission of the European Community for South and Southeast Asia in Bangkok in 1979, and the signing of the ASEAN–EC Cooperation Agreement at the Second ASEAN–EC Ministerial Meeting in Kuala Lumpur in 1980 to assess and monitor ASEAN–EU cooperation. The most recent ASEAN initiatives have been the establishment of regular ASEAN–EU dialogues and Asia–Europe ministerial (ASEM) meetings which began in Singapore in 1996.

On the other hand, the EU policies towards developing countries are designed to stimulate trade and investment. Since 1972 the EU has adopted the Generalized System of Preferences to assist developing countries in gaining access to the EU market. The ASEAN6 countries have been recipients of EU financial and technical assistance to promote industrial development and cooperation in the ASEAN region. However, the introduction of the Multifibre Arrangement has been a major concern for the ASEAN countries as it imposes trade restrictions on their textile exports where they have a comparative advantage.

The future of ASEAN6–EU economic relations depends to a large extent on ASEAN6's continued surge in growth, greater integration in ASEAN, success of the implementation of the agreements under the World Trade Organization (WTO) and future economic conditions in Europe.

6.2 THE NEWLY EMERGING MARKET ECONOMIES OF CHINA AND VIETNAM

Although the newly emerging Asian economies are not ASEAN6 countries' major trading and investment partners, they are fast-expanding markets for ASEAN6 exports and for some capital-rich ASEAN6 countries a growing destination for their capital and managerial expertise. This is particularly true with respect to the newly emerging market economies of China and Vietnam.

6.2.1 China

Before normalization, bilateral trade with China was largely indirect, except for Singapore. Bilateral trade remains small but has been increasing since normalization. In absolute levels, total two-way trade with China rose from US$3.9 billion in 1985 to US$18.7 billion in 1995, faster than the growth of China's global trade.

From the ASEAN6 perspective, China remains a small trading partner, and China's share in ASEAN6's total direct trade slightly decreased from 3.1 percent in 1985 to 2.9 percent in 1995. ASEAN6 is more dependent on China as a source of imports than as a market for exports. However, a new trend seems to be emerging since the latter half of the 1980s as the import share declined from 5.1 percent in 1985 to 3.1 percent in 1995 and the export share rose from 1.3 percent in 1985 to 2.7 percent in 1995. The export shares could be higher if the indirect trade via Hong Kong is fully considered.

Among the ASEAN6 countries, Singapore is China's largest trading partner. In fact, Singapore accounted for 36.5 percent of ASEAN6–China trade in 1995. From China's perspective, the share of ASEAN6 in China's trade increased from 5.6 percent in 1985 to 7.0 percent in 1995.

Promotion of foreign investment has been one important element of China's industrialization programme. A number of incentives have been offered to foreign investors: in Special Economic Zones (SEZs) there is preferential taxation treatment, eased restrictions on entry of foreign personnel, and better access to foreign exchange and working capital; in coastal cities there are infrastructural facilities and preferential treatment. Among ASEAN6 Singapore has the largest number of investment projects in China, which are diverse and technologically sophisticated. While China offers great opportunities to ASEAN6 for its huge market potentials and for ASEAN6's export diversification policy, China is also a source of competition in third country markets. This point will be pursued further in Chapter 14.

6.2.2 Vietnam

From the ASEAN perspective, ASEAN6–Vietnam bilateral trade is very low by international standards. ASEAN6's total exports to Vietnam as a percentage of its total exports is very insignificant with less than 1 percent, although it went up from 0.002 percent in 1985 to 0.89 percent in 1995. Similarly, the ratio of imports from Vietnam was also less than 1 percent, but slightly increased from 0.001 percent in 1985 to 0.20 percent in 1995. However, trade volume is fast increasing. For the same period, bilateral trade between ASEAN6 and Vietnam grew by 148.9 percent per annum on average. But, from the Vietnamese perspective, ASEAN6 is one of its major trading partners. Vietnamese exports to ASEAN6 as a proportion of its total exports was 11.6 percent while its imports from ASEAN6 as a proportion of its total imports was 26.1 percent in 1995.[2] Major exports from Vietnam to ASEAN6 are natural rubber, vegetables and fruits, coal, chromium, and footwear. Its major imports are machinery and equipment, petroleum, fertilizers, corn, maize, sugar, wool and cotton fabrics.

Foreign direct investment between ASEAN6 and Vietnam has also grown in recent years. FDI from ASEAN6 countries accounted for 15.5 percent of Vietnam's total cumulative investments at the end of 1993 compared to a mere 7 percent in 1991. Over the 1995–97 period the ASEAN6 share of total FDI commitments and legal capital has grown significantly. Construction and related real estate have been the main focus of ASEAN6 investments followed by agricultural processing and textiles.

Singapore is Vietnam's top ASEAN6 investor particularly in the areas of tourism and infrastructure. Singapore has worked with Vietnam to promote tourism, build an industrial estate and develop its port and shipbuilding industry. In 1996, the number of licensed projects held by Singapore investors was 120, and the capital pumped in was about US$2 billion (*The Straits Times*, 5 October 1996).

To promote foreign investments, Vietnam has been building its legal framework starting with the promulgation of the new Law on Foreign Investment in 1987. Subsequent amendments in 1990 and 1992 allowed joint ventures between domestic private and foreign firms, the establishment of Export Processing Zones (EPZs), and 100 percent foreign-owned investments with no fixed minimum or maximum amount of FDI stipulated. They also contained various fiscal incentives such as a two-year tax moratorium for joint ventures, tax exemption for certain exports and imports and guarantees against capital expropriation and nationalization (*Vietnam Jewel of Asia*, 1993).

In 1992 Vietnam attracted a total invested capital of US$6.320 billion in 724 projects in the form of joint ventures. Investments are largely from the non-ASEAN countries. Singapore is the largest ASEAN trading and investment partner, accounting for 3.6 percent of total foreign investment in Vietnam in 1992. A number of problems, however, have hindered the inflow of FDI such as underdeveloped infrastructure, bureaucratic delays, massive and widespread corruption, and unclear ownership guidelines.[3]

The prospect for ASEAN6–Vietnam economic relations is bright due to Vietnam's policy of giving priority to developing cooperative relations with neighbouring Asian countries, its political stability, improvement in its bureaucratic machinery and infrastructure, its policy of export market diversification for ASEAN and its membership in ASEAN in July, 1995.[4]

SUGGESTIONS FOR FURTHER READING

For a good general background on ASEAN6 economic relations with their major trading and investment partners such as the US, Japan and the European Union, read Sandhu et al. (eds) (1992, pp. 321–8, 329–34, 335–9). Harris and Bridges (1983) is also worth reading with respect to ASEAN6–EU economic relations. For ASEAN6–China and ASEAN6–IndoChina economic relations, Sandhu et al. (eds) (1992, pp. 340–51) is recommended.

NOTES

1. Singapore is the world's largest producer of hard disk drives and the third largest producer of headphone stereos. Thailand is the world's second largest producer of hard disk drives while Malaysia is the world's third largest producer of radio cassette players. This observation is based on Table 16 of United Nations Economic and Social Commission for Asia and the Pacific (1994).
2. With the fall of the CMEA, Vietnam's trade orientation has shifted from the former Soviet Union and East European bloc to Asia. In 1992 Singapore emerged as Vietnam's top trading partner. The other top four trading partners were Japan, Hong Kong, France and Taiwan.
3. Vietnam has recently amended and simplified its tax and foreign investment laws and procedures to make it easier and more attractive for foreign investors.
4. The economic implications of Vietnam's entry into ASEAN and AFTA will be discussed in detail in Chapter 12.

7. ASEAN and other regional trading arrangements

Another source of serious concern for ASEAN countries in their dealings with developed countries is the likely negative impacts of regionalism in these economies. This chapter will examine the two major regional economic initiatives formed by Western developed countries and their likely impact on ASEAN economies: the deepening and enlargement of European integration and the establishment of the North American Free Trade Area (NAFTA).

The late 1980s witnessed a growing interest in regionalism as an alternative to multilateralism. During this period important steps were taken to establish and deepen existing levels of economic integration. The European Community (EC) led the way by first aiming for a Single European Market (SEM), then forming the European Union (EU) and later a European Economic Area (EEA) that includes four members of the European Free Trade Area (EFTA). Quite recently, the EU has further advanced into a higher level of regional grouping by forming a European Monetary Union (EMU). In 1992 the North American countries, the US, Canada and Mexico, signed a historic free trade agreement (NAFTA), and since then much of the commitments towards trade liberalization within this grouping have been implemented. These developments seem to indicate the emergence of two trading blocs and have caused the fear that the EU and NAFTA could turn into inward-looking blocs, thereby posing a threat to the openness of the world multilateral trading system.

Theoretically, an economic grouping becomes a bloc only when the members adopt a common economic policy in their dealings with non-members and use it to divert trade and investment from the latter. Thus, while an economic union such as the EU can be considered a bloc, a free trade area cannot be because it does not have a common external policy. That is why the US has always insisted that NAFTA would not become a protectionist bloc. In practice, however, the fact that the EU and NAFTA do not benefit non-members means that trade and investment diversion could take place.

The first impact comes in the form of *trade diversion*, the extent of which depends on the degree to which commodity exports to an integrating country, say the United States, overlap that of a partner country, say Mexico, (elasticity of substitution) and on the degree of discrimination against outsiders in the matched commodities (margin of trade preference).

The second impact is in the form of *investment diversion*, as domestic and foreign investment shift away from non-members to member countries within an FTA or a customs union zone. The effect would be particularly pronounced in industries sustaining acute trade diversion.

However, the picture is not all gloomy for non-members if we take into account the dynamic and long-run effect of economic integration. The growth of income in the integrating area will accelerate due to expanded market size, leading to an increase in demand for foreign imports. The size of this increase depends on the income elasticity of import demand. Along with other sources, ASEAN exports to the integrating area will also expand, but this effect may be offset wholly or partly by the dynamic counterpart of trade diversion, which implies shrinkage of the non-member economies as their exports contract.

7.1   ASEAN AND EUROPEAN INTEGRATION

European integration is a process that commenced more than 40 years ago. In the late 1950s, the original six members started the formation of a customs union and Common Agricultural Policy (CAP), a process which was completed ten years later. During the 1960s and 1970s the EC set up a web of preferential arrangements with various countries such as Greece and Turkey, EFTA countries in Europe and associated states in Africa and the Caribbean (ACF). The EC was enlarged in the 1970s from six to nine members with the accession of the United Kingdom, Ireland and Denmark. In the 1980s it was further enlarged to twelve members with the accession of Greece (1981) and then Spain and Portugal (1986). On 3 December, 1992 the Common Market came into being. The EC has recently established a common currency.

7.1.1   Trade Diversion

The European integration poses a protectionist challenge to ASEAN in the form of a trade-diverting common external trade policy where efficient low-cost ASEAN producers may be discriminated against. Since it is impossible to estimate the trade diversion effect without the knowledge of the relevant elasticities, qualitative observations are made here. Trade diversion will come from the following measures adopted by the EC:

- The abolition of all intracommunity non-tariff barriers (NTBs), including the technical barriers to trade, which result from differential product standards between member states. Products where such technical barriers are important are: electrical engineering products, mechanical engineering equipment, medical equipment, pharmaceutical products, motor vehicles, foodstuffs, metal articles, mineral products and rubber products. The abolition of intra-EC NTBs will enhance discrimination against the ASEAN countries.

- The conversion of national quotas on sensitive products into EC-wide quotas. Whether or not this conversion is trade-diverting or trade-creating depends on whether the EC-wide quotas will be more restrictive than the ones now in existence.[1] The uncertainty it creates could be trade-diverting.
- The elimination of national preferences on government contracts and the opening of government procurement bids only to the Community members will discriminate against ASEAN bidders for public contracts.[2]
- The increasing use of anti-dumping measures by EC as a vehicle for protection.

ASEAN exporters of manufactures are expected to be most hurt as the EU imports a large amount of manufactures from ASEAN. EU imports of ASEAN manufactures have increased from 48 percent in 1980 to 64 percent in 1988, as a proportion of total EU imports from ASEAN.

The European integration also poses a competitive challenge in the third markets. Competition among EU firms will intensify due to the extension of trade preferences among themselves, which could lead to more efficiency. Industries that will face strong EU competition are cars, electronic goods, textiles and clothing.

Kreinin and Plummer (1998), using an import-growth approach and a gravity model, estimated the negative implications of the European Single Market Programme (EC-92) on the exports of the ASEAN countries for the years 1994 and 1996, with the effects concentrated in miscellaneous manufactures and electrical machinery. Amongst ASEAN, Malaysia and Thailand suffered the largest trade diversions. These negative diversionary effects were estimated to be larger than the positive income effects so that Malaysia and Thailand were found to have experienced considerable trade deficits due to the EC-92 programme.

7.1.2 Investment Diversion

Apart from trade diversion, there may be investment diversion. Foreign direct investment has been one of the factors responsible for the economic dynamism of ASEAN by providing an important source of capital, technology and management skills and by stimulating exports. The creation of a large EU market means that more firms will establish their operations in Europe to benefit from this enlarged market. Third country investment could also flow in to avoid protectionist barriers maintained by the EU. Investment diversion in ASEAN could occur in machinery and transport equipment, food, chemicals, textiles, metals and electronics.

Substantial trade and investment diversion may slow down ASEAN growth. The effects of trade and foreign investment have generally been favourable for ASEAN in terms of technology transfer and employment creation. If such diversions are great, sustaining the present growth momentum might be a problem.

7.2   ASEAN AND NORTH AMERICAN INTEGRATION

On 17 December 1992 the US, Canada and Mexico signed a trade accord to eliminate trade barriers and form a continental-wide single market. Coming into force on 1 January 1994, it has established a free trade area of 370 million people producing and consuming goods and services valued at US$6.8 trillion a year. An agreement of such a size will certainly have widespread implications for member and non-member countries.

The specific objectives of NAFTA are (a) to eliminate trade barriers, (b) to promote conditions of fair competition, (c) to increase investment opportunities, (d) to provide adequate protection of intellectual property rights, (e) to establish effective procedures for the implementation and application of the Agreement and for the resolution of disputes, and finally (f) to improve further trilateral regional and multilateral cooperation.

When NAFTA came into force, tariffs on approximately 50 percent of the 9000 traded items covered by the treaty were eliminated with immediate effect. Within the next five years, 15 percent more of the items are to have zero tariffs with the remainder following in the next ten years. In addition, remaining licensing requirements and quotas were also eliminated with immediate effect.

To qualify for the preferential access, a commodity must be wholly produced within that particular member country or if imported materials are used, they must be subject to 'substantial transformation' within the country. At least 35 percent of the value of the commodity exported has to be accounted for by the beneficiary country in question. This is known as the 'rules of origin'.

NAFTA investors also receive more favourable treatment in setting up operations or acquiring firms. Existing requirements, including specified export levels, minimum domestic content, preferences for domestic sourcing, trade balancing and technology transfer, are being phased out over periods of up to ten years.

Following the US and Canada, Mexico is committed to the removal of various restrictions on service transactions. Mexico would have eliminated its restrictions on banks and insurance companies by January 2000, and on brokerage firms within ten years so that wholly-owned subsidiaries that may be established will be subjected to non-discriminatory treatment.

US trucking firms, which were barred from carrying cargo into Mexico, have been permitted to carry international cargo into the Mexican states and to the rest of Mexico since the year 2000. Full reciprocal access for trucking firms has also been permitted, with full access for charter and tour bus operations in the cross-border market in all three countries. US railroads are now able to serve Mexico generally. US investments are permitted in landside port services. The majority of Mexico's tariff and non-tariff barriers on telecommunication equipment have been eliminated. And NAFTA allows the three countries to follow their own environmental, health and safety standards.

The same theoretical framework used in the case of the European integration can be used here. The economic implications of NAFTA for the ASEAN countries can be assessed in terms of trade and diversion effects. Also, if the dynamic perspective is adopted, it is possible that the growth-enhancing effects of NAFTA may be significant enough to reduce the negative short-run implications of trade and investment diversion.

Since the US is the largest market for ASEAN, competition from Mexico in the US market has caused the greatest concern among the ASEAN countries, as the Mexican economy resembles the ASEAN economies most, and as the Canadian and Mexican markets are relatively insignificant to ASEAN. Direct competition from Mexico is likely to occur in food, petroleum and petroleum products, organic and inorganic compounds, machinery, telecom equipment, electronics and in miscellaneous manufactures such as clothing and footwear. For these items Mexico has demonstrated some productive capacity and thus its export elasticities in these products are relatively high.[3] Diversion of investments to Mexico, particularly in labour-intensive products, is also likely due to its low labour costs and proximity to the US market.

There are, however, a number of forces which can mitigate the trade and investment diversion effects of the European and North American integration on ASEAN. First, due to the successful completion of the Uruguay Round of Trade Negotiations under GATT, the barriers that Europe and North America have against foreign countries will be reduced substantially over the next 10 years (2003 roughly at the same time as NAFTA and AFTA). The Uruguay Round aims to cut tariffs by 37 percent on average on industrial and farm goods as well as liberalizing trade in agriculture and services. It also intends to replace non-tariffs such as quotas with tariffs. Although it does not have the scope and depth of NAFTA, a successful implementation of the new GATT treaty can mitigate the trade and investment diversion effects of NAFTA from ASEAN.

The ASEAN countries also have a competitive edge over Mexico in terms of infrastructure and management (*The Straits Times*, 27 August 1992). Based on the World Economic Forum (1992, 1994), Mexico was behind Singapore, Malaysia, and Thailand in terms of overall competitiveness. Based on The World Economic Forum (1995), Mexico was ranked behind all the ASEAN5 countries, that is, Singapore, Malaysia, Thailand, Indonesia and the Philippines.

Continued dynamism in the Asian region, fuelled by greater regional trade liberalization and the enlargement of markets with the opening up of China, India and IndoChina, will make ASEAN an attractive region for investments. That is why the US and Canada have increased their trade with ASEAN even after the US–Canada free trade agreement was implemented in 1989.

7.3   COUNTER STRATEGY FOR ASEAN

7.3.1   AFTA and linkages with NAFTA and the EU

The response of the ASEAN countries to the growing regionalism in Europe and North America has been one of retaliation and reconciliation. First, the 1992 decision by the ASEAN countries to establish an ASEAN free trade area by the year 2008 and the recent decision to speed up the process by moving the implementation date to 2002 reflected the ASEAN effort to maintain, if not improve, the attractiveness of the ASEAN region for trade and investment. At the same time, there has been an attempt to forge linkages with NAFTA and EU countries. Such linkages are taking shape already. An initial link between NAFTA and AFTA countries was forged in November 1991 when a trade and investment framework agreement was signed between the US and Singapore. For example, a Mexican manufacturer of sheet glass has a technology-sharing agreement with US firms in glass-making machines and moulds. This firm hopes to manufacture glass products in Thailand and then uses Singapore as a purchasing, distribution and financing centre. Similar arrangements are being sought for textiles and garments manufacturing between Mexican and Indonesian parties.

Dialogues between ASEAN and the EU to discuss the prospects for cooperation on trade with each other have started under the Asia–Europe Meeting (ASEM). An Investment Promotion Action plan under the Asia–Europe Cooperation framework has been proposed to strengthen the multilateral trading system.

7.3.2   Formation of Asia-Pacific Economic Cooperation (APEC)

Since APEC was formed in 1989, it has become the primary regional vehicle for promoting trade and investment cooperation in the Asia–Pacific region.[4] ASEAN has joined APEC initially on the understanding that the grouping is informal, with no legal binding power. But, since 1993 the development of APEC into a more formal grouping is taking shape.[5] This trend is a response to the rising regionalism in Europe and to the possibility of the world splitting into blocs. This grouping can, therefore, be viewed as a cooperative venture between East Asia and North America to promote an open global trading system.

Apart from the vision statement and general framework for trade liberalization in the Asia–Pacific region, the APEC leaders have also expanded the trade and investment facilitation programme to include the endorsement of non-binding investment principles to facilitate investments in the region, improve customs procedures,[6] establish common standards and lower administrative barriers to market access and establish a dispute settlement mechanism to supplement that of the World Trade Organization. They have also agreed to expand regional cooperation in education and training, science and technology, small and medium enterprises, sustainable development and infrastructure (including energy, transportation, telecommunications and tourism).

Given APEC's commitment to the principle of open regionalism, APEC can complement ASEAN's long-term interest in establishing a freer multilateral trading environment. ASEAN have much to gain from APEC not only because the Asia-Pacific region is economically important for them, but also because of the political leverage from being part of APEC. Since APEC will offer to extend its liberalization to non-members who are willing to reciprocate, barriers are likely to fall inside and outside the region.

In the Osaka Summit meeting in November 1995, the action agenda for trade liberalization to ensure compatibility of balance of interests among member countries was approved, but the scope of coverage remained unresolved. APEC members were divided on whether or not certain sectors would have to be exempted from trade liberalization. Japan, South Korea and China wanted to shelter their farmers from free trade while the US and Australia, APEC's biggest food exporters, insisted on no exceptions.

In the APEC Summit Meeting in Subic Bay, the Philippines held in November 1996, the APEC leaders took another step by endorsing a detailed action plan (Manila Action Plan for the Asia–Pacific Economic Cooperation) for achieving the goal of free trade and investment within the region by the year 2020. Each individual member's action plan details a plan to reduce tariffs, commencing in January, 1997, gradually to zero (by 2010 for developed countries and 2020 for developing countries), and to speed up the movement of goods and people throughout the region by harmonizing customs and immigration procedures. On the unfinished issue of coverage, the APEC members have reaffirmed their commitment to a voluntary non-binding structure, instead of the formal and legal structure of other trading arrangements such as the EU and NAFTA. Unlike previous summits, they have also expressed their commitment to improve their less-developed members' ability to compete and benefit from a larger market by fostering a programme of economic and technical cooperation. Further, they have expressed support for a leading role for the private sector in boosting trade and investment in the region and in providing a 'reality check' for political leaders and officials. They have also demonstrated their concern for small and medium-scale enterprises by agreeing to provide training resources and information on potential new markets.

SUGGESTIONS FOR FURTHER READING

For an industry by industry assessment of the trade effects of the North American Free Trade Area (NAFTA) and the Economic Community post-1992 on the Association of Southeast Asian Nations, see Kreinin and Plummer (1992, 1998). For a general assessment of the relationship between the ASEAN Free Trade Area (AFTA) and NAFTA, read Pupphavesa and Geeve (1994, Chapter 8).

NOTES

1. EC-wide quotas are in a way trade liberalizing compared to national quotas. Under the national quotas, if the import quota of EC country A has not been filled, while in country B the quota is binding, it is not possible to use the slack in A to increase imports into B.
2. Products where public procurement accounts for a large share of the market and where discrimination against imports is important are: defence equipment, aircraft and space equipment, electric power-generating machinery, medical equipment, railway equipment, ships, telephone exchanges, computers and metal constructions (Kreinin and Plummer, 1992, p. 1362).
3. A large proportion of ASEAN exports to the US is likely to be affected as the US is the largest export market for the Philippines, Singapore and Thailand and the second largest for Indonesia and Malaysia (*The Straits Times*, 1 October, 1992).
4. The APEC concept was initiated in January 1989 by the then Australian Prime Minister Bob Hawke. At his invitation trade and foreign ministers met in Canberra and created APEC. The founding members include Australia, Canada, Japan, South Korea, New Zealand, the United States and all members of ASEAN. Memberships were subsequently extended to China, Hong Kong, Taiwan, Mexico, Papua New Guinea and Chile, bringing the total membership to 18 nations. This grouping is committed to regional economic cooperation and open regionalism.
5. At the pathbreaking 1993 Summit meeting in Seattle, the APEC leaders issued a vision statement and endorsed the Report of the Eminent Persons Group. At the second Summit meeting in 1994 in Bogor, Indonesia, they produced commitments including the setting of 2020 as the dateline for a free and open trade in the Asia-Pacific and 2010 for the industrialized economies.
6. The APEC Subcommittee on Customs Procedure has reached an accord to adopt common customs checks by 2000. The accord contains nine technical steps needed to ensure that goods pass through the same customs clearance procedures including common rules for valuing goods to assess import tariffs, wider enforcement of copyrights, adoption of a single APEC customs declaration form, and the computerization of clearance procedures in line with UN rules.

8. Regionalism, multilateralism and the World Trade Organization

It is implied from the preceding chapters that the ASEAN countries in negotiating with countries outside the region for freer trade and more secure market access have reinforced their bargaining position by negotiating as a group and taking a common position, rather than acting individually. They have also pursued a regional approach to trade liberalization. But it is quite clear from their policy announcements that they prefer a freer global trade to a freer regional trade and that the multilateral approach is the best tool for achieving a freer global trade. This chapter will explore the factors behind the worldwide revival of interest in regionalism, analyse the major achievements of the last round of multilateral trade negotiations and its implications for the ASEAN countries and the role and challenges facing the World Trade Organization (WTO). The last section considers the advantages and disadvantages of regionalism *vis-à-vis* multilateralism.

8.1 REASONS FOR THE REVIVAL OF REGIONALISM

Created in Geneva on 30 October 1947 by 23 founding nations, the General Agreement on Tariffs and Trade (GATT), now known as the World Trade Organization (WTO), membership increased to over 100 countries. As believers in an open market and fair competition secured through multilateral rules and discipline, the GATT members had over seven rounds of negotiations slashed average tariffs on manufactured goods from more than 40 percent in the 1940s to less than 5 percent today. The rounds were: the Geneva Round in 1947, the Annecy Round in 1949, the Torquay Round in 1950–51, the Geneva Round in 1955–56, the Dillion Round in 1961–62, the Kennedy Round in 1964–67, and the Tokyo Round in 1974–79.

Despite the substantial tariff reduction on manufactured goods, there has been a growing dissatisfaction over the multilateral approach to trade liberalization under the auspices of GATT for a number of reasons. New forms of trade restrictions such as the Voluntary Export Restraints (VERs), Orderly Marketing Arrangements (OMAs), technical standards, customs procedures and others have emerged as disguised forms of protectionism. The large membership of GATT has made negotiations more complicated and difficult to resolve, let alone monitoring compliances. The Western countries, particularly Western Europe and the US, are increasingly disillusioned with GATT and there has been a growing perception that multilateralism has failed to provide a level playing field. The Special and Differential treatment (S&D) accorded to developing countries in the form of the Generalized System of Preferences has been cited as an example.

There has been a perception that the European market is becoming more inward-looking with the establishment of the European Union (EU) and the extension of integration to the European Free Trade Area (EFTA) and Eastern European countries. The decline in US economic dominance and increased competition from Europe and Japan has reduced US commitment to multilateralism and pushed it to form a countervailing bloc. The US–Canada Free Trade Area (FTA) was later followed by the North America Free Trade Area (NAFTA). The enterprise for the Americas' initiative envisages more FTAs with South American countries.

The delayed conclusion of the Uruguay Round[1] has made countries pessimistic about the effectiveness of multilateralism and has driven a number of countries to form regional groupings as an insurance policy. Finally, the faltering support of the US and Western Europe for the multilateral system has created a sense elsewhere that regionalism is the order of the day. Smaller countries are seeking regional trading arrangements with their large neighbours. Ex-President of Mexico, Salinas, pushed Mexico into NAFTA because of concern that European investments would be diverted to Eastern Europe and that domestic reforms in Mexico might be derailed under political pressure. On the other hand, there was the US concern with cross-border problems should the Mexican economy collapse. Due to the above sources of dissatisfaction over the GATT-sponsored multilateral approach, there has been a proliferation of regional trading pacts. According to the WTO report (1995), 109 regional trading arrangements were submitted to GATT between 1947 and 1994. There were 33 registered pacts between 1990 and 1994.

8.2 ACHIEVEMENTS OF THE URUGUAY ROUND AND ASEAN

During these seven rounds the ASEAN countries did not benefit as much as the developed industrialized countries as they chose to remain on the sidelines. The successful conclusion of the Uruguay Round (1986–93), where the ASEAN countries had been more active participants in the negotiation process, has achieved the following agreements beneficial to the ASEAN countries:

(a) Tariff reduction on industrial and farm goods by an average of 37 percent and the replacement of non-tariffs with tariffs. The tariff equivalents are to be reduced by a simple average of 24 percent over a ten-year period for the developing countries and by a simple average of 36 percent over a six-year period for the developed countries subject to a minimum of 15 percent (ESCAP, 1995, p. 90).

(b) The tariffication of non-tariff barriers and reduction of farm subsidies. All border non-tariff measures applied on imports of agricultural products are converted into tariff equivalents and subjected to the same tariff reductions and datelines as in the imports of industrial products. Subsidization of domestic producers of agricultural products is reduced equal to a 20 percent reduction of the aggregate measure of support with the exception of subsidies with a minimal impact on trade (the 'Green Box'), cases where domestic support constitutes less than 10 percent of the total value of production for developing countries or 5 percent for developed countries on a general or product-specific basis and direct payments under production-limiting programmes. The developing countries are provided with exemptions with respect to investment subsidies, agricultural input subsidies, or those applied to encourage diversification out of illicit narcotic crops.

(c) Liberalization of the trade in services. The General Agreement on Trade and Services (GATS) extends basic MFN obligations to services, thus bringing this sector for the first time into the auspices of GATT. Agreements include elimination of limits on the number of service providers, total value of service transactions, kind of legal entity or joint ventures and foreign capital related to maximum foreign participation.

(d) Protection of trade-related intellectual property rights (TRIPs). The TRIPs Agreement establishes disciplines for copyright, trademarks, geographical indications, industrial designs, patents, layout designs of integrated circuits and protection of undisclosed information.

(e) Strengthening of the rules for settling international trade disputes and clarification of the anti-dumping rules. The Agreement provides more detailed rules in defining dumping, and procedures and methods for initiating investigations. These rules are aimed to make domestic legislations more transparent, greater scrutiny of information contained in the complaint, positive action to ascertain industry support for the complaint and reviews of anti-dumping measures within five-year intervals.

(f) Transformation of GATT into a permanent watchdog, called the World Trade Organization (WTO), with status equal to the International Monetary Fund and the World Bank.

The success of the long-drawn-out Uruguay Round has certainly been a boost to the multilateral process as an approach to global trade liberalization. The pessimism that prevailed during Uruguay talks about the inability of the process to strike general agreements on rules governing international trade has been to a large extent translated into new hopes and reinvigorated the world trading environment. Apart from the psychological boost, there are also benefits derived for the ASEAN countries. On the first agreement, a freer trade in agriculture and manufactures will benefit particularly Malaysia and Thailand. Malaysia's exports of palm oil have been facing quotas in the European market with its common agricultural policy. Thailand's exports of rice have faced significant tariffs and global quotas in Japan and the European Community (EC); its cassava exports are subject to the EC's voluntary export restraints (VERs).

The Philippines and Indonesia in particular will also benefit from the agreed phasing out of import quotas under the Multi-fibre Arrangement (MFA), particularly for their exports of textiles, clothing and footwear. The reduction of farm subsidies should also particularly benefit Malaysia's export of palm oil in the EC since soya bean oil (its competing substitute) in the EC is heavily subsidized.

The basic obligations incorporated in the Services Agreement and the commitments undertaken by the countries lay the groundwork for progressive liberalization of international trade in services through successive rounds of negotiations. The impact of this on ASEAN is likely to be varied as their services sectors vary in terms of efficiency and development. Singapore, having the most developed financial sector, is likely to benefit from the liberalization of trade in professional and technical services such as banking and finance, transport, tourism, engineering consultancies, medical services and computer software. But Indonesia, Malaysia and the Philippines may experience substantial deficits in services account resulting from liberalization of trade in services.

The protection of intellectual property rights would seem to inconvenience the ASEAN countries at first reading. But in the long term this agreement would lower the risk of investment for foreign businesses, making the ASEAN region more attractive to foreign direct investment (FDI). Further, an effective enforcement against any breach of copyright will encourage greater indigenous innovation and technological progress.

The agreement on the rules on anti-dumping should also benefit the ASEAN countries as problems relating to the application and administration of anti-dumping systems and the increased recourse to anti-dumping actions have become more pronounced.

8.3 THE ROLE AND CHALLENGES OF THE WTO

The main task of the trading community now is to implement the results of the Uruguay Round in order to bring about a world trade liberalization. This enormous task can better be managed within an institutional framework – the WTO – encompassing the GATT and having the status of an Inter-Governmental Organization like the World Bank. Also, a more credible system for managing disputes has been established within the WTO, which is crucial to the successful enforcement of the commitments under the Uruguay Round.

To be able to effectively implement the Uruguay agreements and become the motor of world trade liberalization, the WTO needs to resolve the following issues:

- The WTO must be able to maintain a motivated Secretariat so that it can be adequately equipped with resources to deal with its enormous work. Although the key posts in the WTO Secretariat are filled, the team in the Secretariat has been overstretched and has been demanding improved pay and work conditions.[2]
- There are over 200 notification requirements arising from the Marrakesh decisions and member countries are behind schedule in meeting many of them.[3]
- The Uruguay Round has agreed on a set of principles to govern services trade, but only a few barriers have been reduced. There is still the remaining task of resolving negotiations in the area of agricultural trade, financial services, telecommunications and maritime transport.[4]

  There are a few dynamic countries that have just been admitted to (such as China and Taiwan) or that are still outside the WTO (such as Cambodia, Russia and Vietnam). Global free trade cannot be achieved if such countries are unable to implement fully their commitments to the WTO principles or are unwilling to align their rules with WTO norms. The challenge is how to accelerate their economic integration into the global community without any sacrifice of principles.
- There are a number of current members of the WTO, mainly developing countries, whose governments and economies are not effectively plugged either to the world economy or the Geneva decision-making process due mainly to low income and high indebtedness. These countries may not see any benefits from an open trading system and from the additional efforts launched in WTO.
- There is a challenge to secure for the WTO and the open trading system the support of the voters whose opinions drive policy in an increasingly democratic world. Despite the unprecedented support for freer trade around the world, considerable protectionist pressures remain. The

WTO is seen in some quarters as contributing to the violation of human rights and labour exploitation. The WTO needs to spearhead a global educational campaign on the benefits of free trade, apart from individual countries' campaigns on the merits of the strategy.

- There is the unsettled issue of whether or not the principle of fairness, human rights, child labour and right to collective bargaining must be linked to trade. The US has proposed that WTO members proclaim the desirability of five core labour standards, and set up a committee to examine the links between trade and the observance of these standards. This question is related to defining the meaning of 'free trade'. Countries are divided on this. Norway has made similar proposals and some EU countries, notably France, are sympathetic. The ASEAN countries have already made their position clear. In contrast to the countries of North America and Western Europe, they prefer to take up this issue under the auspices of the International Labour Organization (ILO), rather than under the WTO. This issue could delay the progress for establishing a freer world trade unless properly managed.

- Finally, the need for the WTO to set the course for the global trading system and for the world economy for the new millennium.

8.4   MULTILATERALISM VS REGIONALISM

Given that there are a number of challenges facing the WTO, it is not an irrelevant question to ask whether or not regionalism is better than the multilateral approach towards worldwide trade liberalization. The case for free trade was advocated by Adam Smith and David Ricardo and later was rigorously proved in a number of theoretical studies (for example, Samuelson, 1939 and Kemp, 1962). Viner's analysis of trade creation and trade diversion has also shown that preferential trading arrangements are not necessarily welfare-enhancing, either from the members' viewpoint or from the world's. Preferential trading arrangements are second-best solutions, as shown by Meade (1955, 1956), Johnson (1958) and others.

The key issues in the multilateralism versus regionalism debate are: Will regionalism in the form of free trade arrangements (FTAs) and customs union (CUs) bring quicker results in trade liberalization? Will regionalism increase or reduce world welfare? Will regionalism ultimately support and reinforce the multilateral free trade system and therefore should it be welcomed, or will it undermine the system and deserve condemnation? Should regionalism be accepted as a second-best solution to the breakdown of the GATT-based multilateral system, given that the first-best solution is unattainable?

Critics of the GATT-based multilateral approach to free trade who are frustrated with the slow progress made under GATT in trade liberalization have translated the GATT acronym as a general agreement to talk and talk. They have argued that regional trading arrangements among like-minded nations produce faster agreements on trade liberalization. On the other hand, supporters of the GATT approach have pointed to the slow implementation of an FTA or CU. For example, the European Community (EC) started in 1957 and the integration process has been slow. It took ASEAN ten years after its formation to draw its agenda for economic cooperation, and 25 years to agree to establish an FTA. The ASEAN FTA immediately faced hitches in implementation and the time frame for implementation was reduced from 15 to 10 years largely because the implementation of the Uruguay Round agreements would be completed within a ten-year time frame.

A regional trading arrangement is designed to promote trade among its members at the expense of non-members. It, therefore, produces a trade-creating effect (generating trade with one more efficient member at the expense of another less efficient member) and a trade-diverting effect (taking trade away from efficient outside suppliers and giving it to inefficient member countries). Which effect would be dominant depends on the proportion of trade between members and non-members, on the expenditure share between imports and domestic production and on the elasticity of substitution between goods. It is not certain that the trade diversion effect is minimized if the regional trade arrangement is confined to proximate countries.[5]

It is suggested that certain disciplines must be observed to minimize the incidence of trade diversion; for example, that the common external tariff in a CU is not higher or more restrictive than the pre-CU level, that duties and regulations in an FTA are not higher than the pre-FTA level, and that greater discipline is exercised with regard to antidumping and VER actions.

Will regionalism support or undermine multilateralism? One view is that regionalism can serve as a building block for multilateralism.[6] The threat of regionalism could produce multilateral trade agreements that otherwise would have been held up. It was reported that one of the forces that prompted the eventual successful conclusion of the Uruguay Round in 1993 was the decision of the EU to form a Single Common Market in 1992. Thus, there could be a positive interaction between regional and global approach to trade liberalization.

In a political economy sense, negotiations and agreements where few parties are involved are easier to achieve than in situations where a number of parties are involved. There are over a hundred countries currently involved in the process of multilateral trade negotiations which makes the achievement of agreements and resolutions under the Most Favoured Nation (MFN) principle much more complex and difficult than if negotiations are conducted with few parties under regional reciprocity. The free rider problem has constrained groups of countries to extend preferential arrangements under the MFN principle.

Further, public support for a regional trading arrangement tends to be more focussed and mobilized than support for multilateralism. The politics of preferential trade arrangements implies that it is easier for businessmen to secure trade diversionary deals in a Free Trade Area or Customs Union than in the non-discriminatory world of the General Agreement on Tariffs and Trade.

On the other hand, regionalism could also undermine multilateralism. The unwillingness of the EC to start the multilateral trade negotiations in 1982 and its foot-dragging in the Uruguay Round reflect to some extent its availability of regionalism as an option. Under this scenario the world will be divided into three or two trading blocs.

To date, regional trading arrangements have been positive forces in driving global liberalization with initiatives to establish free trade between regional groupings.[7] This goal of global free trade is quite feasible. As Table 8.1 shows, over 60 percent of world trade now occurs within regional groupings that have already achieved free trade such as the EU and Australia–New Zealand, or have signed an agreement that will achieve it such as NAFTA and AFTA, or have made a political commitment to do so by a certain date such APEC, the Free Trade of the Americas and EUROMED. On the other hand, the proliferation of regional arrangements could also make it difficult to maintain consistency with the global system. For example, the next potential regional arrangement, a TransAtlantic Free Trade Area (TAFTA) between North

Table 8.1 Regional free trade arrangements (percentage share of world trade, 1994)[a]

European Union	22.8
EUROMED	2.3
NAFTA	7.9
Mercosur	0.3
Free Trade Area of the Americas	2.6[b]
ASEAN Free Trade Area	1.3
Australia–New Zealand	0.1
APEC	23.7[b]
Total	61.0

Notes:
[a] Trade among the members of each regional group.
[b] Excluding trade among the members of their own sub-regional groups.

Source: Bergsten (1996).

America and Europe, could have a negative impact on the global trading system by encompassing new discrimination against the poor by the rich and thus reversing the progress towards North–South trade cooperation.

Whether regionalism will lead to a fragmented world economy or to non-discriminatory free trade through building blocs depends on the willingness of member governments, behaviour of interest groups and the reactions of governments and interest groups in non-member countries.

SUGGESTIONS FOR FURTHER READING

Martin and Winters (eds) (1995) provides an assessment of the concluded Uruguay Round of Trade Negotiations and its implications for the developing countries covering a wide range of issues. Bergsten (1996) and Brittan (1996) provide an introduction into the challenges and opportunities the World Trade Organization (WTO) is facing. On multilateralism versus regionalism, Schultz (1996) is recommended.

NOTES

1. Commencing in 1986, it was finally concluded on December 1993.
2. Taken from the speech of Sir Leon Brittan, Vice President of the Commission of the European Communities, 24 April 1996.
3. Ibid.
4. A new round of negotiations on freeing agricultural trade, which began during the Uruguay Round, was expected to resume in 1999; more talks on services trade began in 1997.
5. For a more detailed discussion of this issue, see Bhagwati (1996).
6. The phrase 'building or stumbling blocks' is owed to Bhagwati (1991, p. 77) who refers to the expansion of membership as a test of preferential trading arrangements (PTA) serving as building blocks for global freeing of trade. He also pointed out that if going down the PTA path itself can trigger multilateral negotiations and their successful conclusion, that too can be a way in which PTAs may serve as building blocks.
7. For example, Mercursor is a free trade agreement between the South American Market and the European Union; Free Trade Area of the Americas is between NAFTA and South America.

9. Role of foreign direct investment (FDI) in ASEAN

We have seen previously that foreign direct investment (FDI) in the form of MNCs has played a significant role in ASEAN5 economic development by providing the required capital, technology and access to the external markets through their international marketing networks. This chapter will discuss in more detail the benefits and costs associated with FDI, and the policies adopted by the ASEAN5 countries to maximize the benefits of FDI and counteract its potential negative consequences.

9.1 FOREIGN DIRECT INVESTMENT

Foreign direct investment is differentiated from other forms of investment by the former's ability to have a direct control over the invested capital. Usually in the form of multinational corporations (MNCs), foreign investors are driven to invest overseas due to their possession of superior technology or some type of comparative advantage, to maintain international competitiveness in the midst of rising production costs at home, or/and to counter certain moves of their rivals.

9.1.1 Forms of Foreign Direct Investment

The activities of MNCs may take the form of *horizontal integration* in which case large corporations open new subsidiaries worldwide, or one or several existing firms competing in the host country may be bought up by a large international corporation, and competition is reduced and market divided in oligopolistic fashion. Horizontal integration may be domestic market-oriented or export-oriented investments. For example, Toyota setting up an assembly plant in ASEAN is a domestic market-oriented investment whereas Sumitomo's chemical complex in Singapore is an export-oriented one. They may also take the form of *vertical integration* by keeping control of the various stages of a production process. For example, Unilever in the Philippines sets up a coconut oil production plant for soap production in its American factories.

9.1.2 FDI Trends in ASEAN

From the late 1970s until the early 1990s the ASEAN region became one of the most attractive investment locations in the developing world. Its share in the total stock of FDI in developing countries increased from 9 percent in 1980 to 24 percent in 1992 (UNCTAD, 1994). Its share in global FDI flows increased from less than 1 percent to 9 percent over the same period (Athukorala and Menon, 1996, p. 77). The growth of FDI into ASEAN5 was rapid particularly in the 1987–91 period (see Table 9.1). The importance of FDI varies, however, among individual ASEAN5 countries. FDI in aggregate plays a more important role in Singapore and Malaysia than in the other three remaining ASEAN5 economies, as Table 2.5 and Table 9.1 reveal.

Developed countries have been the largest source of FDI, accounting for the vast majority of outflows in all years, but the share of developing economies has grown rapidly due to the significant increase in outflows from the NIEs (see Table 9.1). Japan and the US remain the major country sources of FDI.

Foreign firms are directly involved in the host country trade to a large extent complementing the outward-looking strategies of ASEAN5, particularly important in resource extraction, manufacturing and services. The manufacturing sector has been the prime mover of industrial expansion, evident in the rapid rise of MNCs in the ASEAN growth economies.

FDI flows have accounted for a significant portion of total foreign capital flows in ASEAN5, but have been small as a source of ASEAN total investment, as Table 9.2 shows, with the exception of Singapore.[1] This means that capital movements associated with FDI are generally of limited consequences for most of the ASEAN countries. A downturn in FDI flows generally has little implication for their aggregate investment flows.

Although extra-regional investments are still dominant, there is a rising share of Northeast Asian investments, (that is, Japan, Hong Kong, Taiwan, South Korea and China) due to relocation of manufacturing industries and appreciation of currency. The share of NIEs' investment in ASEAN overtook that of Japan in 1990 which emphasizes the NIEs growing importance within ASEAN as a source of FDI.[2] Intra-ASEAN investment is also growing with Singapore as the leading supplier of foreign capital to the rest of the ASEAN region.[3]

It is likely that inward investment in the area of labour-intensive manufactures for the ASEAN5 countries will fall as they are facing increasing competition from lower wage-cost emerging economies of China, South Asia and the rest of Southeast Asia. It is, however, uncertain whether or not the aggregate level of inward investment will fall. It largely depends on how the ASEAN5 countries can maintain their attractiveness to foreign investors. There are other

Table 9.1 Outward and inward FDI flows ($USmillion)

	Average (1976–80)	Average (1981–85)	1986	1987	1988	1989	1990	1976–90	1991
Outward flows									
World	42 030	44 178	92 963	138 196	170 725	212 463	230 305	1 275 693	–
DCs	41 265	43 080	91 058	135 617	164 614	202 666	221 861	1 237 541	–
Europe	19 477	25 467	50 692	73 135	100 984	119 269	136 774	705 570	–
Japan	2 255	5 094	14 480	19 520	34 210	44 130	48 024	197 108	30 726
USA	16 881	7 706	18 690	28 980	17 871	30 167	34 111	252 757	28 197
Others	2 652	4 813	7 196	13 982	11 549	9 100	2 952	82 106	–
Inward flows									
World	32 474	53 115	70 874	126 199	150 750	190 740	187 988	1 154 494	–
ASEAN	1 524	3 012	2 847	4 303	6 983	8 902	11 580	57 291	–
Indonesia	253	237	258	385	576	682	964	5 312	1 482
Malaysia	559	1 083	489	423	719	1 668	2 902	14 412	–
Philippines	69	63	127	307	936	563	530	3 120	–
Singapore	545	1 349	1 710	2 836	3 647	4 212	4 808	26 684	–
Thailand	98	280	263	352	1 105	1 177	2 376	7 763	2 015

Note: –: not available.

Source: Ramstetter (1993, Table 1).

Table 9.2 Ratios of inward flows of FDI to foreign capital flows and fixed capital formation (%)

	1976–80	1981–85	1986	1987	1988	1989	1990	1986–90	1991	1992	1993	1994
Ratios to foreign capital flows												
Indonesia	out	7.4	6.6	18.4	41.2	61.6	40.7	–	–	–	–	–
Malaysia	out	45.8	400.8	out	out	953.1	235.7	–	–	–	–	–
Philippines	5.4	3.4	out	69.1	240.0	38.7	19.7	–	–	–	–	–
Singapore	75.4	179.3	out	out	out	out	out	–	–	–	–	–
Thailand	7.1	13.9	out	21.4	71.2	73.6	57.5	–	–	–	–	–
Ratios to fixed capital formation												
Indonesia	2.4	1.2	1.3	2.0	2.6	2.6	–	2.1	3.6	3.9	3.8	3.6
Malaysia	12.3	10.9	6.7	5.8	8.6	14.9	20.7	11.7	24.0	26.0	23.7	16.1
Philippines	1.1	0.8	3.2	6.2	15.6	7.3	6.2	6.7	6.0	2.1	7.9	9.6
Singapore	17.7	17.8	26.0	39.4	42.3	39.7	36.6	35.0	32.7	13.3	24.6	23.5
Thailand	1.6	3.1	2.9	3.1	6.9	8.4	8.6	6.5	4.9	4.8	3.5	1.1

Notes:
out = net capital outflow; total capital inflows = the negative of the current account balance.
–: not available.

Sources: Ramstetter (1993, Table 3); UNCTAD, *World Investment Report* (1995, Annex Table 5); *World Investment Report* (1996, Annex Table 5).

parameters foreign investors consider important in choosing their investment locations including political stability, proximity to markets and productive resources, infrastructure and administrative efficiency.

9.2   BENEFITS AND COSTS

During their initial stages of economic development the ASEAN5 countries, like other developing countries, were constrained by the shortage of capital. Low output, high unemployment and poverty were largely attributable to low productivity and poor productive capacity. The inflow of foreign direct investment has provided not only more employment opportunities, much required capital and technology to boost its productivity and output, but has also reinforced its export competitiveness through the outward-oriented foreign investments and the foreign firms' international networks and management know-how.

Although the growth in employment has been slower than the growth of FDI flows (see Table 9.3), FDI has provided employment opportunities directly and indirectly resulting from the growth of local ancillary industries via the linkage effect. The direct and indirect employment effects of FDI work through the multiplier effect on income emanating from the increase in investment which raises demand and leads to subsequent expansion of production in other industries, resulting in the expansion of local employment. The possible offsets to such positive effect include the high import intensity of foreign firms and the possible crowding out of indigenous firms due to the large market power of foreign firms. Besides, if the capital intensity of foreign firms is higher than that of local firms, there will be employment displacing effects with the inflow of FDI. For the ASEAN5 countries, FDI has resulted in the generation of employment opportunities due to the substantial linkage effect, less significant crowding out and direct employment effects.

The greater export-orientation of foreign firms, as evidenced by their shares in export sales as compared to domestic firms in ASEAN5 (see Table 9.3), appears to exert a demonstration effect for the local firms. This, coupled with the increasing competitiveness brought about by the diffusion of new technologies as well as management skills of the foreign enterprise, has served to stimulate the host country's exports. Singapore is a striking example among the ASEAN countries that has effectively used FDI to spearhead an export-led growth. The Singapore government has been instrumental in making FDI more export-oriented which subsequently leads to a large FDI contribution to the export sector. In this respect, the government policy of minimal restrictive trade policy has been crucial.

However, there are also costs associated with the inflow of FDI. A significant inflow of capital is usually accompanied by a deterioration of the current

Table 9.3 Foreign firm shares of employment, total sales and exports in non-petroleum manufacturing industries

Countries	1977			1986			1989		
	Employment	Sales	Exports	Employment	Sales	Exports	Employment	Sales	Exports
Indonesia	10.6	21.0	–	8.9	17.2	–	–	16.7	–
Malaysia	33.6	43.9	–	30.3	36.7	–	36.2	40.7	–
Singapore	53.8	72.8	84.7	54.2	63.4	74.9	59.6	76.4	86.1
Thailand	7.6	9.2	11.3	5.7	6.1	15.9	–	–	27.3

Note: –: not available

Source: Ramstetter (1993, Table 10).

143

account, as a rise in domestic demand induces an increase in imports or as the currency appreciates accompanied by a substantial repatriation of profits. It could also lead to inflationary tendencies. The type and size of macroeconomic impacts depend on the size of the foreign capital relative to the resource utilization level prior to the capital inflow and on the exchange rate regime adopted. Under a fixed exchange rate regime, the impact is via the income channel. The deterioration in the current account is due to a higher level of domestic demand and a rise in international reserves. The extent of current account deterioration depends on the import intensity of domestic demand and the resulting decline in the price of tradables relative to nontradable goods. Higher monetary growth could lead to lower interest rates or to higher inflation. Under a flexible exchange rate regime, the deterioration in the current account is due to a currency appreciation. A currency appreciation, *ceteris paribus*, means a lowering of the price of importables and an increase in imports with detrimental effects on export competitiveness.

Having a current account deficit is not necessarily bad. It makes sense for growing economies like ASEAN to import the necessary capital to increase their productive capacities. This investment-driven deficit is sustainable. It is only when the deficit is driven by consumer spending and when the current account deficit leads to unsustainable foreign debt that a current account deficit becomes a real cause for concern. Second, it is also dangerous if it could lead to a money supply-caused asset price bubble that then bursts leaving banks with huge bad loans. Third, it is also a cause for concern if the current account deficit is a reflection of a budget deficit. Based on past experiences, the track record of the private sctor in its ability to settle its debt is satisfactory partly due to the fact that the private sector is usually profit-oriented and thus is likely to ensure they have made calculated risks.

Further, domestic savings might weaken. Reduction in domestic savings may occur when the availability of foreign capital can deter the efforts of domestic financial institutions to mobilize domestic savings, and when it allows the government to increase its expenditure in less or unproductive areas and not to increase taxes which could lead to lower public sector savings.

There is the danger of losing some political autonomy as the economy becomes too dependent on foreign firms and foreign technology. There is also the danger of it becoming a 'dumping ground' of outdated, environmentally harmful and energy inefficient technology.

9.3   MANAGING FOREIGN CAPITAL

During the 1960s the ASEAN5 countries, except Singapore, had looked at MNCs with distrust because of the possible adverse effects of FDI including those that were presented in the preceding section.[4] Japanese MNCs received the strongest distrust due to the rapid expansion of Japanese investment and the fear of Japanese domination in the region (Pussarangsri and Chamnivickorn, 1995). During this period they had adopted restrictive regulations in an attempt to control FDI and thus avoid its possible harmful effects.

Since the late 1970s there has been a change in attitude towards FDI due to several reasons including the debt crisis and the benefits of FDI in the NIEs. Although the ASEAN5 debt crisis was not as severe as that of Latin American countries, it raised some concern to ASEAN5 policymakers, in particular in Indonesia, Malaysia and the Philippines. FDI was consequently accepted as a means to alleviate their debt crises.

9.3.1 Maximization of Benefits of FDI

In an attempt to attract FDI into their respective economies, the ASEAN5 countries have adopted some form of guarantee against nationalization.[5] They have relaxed their restrictive rules and regulations on FDI and changed their policy orientation to create an environment conducive to investment. The change in policy has been moderate in Thailand and Singapore, but has been drastic in Malaysia, Indonesia and the Philippines.

Singapore's attitude towards foreign investment has always been favourable. Its rules and regulations governing the operation of a foreign juristic person have always been quite lenient. Thailand's case is also unique. No significant change in its Alien Business Law has occurred since its enactment in 1957, although the interpretations of the Law are becoming more favourable with more exemptions granted to foreign investors (Pussarangsri and Chamnivickorn, 1995, p. 17). In Indonesia since its trade liberalization in 1986, restrictions and barriers applied to foreign investors have been modified or removed. In the Philippines the rules and regulations for foreign investors have been relaxed with the enactment of the Foreign Investment Act of 1991. In Malaysia many new incentives have been introduced since 1986 with a reduced role of government intervention.

The following are some of the areas where rules and regulations for foreign investment have been relaxed.

Foreign ownership of business

Total foreign ownership of business is allowed in most industries. In many cases exemptions are granted to foreign investors in activities that are closed to foreign investment. In areas where national security and use of domestic natural resources are at stake joint ventures are preferred. However, there is still some variation in terms of restrictiveness within the ASEAN5 countries. Singapore has the most liberal policies on foreign ownership of business with no specific rules and regulations for foreign investors except in banking and brokerage. There are no restrictions on foreign participation even in telecommunications and public utilities. Malaysia's policy on foreign ownership is also quite liberal. Practically, all businesses are open to foreign investors, except in the news media industry. The proportion of foreign ownership allowed is tied to the performance of firms and not to the type of business activities. A 100 percent foreign ownership is allowed when a firm exports at least 80 percent of its production, and 51 percent foreign ownership is allowed if a firm uses high technology in production. The Philippines and Thailand have moderately liberal policies. Based on the Foreign Investment Act of 1991 the Philippines has a negative list of business activities restraining foreign investment. The business activities in the negative list are classified according to the level of restrictions applied to foreign investors. The industries in the most restrictive group are completely closed to foreign investors. The second and third most restrictive groups refer to industries where up to 25 percent and 30 percent of foreign ownership is allowed, respectively. In the least restrictive group foreign investors can own up to 40 percent of the business equity. The rules are rigid with very few exemptions. Similar to the Philippines, Thailand has classified business activities into three types according to the level of restrictions. Under the Treaty of Amity and Economic Relations between the US and Thailand, US companies are not subject to restrictions imposed by their Alien Business Law, except in some specific areas. Indonesia has the most stringent policy towards FDI. Apart from the negative list of industries where foreign investors are restricted, joint ventures are preferred with the majority of shares to be held by the Indonesian partners for at least 15 years, with a few conditions for possible exemptions.

Land ownership
Although the Philippines, Thailand and Indonesia prohibit foreign juristic persons from owning land, they allow foreign firms long-term leasing agreements. In Thailand promoted firms are, however, allowed to own land and foreign juristic persons to own land in industrial estates. Malaysia and Singapore are most liberal with no restrictions on land ownership by foreign investors, although approval from the Foreign Investment Committee is needed in Malaysia.

Foreign exchange control
As discussed in Chapter 2, foreign exchange control in ASEAN5 countries is virtually minimal. International transfers are permitted with a few restrictions. For example, profit remitted out of Thailand is subject to 20 percent tax, except for those promoted firms. In the Philippines a specific amount of capital is

allowed to be transferred abroad each year, and any additional amount to be transferred requires an approval from the Central Bank of the Philippines.

9.3.2 Minimization of Costs

Given that there are potential costs associated with FDI inflows, the ASEAN5 governments have adopted appropriate policies to neutralize or minimize the disadvantages of FDI. Generally, they have relied on three sets of policy measures. The first type, some of which was discussed previously, are the rules and regulations governing FDIs such as equity ownership, restricted sectors, foreign exchange control and performance requirements such as local content, export–production ratio and manpower training. The second set of policies refers to the system of promotion measures and incentives such as income tax reductions or exemptions, import duty exemptions, investment and depreciation allowances. These incentives are tied to certain criteria consistent with their development objectives. The third set refers to policies affecting intra-industrial linkages through subcontracting arrangements.

Deterioration of the current account and inflation

As can be gleaned from Table 2.6, all the ASEAN5 countries, except Thailand, experienced a significant improvement in their current account balance during the 1987–96 period when there was also a massive inflow of FDI into their respective economies. Singapore, being the most FDI-dependent ASEAN country, has the most spectacular achievement in counteracting the negative consequence of FDI in terms of current account deterioration. Apart from Singapore's surplus in the services account, it has been successful in attracting export-oriented FDI with its generous scheme of fiscal incentives, superior legal and physical infrastructure, political and social stability, harmonious industrial relations and liberal trade policies.[6] The export orientation of these foreign firms has contributed greatly to the surge in exports and reinvestments by MNCs and thus more than compensated for the repatriation of profits by MNCs. The negative impact of the appreciation of the Singapore dollar has also been neutralized by the government policy of encouraging firms to produce high value-added products and improve productivity using various incentives. The government's emphasis on education and training has also facilitated the technology transfer.

The other ASEAN5 countries, which were traditionally less open, have reduced import leakages by imposing a local content rule in the production of exportables. Among the ASEAN5 countries the Philippines has relied on this most heavily. Malaysia is the first ASEAN country to adopt positive measures to induce higher local content in the automobile industry. Credits in the form of points are given to producers whose production exceeds the required local content level.

With the exception of Singapore, whose tariffs are already very low, they have encouraged exports by also eliminating or reducing import tariffs on capital goods and raw materials used by export-oriented firms. Virtually all ASEAN5 countries, except Singapore, grant import duty exemptions to imports of raw materials and machineries used for producing goods for export based on the concept of export-processing zones.

There are other incentives such as tax holidays, investment allowances and accelerated depreciation allowances and the 1996 initiatives by Indonesia to allow foreign-owned firms to provide services to export-oriented firms (*The Straits Times*, 5 March 1996).[7] Previously this privilege was only given to joint-venture firms. Further, private firms are now allowed to operate bonded zones.

Prudent fiscal policy has also contributed to a healthy current account balance.[8] Under the twin deficit phenomenon there is a link between trade balance and budget balance. Most ASEAN5 countries had not experienced budget deficits and thus their healthy budgetary positions contributed to their favourable trade balance positions.

Although Thailand's current deficit as a proportion of its GDP did not improve for the 1987–96 period (as Table 2.6 shows), it succeeded in arresting the upward pressure on inflation resulting from the surge of foreign capital particularly during the period 1987–92.[9] Thailand, with its fixed exchange rate regime, was able to contain the inflationary pressures by implementing effective liquidity control measures. Its monetary policy was aimed at neutralizing the monetary impact of the capital inflows while other policies were aimed at encountering the tendency for the inflows in the overall balance of payments. To reduce domestic liquidity, mopping up operations were conducted through the issuance of the Bank of Thailand's own securities while the Bank of Thailand exercised moral suasion asking commercial banks to limit their lending to speculative activities. The monetary restraint was supported by a fiscal policy that emphasized a sizeable fiscal surplus. Central government's budgetary surplus averaging about 3 percent of GDP was maintained from 1987 to 1992. This policy stance helped boost national saving and made room for higher investment and export.

Weak domestic savings
The negative impact of FDI on domestic savings has been neutralized by requiring their residents to save part of their earnings in a provident fund which has become a major source of investment funds. This is particularly true for Singapore and Malaysia through their compulsory savings schemes. In addition, low inflation and an efficient banking system achieved through the process of deregulation have contributed to more confidence in the financial system, and thus to greater savings.

Loss of political autonomy

This was minimized by diversifying the source of FDI and allowing market forces to determine the final composition. In the 1960s petroleum refining, metals and food and beverages were the main sources of growth in Singapore. By the 1980s skill-intensive industries such as industrial electronics, computers, industrial machinery and high value-added petroleum products had taken over.

The local firms have also prospered despite the dominance of the foreign firms. This has been due to the assistance from the ASEAN5 governments and the initiative from local entrepreneurs. For instance, the ASEAN5 governments have tried to forge better relationships between foreign firms and local suppliers of parts and components.

Lack of technology transfer

To ensure a real transfer of technology from the foreign investors to the local firms, the ASEAN5 countries have adopted various measures to promote subcontracting arrangements. Malaysia has the most comprehensive scheme which includes tax incentives and specific institutional arrangements such as the umbrella strategy, vendor development scheme, local content requirement and cluster creation. Under the umbrella strategy one large enterprise, called the umbrella company, provides assistance to small local companies in production and marketing. The umbrella company gets rewards in return, say awarding of government contracts without contest bidding. Under the vendor development scheme MNCs assist local counterparts in the production of parts and components for them. INTEL and PROTON car producers are participants in this vendor development scheme. Under cluster creation small local enterprises are relocated to the same area to become a cluster of vendors of the same industries. Information about buyers (large enterprises) and sellers (small local subcontractors) is conducted by the Subcontract Exchange scheme.

Singapore has introduced a subcontracting scheme similar to Malaysia. However, unlike Malaysia Singapore does not have a local content requirement. The specific institutional arrangement consists of the Local Industry Upgrading programme managed by MNC engineers on a rotational basis in which MNCs are encouraged to provide technical and other types of assistance to small local enterprises. In return the MNC engineers receive compensation from Singapore's Economic Development Board (EDB). Indonesia's subcontract arrangement is called the Foster Father Plan where large enterprises provide financial assistance to and market the products of small enterprises.

The Philippines and Thailand have not promoted interfirm technology transfer as vigorously as Malaysia, Singapore and Indonesia. The Philippines has simply relied on the local content requirement. In addition, Thailand has an information provision and exchange programme operated by Thailand's Board of Investment Unit for Industrial Linkages.

9.4 CONCLUSION

In conclusion, the impact of FDI on the ASEAN5 has been more positive than negative. Effective implementation of appropriate policies played an essential role in ensuring that the FDI flow complemented their national development strategy (such as encouraging the export orientation of FDI which is in line with the export-led growth strategy), assimilating the appropriate technology to local economy and minimizing the negative impacts of FDI. Singapore is a good example illustrating the appropriate use of government policies to ensure the effective use of FDI, which resulted in the overall positive impact of FDI on Singapore.

Greater cooperation in the area of investment will go a long way in increasing the bargaining power of the ASEAN countries and their attractiveness as an investment location in the context of a tighter global capital market. It is heartening to note that the ASEAN countries at their 28th ASEAN Economic Ministers (AEM) Meeting in Jakarta in September 1996 agreed to establish an ASEAN Investment Area (AIA) with the objective to increase substantially the flow of investment into ASEAN from member and non-member sources. They suggested such measures as allowing ASEAN companies to be listed on other ASEAN stock exchanges, establishing an enhanced ASEAN agreement on investment promotion and protection and joint promotion of ASEAN as an investment location. Apart from this, they have also agreed to set in motion another investment liberalization scheme – the ASEAN Industrial Cooperation Scheme – by 1 November, 1996, as mentioned previously.

SUGGESTIONS FOR FURTHER READING

For a general review of the literature on FDI, see Hill (1990) and Pussarangsri and Chamnivickorn (1995). Studies published over the last few years on ASEAN FDI include Ramstetter (1993) and Chia Siow Yue (1993). In addition, there are country studies: on Singapore, see Lim and Associates (1988, Chapter 9); on Indonesia, see Hill (1988) and Thee (1991); on Thailand, see Tambunlertchai (1993).

NOTES

1. The small proportion of FDI in Indonesia and Thailand's total investment is due to their reliance on external borrowings to finance their current account deficits. The Sukarno-led distrust of foreign investors was still prevalent in Indonesia during the time of Suharto, despite the launching of the New Order one aim of which was to secure capital for the economy. This was reflected in an interrupted implementation of deregulation policies in the 1970s and 1980s. Foreign investors in turn have been sceptical and required substantial reforms of the whole economy.
2. Taken from APEC Report: Vision for the conomies of the Asia Pacific Region in the Year 2000 and Tasks Ahead, Report to the Ad Hoc Group of Economic Trends and Issues, APEC, September 1993.
3. Singapore emerged as Malaysia's top foreign investor for the first time in 1996, with total approved investments in the manufacturing sector rising sharply to M$4.8 billion (S$2.7 billion) from a mere M$1 billion in 1995 (*The Straits Times*, 24 January, 1997, p. 80)
4. Other possible negative consequences of great concern to ASEAN5 are excessive repatriation of profits, increase in market concentration and worsening income inequality (Naya and Imada, 1990).
5. Malaysia has the strongest guarantee by constitution. Indonesia and the Philippines are less liberal but also have a guarantee by law. Nationalization is flexible in these countries, but there is a provision of compensation. Thailand and Singapore do not have a guarantee by law but have signed bilateral treaties with their major foreign investors for protection. FDI in ASEAN5 countries is also under the protection of the Multilateral Investment Guarantee Agency which assures against non-commercial risks (Pussarangsri and Chamnivickorn, 1995, pp. 20–21).
6. Singapore has provided a relatively more elaborate incentive scheme such as tax holidays, investment allowances, accelerated depreciation allowances and reinvestment incentives.
7. Indonesia is the only ASEAN5 country that has not offered income tax privileges for foreign investors. However, Indonesia is reportedly considering offering tax holidays to selected companies in strategic industries to lure them away from competing countries (*The Straits Times*, 7 January 1997, p. 38).
8. This point is supported by the twin deficit argument which establishes the link between budget deficit and trade deficit. For more detailed arguments, see Feldstein (1986), Hooper and Mann (1989).
9. The rate of inflation decelerated from 6 percent in 1990 to 5.7 percent in 1991. For detailed explanation, see Nijathaworn (1993, pp. 18–19).

PART THREE

The 1997 Asian Crisis and its Aftermath

10. The causes of the 1997 Asian crisis and its impacts on the ASEAN economies

The recent crisis that swept across the ASEAN region in 1997 and 1998 has not only thrown into doubt the future economic prosperity of the ASEAN countries, but has also raised intriguing questions about the right approach to economic development and the future of ASEAN economic cooperation. The crisis has had devastating economic, social and political consequences for the ASEAN countries, particularly in the hardest-hit economies of Thailand, Indonesia and Malaysia. This chapter will re-examine the origin and causes of the recent Asian crisis, evaluate the impacts it has had on their economies, the economic policies adopted and the impact of the crisis on their extra-ASEAN trade relations.

10.1 GENESIS AND CAUSES OF THE 1997 ASIAN CRISIS

No one had anticipated that the ASEAN economies would experience a severe economic crisis, as the region had generally been performing remarkably well for the past decades. Prior to the crisis, countries such as Thailand and Malaysia had large current account deficits, but not at alarming levels. No ASEAN country had persistent and unmanageable fiscal deficits and foreign debts, nor had experienced excessive monetary expansion. But the economic crisis, which started as a currency crisis and then as a financial crisis, did occur.

Much has been written and said about the causes of the crisis, and they all have agreed that a number of factors were responsible for it. These factors could be classified as financial, political and social in nature. However, there has been some disagreement as to which factor played the most significant role. With the benefit of hindsight, we can now say with greater confidence which of the factors had figured most prominently in the recent crisis.

The 1997 Asian crisis started in Thailand when the Thai baht was floated after the monetary authorities in Thailand decided to stop defending the baht

Table 10.1   The impact of the crisis on ASEAN4 exchange rates

Country	Exchange rates to US dollars		GNP in US billion dollars	
	June 1997	July 1998	June 1997	July 1998
Thailand	24.5 baht	41 baht	170	102
Indonesia	2380 rupiah	14 150 rupiah	205	34
Philippines	26.3 peso	42 peso	75	47
Malaysia	2.5 ringgit	4.1 ringgit	90	55

Source: Updated version from a table in Cheetham (1998).

and freed up its fixed exchange rate regime. The massive speculation against the Thai baht had put tremendous pressure on Thailand's foreign exchange reserves so that before the floating of the Thai currency the Thai government had almost depleted its foreign reserves in order to defend its currency peg to the US dollar. Once the Thai baht was floated, its value depreciated substantially. Other regional currencies also depreciated in value, ranging from 35 percent to almost 500 percent during the peak of the crisis, as Table 10.1 shows.

Currency speculation was, therefore, the triggering factor behind the Asian economic crisis. But behind the speculative attacks on the Thai baht was a more fundamental factor which caused the speculators and investors to lose confidence in the Thai government's ability to defend the baht. Thailand continued to experience robust export growth after the 1985 crisis until 1996 when there was a sudden reversal. In 1996 Thailand's exports experienced a significant fall in volume (5.5 percent) and value terms (1.3 percent) after experiencing a two-digit growth in export value in the first half of the 1990s, mainly due to the loss of international competitiveness caused by the appreciation of its local currency with the strengthening of the US dollar (since its currency was largely tied to the US dollar) and the competition from China, Vietnam and Indonesia in the production of labour-intensive products (such as textiles, clothing and other labour-intensive products) which have constituted a significant portion of Thailand's exports. The major decline in export performance coupled with mounting foreign debt[1]. had contributed to the loss of confidence in the Thai government's ability to defend its currency, the baht, as can be gleaned from Table 10.2.

Krugman (1979) explains that speculative attacks on a currency occur when there are inconsistencies between macroeconomic policies and exchange rate targets. If a government sticks to a currency peg and defends the exchange rate by drawing on its foreign currency reserves in the face of rapid growth in domestic credit and large budget deficits, speculators observing the depletion

Table 10.2   *Current account deficits and export growth rates in ASEAN5 before the crisis*

	Current account balance (% of GDP)			CPI inflation rate (%)		Annual growth (%) of exports in value terms		
	1990–92	1993–95	1996	1993–95	1996	1993–95	1996	1997
Indonesia	–2.9	–2.2	–3.5	9.2	6.5	10.2	9.7	8.9
Malaysia	–4.8	–6.5	–4.9	3.6	3.5	21.9	6.2	3.2
Philippines	–3.7	–4.2	–4.7	8.3	8.4	21.7	16.7	24.0
Singapore	10.1	13.6	14.1	2.4	1.3	23.2	5.7	0.4
Thailand	–7.2	–6.3	–8.0	4.8	5.9	20.1	–1.3	2.3

Source: Rao (1998, Table 3); Ito (1998).

of reserves will attack the currency in the belief that it could lead to an eventual collapse of the peg. The attacks will make the collapse of the currency peg certain. Obstfeld (1986), however, thought that, even when macroeconomic policies are consistent with an exchange rate peg, the belief of speculators or adverse economic conditions may affect the willingness of a government to defend a peg and the peg collapses as in a self-fulfilling prophecy.

Moreno (1995) has provided empirical evidence of currency crises in East Asia. By looking at episodes of speculative pressure in Indonesia, Japan, Korea, Malaysia, the Philippines, Singapore, Taiwan and Thailand during 1980–94, he concluded that episodes of depreciation in East Asia have been associated with larger budget deficits and growth in central bank domestic credits. In addition, inflation tended to be higher and growth tended to be slower during periods of depreciation than during periods of tranquillity. This implies that episodes of speculative pressure may also rise when economic conditions make it costly for the government to maintain a stable exchange rate. The crisis of 1997 is, therefore, quite different from the previous crises experienced in East Asia, which were associated with persistently large deficits, high inflation rates and slower growth.

The currency crisis later developed into a financial crisis. The sudden and massive withdrawal of foreign funds, which were invested in short-term banking instruments, but which were lent out to long-term and unproductive (such as real estate, shares and other projects with no clear feasibility studies) ventures, had caught many banks and other finance companies unprepared and short of liquid assets. Many of them became insolvent. It was reported that by 8 December, 1997 only two of the 58 suspended finance/securities companies were allowed to reopen (Leightner, 1999: p. 370). A weak financial sector in a deregulated financial environment has been blamed by a number of authors (for example, Radelet and Sachs, 1998; Krugman, 1998) as one underlying factor behind the financial crisis. Thailand like other ASEAN countries, as discussed previously, has embarked on financial liberalization and deregulation since the mid-1980s to woo more foreign investments into the economy. Thailand has liberalized its capital account and set up an international banking centre in Bangkok to facilitate the access to foreign funds. High domestic interest rates, a fixed exchange rate regime and Thailand's recent economic success had successfully attracted an inflow of short-term foreign capital. The ASEAN countries saw the advantages of financial liberalization, as described in the previous chapter, but no one realized the danger of financial liberalization under a weak and unprepared financial sector. The banks were not adequately capitalized and lacked transparency in their rules and credit policies, characterized by inadequate supervision and rampant corruption.

The financial crisis then developed into an economic crisis. The closure of many financial institutions, including finance and securities companies due to their insolvency, had led to massive lay-offs. Of the original 91 finance/securities companies, only 35 remained. The share market in Thailand slumped as foreign investors scrambled to sell off their shares to avoid further losses from currency depreciations and as they anticipated further decline in share values. The banks and other financial institutions tightened up their credit policies by raising interest rates and restricting their available loans. Since shares were also used as collateral by companies in their borrowings from financial institutions, the reduction in share values meant a lower valuation of their collaterals and thus their borrowing capacities. Moreover, with the borrowers' asset values down, the lending institutions were forced to increase their interest payments adding further to the liquidity problems experienced by the debtor companies.

10.2   THE CONTAGION EFFECTS

The crisis that started in Thailand was quickly transmitted to other countries in the region via a number of channels. First, Thailand has considerable trade and financial links with other ASEAN countries, and these intra-ASEAN trade links have provided a channel of contagion for other ASEAN countries. For example, a reduction in Thailand's aggregate output due to the crisis was translated into lower imports from other ASEAN exporting countries. Banks and other financial institutions with lending exposure to Thailand were obviously affected, as crisis-hit debtors could no longer service their debts. Moreover, since some products exported by Thailand are similar to the exports of other ASEAN countries, the depreciation of the Thai baht had an adverse impact on other ASEAN countries' international competitiveness, trade and employment, and hence increased the pressure of their respective governments to abandon their own commitment to a pegged exchange rate. Second, the region has been considered as possessing the same characteristics in terms of economic fundamentals and orientation. Thus, when the crisis happened to Thailand, many investors thought that the same thing would happen to the rest of the region. Third, investors' herd instincts due to incomplete information explained the panic and stampede in the withdrawals of funds from the region.

In the Dybvig–Diamond model of a bank run as explained in Radelet and Sachs (1998, p. 6), a panic is an adverse equilibrium outcome in which short-term creditors suddenly withdraw their loans from a solvent borrower. This can occur when three conditions hold: short-term debts exceed short-term assets; no single private market creditor is large enough to supply all of the credits necessary to pay off existing short-term debts; and there is no lender of last resort.

Economic theory provides two distinct explanations for the phenomenon of herding behaviour, which are consistent with individual rationality under imperfect information. One explanation is in terms of the so-called bandwagon effect. The bandwagon gets built up when investors make particular decisions, having noted the behaviour of preceding individuals without giving adequate consideration to their own private information. The second runs in terms of the way money managers are compensated. Money managers are compensated based on their performance relative to other money managers (the median performer). Even when a money manager makes a wrong investment decision in which most other managers commit the same mistake, the chances are that the money manager in question will not be penalized. Thus, there is strong incentive for money managers to act alike (Krugman, 1998).

The currency crisis, experienced by the older market-oriented economies of Southeast Asia, had spread out to the transitional economies of Vietnam, Cambodia, Laos and Myanmar mainly due to their significant trade and investment inter-linkages. Although these economies do not have a significant financial sector and stock markets (as discussed previously, the weakness of the financial sector was a major factor behind the 1997 Asian crisis), they have relied substantially on their Asian neighbours as a source of foreign capital and as markets for their exports. Intra-ASEAN trade and investment have been an important component in their economic development. For example, Singapore has been Vietnam's major trading partner and top foreign investor (more than 70 percent of Vietnam's foreign trade and investment comes from the Asian region) while Thailand is Laos's top source of foreign capital (more than 40 percent of Laos's approved foreign investment licenses was accounted for by Thailand in the 1990s) and its major export market (30 percent of its total exports went to Thailand in the 1990s) due to their geographical proximity and cultural affinity. Further, there was an increasing demand for the US dollar in these economies, as economic agents had lost their confidence in the local currencies and found the US dollar as a more secure form of assets.

Their currency responses to the regional crisis, however, have varied due to their differences in payment policies and vulnerability to regional influences. The Laotian kip has fallen by over 80 percent against the US dollar since June 1997, tumbling even more than the Indonesian rupiah. In January 1999 the kip, which is not freely convertible, had its latest collapse. The black market was offering about 4500 kip to the dollar. In March 1999 the rate was about 6300 kip and further depreciated to almost 8000 kip before stabilizing into around 7840 kip. Due to the Vietnamese government's refusal to follow the other currencies in the region, the Vietnamese dong did not depreciate as much against the US dollar, by only 17 percent after three rounds of devaluation. The rate as at June, 2000 was VND 14 800 to 1 US$. Cambodia's riel fell 15 percent from 3050 to 3518 to the US dollar in the second half of 1997 and continued to slide in 1998, from 3518 to 4015 at the end of May 1998, a further depreciation of 14 percent. Myanmar's currency kyat was only slightly affected, as it depreciated by only 5.3 percent between 1996/97 (before the regional crisis) and 1997/98 (during the regional crisis) which is, like the Vietnamese dong, inconvertible.

10.3   ECONOMIC IMPACTS ON THE ASEAN ECONOMIES

The 1997 economic crisis has had serious and painful consequences for the Southeast Asian region, particularly for the hardest-hit economies of Thailand, Indonesia and Malaysia. Singapore and the Philippines were also not spared from the crisis due to reasons stated above. The transitional economies of Vietnam, Cambodia, Laos and Myanmar were also adversely affected mainly due to their reliance on the other countries as their major source of foreign direct investment and as export markets. These economic impacts are reflected in the significant re-adjustments of their macroeconomic indicators such as inflation and GDP growth, and deterioration of their socioeconomic indicators such as employment, standard of living and level of social services.

10.3.1   Inflation

There are a few channels by which a currency depreciation can lead to inflation. Depreciation may cause producers to mark up prices, which in turn could lead to higher wages, setting off a cost-push spiral. Expectations can also play a significant role in the transmission mechanism. If it is assumed that expectations are regressive, continuous small currency depreciation could generate expectations of sustained depreciation, which in turn could cause an increase in the inflation rate. Further, under a flexible exchange rate system, prices are marked up when there is devaluation, but are not marked down when there is a revaluation. Other factors include import prices and excess money supply. In a small open economy where imports form a sizeable portion of GDP, the effects of exchange rate and import price changes on domestic prices will be strong and will also affect wages and producer prices. Based on the monetarist model, inflation arises from money supply growth in excess of the growth in money demand.

With regards to the four ASEAN economies hard-hit by the crisis (that is Indonesia, Thailand, Malaysia and the Philippines), inflation did not rise significantly until 1998 as a result of a weaker currency brought about by the currency crisis. Indonesia's inflation rate rose by 75 percent in 1998, the highest among the four, as a result of the massive collapse of the rupiah. When the Indonesian government decided to float its currency in 1998, the rupiah went as low as Rp 16 000 (for 1 US$) in June, 1998. Since they are largely open economies with substantial reliance on imports particularly of capital and intermediate goods, the rise in the prices of imported goods and services led to a rise in the cost of living. As Table 10.3 shows, all the ASEAN10 countries experienced a significant rise in inflation, with the exception of the Philippines, compared to the 1996 pre-crisis period when they all experienced moderate inflation rates.

Laos experienced uncontrolled inflation running at more than 100 percent in 1998. This is quite enormous considering Laos's annual average inflation running at 13.0 percent and 19.3 percent in 1996 and 1997, respectively. Vietnam experienced a significant setback in its inflation control achievements. One of Vietnam's major economic achievements was its ability to reduce its inflation rate, which used to be in double-digit levels prior to 1992, to single-digit levels in 1996 and 1997. As Table 10.3 shows, its inflation rate went up to 10.0 percent in 1998 due mainly to the crisis. In 1999, one year after the crisis, inflation declined to 2.0 percent, reflecting significant declines in food prices resulting from a bumper rice harvest and relatively stable non-food prices.

Cambodia's inflation rates averaged 9.0 percent in 1996 and 1997, respectively. This went up to 12.6 percent in 1998. Both the regional crisis and the July 1998 fighting, which caused widespread disruption of production and supply leading to increases in food prices and loss of confidence, were responsible for this increase in the inflation rate. It was reported that food prices doubled and supplies were running low. Large price increases were also recorded for non-food items such as housing, utilities, home furnishings and medical care. After the crisis and with the resolution of the political crisis, inflation rates declined to 0.0 percent in 1999. Cambodia's Ministry of Economy and Finance predicted that inflation would be at around 5.0 percent for the year 2000 and 2001, respectively.

Table 10.3 *Macroeconomic indicators before and after the crisis*

ASEAN10 Countries	Exchange rates (vs US$)					GDP growth (%)					Inflation (%)				
	1996	1997	1998	1999	2000	1996	1997	1998	1999	2000	1996	1997	1998	1999	2000
Brunei	1.41	1.48	1.67	1.69	1.74	3.6	4.1	1.0	–	–	2.0	1.7	0.0	–	–
Indonesia	2 342	2 909	7 550	7 855	9 400	8.0	4.7	–15.0	0.3	4.8	6.5	11.6	75	20.5	9.3
Malaysia	2.5	2.81	3.8	3.8	3.80	8.6	7.7	–6.0	6.0	8.5	3.5	2.6	5.0	2.8	1.52
Philippines	26.22	29.47	40.89	39.09	47.0	5.5	5.1	–0.2	3.2	3.9	8.4	5.1	8.0	6.6	4.4
Singapore	1.41	1.48	1.67	1.69	1.74	6.9	7.6	1.0	5.4	9.9	1.4	2.0	2.0	0.02	1.3
Thailand	25.24	31.36	36.73	37.81	42.0	5.5	–0.4	–8.0	4.2	4.4	5.8	5.6	8.0	0.32	1.2
Vietnam	11 700	11 745	13 897	13 939	14 800	9.3	8.8	5.8	4.8	5.0	4.5	4.0	10.0	2.0	–
Laos	954	2 152	4 274	8 000	7 840	6.0	7.2	4.0	5.8	5.2	13.0	19.3	142.0	60.0	10.5
Myanmar**	5.9	6.2	6.4	–	6.4	6.9	6.4	5.7	5.8	10.9	16.0	20.0	35.9	49.1	11.4
Cambodia	2 624	2 946	3 750	4 015	–	7.0	1.0	1.0	4.3	–	9.0	9.0	12.6	0.0	5.0*

Notes: –: not available; * forecast; ** For Myanmar, the years are fiscal years (for example, 1996 = 1996–97, etc.).

Sources: Foundation for International Human Resource Development (1999); Asian Development Bank (1999, 2000), *Asian Development Outlook*; International Monetary Fund (2000), *International Financial Statistics*; IMF (1999), *Brunei Darussalam: Recent Economic Developments*. IMF Staff Country Report No. 99/19; Myanmar Ministry of National Planning (Restricted); http://www.us-asean.org; State Bank of Vietnam, Annual Report 1999.

Myanmar's inflation rate has been in the double digit since 1988–89, but it further went up during the crisis years, running at 20.0 and 35.9 percent for 1997–98 and 1998–99, respectively.

10.3.2   GDP Growth

In contrast to their impressive growth rates in the second half of the 1980s and the first half of the 1990s, all the ASEAN5 countries (Indonesia, Malaysia, the Philippines, Singapore and Thailand) experienced declining or negative growth figures in the years 1997 and 1998. As Table 10.3 shows, the economies of Thailand, Indonesia and Malaysia, which bore the brunt of the crisis, posted significant declines in output. The output declines resulted mainly from the decline in private investments, private consumption and exports. With rising lending interest rates and tighter credit policies adopted by banks and other financial institutions under a pessimistic business outlook, domestic private investments slowed down significantly. Faced with non-performing loans, the banks' cautious and restrictive stance had only contributed to the already deteriorating financial position of many highly-geared companies. The liquidity problem, weak external demand particularly in light of the sluggish Japanese economy and unstable exchange rates constrained the ability of many enterprises in the affected countries to take full advantage of the depreciation of currencies. As can be seen from Table 10.4, the Philippines was the only country among the ASEAN5 that enjoyed a positive export growth in 1998. Its exports rose by a hefty 16.9 percent, despite the regional crisis, partly due to the continued robust growth of the US economy on which it depends highly as an export market and source of foreign investment, and partly due to its relatively less reliance on the regional market.

The unstable and uncertain macroeconomic environment caused by the crisis had also driven away existing and potential foreign investments from the region. Based on recent estimates by the Institute of International Finance, South Korea and the four ASEAN countries (that is Indonesia, Malaysia, the Philippines and Thailand) together suffered net private capital outflows of US$12 billion in 1997, compared to net flows of US$93 billion in 1996, with commercial banks experiencing the sharpest decline. Portfolio investment suffered a large outflow of as much as US$12 billion in 1997, in contrast with an inflow of about US$12 billion in 1996 (Asian Development Bank, 1998, p. 33). Racial riots in Indonesia and further political uncertainties after the stepping down of the former President Suharto in 1998 after 35 years in power have also contributed to the massive outflow of capital (domestic and foreign) from Indonesia. The handing over of political leadership to B.J. Habibie did not help restore the confidence of the people and investors as he was seen as a protégé of Suharto. Thus, with political instability, higher prices, declining

The 1997 Asian crisis and its aftermath

Table 10.4   ASEAN export performance before and after crisis (US$ million)

	1996	1997	1998	1999	2000
Brunei	2 493.3	3 048.5	1 816.1	2 340.7	–
	(–10.0)	(22.3)	(–40.4)	(28.9)	
Indonesia	53 844.5	51 274.3	48 847.6	48 665.5	61 100
	(18.6)	(–4.8)	(–4.7)	(–0.37)	(25.6)
Malaysia	74 246.7	77 457.6	77 098.6	84 287.9	97 852.2
	(10.6)	(4.3)	(–0.46)	(9.3)	(16.1)
Philippines	19 533	25 227.7	29 496.4	35 012.2	39 038.68
	(12.3)	(29.2)	(16.9)	(18.7)	(11.5)
Singapore	117 349.4	128 174.3	115 958.5	121 251.5	148 290.6
	(12.2)	(9.2)	(–9.5)	(4.6)	(22.3)
Thailand	55 894.7	57 822.0	49 481.6	56 110.9	67 333.08*
	(–5.8)	(3.5)	(–14.4)	(13.4)	(20.0)
Vietnam	7 256	9 300	9 486	10 814	–
	(33.2)	(24.0)	(2.0)	(14.0)	
Laos	321.4	316.8	340.8	–	–
	(2.6)	(–1.4)	(7.6)		
Myanmar	928.5	1 010.8	1 232.9	1 126.6	–
	(3.5)	(8.9)	(22.0)	(–8.6)	
Cambodia	643.5	735.8	795.0	934.0	–
	(10.2)	(14.3)	(8.1)	(17.5)	

Notes: Figures in brackets are percentage growth rates; –: not available; * means 'estimates'.

Sources: ASEAN Secretariat Database; UN, International Trade Statistics Yearbook (1996); Bank of Lao PDR (2000); The World Bank (1999); Cambodia, Ministry of Commerce (2000); Myanmar's Central Statistical Office (January-February 2000); http://www.us- asean.org.

incomes and pessimistic job outlook, private consumption was adversely affected.

The growth of transitional economies decelerated as they experienced a slowdown in exports, despite the currency depreciation, mainly due to low price elasticity for their exports, supply bottlenecks, falling demand in the ASEAN region and their high degree of dollarization. Due to its heavy reliance on Thailand and Vietnam as export markets (accounting for about 65.0 percent of its total exports in 1997), Laos experienced a fall in exports during the crisis of 1997.[2] As Table 10.4 shows, the significant currency depreciation in 1997 did not contribute to an increase in overall exports until 1998 when total exports started to recover. Laos's main export is in the wood products category consisting of logs, timber and other semi-finished products. The other important export item is garments. The income effect of the crisis has further reduced the market potential of Thailand. The fall in exports to

Thailand, combined with the declining trend of Laos's exports to the European Union, which mainly consisted of garments exports, has only aggravated Laos's overall poor export performance. Following the suspension of the Generalized System of Preferences (GSP) in the EU for Laos at the end of the financial year 1995, their exports of clothing started to slow down quite sharply.[3] This preferential access was later restored sometime in 1998. Despite the recovery of exports starting in 1998, the value of the kip continued to slide mainly due to the fall in foreign investment and loss of confidence in the kip.

Cambodia does not rely on Thailand as much as Laos does as a market for its exports. Cambodia's exports of garments continued to enjoy preferential access to markets external to the region (mainly the US and the EU). Consequently, its overall export performance was only slightly affected by the regional crisis. As shown in Table 10.4, there was only a slowdown in export growth in 1998 with a strong export recovery registered in 1999.

In terms of services exports, however, a noticeable reduction was registered in 1997. Tourism was hit by the crisis due mainly to the dollarization of Cambodia, which meant that the cost of tourism activities in Cambodia increased substantially as currencies in other ASEAN countries depreciated against the US dollar. Cambodia still relies heavily on the US dollar as a medium of exchange and store of value. Its reliance on the US dollar has to some extent insulated the economy from the crisis-induced currency depreciation, but has opened the way for rapid repatriation of dollar-denominated domestic savings in the shorter and longer terms. Further, because of high degree of dollarization, Cambodia has not benefited from the crisis in terms of increased cost competitiveness because the labour sector is paid in US dollars, while its neighbouring countries are paid in their local currencies.

FDI from the ASEAN countries slowed down during the regional crisis. The registered capital and fixed assets from Singapore, Malaysia and Thailand, which peaked in 1995, drastically declined in 1997 and 1998. Thailand registered no investment in Cambodia in the first quarter of 1998. Preliminary estimates from the Council for the Development of Cambodia (CDC) indicated that the number of applications for investment licenses fell by about 20 percent between 1997 and 1998. A number of applications from Thai investors in particular that were granted a license prior to the crisis applied for postponement in commencement dates, while a number of other projects that had commenced just before the crisis had stalled. The garments industry, in contrast to other sectors, however, has experienced an increase in FDI due to the preferential access Cambodia has enjoyed under the Generalized System of Preferences (GSP) and Most Favoured Nation (MFN) treatment granted by the European Union and the US, respectively. Recent inflows of FDI have been concentrated in small and medium-sized enterprises, particularly in the garments sector induced by GSP access to the US and the EU markets. It was gathered from Cambodia's Ministry of Commerce that, despite the continued economic recovery in Thailand and other crisis-hit Asian countries, the inflow of FDI into Cambodia has remained sluggish.

Most of Vietnam's trade and foreign investment (more than 70 percent) comes from the Asian region. Vietnam's exports to ASEAN as a proportion of its total exports increased significantly after 1994. In 1995, its exports to other ASEAN countries accounted for about 19 percent of its total exports and in 1996 accounted for about 25 percent. Currently, 60 percent of its exports go to the Asian region. Singapore is Vietnam's main ASEAN export market. Vietnam has, therefore, been affected by the crisis in terms of slow down in exports to the crisis-hit region. As shown in Table 10.4, there was a marked slowdown in its exports one year (1998) during the crisis.

This slowdown in exports was mainly due to Vietnam's loss of international competitiveness *vis-à-vis* its ASEAN member countries. Although the Vietnamese currency has depreciated, it has remained overvalued in real terms relative to other regional currencies, which have fallen by at least 40 percent. This loss of competitiveness has also resulted from many other longstanding factors including its complex but unclear legal and administrative framework, inconsistent and ambivalent policies, and inefficient and corrupt bureaucracy, which already existed even before the 1997 crisis. The crisis has only aggravated the problem.

The year 1999, however, saw a dramatic pick-up in Vietnam's exports accompanied by a jump in the share of the private sector in total exports. For the first time, nearly half of total exports were conducted by domestic private firms and by foreign invested enterprises, and the share of the domestic private sector in exports jumped from 4.0 percent in 1997 to 14.0 percent in 1999. Growth in exports of crude oil, seafood, garments and footwear led to the strong pick-up in total exports. A strong recovery in regional demand was the key factor, although increased garments and footwear exports to Europe and Asia contributed significantly to the export growth. The availability of additional capacity allowed Vietnam to respond quickly to the recovery in regional demand. It is also most likely that exports would continue to grow in 2000 based on the available first-six months trade data.

However, there are no signs that foreign investment will recover. Foreign investment, which contributed an average of US$2 billion to the Vietnamese economy a year for three years until 1997, dropped to US$800 million in 1998. It recovered slightly in 1999 when actual foreign investment disbursement amounted to US$1.5 billion, but this is still much lower than during the pre-crisis years. Further, there has been a significant decline in FDI commitment since 1996. The biggest decline came from East Asia and Japan. Regional investors, buffeted recently by the crisis at home and saddled with uncompetitive costs in Vietnam, are trimming operations or closing altogether. In 1999 three times as many foreigners were leaving or arriving. In Ho Chi Minh city the ratio was 6 to 1. In Dong Nai, a manufacturing centre outside Ho Chi Minh city, at least 11 Asian companies had withdrawn from scheduled projects in 1999. All eight Korean banks planned to close shop. Companies that export low-end products to Asia, such as Nike athletic shoe producer Sam Yang Inc. have announced massive layoffs (Tribune Business News, 18 March 1999). Bureaucratic inefficiency, widespread corruption, the dual pricing system, the government's cautious approach, prohibitive infrastructure costs and high tax rates have been considered responsible for the uncompetitive costs leading to the declining trend in foreign investment inflow to Vietnam.

Myanmar's exports continued to enjoy positive growths until 1999–2000 when total exports declined considerably, as Table 10.4 shows. The underlying cause for this decline could not be ascertained, but the decline was recorded almost across all principal commodities traded. Although Myanmar's currency and exports were less affected by the regional crisis, the inflow of foreign investment was significantly affected because it has been relying on foreign capital from its regional neighbours (such as Singapore, Thailand, Malaysia and Indonesia), most of which were badly hit by the crisis. As a result, economic growth slowed down from 6.9 percent in 1996–97 (before the crisis) to 5.7 percent in 1998–99 (during the crisis). No recent data on economic growth are available.

10.3.3 Unemployment and Standard of Living

Due to a significant fall in national output, the ASEAN4 countries (Indonesia, Malaysia, the Philippines and Thailand) suffered severe unemployment, with Indonesia registering the highest unemployment rate of 20 percent in 1998, a marked increase from 4.9 percent in 1996. Since employment follows recovery in output with some time lags, Indonesia's unemployment rate is expected to remain high for some time. For the year 2000 Indonesia was expected to have an unemployment rate of 29 percent – 40 million unemployed out of 138.6 million workforce (*The Straits Times*, 19 January 2000, p. 34). The Philippines had the second highest unemployment rate at 10.9 percent in 1998, a considerable increase from its average unemployment rate of around 8 percent for the 1990–96 period, resulting from a significant incidence of firms' closures and retrenchments. Of the 3000 reported closures (compared to only more than 1000 firms in 1996 and 1997), more than 2000 firms retrenched and around 600 closed down – translating to more than 76 000 permanently laid off workers, more than 50 000 temporarily laid off and another 27 000 transferred to shorter work hours (Pasadilla and Terosa, 1999, pp. 9–10). The most affected sectors in the crisis were manufacturing, wholesale/retail trade, financing, insurance and real estate.

Thailand and Malaysia's unemployment rates increased less sharply from 2.6 percent and 2.5 percent in 1996 to 4.8 percent and 4.9 percent, respectively, in 1998. The relatively small rise in the unemployment rate, despite the severity of their output contraction, was largely due to a large decline in foreign workers, who absorbed the brunt of the labour market adjustments. Moreover, pay cuts, rather than lay-offs, were preferred by most firms in the light of hiring and retrenchment costs. Most of the lay-offs that did take place came at the expense of migrant workers, who represented a high proportion of agricultural workers. The Malaysian government also became more restrictive with respect to its foreign labour policy in 1998 by giving increased emphasis on measures to reduce reliance on foreign workers (as outlined in the seventh Malaysia Plan, 1996–2000).

Due to a significant fall in foreign direct investment and economic activity, Vietnam's industrial production in 1998 grew only by 8 percent – down from 12 percent in 1997. Agricultural production grew only 2.7 percent. As a result, urban unemployment has risen for the second consecutive year in a row, though the Vietnamese government maintained that the figure is a respectable 6.9 percent. The rural underemployment rate also increased from 25.5 percent in 1997 to 28.2 percent in 1998. Despite the regional economic recovery resulting in export pick up for Vietnam, unemployment remains a serious challenge. In 1999 the urban unemployment rate increased to 7.4 percent.

Data on unemployment due to the crisis are not available for Laos and Cambodia. But they have identified sectors mostly affected by the crisis. These are the retail, hotel and hospitality sectors. For example, tourist arrivals in Cambodia were about 25 000 a month before the crisis, but after the crisis there were only about 8000 tourists a month. Consequently, a number of hotels and travel agencies have either closed down or resorted to laying off some staff or reducing working time. It is estimated that there were about 40 000 people who lost their jobs in hotels, restaurants and tourist agencies in Phnom Penh alone. Despite the Cambodian government's effort to promote major tourist attractions such as the ruins of Angkor Wat, the tourism industry in Cambodia remained depressed during the crisis period (Kuyly, 1998, p. 22). With improving political stability and the government's recent efforts to promote major tourist attractions, such as the ruins of Angkor Wat, the tourism industry in Cambodia is poised to pick up and benefit from the region's continued economic recovery.

A fall in foreign direct investment from other ASEAN countries, as described in the previous section, played a significant role in the rise of unemployment in Cambodia. Its agricultural sector, however, was least affected by the crisis, except for those without land and those who went to Thailand illegally in search for jobs. Those who could not find jobs have turned to begging while others have been lured into prostitution, drug trafficking and other illicit activities (*The Straits Times*, 12 June 1999, p. 38). Consequently, Thailand has put a tighter restriction on illegal workers while Thailand itself faced an acute unemployment problem caused by the crisis. Many of these illegal entrants that were caught were forcefully repatriated back to Cambodia.

Unemployment and inflation have affected adversely their standards of living as their real income fell, thus driving more Southeast Asians into poverty. The per capita income of Indonesia, the most populated ASEAN member, declined sharply from US$1110 at the start of the crisis in 1997 to US$515 in 1998 in the middle of the crisis. Consequently, poverty incidence increased from 34.5 million or 17.7 percent of total population in 1996 (based on the poverty line defined as Rp 42 032 or approximately US$17.64 per month in urban areas and Rp 31 366 or US$13.16 in rural areas) to 49.5 million or 24.2 percent of total population, with more people slipping into extreme poverty (National Development Planning Agency, 2001). In the case of Thailand, real money wages fell by 6 percent across all worker categories between February 1997 and February 1998 (National Statistics Office of Thailand, 1998). The World Bank (2000) reported that poverty incidence in the Philippines may have increased from 25.1 percent in 1997 to 27.8 percent in 1998. No data on crisis-induced poverty in Malaysia can be obtained at the time of writing, but given that the rise in unemployment in Malaysia was less severe, it is more likely that the increase in poverty incidence there due to the crisis was mild.

In Laos civil servants have seen the value of their salaries fall from about US$50 a month to a little more than US$5. Those working for foreign companies or aid agencies were partly cushioned by their dollar-based salaries. Others who earn foreign currency from tourism were also spared somewhat, as well as those who have sufficient land and access to markets. But those without land or insufficient land to provide for themselves and who have to go to the labour market to survive, have found it increasingly difficult. Examples of these difficulties include some households unable to meet their daily food requirements, school costs and/or medical costs.

10.3.4 Social Services and Public Expenditure

Just as the crisis has caused enormous social costs and human sufferings, the ASEAN governments' ability to provide basic social services and expenditure programmes to ameliorate the situation was limited by lower revenue generating capabilities. Apart from the substantial reduction in the revenue base (as output, investments and exports declined), the Philippine government's level of social services was further hampered by its 25 percent mandatory savings rule. Revenues from international trade taxes have constituted a significant portion of total government revenue in some of these countries, particularly

Indonesia, Thailand and the Philippines. Customs duties have accounted for about 50 percent and 25 percent of total revenue in Cambodia and Vietnam, respectively. Their revenue bases are, therefore, quite sensitive to the fall in international trade and investment due to the crisis. Consequently, these countries have experienced a significant shortfall in revenue collection due to the recent crisis.

Important areas of public and social services that have been seriously affected by the fall in government revenue due to the crisis are education, health and rural development. Expenditures on education, health and rural development have been severely affected by austerity measures. Despite the increasing demand for public social services such as government-funded educational and medical facilities and services resulting from population growth and increasing poverty incidence, budgets for these expenditures had to be cut substantially. The transitional economies were particularly most susceptible to budgetary cut options, as they have been reliant on international aid and loans to fund the budget deficit. For example, Cambodia experienced 10–25 percent cuts from the 1997 budget, as many major donors have suspended their aid and most lenders have not resumed lending since 1998.

10.4   POLICIES ADOPTED TO REVIVE THE ASEAN ECONOMIES AND AVOID ANOTHER CRISIS

10.4.1   Short-term Measures

Indonesia and Thailand turned to the IMF for financial assistance. In the case of Thailand, the IMF assistance was necessary because of its nearly depleted foreign reserves, massive (over US$30 billion in short-term debt) foreign debt and the need to beef up confidence in the Thai economy after the baht depreciated by more than 20 percent. In return, Thailand had to comply with the IMF conditionalities: to reduce its current account deficit to 5 percent of GDP in 1997 and 3 percent in 1998, achieve fiscal surplus of at least 1 percent of GDP in 1998, make the VAT go up from 7 to 10 percent, prices of utilities and petroleum products to go up, stop assisting unviable financial institutions, institute financial restructuring, and augment foreign exchange reserves to 4.2 months of imports in 1997 and 4.4 months in 1998.

Indonesia signed the IMF standby agreement on 31 October 1997 for a 36-month programme involving assistance of US$40 billion made up of contributions from IMF ($10 billion), WB and ADB ($0.8 billion) and the balance from various countries including Japan and the US. The Indonesian government announced a package of measures to boost up confidence in the ailing financial sector: (i) government guarantee for a period of two years for debts and deposits of all Indonesian banks; (ii) government guarantee for payments of imports of essential goods with the Bank of Indonesia covering any defaults; (iii) removal of all restrictions on foreign ownership of banks; and (iv) setting up of a committee for voluntary debt renegotiations. The committee is tasked to bring together private corporate borrowers unable to service their external debt and the concerned international lenders to work out rescheduling plans.

After a year of high interest rates and credit squeeze coupled with a cut in public spending, Malaysia decided to impose capital and currency controls sometime in September 1998 to curb currency speculation, which was considered by the Malaysian government as mainly responsible for the currency collapse and the economic crisis in Malaysia. Under this policy, restrictions are imposed on the repatriation of profits made by foreigners from trading shares, an end to offshore trading of the ringgit and the pegging of the ringgit to the US dollar at 3.80. Under this predictable exchange rate regime, Malaysia was able to adopt an expansionary fiscal and monetary policy, which is different from the approach adopted by Thailand and Indonesia as prescribed by the IMF, without impeding the inflow of foreign direct investment.

At the onset of the Thai baht devaluation, the Philippines Central Bank (BSP) mounted a vigorous defense of the peso. It raised the overnight lending rates from 15 to 24 percent. The estimated costs of the defence were approximately $2 billion of its $11 billion international reserves. Finally the peso was allowed to float on 11 July 1997. The IMF subsequently extended $1.1 billion in financial support to the Philippines. The BSP also tried to dampen speculative attacks on the peso by requiring a prior clearance on the sale of non-deliverable forward contracts. This was seen as a reversal of the open capital account policy, which could have risked more capital flight from the Philippines.

On the fiscal front, the government ordered an across-the-board 25 percent cut in government spending. Tax revenues declined significantly leading to a weakening of its fiscal position. The weakness in fiscal finances forced the government to accelerate the rolling over of domestic debt and spurred the higher domestic interest rates. In December 1997, Congress passed a comprehensive tax reform programme, which was a key provision of the IMF Extended Fund Facility (EFF). The EFF was subsequently extended to the end of March 1998 as a precautionary measure to support the Philippines government's fiscal position.

A public debate broke out in early 1998, regarding the high interest rates banks were charging for their loans. It was alleged that the banks were charging interest rates far beyond their costs of funding. This led to the BSP governor publicly chiding the domestic banks to lower their lending rates and resume loan growth to the business sector. The rather conservative credit practices of the domestic banks probably helped preserve the soundness of the domestic financial system. Their high margin from lending allowed the banks to write off their non-performing loans much faster than Thai and Indonesian banks. To help reduce the costs of funding, the Central Bank reduced the reserve requirements from 13 to 10 percent effective from 31 March 1998. Suggestions were also made to allow easier entries of foreign banks into the Philippines to encourage more competition and lowering of the lending rates.

The currency crisis did not have too big an impact on Singapore. Nonetheless, Singapore's Finance Minister announced in the 1998 Budget statement several tax concessions to lower business costs and to help local companies tide over the tight liquidity. In June 1998, the Singapore government unveiled a $2 billion package to help cut business costs and boost the Singapore economy (*The Straits Times*, 30 June 1998, pp. 28–9). The package consisted of reductions in government rentals, increase in government spending on economic infrastructure and measures to stabilize the property, financial and hotel sectors.

To help local businesses cut rental costs, three measures were implemented – additional property tax rebate, rental rebates by Jurong Town Council (JTC) and Housing Development Board (HDB), and rental rebates by Civil Aviation Authority of Singapore (CAAS). Labour costs were also kept low by appropriate wage restraints, which complemented the government's efforts in the training, job-matching and upgrading of skills. Some of the initiatives in this aspect included the Education Training Fund under the Economic Development Board's (EDB) Economic Development Assistance Scheme (EDAS) and the Skills Redevelopment Programme (SRP). The government ensured the availability and affordability of capital during the economic turmoil by supporting the Local Enterprise Financing Scheme (LEFS). This scheme enabled the government to share the credit risks with the banks while allowing them to conduct the necessary credit assessment. The reduction of fees and service charges was also aimed at reducing business costs. The measures in this area included the suspension of parking surcharge scheme where the owners of car parks were encouraged to pass on their savings to their tenants in the form of lower parking charges, lowering of port-related charges, telecommunications, electricity and water tariffs.

As for infrastructure, the Singapore government hastened several existing projects and also implemented suitable new ones. Furthermore, the government also provided extra funds for EDB's EDAS Phase III, which gave loans and grants to companies and manpower initiatives, and for the Trade Development Board to promote and facilitate trade. The measures drawn up by the government were pragmatic in that they addressed the primary cause of Singapore's economic downturn, which was a fall in external demand, by focusing on export-driven demand stimulation.

The transitional economies of ASEAN adopted short-term macroeconomic measures following the rise in inflation caused by the depreciation of their respective currencies. Generally, they adopted mainly demand-management measures aimed at affecting the various components of aggregate demand: private consumption, private investment, government expenditure, exports and imports. These have come in the form of a tighter fiscal policy through a reduction in government spending and raising taxes, and a restrictive monetary policy through a reduction in money supply. Their central banks issued securities and treasury bills, offering higher than market interest rates, to mop up excess liquidity, and directives to increase the minimum deposit rates to encourage savings and discourage borrowing. At the same time, they took measures to accelerate revenue collection.

10.4.2   Long-term Measures

Recapitalization of banks

Massive bank restructuring – which looks likely to end up costing substantially more than current estimates of around US$60 billion – is a prerequisite for economic revival in the three crisis countries of Thailand, Indonesia and Malaysia.

One important aspect of this bank restructuring is the recapitalization of those banks saddled with non-performing loans (NPLs) so that they can lend funds needed to fuel economic recovery. Governments can play a significant role here by providing a deposit guarantee and liquidity support. Moreover, they can create an asset management company to buy the NPLs at discounts to reflect market values and hence improve the banks' asset quality. Alternatively, they can force the banks to re-capitalize or perish through license withdrawal. Where private capital is not available, they can pump in public funds (financed through the issue of government bonds) in exchange for shares in the banks. In theory, the government should be able to recover its funds through the sale of the assets underlying the NPLs, and eventually through a disposal of its stakes in the rehabilitated banks. Accordingly, the government of Malaysia has set up Danaharta to handle the NPL carve-up and disposal of assets, and Danamodal to re-capitalize the banks. Indonesia has set up IBRA (Indonesian Bank Restructuring Agency) and its AMU (Asset Management Unit) while Thailand has its Financial Sector Restructuring Authority (FRA) and an Asset Management Corporation (AMC). They have also mandated the merger of banks to strengthen their banking systems.

Improvement in governance and institutional framework

Recapitalization of banks is not the only component of the financial restructuring programme of the crisis-hit ASEAN economies. It also involves an improvement of their regulatory and supervisory mechanisms to ensure that the banks' investment funds are effectively and efficiently allocated and channelled to the right usage. To this end the governments of Indonesia, Malaysia and Thailand have taken major steps to upgrade their legal and regulatory framework for bank supervision and supervisory capacity. Thailand's bankruptcy and foreclosure laws, which dated back to 1940, were revised in March 1998. A special bankruptcy court was also opened in August 1999. The previous 49 percent foreign ownership restriction on foreign investment in the domestic banking sector was also eased, with the Board of Thailand (BOT) having the discretion to approve 100 percent foreign ownership.

For corporate restructuring, the Thai authorities have created a voluntary framework for out of court debt settlement via the Corporate Debt Restructuring Advisory Committee (CDRAC). As small and medium enterprises (SMEs) account for more than two-thirds of the corporate debts in Thailand, a special fund for SMEs was set up to deal with potential difficulties in debt restructuring. The government has also introduced a number of tax measures to encourage speedy restructuring, but the actual resolution process has been left to debtors and creditors.

Changes were also made to the legal and regulatory framework of Indonesia. Previously, Indonesia's bankruptcy laws were even more outdated than those of Thailand, dating back to 1908. New bankruptcy laws were enacted in April 1998 and a special commercial court was established in August that same year. Additional measures are being undertaken to strengthen the judiciary so that the courts may handle litigation under the new bankruptcy code. Plans are also underway to bring regulation and supervision of the Indonesian banking system into line with the Basle accords. On top of these, restrictions on foreign ownership have been eliminated.

Under corporate restructuring, the Indonesian government has sponsored the Jakarta Initiative to facilitate voluntary out-of-court settlements, which can be achieved by requiring indebted companies to reorganize and restructure their operations in return for loan rescheduling or by accepting equity as payment to creditors. This scheme was combined with the Frankfurt Agreement for debts to foreign commercial banks. The Indonesian Debt Restructuring Agency (INDRA) was established to guarantee access to foreign exchange for indebted companies. The terms on which foreign exchange would be made available were revised in late 1999 to better reflect market conditions, as the original terms did not appeal to corporations.

Major reform emphasis in Malaysia has been on strengthening banking and corporate supervision. Malaysia's bankruptcy and foreclosure laws were up to date and had adequate supporting legal framework even before the crisis. While some regulatory standards have been tightened, others have been relaxed to ease the liquidity position of banks. The Corporate Debt Restructuring Committee (CDRC) was established for the purpose of out-of-court corporate debt restructuring for viable companies with over RM 50 million of debt involving at least three banks. There are various rules to guide restructuring, but there are no penalties for non-compliance. Further, the Malaysian government has also required a greater disclosure of financial statements and accountability to increase transparency of corporate activities.

The Central Bank of the Philippines announced further measures to strengthen its banking system. Rules for reporting and provisioning of doubtful loans were introduced to reform the banking system. On the political front, the crisis has prevented the Ramos administration from seeking to amend the constitution to allow the incumbent to run for a second term in office. It also appeared that the development programme started in the Aquino government and extended by the Ramos government would be continued after the crisis by the new administration.

Economic restructuring
The ASEAN5 countries have also embarked on the following long-term strategies to avoid another crisis and achieve sustainable growth: diversification of exports and reduction of their heavy reliance on electronics; promotion of agriculture and other resource-based products; enhancing the role of the services sector as a new source of growth; deepening the capital market and rationalization of their capital markets.

10.4.3   ASEAN Joint Efforts

The 1997 Asian crisis has taught the ASEAN countries that their respective economies are indeed interdependent so that what affected one member country adversely could quickly be spread to the other members of the grouping. Hence, they have realized the importance of making collective and coordinated efforts to revive their economies and to avoid a re-occurrence of similar crises in the future. At the regional level, the joint initiatives adopted include the establishment of an ASEAN surveillance mechanism, encouraging the use of ASEAN currencies for settling intra-ASEAN trade payments, acceleration of regional economic integration and enhancement of the investment climate in the region.

At the sixth ASEAN Summit in Hanoi on 16 December 1998, the ASEAN leaders agreed to adopt an ASEAN surveillance mechanism to try to anticipate and highlight emerging risks, using sophisticated early-warning indicators and head-off any future crises by recommending appropriate policy responses and early actions. Although this mechanism is empowered to recommend appropriate policies to individual members, the decision to take up such advice is still voluntary in line with the principle of national sovereignty.

The leaders of the ASEAN6 countries have also agreed to advance the implementation of AFTA by one year from 2003 to 2002. They have agreed to achieve a minimum of 90 percent of their total tariff items with tariffs of 0–5 percent by 2000. The new members of ASEAN have also agreed to maximize their tariff lines between 0 and 5 percent by 2003 for Vietnam and 2005 for Laos and Myanmar. Vietnam has committed to expand its tariff lines at 0 percent by 2006 while Laos and Myanmar by 2008. These initiatives were complemented with the facilitation of trade and investment especially in the area of customs and standards.

The ASEAN members have adopted short-term measures to enhance the ASEAN investment climate, which include a minimum three-year corporate income tax exemption or a minimum 30 percent corporate investment tax allowance; allowing a 100 percent foreign equity ownership; granting of speedy customs clearance and duty-free imports of capital goods under approved investment projects through the ASEAN Green Lane or equivalent procedures adopted by the ASEAN member countries for all raw materials and capital goods required by investment projects; domestic market access for foreign-invested companies; minimum industrial land leasehold for 30 years; and employment of foreign personnel. Further, a more relaxed policy has been adopted on the approval of required foreign professionals, managerial and technical personnel, necessitating the relaxing of the restrictions and levies on employment of foreign personnel and their multiple entry visas (one year renewable multiple entry visas are now allowed). To provide greater scope for industrial cooperation in the region, member countries have agreed to waive the 30 percent national equity requirement under the ASEAN Industrial Cooperation (AICO) scheme during the period 1999–2000.

The effectiveness of the measures to attract FDI will vary from country to country. The above measures are only broad guidelines, and individual member nations reserve the right to impose specifications unilaterally. For example, for the duty exemption on the import of capital goods, the Philippines only allows it in export zones, free ports and other selected sectors covered by special laws. Hence, the ability of individual members to attract FDI will depend on the number of restrictions they impose unilaterally on the proposed measures.

ASEAN countries have strengthened their commitment to forge greater economic cooperation with their East Asian neighbours (that is China, Japan and South Korea). The ASEAN + 3 grouping, which has already held its own summits for three successive years, has announced a region-wide system of currency swaps to deal with future Asian crises. At the meeting between ASEAN finance and central bank deputies and their counterparts from Japan, China and South Korea – the so-called 'plus three countries' – on 24 of March 2000, it was agreed to set up an Asian Support Fund to help regional economies fight future financial crises, with strong support from Japan and China. Although the details of the fund are still being worked out, this fund is expected as an effective form of joint intervention arrangement among the ASEAN + 3 countries (*The Straits Times*, 25 March 2000, p. 49).

10.5 IMPACT OF THE ASIAN CRISIS ON ASEAN EXTERNAL ECONOMIC RELATIONS

As discussed previously, intra-ASEAN trade has been growing in importance to the ASEAN countries so that in 1996, just before the crisis hit the region, 25 percent of their exports were destined for the ASEAN region, a share larger than that held by any of their traditional export markets. From 16.5 percent in 1992, the share of intra-ASEAN exports went up and was hovering at around 23 percent in 1994 and 1995 before it increased to 25.0 percent of their total exports in 1996. The onslaught of the 1997 crisis has certainly reduced its importance, and there is an indication based on the latest available trade data that the US has reasserted itself as the largest market for ASEAN exports. The Asian crisis has adversely affected the growth of intra-ASEAN trade and re-emphasized the importance of the US market. As demand from crisis-hit economies fell due mainly to liquidity constraints and a significant fall in general economic activity, a significant proportion of exports were redirected towards the non-ASEAN markets such as the US and the EU markets. The share of economically depressed Japan in ASEAN exports has further declined during the crisis, thus contributing to the overall decline in ASEAN export performance in the crisis period.

The Asian crisis and the continued strength of the US economy in the late 1990s have made the ASEAN countries as a group more dependent on the United States as their export market, accounting for about 20 percent of total ASEAN exports. Between 1980 and 1993 ASEAN exports to the US as a proportion of total ASEAN exports increased from 16.9 percent to 20.33 percent, but remained around that level from 1993 to 1998. It is likely that this share would have further increased in 1999. In contrast, the importance of Japan as a market for ASEAN exports has been declining from 26.8 in 1980 to around 11 percent in 1998. Japan was also overtaken by the US as the ASEAN countries' largest source of imports outside the region.

10.6   CONCLUSION

The recent Asian economic crisis has certainly set back the economic and social progress made by the ASEAN countries for the past decades. The account of its origin and causes, however, has shown that the crisis was mainly the result of a fragile financial system in dealing with the surge of foreign capital, loss of confidence and contagion effects discussed above. Certainly, the recent crisis, unlike the other crises affecting Mexico and other Latin American countries, was not due to weak economic fundamentals or adoption of an inappropriate approach to economic development. The policy of export-oriented industrialization and financial deregulation *per se*, for example, did not cause the recent crisis. It has certainly taught the ASEAN countries to strengthen their financial sector and to give this sector more attention in their future economic cooperation agenda particularly in the area of regulation and supervision. The experience has also highlighted the importance of institutions (including the quality of government intervention and effective implementation of policies) in achieving a sustainable growth and development.

SUGGESTIONS FOR FURTHER READINGS

The following references are highly recommended for a good account of the origin, lessons and future paths of the recent Asian crisis: Montes (1998), Krugman (1998) and Arndt and Hill (1999). For a supplementary reading on the social impact of the Asian crisis for the hardest-hit countries of ASEAN, see Yun-Peng Chu and Hill (eds) (2001).

NOTES

1. Lopez-Mejia (1999) and the World Bank (1997) noted the massive accumulation of foreign debt in Thailand which was one of the ten largest emerging market recipients of net private capital flows (together with Malaysia and Indonesia) prior to the 1997 crisis.
2. Laos, a landlocked least developed country, also depends on Thailand for transiting its goods for export.
3. This decision was made on the basis of a recommendation of an EU customs delegation that visited Laos in 1995 and found that minimum domestic content requirements based on rules of origin were not being met. Apparently, many Thai manufacturers of garments were also using the made-in-Lao label to gain GSP access to the EU.

PART FOUR

Future ASEAN Economic Cooperation and
Challenges

11. Prospects for ASEAN economic cooperation

If one has to assess the performance of ASEAN as a political and economic grouping since its formation in 1967, two remarkable political achievements can be noted: first, ASEAN has promoted peace and stability in the region; second, it has strengthened ASEAN's bargaining position and influence in international negotiations. But ASEAN's efforts at trade liberalization, as indicated by the level of intra-ASEAN trade, and industrial cooperation have met only with limited success due to a number of factors, as explained in previous chapters. The 1992 agreement at the Fourth ASEAN Summit in Singapore to form a free trade area among the ASEAN countries by the year 2008 (the target date was later moved forward to the year 2002) represents a milestone as well as a greatest challenge in the entire history of ASEAN economic cooperation.

At the Fifth ASEAN Summit in December 1995, ASEAN took another important step forward. The focus was to look for an enhanced model of economic integration with the aim of bringing ASEAN towards a more closely integrated, dynamic and prosperous enlarged family beyond the year 2002 after AFTA is realized. A bold regional arrangement for investment was agreed in the form of an ASEAN Investment Area (AIA) to enhance the attractiveness and competitiveness of the region. At the inaugural meeting of the AIA Council in October 1998 in Manila, the ASEAN member states signed the Framework Agreement on the ASEAN Investment Area.

This chapter discusses the prospect for greater ASEAN economic cooperation and the challenges facing the ASEAN countries in the process of achieving this vision. Specifically, it tries to examine the economic benefits and challenges that the two agreements can present for these economies.

11.1 RATIONALE OF AFTA

The 1992 ASEAN Free Trade Agreement (AFTA) is a watershed, as it represents a significant change in the economic policy orientation of the ASEAN countries, with the exception of Singapore which has long cherished the idea of regional free trade. A number of internal and external developments have made free trade politically acceptable. First, the ASEAN economies have become more diversified in production structure and more complementary to each other, raising potential for greater regional trade. Growing intra-industry trade resulting from the activities of MNCs and increasing levels of industrialization achieved by most ASEAN members have strengthened this complementarity. Second, since the 1980s ASEAN economies have been undertaking unilateral policy reforms to liberalize trade and deregulate foreign investments, resulting in a more outward-oriented industrial sector. Third, perceived protectionism in their major Western trading partners in the form of emerging regional arrangements (such as NAFTA and the EU) and emergence of non-tariff barriers (such as VERs and anti-dumping duties) pointed to the need to reinforce intra-ASEAN cooperation as a safety net and as a counterstrategy to maintain their bargaining position *vis-à-vis* these emerging trading blocs in market share and in attracting investments. Fourth, the newly emerging market economies of China, Indo-China and Eastern Europe have posed a new threat and challenge for investment attraction as these countries have huge domestic markets or/and highly competitive cost structures. Last, but not least, the private sector, realizing the potential benefits of greater regional integration and frustrated with the slow progress in trade liberalization, have intensified their pressure on their respective governments to achieve greater ASEAN integration.

11.2   OBJECTIVES OF AFTA

The main objective of AFTA is to increase the international competitiveness of ASEAN industries and the ASEAN region as an investment location. Specifically, the objectives are to increase intra-ASEAN trade by abolishing intra-regional trade barriers while allowing member countries to keep their respective trade policies towards the rest of the world, to attract local and foreign investors to invest in the region and to make their manufacturing sector more efficient and internationally competitive within a liberalizing global market. An integrated regional market is expected to produce economic benefits from greater consumer surplus, exploitation of economies of scale, competition-induced efficiency, industrial rationalization, inter-industry linkages and intra-industry trade.

To realize these benefits, the ASEAN Free Trade Agreement (AFTA) seeks to reduce tariffs on all commodities traded within the member countries to between 0 and 5 percent *ad valorem* and remove all other trade restrictions by the year 2002 under the Common Effective Preferential Tariff (CEPT) – the main instrument of AFTA. The agreement also lays down the rules for fair competition and identifies a number of measures to enhance economic cooperation such as harmonization of standards, macroeconomic consultations and improved reciprocal recognition of product testing and certification, coordination of foreign investment policies, joint investment promotion strategies and cooperation in transport systems. Further, it contains measures of contingent protection and allows the reintroduction of trade barriers in case of balance of payments difficulties.

11.3 ELEMENTS OF CEPT SCHEME

To ensure that the benefits of the scheme are restricted within the member countries a minimum of 40 percent of value must originate within AFTA, if the products are not wholly produced within AFTA countries.

The tariff reduction schedules are classified into two tracks. The list of products subjected to accelerated tariff reductions are in the fast track. Those products in the fast track with tariffs at 20 percent or less will have their tariffs reduced to 0–5 percent by 1998, and those whose tariffs are above 20 percent will have their tariffs reduced to 0–5 percent by year 2000.[1] Other products are in the normal track. Under the normal track tariffs at 20 percent or below will be reduced to 0–5 percent by the year 2000, and tariffs above 20 percent by the year 2002.

There are also exclusions (products that will not be given preferential tariffs, if exported). The first type of exclusions refers to those products in the Temporary Exclusion List (TEL). These products will be gradually transferred, in equal instalments, to the Inclusion List starting in 1996 and finishing in 2000. Motor vehicles and mineral fuels are examples. The second type refers to the goods excluded for national security reasons, protection of public morals, human, animal and plant life and health, and the protection of articles of artistic, historic or archaeological value. Examples of items in this list are armaments, live plants and animals and alcoholic beverages. The third type refers to those products in the Sensitive List. These products, due to their special nature and political importance, are accorded special treatment compared to the products in the Inclusion and Temporary Exclusion Lists. This means that the timeframe may be longer than 2002 and tariff rates are not required to be reduced to the 0–5 percent range as in the CEPT. A working group under the purview of both the Senior Economic Officials Meeting (SEOM) and the Senior Officials of the ASEAN Ministers on Agriculture and Forestry (SOM AMAF) has been created to work out the features of the special arrangement. This working group has held a number of meetings, including the one in Jakarta in December 1994 and the one in April 1995 in Kuala Lumpur. The outcome of these meetings has been the submission of the three lists from each country as well as initial discussions on the features of the special arrangement.

A key feature of the CEPT is that the concessions are granted on a recipro-cal, product-by-product, basis. There are two conditions for a product to be eligible for concessions under the CEPT, apart from the local content require-ment: the product has to be included by both the importing and the exporting countries; to receive all concessions, the product must have a CEPT tariff of 20 percent or below. If the tariff on a product that a country has included in the CEPT is above 20 percent, then it is eligible for concessions only in those member countries that also impose a CEPT rate that is higher than 20 percent. In the short run, the reciprocal nature of the CEPT scheme provides incentives for the member countries to include their commodities in the Inclusion List (IL) and to reduce tariffs below 20 percent to receive concessions. The CEPT also involves a phased reduction in tariffs.

Another important feature of the CEPT is that the member countries are required to eliminate quantitative restrictions on products immediately on receiving CEPT concessions on that product and eliminate other non-tariff barriers (NTBs) within a period of five years after the enjoyment of the concessions. Based on the UNCTAD classification of NTBs, a working defin-ition of NTBs has been agreed upon in ASEAN. This covers para-tariff measures, price control measures, finance measures, monopolistic measures, and technical measures (ASEAN Secretariat, 1995).

Most products are now covered by the CEPT. As of 1994, 87 percent of all tariff lines were covered by the CEPT and in 2002, it is expected that 99 percent of products will be brought under the CEPT.

11.4 FREE TRADE AND ECONOMIC OPPORTUNITIES

Existing theories of regional integration, which provide a general frame-work for what economic results to expect from joining a free trade area, have already been discussed in Chapter 3. In static terms, the welfare effects of regional integration on member countries would be positive or negative, depending on the relative magnitudes of trade creation and trade diversion.

Under this framework, two prominent studies on AFTA's implications for member countries have shown quite varied results. A study by Imada et al. (1991), using a partial equilibrium framework, shows that AFTA would result in a net welfare gain for the ASEAN members. With free trade the growth of intra-ASEAN imports would increase between 40 percent (for Malaysia) and 70 percent (for Thailand). The only exception is Singapore whose imports will only increase slightly. This increase is partly due to the diversion of imports from non-partner countries, but the trade-diverting effects are lower than the trade-creating effects.

Total exports of ASEAN would increase between 1.5 percent (for Singapore) and 5 percent (for Thailand). The increase in exports would not be at the expense of exports to the rest of the world. It also shows that there would be shifts in the distribution of industrial activities, but that no country will dominate the region.

A recent study by Teh (1999), using a computable general equilibrium framework, has found that ASEAN countries would experience net welfare gains, except for the Philippines and Thailand, under zero tariff assumption. Intra-ASEAN trade would rise by 44.2 percent, but exports would rise at the expense, to a great extent, of reduced extra-regional exports. The results are to some extent different from the previous one (mainly due to the different methodology used), and the estimated increases in exports and changes in welfare were fairly small.

It should, however, be pointed out that both studies are dealing with the static effects of trade liberalization without taking into account the dynamic effects. Apart from the static gains, there would also be dynamic gains associated with the growth of internal markets, greater intra-ASEAN trade and investment and others, which are not captured by the partial and general equilibrium framework. These dynamic effects have already been discussed in Chapter 3. If the dynamic effects are taken into account, the net welfare effects are likely to be positive for all ASEAN countries.

11.5 RATIONALE AND OBJECTIVES OF AIA

Recognizing the strong link between trade and investment in the region, the ASEAN countries have also taken another significant decision to establish an ASEAN Investment Area (AIA). The main aim of AIA is to help ASEAN attract greater and sustainable levels of foreign direct investment (FDI) flow into and within the region. This is to be achieved by undertaking collective measures that would enhance the attractiveness, competitiveness and the complementarity of the region for FDI. AIA envisages greater private sector cooperation, freer flow of capital, skills and technology among member countries, transparency of investment policies, rules, procedures and administrative processes, coordinated ASEAN investment cooperation, facilitation and promotion and, where possible, national or preferential treatment for ASEAN and non-ASEAN investments. All industries, with some exceptions as specified in the Temporary Exclusion and Sensitive Lists, would be open to ASEAN investors by 2010 and to all investors by 2020. The granting of national treatment would also be granted to ASEAN investors and non-ASEAN investors by 2010 and 2020, respectively.

11.6   COSTS AND CHALLENGES UNDER ASEAN ECONOMIC INTEGRATION

The foregoing discussion has emphasized the potential economic benefits from the establishment of a free trade and investment area based on existing theories of regional integration. However, what are not clearly spelled out are the possible social costs and adjustment problems associated with trade and investment liberalization.

First, the perfect competition assumption of the above model of integration may be violated in the real world (for example, the energy, chemicals and other heavy industry markets are dominated by a few large multinational companies (MNCs)). Thus, the enlargement of markets caused by economic integration is likely to lead to market consolidation by the big MNCs through mergers and acquisitions which already have significant market power based on their capital, technology, marketing and management advantages to keep away potential competitors. Under these market conditions oligopoly or monopoly might be a more appropriate model to use in analysing the effects of ASEAN economic integration.

The loss of national control and regulation over certain industries, resulting from economic integration, may lead to the entrenchment of MNCs' market power to the possible detriment of consumers and workers' welfare. This happens when their oligopolistic or monopolistic power is being exploited to increase or consolidate their control over resources and profits.[2]

Further, greater competition fostered by the enlargement of markets will further reinforce the trend in MNCs towards restructuring and rationalization to concentrate on their core activities. These industrial changes have already caused a significant decline in employment security and job losses. In particular, these have resulted in the replacement of permanent workers by externally-hired contractors. Consequently, there has been a growing army of casual or part-time workers without enjoying the benefits of job security. Due to the multi-nationalization of production, occupational and health hazards have increased for workers everywhere. Attempts to impose high health and safety standards in the workplace have been constrained by the use of outside contractors to maintain and run the plant and machinery, and by the desperate need for foreign direct investment in some developing countries (ICEF–MIF Merger Congress, *World Industry Trends*, 1995).

Second, the establishment of an ASEAN economic integration will produce equilibrium adjustments involving other variables, apart from the abolition of trade impediments such as tariffs and non-tariff barriers, affecting the entire member country economies. There will be adjustments in production, employment, price, wage structures and exchange rate alignments, as the cost structure and resource allocation in the region changes.

Shifts in production, employment and wage structures will occur based on the principle of comparative advantage. The ASEAN region is heterogeneous in terms of resources, and thus based on the principle of comparative advantage, industries that use relatively large amount of labour and natural resources are likely to shift their labour-intensive and natural resource-intensive operations to relatively labour- and natural resource-rich countries such as the Philippines, Thailand, Indonesia and Vietnam. In fact, this shift is already occurring in the region and the abolition of trade and investment barriers under AFTA and AIA will reinforce this trend.[3]

We will, therefore, expect with high probability, employment levels and wages for certain industries in some countries to decline. But wages in other lower-cost countries, where the relocation of production takes place, may not increase (although employment levels are expected to rise in the short run) in the short and longer terms as long as there is an infinite supply of unskilled labour available to take on the labour-intensive operations of the MNCs. This type of wage adjustment will be reflected in greater profits for the MNCs, and may not be reflected in lower consumer prices. Under this scenario there will be repercussions on the price structure of the area and on real exchange rates of member countries.

Third, there will be obvious fiscal implications. The role of international trade taxes as a major source of government revenue will lose its significance and this may create financial problems for the ruling government. Governments that are unable to restructure their source of fiscal revenue will have to resort to social expenditure-cutting measures to the detriment of the needy and the disadvantaged. The under-provision of public goods will have significant ramifications for the rest of the economy.

Fourth, as trade liberalization proceeds, the growing interdependence among member economies will reduce a member nation's degree of national autonomy in terms of effective policy making. As economies become more interdependent, the need for coordination of policies becomes essential. Economic interdependence in Asia is already occurring due to greater intra-regional trade and investment.

Intra-regional trade is likely to gain further momentum in the coming years due to the following factors: the rapid growth and expanding markets of the region's developing economies, increasing outward orientation in trade policies, increasing intra-regional investment and relocation of production facilities from Japan and the NIEs to other countries in the Asian region.

The last factor is particularly important in the context of the recent decision to eliminate the performance requirements and trade-related investment measures (TRIMs) by the members of the World Trade Organization (WTO). Intra-regional investment within ASEAN and recent booming investment from

ASEAN5 to the transitional economies of Cambodia, Laos, Myanmar and Vietnam indicate that ASEAN has begun to build up its own outward investment momentum and may emerge as an important regional capital supplier in the future.

As investment deregulation brought about by trade liberalization under AFTA and AIA will further reinforce this growing regional interdependence, the need for policy coordination implies giving up one's national autonomy and independence in policymaking. It means an equalization and/or enforcement of regulatory framework not only in relation to customs procedures and other non-tariff barriers, but also in relation to labour and environmental standards. Labour standards are particularly important and vary within the ASEAN member countries. In the process of policy coordination national governments may lose control over the activities of the MNCs especially in relation to individual governments' policies on wages and enforcement of national environmental standards. Due to ASEAN's different levels of economic development and differences in priorities, the ASEAN countries tend to adopt different policies with respect to these areas.

Finally, there is the issue of division of costs and gains. An increase in output could occur at the cost of greater inequality across countries as well as within countries. The relocation of resources from high-cost to low-cost countries will not only result in lower wages but will also cause inequality in wages. Competition for foreign investment and for exports to other countries outside ASEAN could lead to greater problems associated with the distribution of gains. Unlike the European Union where intra-trade accounts for a substantial portion of each member's total trade, intra-ASEAN trade accounts for only about 20 percent of their total trade. The bulk of their trade is external. Consequently, an ASEAN FTA is likely to result in substantial trade diversion.

Since there are benefits and costs associated with trade and investment liberalization, it is uncertain whether the creation of AFTA and AIA will be overall beneficial.[4] This brings us to the next point: Is economic growth necessarily incompatible with the attainment of social objectives of poverty alleviation and reduced income inequality?

As discussed in Chapter 2, the experiences of most ASEAN countries have shown that the economic objectives of growth and efficiency can be achieved under a liberal regime without necessarily sacrificing the social dimensions of development. This was made possible by their effective implementation of appropriate polices that minimize or neutralize the social costs of trade liberalization. This remarkable economic achievement has been fuelled, among other things, by the massive inflow of foreign direct investments fostered by their liberal policies.

11.7 FACTORS AFFECTING THE IMPLEMENTATION OF AFTA

Will the ASEAN countries be able to implement their commitments to trade liberalization and thus promote economic growth by increasing intra-ASEAN trade and investment? A successful implementation of AFTA depends very much on how they can resolve the following:

(a) low economic complementarity and trade diversion effects;
(b) macroeconomic imbalances;
(c) high and variable inflation in some member countries;
(d) losses of fiscal revenue;
(e) uncoordinated policies;
(f) divergent views on the degree of market decentralization and government intervention;
(g) an unbalanced distribution of costs and benefits and acceptance of the overall social benefits; and
(h) absence of adequate institutions.

11.7.1 Low Economic Complementarity and Trade Diversion Effects

According to Meade (1955), the trade diversion effects will be smaller if countries are initially competitive but potentially complementary or dissimilar. This means that due to protection, similar goods are produced before the integration. After the integration, the differences in unit costs in the previously protected industries will be large, providing greater opportunity for more efficient producers to expand trade in an enlarged market.

Although most ASEAN economies have achieved a high degree of industrialization with a dramatic increase in the share of manufactured goods in their overall exports and a large increase in intra-industry trade in manufactured goods, the degree of complementarity particularly in the primary and low value-added sectors is still generally low due to similarity of factor endowments. Similarity of factor endowments (as indicated by the fact that ASEAN's extra-regional trade still accounts for the bulk of ASEAN's total trade) will produce significant trade diversions,[5] thereby increasing the need for macroeconomic adjustments. Price and wage flexibility and factor mobility will be necessary. These are attributes that most ASEAN countries do not possess.

11.7.2 Macroeconomic Imbalances

The experiences of the Central American Common Market (CACM) and the Latin American Integration Association (LAIA, formerly LAFTA) have shown that macroeconomic imbalances such as external and fiscal disequilibria will not only cause real exchange rate overvaluation but also large real exchange rate variability. In 80 percent of trade liberalization reversals in Latin America, persistent external and fiscal deficits were the cause.

As pointed out in Chapter 9, current account deficits are not necessarily bad. However, at some level a deficit becomes unsustainable. Indonesia, the Philippines and Thailand already have larger foreign debts as a share of GDP than did Mexico in 1994. Indonesia, the Philippines and Vietnam are still running huge fiscal deficits, although there has been an improvement in their budget deficits. All these will make trade liberalizaton for these ASEAN countries more difficult.

11.7.3   High and Variable Inflation

High and variable inflation in some member countries reduces the static and dynamic gains of market integration by increasing real exchange rate variability, by hindering the development of capital markets and by increasing the risk of longer-term projects (related to horizontal and vertical integration). In the period 1968–85 ASEAN countries that had relatively high inflation also had more exchange rate variability (Nadal De Simone, 1995).

11.7.4   Losses of Fiscal Revenue

As pointed out earlier, in the process of trade liberalization, there will be a substantial loss of fiscal revenue for countries which are relying on international trade levies. With the exception of Singapore, whose reliance on these sources is very little, all other ASEAN member governments, especially Indonesia, Philippines, Thailand and Vietnam, will be losing a significant source of fiscal revenue.[6] Thus, the formation of an AFTA will require a restrictive policy stance in most ASEAN countries, or structural fiscal reforms and the establishment of efficient transfer mechanisms. The required structural reforms may meet with political opposition which may impede the process of fiscal reforms.[7]

11.7.5   Uncoordinated Policies

As market integration proceeds resulting in growing economic interdependence within ASEAN, brought about by increased intra-ASEAN trade and investments, uncoordinated policies will increase the variability of real exchange rates and the international spillover effects of domestic policies, and thus reduces the gains from integration. Moreover, the lack of coordinated policies with respect to foreign investment reduces the attractiveness for and the ability of ASEAN to maximize the benefits from foreign investment. However, AFTA does not include measures for effective policy coordination.

11.7.6 Divergent Views on the Degree of Market Decentralization and Government Intervention

If there are large gaps in national lobby groups' preferences and the level of government intervention, constraining national sovereignty in a free trade agreement may become too costly for a government, as it will bear the full cost of a failure to satisfy politically important groups. The inclusion of untraded and irrelevant items within the ASEAN PTA and the existence of products in the Sensitive and General Exclusion lists are the manifestations of strong import-competing groups that led governments to refrain from fully liberalizing trade.

11.7.7 Unbalanced Distribution of Costs and Benefits

An unbalanced distribution of costs among the ASEAN countries due to significant disparities in per capita income, investment rates and in unemployment rates will render AFTA unstable. The solution is usually to provide training programmes and safety nests. Fiscal expenditures will rise. It is therefore necessary for the richer member countries to compensate poorer members to settle disputes over an unbalanced distribution of the costs and benefits of AFTA. But AFTA does not have this provision and thus this reduces AFTA's chance of success.

11.7.8 Absence of Adequate Institutions

Institutions and rules introduce stability and continuity in the process of integration by increasing the probability that future policymakers will consider the effects of their policies on the current decisions of economic agents. The EU provides an example where institutions have played an important role in its evolution from a free trade area to a common market and now on its way towards complete economic integration. The ASEAN countries are now in the process of harmonizing standards, tariff classification, customs valuation and procedures. But in ASEAN there is still a need to establish a mechanism to enforce AFTA decisions and rules, and a clear procedure for monitoring and settling disputes.

11.8   THE ASIAN CRISIS AND THE FUTURE OF AFTA

The recent crisis has obviously had negative implications for the future of ASEAN cooperation. As discussed previously, trade liberalization entails short-term adjustment costs and a reallocation of human resources consistent with the principle of comparative advantage. During the transition period workers that cannot re-equip themselves with the appropriate skills can find themselves structurally unemployed. In countries such as Indonesia and Thailand where unemployment and poverty have risen from their pre-crisis levels due to the crisis, the costs of adjustments would become more severe and difficult. A corollary to this is the issue of division of gains and costs. The crisis has reinforced the fear that trade liberalization would only benefit the more developed and competitive member countries at the expense of surrendering one's national priorities and autonomy in policy setting. For example, despite its recent official agreement to accelerate AFTA's implementation, there were indications that Vietnam's pace of implementation of its trade liberalization commitments has further slowed during and after the crisis. Vietnam's economic development strategy for 1999 emphasized agricultural development with domestic market orientation and importance of the state-owned enterprises (*The Economist*, 14–20 November 1998). This indication was confirmed by Vietnamese officials' admission that the regional crisis has slowed down their economic reforms and forced them to be more inward-looking (*Dow Jones International News*, 2 January 1999). Vietnam has not made any reference to their efforts to join the WTO or their commitment to tariff reductions until recently with the signing of the historic US–Vietnam bilateral trade accord and the impending membership of China in the WTO.

The crisis, by causing greater debt servicing commitments and exchange rate instability, has also accentuated the major concern that countries with higher levels of protection, such as Indonesia, the Philippines and Thailand, will have to give up more in terms of tariff revenue loss, current account deterioration and job losses than countries with lower levels of protection such as Singapore and Malaysia. It has highlighted the question of mutuality of external trade and investment gains from AFTA. It has also intensified intra-ASEAN competition for non-ASEAN export markets and foreign investments, and could further raise this longstanding question of division of external gains among the ASEAN countries.

Despite these negative implications, the crisis seems to have strengthened their political will and resolve for closer economic cooperation. The crisis has invoked the ASEAN sense of 'shared destiny' and thus reinforced their sense of determination to forge a greater level of economic cooperation; further, the contagion effect of the financial crisis has demonstrated their high degree of economic interdependence, and therefore highlighted the need for some policy coordination. It can be argued that the crisis has not derailed the implementation of their AFTA commitments at all. The progress made in meeting their AFTA commitment has been well on track. As Table 11.1 shows, in the area of Common Effective Preferential Tariff (CEPT) commitments, it is most likely that the ending tariff rates of 0–5 percent will be achieved well ahead of the target year 2002.

Moreover, they are now more committed to realize the vision of free trade amongst themselves by signing an agreement at the September 1999 ASEAN Economic Ministers Meeting in Singapore to adopt a target of zero tariffs to be achieved by 2015 for the six old members of ASEAN and by 2018 for the four new ones (the transitional members of ASEAN).

Apart from the deepening of tariff cuts, they have also resolved to expand further the commodity coverage of AFTA. After deciding to include the politically sensitive unprocessed agricultural products (UAPs) into the CEPT scheme, to be phased into the Inclusion List in five equal instalments, significant progress has been made since 1996. Out of a total of 1 995 UAP tariff lines, 1 358 tariff lines were phased into the Inclusion List in 1996 and another 402 tariff lines were given TEL status to be phased into the CEPT scheme in seven equal instalments between 1997 and 2003.

Due to ASEAN efforts to review and shorten the General Exclusion List (GEL), some 230 tariff lines (29 percent) have been transferred out of the GEL into the Inclusion List at the Thirteenth AFTA Council meeting in September 1999. Consequently, the Inclusion List now covers over 98 percent of all tariff lines for the ASEAN6 countries, as shown in Table 11.2.

Although the Inclusion Lists for the transitional member economies are not as large, they are still significant. Vietnam's Inclusion List has also expanded since her first submission of CEPT product list in 1996. See Table 11.3.

Some progress has also been made with regards to the inclusion of sensitive products. Some UAPs are classified as 'sensitive' or 'highly sensitive' which called for a special arrangement. At the Thirty-First ASEAN Economic Ministers Meeting in October 1999 they have endorsed a Protocol on the Special Arrangement for Sensitive and Highly Sensitive Products which set out the mechanism for the integration of sensitive products into the CEPT scheme by 2010 with 0–5 percent tariff rates subject to no quantitative restrictions (QRs) or non-tariff barriers (NTBs). Rice was, however, exempted from this mechanism by allowing it to have an end-tariff of over 5 percent, but with no QRs or NTBs. Rice has always been a very difficult commodity to be liberalized due to the fact that each ASEAN member country, particularly Malaysia, Indonesia and the Philippines, would like to develop self-sufficiency in this commodity as a matter of economic and political security. Recently, motor vehicles and parts was also exempted from the 2002 deadline

Table 11.1   ASEAN6 average CEPT tariff rates (%, 1997)*

Country	1996	1997	1998	1999	2000	2001	2002	2003
Brunei	1.58	1.58	1.21	1.16	0.90	0.87	0.87	0.84
Indonesia	9.05	8.53	7.05	5.82	4.92	4.61	4.20	3.72
Malaysia	4.62	4.04	3.41	3.01	2.58	2.41	2.27	1.97
Philippines	9.22	9.20	7.71	6.79	5.45	4.96	4.68	3.72
Singapore	14.4	13.10	10.46	9.65	7.29	7.27	5.93	4.63
Thailand	1							
ASEAN6	6.68	6.08	4.97	4.41	3.52	3.35	2.93	2.48

Note: *All figures are mutually agreed tariff commitments, except for 1996 and 1997, which are actual CEPT tariff rates.

Source: ASEAN Secretariat (1997).

Table 11.2   CEPT product list for the year 2000: ASEAN6

Country	Inclusion List	Temporary Exclusion List	General Exclusion List	Sensitive List	Total
Brunei	6 276		202	14	6 492
Indonesia	7 158	21	69	4	7 252
Malaysia	9 092		63	73	9 228
Philippines	5 571	35	27	62	5 695
Singapore	5 739		120		5 859
Thailand	9 103			7	9 110
ASEAN6	42 939	56	481	160	43 636
Percentage	98.4	0.13	1.10	0.37	100.0

Source: ASEAN Secretariat (2000).

195

Table 11.3   CEPT product list for the year 2000: CLMV

Country	Inclusion List		Temporary Exclusion List		General Exclusion List		Sensitive List		Total	
	1996	2000	1996	2000	1996	2000	1996	2000	1996	2000
Cambodia		3 114		3 523		134		50		6 821
Laos		1 247		2 126		90		88		3 551
Myanmar		2 356		2 987		108		21		5 472
Vietnam	857	3 573	1 189	984	146	219	26	51	2 218	4 827
Total		10 290		9 620		551		210		20 671
Percentage		49.78		46.54		2.67		1.02		100.0

Source: ASEAN Secretariat (1997, 2000).

and was given an extra-grace period of four years before its inclusion mainly due to the strong objection from Malaysia.

In most cases, unilateral tariff reductions have been undertaken with the assumption that even without reciprocity trade liberalization would be in their long-term economic interests. Moreover, the private industry sector, having realized the economic benefits of trade liberalization in a sub-regional framework, has been pressuring their respect governments to expedite the process of trade liberalization under AFTA.

11.9 CONCLUSION

The emergence of new domestic and external developments has made the formation of AFTA politically acceptable. The recent decision to speed up the process by advancing the target date to the year 2002 from 2008 is a clear manifestation of a high level of political commitment and confidence in greater regional integration, despite its accompanying short-term costs and sacrifices. The onslaught of the crisis has further strengthened their resolve and political will to bring about closer economic integration in the region.

But whether or not AFTA can in fact increase intra-ASEAN trade and promote regional growth depends on their success or failure in resolving the macroeconomic problems discussed. Apart from policy coordination, macroeconomic policy discipline is required to reap the benefits of integration. The ASEAN countries have to resolve the following problems: low production and trade complementarity, macroeconomic imbalances, high inflation, the need to reduce reliance on international trade taxes, unbalanced distribution of costs and benefits and the absence of institutions to enforce decisions and to ensure coordination in policymaking.

AFTA is only at an early stage of its development. Many technical issues, therefore, have to be resolved. Given the strong political will to surge forward, overcoming these obstacles is not insurmountable. Already significant progress has been made in the implementation of their trade liberalization commitments under AFTA, despite the growing economic and political difficulties faced by some member countries engendered by the recent economic crisis and other inherent structural and institutional weaknesses. Unilateral liberalization process in ASEAN has also begun, particularly in previously high tariff economies of Indonesia, the Philippines and Thailand. This has resulted in the harmonization of tariff structures to a considerable degree. Deregulation and privatization have also complemented this trend. On the assumption that these trends continue, it is highly likely that AFTA will achieve its objectives.

SUGGESTIONS FOR FURTHER READING

AFTA Reader regularly provides an update of decisions, developments and statistical data on AFTA and progress made in the implementation of AFTA commitments by individual ASEAN countries. For further discussion of the prospects and problems of AFTA, see Naya and Barretto (1994) and Nadal De Simone (1995). For a more detailed description of the rationale and basic principles of the AIA, consult the ASEAN Secretariat's website, *http://www.aseansec.org*, under the section on investment.

NOTES

1. The products in the Fast Track List are: electronics, copper cathodes, ceramics/glass, leather, gems/jewellery, fertilizers, pharmaceuticals, wooden/rattan furniture, chemicals, cement, pulp/paper, rubber, vegetable oil, plastics and textiles.
2. The 1994 European Energy Charter signed by countries including Japan, Australia and other non-European countries, which seeks to establish a level playing field for multinational companies in the signatory states, does not contain a social dimension protecting workers within the industries affected.
3. This is demonstrated worldwide particularly in the chemicals industry. A number of chemicals companies based in Europe have already shifted their production operations to some low-cost economies of Asia such as India, Vietnam, China and Indonesia. The rise in investments in Asia contrasts with the decline in Europe where capital investment by the chemicals industry declines (ESCAP, 1994, p. 51).
4. It is impossible to quantify the gains and costs of trade liberalization unless we can disentangle the equilibrium adjustment process.
5. The competitive nature of their agricultural sector is demonstrated by Thailand's initial reluctance to include palm oil in the CEPT, fearing that it will face competition from more productive Indonesian and Malaysian palm oil producers, once the market is liberalized.
6. Vietnam and the Philippines are considerably dependent on tariffs as source of fiscal revenue, accounting for about 23 to 28 percent of their budget (Le, 1995, p. 11).
7. The recent experience of the Philippines, when the introduction of the value-added tax (VAT) was delayed due to the strong opposition from political and civil groups, is one example.

12. ASEAN free trade area and the transitional Southeast Asian economies

The admission of Cambodia to ASEAN in 1999 marked the fulfilment of the ASEAN founding fathers' long-cherished dream to establish an ASEAN10, a grouping covering all countries in Southeast Asia. This was indeed a significant event in the history of ASEAN economic cooperation because Cambodia was the last country in Southeast Asia to be admitted to the fold due to its long history of domestic conflicts and associated political issues affecting its relationship with the rest of the region.

Vietnam became officially the first Southeast Asian transitional economy to become a member of the Association of Southeast Asian Nations (ASEAN) on 28 July 1995. As an official member of ASEAN, it has also committed itself to trade liberalization based on the principles of AFTA.[1] At about the same time Myanmar, emerging from its self-imposed isolation, ceded to the ASEAN Treaty of Amity and Cooperation and opened up to join the rest of Southeast Asia in terms of economic orientation and objectives. At the Thirtieth Annual Ministerial Meeting in Kuala Lumpur in July 1997, Laos and Myanmar were admitted as full members of ASEAN. Membership of ASEAN brings with it a commitment to the establishment of AFTA.

As ASEAN members, these newly emerging Southeast Asian economies will have to deal with the important question of how they can maximize the benefits of trade liberalization, as proposed under AFTA. In light of this question, the objective of this chapter is to consider and assess to what extent they meet the requirements to enjoy the benefits of AFTA. More specifically, it deals with the following policy questions: What are the potential benefits associated with their becoming AFTA members? Which areas require further economic reforms in order to make these countries ready to become active and benefiting members of AFTA?

The balance of this chapter is organized as follows: Section 12.1 deals with the potential benefits from the membership of these transitional economies, and Section 12.2 examines how they have measured up to the preconditions required to benefit from regional integration, followed by recommendations on what should be done to make them ready to reap the economic benefits of economic integration.

12.1   POTENTIAL BENEFITS FROM ASEAN MEMBERSHIP

12.1.1   From the ASEAN6 Perspectives

The membership of these transitional economies in AFTA can bring in additional benefits to other ASEAN countries. In economic terms, they offer a substantial market and are a good source of cheap labour and natural resources. Thus, with their abundant human and natural resources they can complement the capital-rich and technology-rich members of AFTA (especially Singapore and Malaysia), which are facing severe labour and natural resource constraints. The 'flying geese' model of development is more likely to take place under a liberal regional trading environment. In a political sense, the engagement and integration of these economies into the region reinforces the foundation for regional political peace and stability. It must be remembered that Vietnam was once considered a source of threat to the democratic and capitalistic systems of ASEAN, but its recent policy of economic renovation (*doi moi*) under a market-oriented philosophy and its adoption of an export-oriented strategy augur well for the region's future. Any potential conflicts can be resolved diplomatically and peacefully using the institutional machinery of ASEAN, and thus reduce the possibility of a violent confrontation.

The continued political uncertainty in Myanmar, caused by the military's alleged refusal to hand over the political leadership to the winning National League for Democracy Party in the 1990 national election, and the antagonistic policies by the West against Myanmar for the latter's alleged violation of human rights, can also be better settled through an open and constructive dialogue with the military junta in Myanmar in the context of ASEAN than through confrontation.

The recent establishment of peace and political stability in Cambodia and Laos can only be secured and maintained with strong cooperation from other ASEAN members as they are faced with potential threats from internal conflicts and anarchy. The threats to the region's long-term political stability, particularly in the Mekong region, that have come from the ongoing trafficking of drugs and human beings and other border problems, can best be addressed and resolved within the framework and spirit of regional cooperation.

12.1.2   From Transitional Economies' Perspectives

The potential benefits the transitional economies can derive from joining ASEAN and AFTA are enormous both in political and economic terms. In political terms, Vietnam shares the same security and political interests with the other ASEAN countries. Vietnam considers joining ASEAN as an opportunity to make friends with other countries in the region and thus to contribute to the creation of a more friendly and conducive environment for economic development. Vietnam also needs ASEAN to have a more significant and influential voice in the international arena. In addition, its membership is necessary in order to maintain the balance of power in the region. The emergence of China with its potential to become a super military power must be balanced in order to avoid any dominance by one country in the region. The superpower vacuum that has been created in the region with the end of the Cold War must not be filled in. Further, Vietnam's entry into ASEAN and AFTA is necessary as an important step in its policy of transition from a centrally-planned to a market economy and thus of integration into the world community.

Myanmar's successful entry into ASEAN and AFTA is important to the present military junta in the light of persistent calls for an imposition of economic and political sanctions on Myanmar due to the ruling government's alleged violation of democratic principles and human rights. While the ASEAN countries have repetitively declared their policy of constructive engagement for Myanmar, its membership can be perceived as a victory for the current leadership and thus as indication of a lack of political support for the opposition party.

Cambodia and Laos' official membership in the regional grouping will serve as a seal of approval on the countries' political security and confidence in its long-term stability. After years of isolation and civil strife, their membership in the regional organization can send a signal to the outside world that they are seriously committed to economic reforms for a full integration into the global economy.

The potential economic benefits are more contentious and more difficult to identify. As discussed in the previous chapter, there are economic benefits and costs from trade liberalization. The theory of economic integration has also predicted two opposite outcomes, and posited that in the short run trade creation must outweigh trade diversion in order to have a beneficial trade liberalization. The main factors largely influencing this outcome are the degree of complementarity amongst the member countries, the ability of the member countries to respond to the opportunities offered in a larger and more liberalized market and the degree of their trade links with the non-member countries.

On the first two factors, it is fair to say that relative to their other ASEAN neighbours these countries enjoy a comparative advantage in the production of mineral products such as oil and gas, agricultural commodities such as rice, marine products, timber and wood products, rubber and soybean, and low skill-intensive and labour-intensive manufacturing. These products are facing increasing demand in the fast-growing resource-poor economies in the Asian region.

AFTA will also reinforce further investment flows into these economies from firms seeking a cheaper source of raw materials and labour in areas of economic complementarity such as tourism, infrastructure projects, trade and banking. Manufacturing opportunities can take the form of agricultural and marine processing, textile production and assembly of electrical and labour-intensive electronic components.

Le (1995) has shown that since Vietnam embarked on economic liberalization, its total volume of exports has grown rapidly, averaging 20 percent annually for the period 1990–95. Trade deficits have also gone down during the same period, from US$1.5 billion in 1987 to US$600 million in 1989. Vietnam then achieved a trade surplus in 1992. Although Vietnam's trade balance went to a deficit again in 1993, there is a decreasing pattern.

On the third factor, Vietnam trade links with its old allies have been on a decline, but its trade with its ASEAN neighbours has grown in recent years by leaps and bounds, for example from US$163.2 million in 1989 (when the economic transformation started) to US$1 643.8 million in 1992. Singapore is Vietnam's main ASEAN export market and Vietnam's exports to Singapore have increased about tenfold for the period 1985–93.

Cambodia, Laos and Myanmar, on the other hand, since they ended their self-imposed isolation, have increased their trade and investment links with their ASEAN neighbours, especially Singapore, Thailand and Malaysia. Thailand is Cambodia and Laos's major export market and top source of foreign investment. Although the share of exports to Thailand has been falling since the 1990s, Thailand still constitutes roughly between 26 and 30 percent of their total export market. Thailand is the largest investor in Laos and is one of the top six investing countries in Cambodia, together with other ASEAN countries including Malaysia and Singapore.

There are, however, challenges and specific-country costs that deserve some discussion. In addition to the costs associated with AFTA as mentioned in the previous chapter, the enlargement of ASEAN as an organization with the entry of these transitional economies makes it more difficult to arrive at decisions by consensus which is the ASEAN mode of decision making. We saw previously that the different levels of economic development and priorities among the member countries have been one of the underlying factors behind the slow progress in regional economic and political cooperation. The admission of new members with significantly different economic and political orientation will only make the progress in regional cooperation and integration more difficult.

Moreover, there are potential short-term adjustment costs specific to their economies. Unemployment has already emerged as a serious problem in the process of their transition. In addition to the impact of the repatriation of Vietnamese and Myanmar refugees and the restructuring of their state-owned enterprises, there will be those that will be laid off as weaker industries close down in the face of greater competition. Further, it is expected that producers in these countries will face strong competition in skill-intensive and capital-intensive industries such as vehicles, electronics, petroleum products, chemicals, machineries and consumer items. Adverse revenue implications for Cambodia, Laos and Vietnam would be high, given that their trade tax receipts as a proportion of their government revenues are relatively significant, accounting for 45.5 percent, 23.3 percent and 25.0 percent, respectively (Fukase and Martin, 1999, p. 11).

Another potential problem is the increasing pressure that will be exerted on their existing institutions, as they become more in contact with the relatively liberal regimes of their ASEAN neighbours. The existing institutions and political machineries are currently geared for a centrally-planned economy, although there have been concerted efforts since the 1980s to restructure their institutions in line with their policy of economic transformation. The liberal concept of private ownership and free market enterprise will put increasing pressures on the present system of ownership and the dominant role of the government in their economies.

12.2 PRIORITY AREAS REQUIRING FURTHER REFORMS

There are certain areas requiring further reforms in these economies to make them ready to benefit from a greater regional market and cope with the costs of adjustment. This section will focus on the priority areas requiring further reforms.

12.2.1 Development of an Internationally Competitive Private Sector

The economic benefits of free trade can only be reaped by the most competitive economy or industry. Under a more competitive environment a country must continually improve its international competitiveness. Further, to have a strong private sector is an important requirement given that the performance of their state sector has so far been poor based on economic criteria. Since private capitalism is new to these economies, the promotion of an environment conducive to the development of the private sector should be given top priority in order to be best prepared for the AFTA challenge and opportunities.

As public enterprises face the problem of restructuring due to inefficiency

Table 12.1   Vietnam's gross output of industry by ownership types(%)

Year	1990	1991	1992	1993	1994	1995
Industry total	100.0	100.0	100.0	100.0	100.0	100.0
State	67.6	68.5	70.5	71.3	72.4	72.4
Non-state	32.4	31.5	29.5	28.7	27.6	27.6
of which:						
Cooperative	9.1	4.8	2.8	2.1	1.1	–
Private	1.0	1.5	2.9	4.5	5.1	–
Household	22.3	25.2	23.8	22.1	21.4	–

Note: –: not available.

Source: Vietnam's General Statistical Office, *Statistical Yearbook 1993, 1995.*

and lack of financial resources accompanied by cuts to employment, the private sector can also be the answer to the output and unemployment problems.[2] Table 12.1 shows the distribution of industrial output by various ownership types (in percentages) in Vietnam for selected years.

The state sector, consisting of state-owned enterprises (SOEs) and large and medium joint state–private enterprises (JSPEs), accounted for about 70 percent of the gross industry output, whereas the non-state contribution largely attributed to the private household sector accounted for less. However, the percentage change in gross output for the private sector had generally increased while that of the cooperative had declined, which meant that the rate of expansion of the private sector had generally been above that of other sectors, signifying its growth potential.[3] In terms of employment, the private sector accounted for a larger portion of national employment, and a dominant portion of the total private employment has been in the agricultural, forestry and construction sectors. Agriculture has accounted for the largest share of total employment in Vietnam. The capital/labour ratio of the private sector is less than that of the state sector, which means that the same amount of capital in the private sector can provide more employment opportunities than the state sector (Ronnas, 1992). This indicates a great capacity for employment generation in the private sector for labour-abundant Vietnam. While the promotion of an internationally competitive private sector should be given priority, the important role of SOEs in Vietnam's economic development, however, should not be ignored. The reformation of SOEs should continue to make them more efficient.

Vietnam has rightly embarked on privatization. Vietnam has prepared some SOEs for privatization with the help of foreign financial institutions. It indicates the present government's intention to stop the draining of public funds, promote competition, to increase state revenues and to move towards the reintroduction of private ownership. However, the authorities have been slow and cautious. There is a growing concern that it could lead to more job cuts and the worry that the government may lose control of the economy. In this case the government should be selective and adopt an effective regulatory scheme. It should be pointed out that the mere transfer of assets and service functions to the private sector is not a sufficient condition for the establishment of an internationally competitive private sector. It must result in greater competition for privatization to become effective.

Laos and Myanmar's private sectors are still weak compared to other ASEAN countries. Their respective governments must create an environment conducive for the development of an internationally competitive private sector. There is a strong tendency for the governments in Laos and Myanmar to revert to their old policy of isolationism and protectionism. But the experiences of the most successful economies of ASEAN have shown that protectionism is not the answer. To develop an internationally competitive private sector, an introduction of market-oriented policies and incentives, where success is based on merits and hard work is appropriately rewarded, is essential. Further, the development of private entrepreneurship can only occur in a liberal environment and in an atmosphere of open competition.

Although Cambodia has gone faster down the path to privatization than Vietnam by giving their SOEs greater autonomy and privatizing some of them for local and foreign investment, its domestic private sector still remains quite limited and weak due to the lack of local entrepreneurship and macroeconomic and political stability. It was only recently that Cambodia has begun to experience some peace and political stability after the 1998 successful UN-led national election.

However, a strong and internationally competitive private sector, although necessary, is not a sufficient condition for realizing the benefits of AFTA. There are other policy-related domestic prerequisites that these countries must meet to derive the potential benefits from a free trade area.

12.2.2 External Stability

Sound economic management, as reflected in manageable current account and fiscal deficits, will not only lead to a greater level of investors' confidence, but will also result in economic stability and strong currency. In contrast, huge and persistent external imbalances will result in real exchange rate overvaluation and instability, thereby making trade liberalization more difficult and less sustainable. Countries with severe current account deficits usually have a high real exchange rate variability and overvalued currency, which in turn produces balance of payments crises. Exchange rate misalignments may hamper integration by distorting the functioning of clearing and payments systems.

Although Vietnam has reduced significantly its current account deficit from 17 percent of its GDP over the 1980–86 period to 7.9 percent of its GDP over the 1987–96 period (see Table 2.6), it is still high relative to its ASEAN neighbours. The rapid growth of imports, fuelled by the easy credit policies of the State Bank and by the increase in government expenditure, has been the main factor behind this large current account deficit. Wide fluctuations in annual growth of imports and exports have also occurred, indicating external instability. Government expenditure rose at a rapid rate, mostly for recurrent items, resulting in large budgetary deficits. This points to a growing need for resources to finance these deficits, but with a small amount of international reserves, Vietnam is unlikely to benefit from the trade liberalization within the region under AFTA. Since 1993 Vietnam has continuously experienced trade and current account deficits with the trade deficit reaching an alarming 15 percent of GDP in 1996. Having a current account deficit is not bad *per se*, especially when the excessive rise in imports is due to imports of necessary inputs for productive capacity expansion and long-term growth. Although the bulk of Vietnam's imports have been in the form of raw materials and capital goods used for investment and production, the destination of these imports has been for import-substituting industries with the structure of imports determined by trade policy rather than by pure market forces.

For Vietnam to be ready for a beneficial free trade, the government must focus its activities more sharply and give a greater role to the private sector. More fiscal incentives for exporters must also be considered to stimulate more exports. Since the link between monetary policy and external deficit is very direct inasmuch as much of the country's money supply consists of foreign currency deposits, a tighter monetary policy may be called for to reduce its external deficit.

Compared to other ASEAN countries, Myanmar's past record in this area indicates that a lot of work is required. Myanmar's huge external debt and poor export performance, aggravated by the wide fluctuations in annual growth of its exports, have been the main factors behind its large current account deficit. A low savings rate and a limited inflow of foreign capital due to its present political instability have constrained the process of its economic transition. Without a significant improvement in this area, Myanmar would be unable to benefit from the trade liberalization under AFTA.

Despite the recent Asian economic crisis, Cambodia has enjoyed an exponential growth in exports since 1994 mainly due to the strong performance of their garment exports. However, its current account deficit is still quite high in proportion to its GDP running at two-digit levels due to the continued robust growth of its imports. The impact of the crisis has been mitigated by the highly dollarized nature of the economy so that the increase in the price of imports was lessened by significant declines in dollar-denominated prices of imports from neighbouring countries.

12.2.3 Price Stability

Vietnam is one of the most successful historically planned economies in reducing inflation. After experiencing a double- and triple-digit inflation in the 1980s and early 1990s, Vietnam has enjoyed a record of single-digit inflation since 1993, which was only interrupted by the recent Asian crisis. Its inflation rate was estimated at 8.3 percent and 6 percent for 1993 and 1994, respectively, comparable with other ASEAN neighbours, but was at 10.0 percent in 1998. An important task for the government now is to consolidate these gains and to develop the monetary policy instruments that will permit effective control of inflationary forces. This includes developing indicators and instruments, as well as skills in interpreting and utilizing them.

Myanmar's rampant inflation, which was officially about 20 percent to 30 percent per annum before the crisis, soared to around 36 and 49 percent in 1998 and 1999, respectively. This is not only reducing Myanmar's competitiveness, but is also discouraging short-term and longer-term investments. An important task for the government of Myanmar now is to develop policies effective enough to control this rampant inflation. A low and stable inflation rate is conducive for long-term and substantial investments. On the other hand, a high and variable inflation hinders the development of capital markets. Further, it increases the risk of longer-term projects, and thus reduces the level of long-term investments crucial in developing the infrastructure of a developing economy.

Laos experienced uncontrolled inflation running at 142.0 percent in 1998 as a result of the massive depreciation of the kip during the height of the Asian crisis, and recent available indications suggest that this would still remain high as the the value of the kip has not yet improved. This inflation is quite enormous considering that Laos's average inflation rate before the crisis was running at 7.0 percent.

12.2.4 Adequate Institutional Environment

The existing economic institutions and political machinery of the transitional economies of Southeast Asia are currently geared for a centrally-planned economy and may constrain their ability to take advantage of the opportunities offered by ASEAN and AFTA. The concept of private ownership and free market enterprise is relatively new as their economies are government-dominated. To face the challenge of greater competition and take advantage of greater economic opportunities, one must have an institutional capacity: an appropriate and adequate legal, political and regulatory framework. If this framework is deficient, investments and other risk-taking activities (such as business ventures and adoption of technological advances) will be reduced. Relevant indicators of institutional environment include quality of bureaucracy, degree of corruption in government, presence/absence of guarantee against expropriation of private investments and repudiation of contracts by government, and infrastructure quality.

The principal consequence of an inadequate institutional environment is insecure property rights (which can be broadly defined as the rights of a firm or individual to assets, to the revenue streams generated by assets and to any other contractual obligations due to a firm or individual). Inadequate protection of property rights adversely affects the development of an internationally competitive private sector. Competitiveness requires the adoption of new technologies, which are usually embodied in highly expensive capital assets. Local and foreign entrepreneurs will be reluctant to invest in these assets in an environment where property rights are uncertain. The greater risks implied by the long-term nature of investments are likely to encourage entrepreneurs to prefer to engage in short-term investments.

It is obvious from the above that the private sector has great potential to become the engine of growth for these economies, but there have to be sound policies and supportive environment before it can effectively play a significant role in their economic transformation. A legal and contractual framework needs to be further developed to facilitate transactions and protect private property. Since the transitional economies of ASEAN decided to move away from a centrally-planned model to a market-oriented model of development, they have enacted a number of changes in law and legal infrastructure to meet the new demands of the market economy. New laws have been enacted in specific areas, such as foreign investment, contracts, companies and private enterprises, which clarify and protect the right of private ownership. Other specialized laws have also been enacted, such as land law, bankruptcy law, environmental protection, labour code, civil code, commercial and domestic investment promotion law.

Despite some progress in building up an institutional framework, there are still some implementation constraints, which affect the development and expansion of the private sector. Vietnam, the first transitional economy to join ASEAN, is a case in point.[4] It has been argued that remaining constraints facing domestic private firms relate to difficult conditions for establishing and expanding businesses, insufficient incentives for investment, inadequate access to imported inputs and new export markets and weak institutions supporting market and private firms (World Bank, 1999, p. 13). Although the new Enterprise Law has just been promulgated, which is supposed to ease private entry significantly, it is not known whether the content of the implementing regulations will strengthen the character of this Law. The legal framework for private enterprises is not fully unified yet, and there is no government body that is responsible for making sure that all implementing regulations are consistent with the intent and content of the primary laws that are to be implemented. The absence of clarity about rules under which private firms receive permit licences leaves considerable scope for interpretation and discretion. Under these circumstances officials tend to favour state agencies over private agencies. For example, although market management boards are legally bound to inspect all types of business, it is reportedly the case that permission from supervisory authorities is required to inspect SOEs, but not to inspect private SMEs.

The ability of businesses to access, use and transfer land more freely and easily and to use land as a collateral is an important factor to facilitating private sector development. Although there have been improvements in respect of land use (for example, private firms are now allowed to contribute their land-use rights as equity in joint venture enterprises and land use rights can now be granted to foreign companies investing in industrial and export-processing zones), land-use rights are differentiated based on the status of the holders. For example, it is easy for household business entities to mortgage land and buildings constructed on residential land-use rights, but identical businesses owned by companies and constructed on short-term leasehold land cannot. Land-use rights under leasehold along with immovable assets are not transferable without government approvals on a case-by-case basis. This causes difficulties in respect of constructing buildings on the land and later selling that building. Moreover, there is no unified and comprehensive land registration system. Although both domestic and foreign firms can now export directly, the time taken for processing exports is still too long. On the import side, the problems are greater. Rights of firms to import products not listed in their business license are restricted. Firms require import licenses from the Ministry of Trade for each consignment or require new business licenses with the relevant products listed, neither of which have been easy to obtain. Many imported inputs are subject to non-tariff import restrictions requiring another license to import. Customs clearance remains a time-consuming and costly process.

Access to medium-term investment capital remains insufficient mainly due to the fact that the banks' deposit base is mostly short-term and private firms have problems fulfilling collateral requirements. Not only are collateral requirements too high, valuations too low and categories of acceptable collateral too narrow, but also SOEs do not need collateral to obtain loans. Without access to investment capital for new equipment purchases and facility expansions, private SMEs continue to operate with mismatched, or otherwise suboptimal production equipment and cramped factories.

Institutions to support markets are still evolving and developing. Courts, public information agencies, accounting services, trade promotion agencies and universities are just beginning to support the market system and private enterprises. However, there is still a need to develop Vietnamese private business associations as channels for accessing information. Getting up-to-date and reliable information is extremely difficult. Availability of business support services is limited.

There is a need for an adequate infrastructure such as the provision of efficient telecommunications, transport and power supply for the private sector to function efficiently. Laos, a landlocked country, relies on Thailand as a trading and investment partner and as a transit point for its overseas trade. Being a small country with a very limited domestic market, it has to depend on international trade for its long-term economic growth and economic stability. But in transporting its good for other export markets, Laos has to transit its goods through Thailand. However, it was reported by the Lao Ministry of Commerce and Tourism that it would cost Lao exporters to transport their cargoes between Vientiane and the port of Bangkok as much as it is to transport their cargoes between the port of Bangkok and the final markets.

Trade liberalization within AFTA would bring about costs in the form of unemployment particularly in weaker industries. This requires labour market regulations to increase labour mobility. The setting up of training programmes and safety nets, for example, may be required.

Although they have already launched a number of initiatives to ensure protection of property rights, there is still some feeling of insecurity to the extent that political and legal institutions can still make unilateral decisions that reassign rights. What are needed are independent judiciaries and well-defined administrative procedures to make firms and individuals feel secure from violation of their property rights.

One factor that may stand in the way of establishing adequate institutions is the poor quality of government intervention particularly in the area of implementing the required policy reforms, as pointed out in Chapter 5. Corruption, red tape and inefficiencies in the process of administration have largely been blamed for the failure of these transitional economies to achieve a significant economic progress.

12.2.5   Reform of International Trade Policies

The Vietnamese government has initiated major steps towards full liberalization of its trade sectors. The granting of the authority to export and import is now solely based on the condition that the enterprise has prospects for receiving an export order. Similarly, export permits and shipment licensing requirements have been lifted for all items, except for products of national and strategic interest. Products are no longer subject to export quotas except for a few items such as rice and garments, and export taxes have been eliminated or reduced to minimal levels, except on raw materials and other goods considered as prohibited or restricted. In Vietnam, the duty exemption system for inputs used to produce for export was improved in 1994 so that exporting firms need not pay import duties on imported inputs, provided that they are processed for export within three months. In 1999 Vietnam undertook another round of trade liberalization including the further freeing up of the rights of all firms to export/import directly without requiring license (for example private firms can now export rice, 20 percent of the export quotas for garment exports are auctioned, and foreign exchange surrender requirement is reduced from 80 percent to 50 percent of available balances), reduction of implicit and explicit export taxes, lowering of the maximum tariff and the number of tariff rates (The World Bank, 1999, pp. 7–8). A three-year agenda has also been adopted to further open up its international trade: to implement a phase-out plan for import licensing restrictions, to continue to expand the auctioning of garment export quotas and improve the terms of auction, increase the share of rice export quotas allocated to private firms, cease granting of new discretionary exemptions on import tariffs and new import restrictions, eliminate remaining restrictions on firms' importing rights, remove the foreign exchange surrender requirement and sign the US–Vietnam trade agreement to expand export markets and move towards WTO accession (which was done in November 2000).

However, there are still a few areas that need further reforms to make the export sector internationally competitive. Apart from providing export incentives, the export-oriented industries must be exposed to greater competition. Although the Vietnamese government has recently announced it will reduce most of its tariffs for imports from other ASEAN nations to below 60 percent as part of its steps towards joining the planned free trade area, its trade regime is still more restrictive relative to its neighbours, while the structure of its tariffs is still complex and designed to provide greater protection to higher value-added industries.

Another issue of concern is the appropriate speed for tariff reduction. The transitional economies of ASEAN have been allowed extra time to cut their tariffs to between zero and 5 percent for most goods due to the relative weakness of their economies and poor tax base. It is therefore advisable that their respective government authorities start to consider alternative sources of revenue to compensate for the revenue loss from tariff reductions.[5]

12.2.6 Consistent Policy Reform Goals

To maintain a conducive environment for international competitiveness, the government must be credible in its policies. Inconsistent policies are not only confusing, but could also have a negative impact. The decision by the Officials of the National Assembly and the Vietnamese government to examine a new land law that would allow companies to mortgage land, use it as a collateral or transfer it to other parties is a reversal of their previous land law which revoked the land-use rights of local businessmen and which required them to lease land from the state. The government did a U-turn on a ban on converting rice fields for industrial use after foreign investors complained.

Despite official announcements that Vietnam is committed to trade liberalization under AFTA, certain government directives were issued that seemed to contradict AFTA's spirit of openness and free market orientation. Apart from introducing a new set of special taxes on certain imports, in 1997 the Vietnamese government issued a decree banning the import of motorcycles and drafted a plan to protect certain industries against foreign competition (Tongzon, 1999, p. 152). All these are cases of inconsistent economic policies.

12.3   CONCLUSION

There are benefits as well as costs associated with being a member of a free trade area. The transitional Southeast Asian economies, by joining ASEAN and announcing their intention to become AFTA members, indicate their sense of confidence that AFTA membership will bring with it a number of opportunities, outweighing its associated costs, mostly costs of transition. This chapter argues that they must meet certain requirements in order to maximize the benefits from greater regional integration. First, an internationally competitive private sector must be developed to take advantage of the economies of scale and larger market in the face of greater competition. Although some degree of complementarity exists between them and their other ASEAN partners, there is also some degree of substitution and hence a fair degree of competition is expected. Crucial to the development of the private sector is the provision of an adequate and appropriate institutional environment. Vietnam and other transitional economies must also consolidate their economic reform process and meet the criteria of macroeconomic stability. Until these criteria are fully satisfied, they are unlikely to maximize the economic benefits that can be derived from their membership in AFTA.

SUGGESTIONS FOR FURTHER READING

For more discussions on the economic opportunities, challenges and implications of Vietnam's entry into ASEAN and AFTA, see Piei and Khalifah (1996), Dollar (1996) and Tongzon (1999). A succinct analysis of the economic and political implications of Myanmar's admission to ASEAN can be found in *Myan View* (1997, pp. 1–3). Menon (1997) provides a preliminary assessment of the likely economic impact on the Lao economy of joining AFTA. Fukase and Martin (1999) analyse the economic implications of AFTA for Cambodia.

For a collection of articles covering a wide range of issues on economic management and transition of historically planned economies of Asia towards a market economy, see Chin and Ng (eds) (1995).

NOTES

1. As discussed in the previous chapter, the target date for the implementation of AFTA has been set for the year 2002. However, as an exception, the transitional economies of ASEAN were granted an additional grace period to complete their transition to AFTA: 2006 for Vietnam, 2008 for Laos and Myanmar and 2010 for Cambodia.
2. The private sector in Vietnam consists of the private capitalist sector, the household and individual sector, but not the collective sector.
3. The collective sector, consisting of agricultural, industrial and commercial cooperatives, was on decline due to reforms favouring the household and individual sector. The number of state-owned enterprises in Vietnam has declined from 14 000 in 1992 to 6 000 in 1994. Only 300 of these are making profits. In contrast, private enterprises increased from 3 000 in 1990 to 280 000 in 1994.
4. The following observations are mostly drawn from World Bank (1999).
5. To reduce its dependence on taxes from international trade, Vietnam's emphasis so far has been to improve their export performance and the efficiency of their tax collection.

13. Domestic capital development and the environment

Foreign direct investment has played a very important role in ASEAN economic development, as Chapters 2 and 9 show, as an important source of capital and technology. But the ASEAN economies and developing countries in general must develop their own local capital and home-grown technology to achieve a sustainable economic development. The importance of developing domestic capital and entrepreneurship has been emphasized on many occasions by the respective ASEAN governments.[1] This is because domestic capital can become a vanguard of economic development by fostering technology development, as demonstrated in the West. Further, it is a good way to reduce ASEAN's reliance on foreign capital and technology which is good for their long-term economic and political stability.

Another challenge confronting the rapidly industrializing ASEAN economies today is to ensure that economic success does not come at the cost of environmental degradation and lack of sustainability. Their depletable natural resources must be transformed into man-made resources while the rate of depreciation must not be more than the rate of growth of their renewable resources in the process of satisfying their economic needs. However, rising population and expectations are likely to put more pressure on their natural resources including water, forests, coral reefs and other threatened natural resources.

Rapid growth and industrialization have constrained the capacity of the ASEAN countries' environment to provide suitable human habitats and ecological support systems. The negative side-effects of industrial growth, which is centred around the capital cities, such as pollution, hazardous waste and congestion have caused so much concern that environmental considerations are now taken into account in their planning and policy decision making.[2] In this chapter a more detailed account of the rise of domestic capital in ASEAN is made with specific attention given to its major characteristics and accompanying problems. It will also provide an overview of the environmental issues in ASEAN and discuss the various measures that can be undertaken to deal with environmental problems.[3]

13.1   RISE OF DOMESTIC CAPITAL

Political independence and economic nationalism were the main factors behind the rise of domestic capital in ASEAN. As pointed out in Chapter 2, all the ASEAN countries with the exception of Thailand were colonies of Western powers, either under the British, Dutch, French or Spanish rule, at one time or another, and understandably their economies during the colonial times relied on capital from their previous colonial masters. The ensuing achievement of political independence by these countries without sufficient local capital and entrepreneurial class has left an economic vacuum. This in most cases prompted their respective governments to take over certain enterprises left behind by their former colonialists and at the same time to stimulate development of indigenous enterprises. Economic nationalism was higher in countries where political independence was attained by force such as Indonesia and the Philippines.

13.2   MAJOR CHARACTERISTICS OF ASEAN DOMESTIC CAPITAL

One major characteristic that distinguishes ASEAN domestic capital from foreign capital is that the bulk of domestic capital is from family-owned firms where there is no separation between management and capital. They are highly concentrated in such sectors as property development, have substantial positions in banking, construction and light manufacturing but have minor interests in areas where sophisticated technology and large capital are required.

Another important characteristic is that these businesses are largely ethnic Chinese-owned in all sectors relative to private indigenous capital, especially in banking, trading and light manufacturing. Ethnic Chinese business in Southeast Asia has undergone a significant transformation from petty traders and emigrant workers in the early half of the twentieth century to today's significant economic force. Over the last 20 years or so more than 70 large corporate conglomerates have emerged in the ASEAN countries, mostly owned or controlled by ethnic Chinese. For example, in Indonesia there was only one indigenous-controlled bank in 1988 among the top 10 private banks and one among large manufacturing companies. It was reported that 30 percent of the Indonesian economy is owned by 10 ethnic Chinese conglomerates (*The Straits Times*, 11 December 1993), and that 70 percent of the Indonesian economy is owned by the ethnic Chinese which account for only 3 percent of the 200 million Indonesian population (*Asiaweek*, 24 January 1997). It was also reported that Indonesia's wealthiest ethnic Chinese businessman has assets more than 12 times the asset value of the wealthiest indigenous businessman.

Table 13.1   Ethnic Chinese in ASEAN (1931 and 1981 in millions)

Countries	Chinese population		% of population (1981)
	1931	1981	
Indonesia	1.2	4.1	3.0
Malaysia	1.7	4.2	33.0
Philippines	0.1	0.7	1.5
Singapore	0.5	1.8	77.0
Thailand	0.5	6.0	13.0

Source: McVey (1992, p. 163).

In Malaysia, despite the implementation of the New Economic Policy in 1971, *Bumiputra* investors still own a smaller portion of corporate equity. The ethnic Chinese still own 40–50 percent of corporate assets in Malaysia. In Thailand they own 90 percent of manufacturing and 50 percent of services (Yeung, 1997, p. 1). It is only in the Philippines that indigenous Filipinos own a more significant share than the ethnic Chinese. However, their economic presence is still significant as they control over a third of the 1 000 largest corporations in the Philippines. Their economic strength is more appreciated if we consider their numbers, as Table 13.1 shows.

What accounts for the rise of Chinese capital over the indigenous capital? The literature on this issue cites a number of cultural and economic factors, but only the major ones are highlighted.[4]

13.2.1   Personal and Business Networks

The Chinese in Southeast Asia are reported to have a penchant for networking which is a function of insecurity inherent in an immigrant community. Culturally, they rely on business networks to facilitate transactions and circumvent host country discrimination. The importance of networking in business (*guanxi*) cannot be overemphasized as it is not only a source of capital but also of know-how and operational flexibility.[5] In the pre-war Indonesia and Malaysia there was no bank to which they could turn for capital, nor could the indigenous population get supplies on credit since it was the Chinese who controlled the distribution network and the latter did not trust indigenous traders. The indigenous population did not have enough exposure to business, as most of their kin were probably farmers. Thus, they were usually barred from the Chinese networks.

The less organized indigenous traders, except in the Philippines, were unable to link with a foreign network. The Philippine situation was unique. The Chinese penetration into the economy was limited to only a few sectors due to the relatively small number of Chinese immigrants.[6] Second, the indigenous entrepreneurship in the Philippines was relatively strong. Third, the indigenous population in the Philippines included the *mestizos* who were more willing to exploit the commercial opportunites than the non-*mestizo* indigenous group and were helped by foreign contacts.

13.2.2   Institutional Factors

It is often argued that the political–economic alliances developed by ethnic Chinese business firms have given them access to markets and resources. It was reported, for example, that in the case of the Salim Group, its rapid expansion and diversification in the past three decades was facilitated to a certain extent by the personal patronage of former President Suharto (Yeung, 1997, p. 24).

Second, the Southeast Asian indigenous market economy before the sixteenth century was underdeveloped compared to the contemporary market economy of China. There is considerable evidence indicating that this was so, although there was no doubt an indigenous market.[7] This underdevelopment had prompted Thailand to introduce institutional measures such as the preferential tax treatment to Chinese immigrants to lure them to come to Thailand. On the other hand, the past requirement by the Thai government on the Thais to perform *corvee* labour had limited their ability to enter business (Yoshihara, 1988, p. 55).

13.2.3   Responsiveness to Commercial Opportunities

The Chinese are more responsive to commercial opportunities and more willing to work hard to exploit them for profits. This is largely due to the fact that the Chinese immigrants ventured for better economic opportunities and wanted eventually to return to China. They never, of course, returned and learned to love their country of residence. The Chinese from the second generation onwards tended not to work hard for money, but the constant influx of new Chinese immigrants in the pre-war period kept alive their work ethic and commercial orientation. The inflow of Chinese stopped in the post-war years, but the need for survival in the midst of discrimination and uncertainty has kept their work ethic and commercial orientation alive.

13.2.4   Nature of the Indigenous Society

The indigenous societies' emphasis on leisure and adaptation of man to nature than on money and materialistic pursuits may explain why they are less hardworking than the Chinese. Also, historically, life in Southeast Asia was not as hard as in South China where the population density was higher and which was often stricken by natural disasters (Yoshihara, 1988).

13.3   AREAS REQUIRING FURTHER IMPROVEMENTS

13.3.1   Low Level of Technology

Although the role of domestic capital has grown significantly in importance over the years, particularly in the downstream and less capital-intensive areas, its importance in technology and capital-intensive production is still marginal compared to foreign capital. The recent industrial transformation of the ASEAN countries, as described previously, has been driven mainly by foreign technology and capital. For example, MNCs are highly involved in the production of electrical and non-electrical machinery (the dominant item in their manufactured exports) in the ASEAN countries. The recent policy emphasis in the ASEAN countries on research and development to develop home-grown technology and on technology transfer is a clear indication of the low technological development in the ASEAN countries.

13.3.2   Quality of Government Intervention

We have already highlighted the importance of the quality of government intervention to a country's economic development in Chapter 5. On this count the ASEAN countries in general have fared much better than the other developing countries particularly in Latin America and Africa. However, there is still much scope for improvement in this area. Administrative and bureaucratic efficiency needs to be improved as they are facing greater competition in maintaining their international competitiveness.

13.3.3   Economic Rationality

The economic ascendancy of the ethnic Chinese in all sectors has generated some resentment, particularly in Malaysia and Indonesia. The prevalence of anti-Chinese feelings in these countries has resulted in certain affirmative policies in favour of the indigenous population. In Malaysia the racial riot of 1969 marked the beginning of an economic policy aimed at reducing the economic dominance of the Chinese by improving the share of the indigenous people in corporate equity and by granting them preferential access to Malaysia's institutions of higher learning. In Indonesia discriminatory measures against the Chinese started much earlier with its Benteng Programme of 1950 which gave preference to *pribumi* traders in the allocation of foreign exchange, similar to the Import Control Act of the Philippines. The Chinese discrimination, however, in Indonesia included all Chinese, even those with Indonesian citizenship. The other discriminatory measure was the government directive, called Regulation No. 10, barring Chinese traders from the rural areas. The government also nationalized a number of Chinese-owned enterprises and statized the economy. Discrimination in business stopped after Suharto came to power. During this time the Chinese did so well that anti-Chinese feelings heightened again among the *pribumi*. This, combined with other factors, led to the Malari Riot during the former Japanese Prime Minister Tanaka's visit in 1974. This incident forced the government to revise its economic policy and announced a *pribumi* policy as one of the remedial measures. Although this is in force today, the policy lacks clear-cut programmes like those of Malaysia's New Economic Policy.

This problem can only be resolved with economic rationality. So far there are indications that the ASEAN governments are acting with economic rationality. The decision by former Philippine President Ramos to form a consortium comprising the six 'taipans' to invest in the infrastructure development of the Philippines is one example. The current policy in Malaysia to forge greater cooperation and understanding between religious sects in Malaysia and the decision to allow the establishment of Chinese schools in Malaysia are examples of economic rationality. Its current policy of adopting English as a second language in schools and as a medium of instruction in certain technical courses suggest the government's flexibility. The long-term solution lies in the integration of the Chinese into the larger community.

13.4   ENVIRONMENTAL ISSUES

The overall quality of life in many ASEAN cities is deteriorating as a result of rapid industrialization and urbanization. The concentration of industrial activities in the capital cities and urbanization has caused pollution, congestion and hazardous waste. Thus, they have become victims of their own economic success.

13.4.1   Deforestation

Deforestation is one of the serious problems of environmental degradation in the region.[8] Clearing lands for farming and generating timber for exports have been the main source of deforestation. Previous studies have shown that deforestation has resulted in such a substantial decline of ASEAN's forested area that it has evoked an international effort to campaign against

Table 13.2 Annual rates of tropical deforestation

Country	Forest and woodland (100 000 ha	Annual average deforestation ('000 ha)	% of remaining forest area	% annual rate of deforestation
Indonesia	1215	600	1.4	0.5
Malaysia	198	255	3.1	1.2
Philippines	112	91	5.4	0.3
Thailand	148	244	8.4	2.4
Myanmar	322	102	3.3	0.3
Laos	131	100	1.5	1.2
Vietnam	131	60	5.8	0.6

Sources: Myers (1988), World Resources Institute (1990).

deforestation, especially of tropical rain forests. About 25 percent of the remaining tropical rain forests are located in Southeast Asia (Seda, 1993, p. 23).

This problem is most relevant to Indonesia and Malaysia, which supply about 80 percent of the world's tropical timber trade and have higher average rates of deforestation. As Table 13.2 shows, the annual average rate of deforestation is 600 000 ha for Indonesia, 255 000 ha for Malaysia, 244 000 ha for Thailand, and 91 000 ha for the Philippines. The Asian Development Bank (1995) estimated that between 1980 and 1990 Asia's total forest cover was reduced by 45 million ha or 9 percent (*The Straits Times*, 7 March 1995). It reported that the yearly average forest loss of 4.5 million ha was nearly double the replacement rate of 2.1 million ha. Among the six worst-affected nations during the period, four were in Southeast Asia with the following annual deforestation rates: Thailand (515 300 ha), Myanmar (400 500 ha), Malaysia (396 000) and the Philippines (316 100 ha).

13.4.2 Air Pollution

This problem is quite serious in most ASEAN capital cities. In Jakarta the annual cost of air pollution was estimated at about US$600 million and in Bangkok more like US$2 billion. Air pollution is largely generated from industries and transport. Motor vehicles, for example, are major generators of air pollutants such as carbon monoxide, nitrogen oxide and lead.[9] To keep air pollution within acceptable levels, the ASEAN countries have adopted a standard pollution index (SPI) and resolved to attain a PSI of below 100 by the year 2010.[10] ASEAN nations have prepared individual national programmes to achieve the target.

13.4.3　Traffic Congestion

Traffic congestion has become increasingly a serious problem in all the ASEAN capital cities due to the proliferation of car ownership as more people can afford to buy cars.[11] Apart from the convenience they offer, cars are also considered a status symbol in the car-cultured ASEAN societies. In 1984 it was estimated that the Philippines had over 1 million vehicles. About 471 000 vehicles were reportedly operated in Metro Manila alone (Seda, 1993, p. 87). It was reported that in 1996 about 1.5 million vehicles were operating in Metro Manila (*The Straits Times*, 1 August, 1996). In Bangkok, it was reported that in 1982 there were about 600 000 vehicles. Between 1984 and 1988 the average annual growth in the number of motor vehicles reached 9 percent in Thailand, compared with about 2 percent in the US and 3 percent in the UK (Seda, 1993, p. 87).

Traffic congestion costs the Philippines about 15 million pesos (S$850 million) a year in lost man-hours, bills for repair, maintenance and fuel (*The Straits Times*, 1 August 1996). The average speed around the centre of Makati, where big companies and MNCs are located, has slowed to 13kmh. The average speed in the Thai capital is just 7kmh (*The Straits Times*, 1 August, 1996).

13.5　ALTERNATIVE MEASURES TO DEAL WITH ENVIRONMENTAL PROBLEMS

Economists argue that the inefficient use of natural resources and environmental degradation can be primarily attributed to market failure, that is, the market's inability to function efficiently due to the presence of external costs not borne by the producer and imposed on the public at large.[12]

Theoretically, there are a number of ways to deal with environmental problems caused by externality-induced market failure. Each of them has advantages and disadvantages, and the choice of which measures to use depends upon the objectives, criteria adopted and weights attached to the criteria. The following criteria are usually adopted: efficiency, acceptability and effectiveness, equity and flexibility.

13.5.1　Regulation

The most common form of regulation is the setting of environmental standards and penalties in relation to the use of the common resource. This could involve imposing certain limits on the extent and duration of deforestation, pollution emissions and other activities producing external costs. In ASEAN, for example, concern about the health and environmental effects of air pollution has prompted the introduction of emission standards such as the fitting of catalytic converters for motor vehicles. To control deforestation ASEAN countries have limited logging concessions to a certain number of years. To control traffic congestion in certain areas, they have adopted an area licensing scheme and in some instances resorted to virtual prohibition.[13]

Although this measure is theoretically effective and efficient provided the source of external costs can be easily traced, in practice it is difficult, if not impossible, to determine the optimal level of access and output. Under a market system the optimal output is determined without any government judgement. However, under regulation the regulators need to estimate the characteristics of the users' demand and producers' costs for the products of the common resource.

To illustrate the point, let us consider the regulation of air pollution,[14] as represented in Figure 13.1. The external costs of air pollution are manifested in the reduced welfare of others such as poor health, unsightly environment, lower property values, reduced productivity and income. There are also

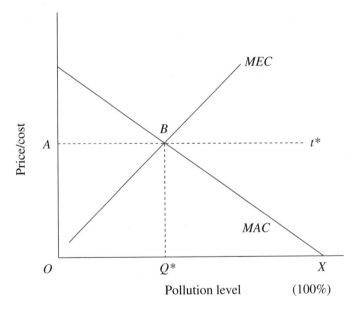

Source: Sathiendrakumar (1993).

Figure 13.1   Externality and government regulations

private costs to abating air pollution. The polluter may have to change his production method, or buy abatement equipment or reduce output. The external costs of pollution are represented by the *MEC* curve, and the private costs by *MAC*. *MAC* rises because it becomes increasingly costly to clean up air or water the stricter the standards, or the lower the level of contamination.[15]

To achieve the optimal level of pollution, the standards should be set at Q^*. But to be able to know this optimal level, the regulator must know the external costs of pollution as a function of the levels of pollutants. This implies some method of finding the values placed by the affected individuals on environmental amenities such as clean air, water and soil. Survey and other methods are being developed but they are still experimental and beyond the scope of governments in many developing countries. There is also the problem of overstatement of the cost of abatement by firms so as to produce more output or avoid abatement costs.

In the absence of information on costs, regulators must and do set arbitrary standards based on previous studies on the impact of pollution on human health, animal survival and the like. Due to the uncertainty of these estimates and the conflicting objectives of environmental policy, setting standards becomes a political issue, subject to contention by interest groups. Policy struggles, the establishment of compliance staff and ensuing law suits all add significant costs to the imposition of standards and thus reduce the gains to society. In societies where rent-seeking is an important feature of legal and political systems, polluting industrialists are likely to use their financial and political muscle to influence the nature of environmental regulation.

Another source of inefficiency is that regulators are unlikely to know the various techniques of pollution abatement and have little incentive to find the most efficient way to reduce pollution. Their required method of achieving the optimal level of pollution is, therefore, likely to raise the *MAC* schedule above its minimum and so unnecessarily raise the cost to society. The costs of abatement, although they are directly borne by the polluters, are also costs to society because they entail less savings which might otherwise have been invested in other goods and services people want.

There is the problem of monitoring and prosecuting any violators of the regulations. The probability of catching a polluter is very low in areas where there are a large number of polluters and each is contributing a small amount to the total level of pollution. Thus, to find out whether the polluter will pollute a certain amount is to take the probability of being caught and prosecuted, multiplied by the penalty, and compare it with the marginal cost of abatement. Thus, the actual level of pollution will be higher than the expected level if the probability is less than 100 percent. The above factors may have explained the low compliance rate of emission in ASEAN's capital cities (Seda, 1993, p. 88).

13.5.2 Taxation

Another way of achieving the socially optimal level of resource utilization is by requiring the user to bear the external cost of resource utilization. Known as the Pigouvian tax, it could mean the imposition of a tax on the level of externality or on the output, equal to the cost of externality. Theoretically, this would push the private marginal cost schedule to coincide with the social marginal cost schedule so that the optimal output is obtained. Based on the pollution example above, if a tax of t^* is imposed on each unit of the level of pollutant, equal to the cost of externality, a socially optimal level of pollution Q^* can be achieved. From a 100 percent level of pollution up to Q^* level of pollution, the cost of pollution control is cheaper than the per unit tax of t^*. Therefore, the firm will control pollution up to Q^*. Any control beyond Q^* (to the left) will make the cost of pollution control to exceed the per unit tax. Thus, the firm will pay the tax beyond Q^* level of pollution.

Apart from the inbuilt optimality property of taxation, it also has the advantage of allowing the firm to find the best way of reducing its production costs and of generating revenue for the government. There are, however, problems similar to the regulation measure. To obtain the optimal level of output or externality requires knowledge of the externality costs, producers' private costs and, if there are a few producers, the contribution of each firm to the total cost of externality.

There is also some uncertainty about the justice of the Pigouvian tax. Based on the standard producer pays (SPP) principle, the producer only bears the cost of optimal efficient control, which is equal to Q^*BX and not for the pollution damage done by the remaining optimal effluent, equal to area OBQ^*. According to the extended producer pays (EPP) principle, the producer must pay the cost of optimal effluent control as well as the pollution damage caused by the remaining optimal effluent. It is argued that industry might tolerate the SPP principle, but not the EPP principle. In the case of the Pigouvian tax, the producer is expected to pay, in addition to what the EPP prescribes, the cost, equal to *ABO*.

13.5.3 Assignment of Property Rights

Coase (1960) argued that the problem of externality was due to the lack of property rights. By establishing property rights, regardless of who has the property rights, an optimal level of resource utilization and level of externality will be achieved through the process of bargaining. With a clear definition of property rights, resources will be put to their highest value without the need for government intervention. There are, however, essential conditions for this approach to work. First, the transaction cost must be low enough for the bargaining process to occur. If the transaction costs become so high that the expected benefit from the bargaining process is lower than the transaction cost, then the bargaining process may not occur. In many party cases, it is clear that the transaction cost will be prohibitive in achieving an optimal bargaining solution. Second, the sources and victims of the externality must be identifiable. If there are many parties involved, the identification of how much each party contributes to the externality may be hard to find and thus the process may break down. Third, the preferences of the parties involved must be accurately represented. However, when many parties are involved, there will be an incentive for each party to engage in strategic misrepresentation of preferences to maximize their private benefits. Therefore, when the externality is a public 'bad', the conditions necessary for the Coase theorem to work will not be met. Further, the Coase theorem is based on the assumption that the willingness to pay and the willingness to accept are equal to one another. But empirical evidence shows the lack of equivalence between the willingness to pay and willingness to accept compensation, as people ascribe different values to gain as opposed to losses (Knetsch, 1990, p. 230). Fourth, to make violators pay requires effective policing, but effective policing requires an efficient property right structure. And an efficient property right structure has two important characteristics of exclusivity (that is, when all benefits and costs resulting from owning and using the resource accrue to the owner of the resource) and enforceability (that is, the property right is secure from involuntary seizure for encroachment by others). Thus, in the case of fund pollutants, market bargaining, as suggested by Coase, may be constrained by a large number of people that are affected and the inability to define clearly individual property rights to a clean environment.

13.5.4 Marketable Permits

The regulatory authority decides on the allowable level of externality in a given area, and issues permits for this level of externality. These permits are transferable. Going back to our pollution example in Figure 13.1, if the authority seeks an optimal level of pollution, then it should issue OQ^* number of permits and the optimal price for these permits is OA since the MAC is also the demand curve for pollution permits. At price OA, the producer will buy OQ^* number of permits, as it is cheaper to abate pollution from X back to Q^*. To the left of Q^*, it is cheaper to buy permits than to abate pollution.

This approach has several advantages. In terms of efficiency, the regulator does not have to know the marginal cost of pollution control for each and every firm. This kind of information, as discussed earlier, is difficult, if not impossible, to obtain. But, even without this information, it can control the level of pollution in the most efficient way by letting the market do the rest.

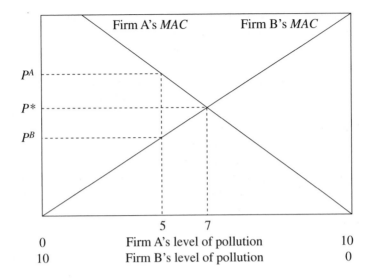

Source: Sathiendrakumar (1993).

Figure 13.2   Externality and marketable permits

For example, let us suppose there are only two firms in an area, each emitting ten units of pollutants. The authority wants to limit the level of pollution to ten units, and thus sells ten permits to the industry where each permit is equal to one unit of pollutant. Suppose initially two firms purchased five units each at a price equal to P^* (see Figure 13.2). Since the marginal cost of pollution control of firm B (MAC_B)is less than the marginal cost of pollution control of firm A (MAC_A), it is mutually profitable for firm A and firm B to trade. In this case there is an incentive for firm A to buy pollution permits from firm B at a price lower than its *MAC*. On the other hand, it is profitable for firm B to sell some of its permits to firm A, provided the selling price is higher than its *MAC*. A transfer of permits will take place until the price of the permit is equal to the marginal cost of pollution control of both firms. In the figure, this is achieved when firm A has seven units of permits and firm B has three units of permits. At this point the price of the permit is equal to P^*. The permit system reinforces competition in the industry by allowing for new entrants. There is of course a unique scenario where the biggest and lowest cost firm may be able to buy all the permits. But this scenario could happen even without the introduction of marketable permits. An oligopolistic or monopolistic industry has to be regulated through other means so that their pricing policies do not harm the welfare of the consuming public.

The system also allows for the price of the marketable permits to reflect and adjust to macroeconomic conditions. Inflation erodes the effectiveness of the tax system unless the nominal value of the tax is adjusted accordingly. In the case of the permit system, the price of permits reflects the demand and supply conditions and thus it can factor in inflation. Since the firm only pays the cost of controlling pollution from X to Q^*, and not from O to X, it is considered to be fairer and more acceptable as it is consistent with the standard producer pays (SPP) principle. There are many possible applications and versions of marketable permit systems. The Singapore government has been successful in avoiding traffic congestion and thus minimizing pollution from motor vehicles by adopting a system of certificates of entitlement (COE). The way it works is similar to the pollution permit system in that a certain number of permits (COEs) are determined and issued by the Singapore government every year for auction. The permits are also transferable.[16]

13.6 CONCLUSION

Although foreign direct investment has brought a number of benefits to the ASEAN countries, it cannot assure their long-term economic security. Thus, the importance of developing their own domestic capital, entrepreneurship and technology cannot be ignored and undoubtedly constitutes a major challenge facing the ASEAN countries. To promote domestic capital, entrepreneurship and technology, most of the ASEAN countries must find ways to deal with the prevalent resentment against the overseas Chinese capitalists who have been a significant source of domestic capital and potential source of technology.

Another challenge is how to maintain their robust economic growth without necessarily sacrificing their environment and long-term sustainability. With increasing industrialization and urbanization in ASEAN it is most likely that deforestation and environmental degradation will worsen over time. Environmental policies are, therefore, required to protect the environment as well as to ensure that the rate of resource utilization does not exceed the replenishment rate in relation to ASEAN renewable resource. In the case of depletable resources, it is important that they are converted into man-made resources to ensure a sustainable development.

The above discussion of alternative measures to deal with the environmental problems points to the importance of government intervention. An honest, efficient and competent government and bureaucracy are again necessary for an effective adoption of appropriate policies.

Although some aspects of resource management and environmental problem are country-specific, others appear to be common to almost all ASEAN cities and transcend national boundaries.[17] Under the latter it is important to enhance ASEAN cooperation on the management of natural resources and on the control of external costs. The ASEAN countries are so far heading in the right direction. They have agreed to regard the entire region as one eco-system and to enhance cooperation on the management of their natural resources. They have agreed to set up a regional early warning and response system to enhance their capacities to deal with natural disasters. They have also emphasized the need for increased consultation and cooperation with regards to issues raised at international conventions.

SUGGESTIONS FOR FURTHER READING

For studies on the development and role of local capitalists in the ASEAN economies, read McVey (ed.) (1992) and Yoshihara (1988). There is a vast and increasing literature on environment and development, but little attention has so far been paid to the links between economic sustainability and environmental concerns in ASEAN. To explore the different environmental concerns or issues and relevant environmental policies pursued by the ASEAN countries, Seda (ed.) (1993) is recommended. For a good economic evaluation of alternative policy options, read Gillis et al. (1996, ch. 7) and Sathiendrakumar (1993).

NOTES

1. Prime Minister Goh Chok Tong of Singapore has, for instance, made a strong call that Singapore must nurture a new breed of MNCs (*The Straits Times*, 25 March 1995).
2. In Malaysia a plan to build a hydroelectric dam was suspended due to environmental consideration. In the Philippines, a Taiwanese-led consortium's proposal to build a cement complex in the North of Manila was not approved due to anticipated environmental damage.
3. Environmental problems may be classified into two categories: the 'population basic needs' category and the 'natural cycles and processes' category. The former includes issues relating to the need for shelter, food, social services and amenities, work mobility and rural–urban migration. The latter includes the transformation and in many cases degradation of the biophysical environment as a result of human activities. This chapter will only discuss the major issues relating to the latter.
4. The following discussion on ASEAN domestic capital will be based mainly on Yoshihara (1988).
5. Prime Minister Mahathir of Malaysia attributed the absence of the bumiputra in business to their lack of networks. See Mahathir (1970, p. 53).
6. The American Administration restricted Chinese immigration to prevent the Chinese from using the Philippines as a gateway to the United States. On the restriction of Chinese immigration in the Philippines, see Khin (1956).
7. This is based on the argument by Yoshihara (1988, p. 56).
8. See ASEAN Experts Group (1987), *Environmental Programme III, 1988–1992*, p. 21.
9. Air pollution in Thailand is frequently singled out as the worst among all countries in Asia. Carbon monoxide is reportedly 50 percent above the WHO standard, while the level of lead is double the standard. See, *Far Eastern Economic Review*, September 1991, pp. 37–57.

10. PSI ratings between zero and 50 indicate good air quality, between 50 and 100 moderate, and above 100 points to unhealthy or hazardous air.
11. Singapore and Brunei are exceptions. Singapore's policy of controlling car ownership through the allocation of entitlements due to its spatial constraints is mainly responsible for relatively smooth traffic flows. Brunei's small population and large space is the main factor.
12. Apart from market failure, policy failure has also been blamed for the inefficient use of natural resources in developing countries. For a detailed discussion of these issues, refer to Todaro (1997) and Gillis et al. (1996).
13. The Philippines, in dealing with its serious traffic congestion problem in Metro Manila, has adopted an odd–even system in which only cars with certain registration numbers are allowed in on certain days.
14. This is one of the most common environmental problems faced by the ASEAN countries and most commonly discussed environmental problem in the literature. Pollutants are classified into stock and fund pollutants, based on the absorptive capacity of the environment. Fund pollutants are those for which the environment has some absorptive capacity, whereas stock pollutants are those for which the environment has little or no absorptive capacity.
15. This approach to the economics of pollution abatement is based on the treatment by Pearce and Turner (1990, chaps. 4–7).
16. For a detailed discussion of Singapore's system of certificate of entitlement, see Phang Sock Yong (1993, pp. 329–36).
17. Occasional haze over Malaysia and Singapore as a result of forest fires in Indonesia is an example of pollution that transcends national boundaries.

14. China's accession to the WTO and its impact on ASEAN countries

A new development, which could pose a serious challenge to the ASEAN countries' future economic progress and security, is the membership of China in the World Trade Organization (WTO). As discussed in the preceding chapters, exports and inward foreign capital have been the ASEAN countries' engines of growth and economic development. For the past three decades they have achieved remarkable economic and social progress largely due to their successful export-oriented and pro-foreign investment policies, which was only interrupted by occasional economic crises: one was in 1985 and most recently in 1997 and 1998.

Political considerations aside, the admission of China into the WTO will certainly have some positive implications for the world economy as it offers a large market potential and would generally provide stability and predictability with China, who will be bound by the same rules, opening up vast opportunities for market niches. But at the same time its membership has also raised serious concern for those developing countries whose export structures are similar to China's. The ASEAN countries in particular are concerned about its likely negative impact on their export and growth potentials. To what extent are their exports competitive or complementary? In which commodities are they likely to compete? What implications will China's WTO membership have for their exports and inward foreign investments?

In view of the membership of China in the WTO and the ASEAN serious concern about its trade and investment impacts, the main objective of this chapter is to evaluate the likely trade and investment impacts of China's accession to the WTO on the ASEAN economies based on previous empirical studies.[1] Before presenting the empirical evidence provided by these studies with respect to the likely economic impacts of China's WTO membership, the chapter will first describe briefly the obligations and privileges of China as a WTO member and the specific issues of major concern to the ASEAN countries.

14.1   CHINA AND THE WTO

With the ratification of its own parliament, China has become an official member of the global trade body, the World Trade Organization (WTO) in November 2001, after the WTO has formally recommended its membership at a meeting of trade ministers on 17 September 2001. As a WTO member, China would have to comply with the terms of the recent Uruguay Round Agreement and other principles of the WTO. This means that China would have to reform its foreign trade regime and further open up its market. Implementing these reforms according to the WTO principles and rules implies, among other things, substantial reductions in tariffs and non-tariff barriers to trade.

China was once a member of the General Agreement on Tariffs and Trade (GATT) but withdrew its membership from the GATT in 1950. Since 1986 China has applied to join the WTO, its successor and thus, a series of liberalization measures have been implemented in a bid to strengthen its case for readmission. At the beginning of 1993 China reduced its tariffs on 3 371 import items and abolished import control of more than 367 commodities. This action reduced the trade-weighted average tariffs by 7.3 percent (Zhang and Warr, 1995). At the 1995 Asia Pacific Economic Cooperation (APEC) meeting, China's President Jiang Zemin further made a commitment to cut average tariffs by at least 30 percent in 1996. According to China's General Administration of Customs, this new liberalization effort includes substantial tariff cuts on 4 994 tariff lines and has lowered China's simple average tariff to 23.2 percent. It has also eliminated quotas, licensing and other import controls on 176 tariff lines, or more than 30 percent of commodities subject to these restrictions. These trade liberalization measures implemented by China are summarized in Table 14.1.

Despite the dramatic decline in tariff barriers, China's level of trade protection was still considered too high to justify its entry to the WTO. After eight rounds of multilateral trade negotiations, average tariff rates of developed countries have dropped from 40 percent in 1948 to 4.7 percent in 1995, while most developing countries have dropped their tariff rates to a simple average of 15 percent. After implementing their commitments under the terms of the Uruguay Agreement, the rates of protection of the WTO contracting parties are expected to fall even further.

China, therefore, needs to continue implementing its commitments to trade liberalization in order to comply with the WTO guidelines. The recently-signed US-China Trade Agreement, detailed information of which can be found in the White House website (www.chinapntr.gov), marked a significant progress in China's commitment to trade liberalization within the multilateral framework. China also needs to implement transparency in investment regulations, protection of intellectual property rights and other terms of the Agreement.

Table 14.1   Trade liberalization measures in China (1991–97)

Date	Trade liberalization measures	Tariff rates after revisions
1991	Abolition of export subsidy for export tax refund	
1992	Tariff rate reduction, 2898 items	Average tariff rate: 43.2%
1993	Tariff rate reduction, 3371 items	Average tariff rate: 35.9%
1993	Abolition of import control, >367 items	Average tariff rate: 7.3%
1996	Tariff rate reduction, 4994 items	Average tariff rate: 23.2%
1996	Abolition of import permits/quotas, 176 items	
1997	Tariff rate reduction, 4874 items	Average tariff rate: 17%

Sources: Wang (1997, p. 1); Ezaki and Lin (2000, p. 3)

Under the newly-signed US–China agreement, China's tariffs will be cut to an average of 9.4 percent overall. Tariffs will be eliminated for Information Technology Agreement products such as computers, telecommunications equipment, semiconductors, computer equipment and other high-technology products. China will cut tariffs from the current 100 percent or 80 percent level to 24 percent for the auto sector and for the auto parts to an average of 10 percent by 2006. Significant cuts will also be made in the wood and paper sectors going from the present levels of 12–18 percent on wood and 15–25 percent on paper down to levels generally between 5 and 7.5 percent.

As a WTO member China will enjoy the rights and privileges enjoyed by other contracting parties. China prior to its membership enjoyed a most-favoured nation (MFN) treatment from the US, this was not permanent and is subject to annual reviews. Its WTO membership will give China an MFN treatment on a permanent basis and this treatment will also be accorded by other contracting countries other than the US. China will also face less discrimination in other contracting countries' export markets particularly for its labour-intensive exports of textiles and clothing. Based on the Uruguay Round Agreement, trade in textiles and apparel will be under the normal GATT disciplines with the commitment by developed countries to eliminate quota restrictions under the Multi Fibre Arrangement (MFA). Under the Agreement the elimination of the bilateral MFA quotas will take place gradually. It involves increasing the growth rates of MFA quotas during a ten-year transition period and progressive reintegration of certain export categories under WTO disciplines followed by the termination of all remaining quota restrictions by the year 2005. China will benefit not only in terms of less discriminatory market access for its exports, but also in terms of building a more predictable and more transparent trading environment in China as well as in other member countries.

14.2 MAJOR ISSUES OF CONCERN

Self-sufficiency and self-reliance were emphasized in China for three decades following the founding of the People's Republic of China in 1949. Thus, foreign trade was viewed as rather unimportant and grew slowly especially in the 1950s and 1960s. There was also an attempt to reduce the exports of industrial goods that were relatively overpriced in the domestic market. However, since China opened its door and introduced market reforms, foreign trade has started to grow strongly. The year 1994 was the year when China really entered into the global market as its exports and imports grew by 97 percent and 66 percent, respectively, partly as a result of the government's intensive call for a more radical economic reform and a further opening up of China. In 2000 China exported US$250 billion worth of goods to become the seventh largest exporting nation. The historic tour of Deng Xiaoping in South China in the spring of 1992 marked a radical shift in China's economic orientation towards a trade-oriented development, which has been adopted by the post-Deng leadership. Further, despite the current global slowdown China continued to post significant gains in the export markets. While many Asian economies have experienced export downturns since the start of 2001, China's export performance has remained robust, up by 7 percent for the past eight months of 2001.

A continued surge in China's exports is predicted to continue and its membership of the WTO is viewed as another opportunity for China to increase its share in world trade. However, while there are opportunities associated with China's emergence as a major exporter/importer, it also has caused some concern particularly for the ASEAN countries. The first cause for concern associated with China's accession to the WTO is its likely impact on their exports in third country markets, particularly with respect to their labour-intensive products. China is known to be a very competitive producer in labour-intensive products because of its abundant and relatively cheap human resources. Thus, ASEAN exports of labour-intensive products are likely to face greater competitive pressure, and one possible trade impact would be a decline in their exports to third country markets (trade diversion). With more supply of these products in the world market, it is also possible that the export prices of these products will decline (export price deterioration).

The extent of trade diversion depends on the degree to which China's exports to a third country, say the US, overlap those of ASEAN countries, the elasticity of substitution between their exports and China's exports, and the degree of price reduction in China's exports in third country markets as a result of China's WTO membership. Further, there are other non-price factors, which could lead to trade diversion such as the elimination of the uncertainty generated by China being outside the WTO, improvement in transparency and predictability and greater sense of security as China complies with the rules of the WTO.

Apart from the trade diversion and price reduction of labour-intensive products, the prices of capital-intensive and some agricultural products are expected to increase as world demand for these products increases. China is a net importer of capital-intensive and some agricultural products and its entry into the WTO is expected to boost the overall demand for these types of imports. Those countries, that are net importers of these products, will therefore face increased prices of these imports. Consequently, this could mean terms of trade deterioration and loss in welfare for these countries, if their average price of exports relative to their imports declines.

Further, there could be a foreign investment diversion. Foreign direct investment (FDI) in particular has emerged as one of the main factors responsible for the economic dynamism of ASEAN in the 1980s and early 1990s by providing an important source of capital, technology and management skills, and by stimulating exports. However, since 1992 the share of FDI going to ASEAN has been declining partly due to the emergence of China as an attractive destination for foreign investment. China's accession to the WTO would only lead to more investment diversion in the absence of any effective counter measures to be adopted by the ASEAN countries. China's commitment to more liberal trade and investment policies, transparency in investment regulations, protection of intellectual property rights and other terms of the Uruguay Agreement would make China even more attractive for foreign investment. Thus, these substantial trade and investment diversions could further slow down ASEAN's overall exports and economic growth.

The overall future economic scenario may not, however, be at all gloomy for the developing countries of ASEAN. The opening and huge size (actual and potential) of the Chinese market could offer many economic opportunities for its geographically close countries, resulting in more trade between China and the ASEAN countries, and a more diversified market for their exports by reducing its heavy trade orientation towards their Western trading partners (that is, the US, Japan and Western Europe). These economic opportunities, if managed properly, could offset the negative implications expected in third country markets.

14.3   ECONOMIC IMPLICATIONS FOR ASEAN COUNTRIES

Having discussed the major issues of concern to the ASEAN countries resulting from China's entry into the WTO and how in theory its membership could
affect their export and growth prospects, this section will now evaluate the
question empirically. Before looking at the overall economic implications of
China's WTO membership for the ASEAN countries, this section will first
identify the export items where competition from China is likely to occur in
third country markets and assess how ASEAN countries have performed and
how competitive they are relative to China with respect to their major export
items.

14.3.1   Areas of Trade Diversion

There is certainly a good reason for the ASEAN countries' concern that
China's entry into the WTO could pose a threat to their exports. The threat
comes from the fact that China's major exports are in direct competition with
ASEAN countries' major exports, as both are major exporters of labour-intensive products and are competing for the same markets.

As Table 14.2 shows, for 1993–98 period labour-intensive manufactures
such as textiles and apparel, footwear and other miscellaneous manufactures
(such as toys, games and sports requisites, and furniture furnishings) constituted a considerable proportion of China's total exports, accounting for about
36 percent of its total exports. They are also the largest contributors to China's
large trade surpluses starting from 1995. Although textiles and apparel exports
in particular have not been growing consistently due to the restrictions
imposed under the Multi-Fibre Arrangement (MFA), they are still China's
most important export items for the period. China's relatively low labour
costs, the industrial restructuring adopted by many developed and newly
industrializing countries away from labour-intensive to capital-intensive
industries and China's deliberate modernization policy are largely responsible
for this trend.

Another fast-growing labour-intensive export sector in China, which could
pose a serious threat of trade diversion to the ASEAN countries, is machinery
and electrical appliances. This sector's share in China's overall exports
increased from 2.82 percent in 1986 to 23.7 percent in 1998. However, disag-
gregating this further reveals that China's main exports in the machinery and
electrical appliances category are mainly comprised of telecommunications
and equipment, such as sound recorders and reproducers, television and parts
and other accessories. These are relatively labour-intensive. Unlike the former
group of labour-intensive products, China is a net importer of machinery and

Table 14.2   China's trade structure by major commodity groups: 1993–98 (US$Millions)

Chapter	Description	1993 Exports	1993 Imports	1993 Net exports	1994 Exports	1994 Imports	1994 Net exports	1995 Exports	1995 Imports	1995 Net exports
01–05	Live animals	2 562.6	548.7	2 014	3 619.8	815.8	2 804	4 484.7	865.4	3 619.3
06–14	Vegetable products	4 371	1 277	3 094	5 458.4	1 612.4	3 846	4 139	4 140	–1
15	Fats and oils	206.5	515.6	–309.1	501.3	1 826.6	–1 325.3	459.4	2 623.5	–2 164.1
16–24	Prepared foodstuffs	3 611.8	841.1	2 771	3 837.2	1 037.7	2 799.5	4 627	1 926.5	2 700.5
25–27	Mineral products	4 873.9	7 157	–2 283	5 014.4	5 529.8	–515.4	6 720.7	7 229.4	–508.7
28–38	Chemicals	4 398.3	5 608	–1 210	5 769.3	6 963.1	–1 193.8	8 420.6	10 402.7	–1 982.1
39–40	Plastics	2 198.2	5 553	–3 355	3 124.5	6 942.1	–3 817.6	4 281.5	9 00.3	–4 718.8
41–43	Hides and leather	3 442.8	1 842	1 600	4 812.9	2 251.4	2 561.5	5 642.6	2 486.5	3 156.1
44–46	Wood and wood articles	1 254.3	1 591	–337.1	1 641.2	1 638.5	2.7	2 147.1	1 576.1	571
47–49	Pulp and paper	629.6	2 035	–1 405	745.2	2 664.6	–1 919.4	1 108.4	3 343.1	–2 234.7
50–63	Textiles and apparel	26 063.6	9 669	16 395	34 216.5	12 858.5	21 358	35 877.7	15 819.1	20 058.6
64–67	Footware	6 290.8	512.6	5 778	7 389	453.9	6 935.1	8 158.6	450.9	7 707.7
68–70	Stone/ Cement/ Ceramics	1 328.8	549.7	779.1	1 993.2	732.9	1 260.3	2 662.9	948.3	1 714.6
71	Gems	881.4	848.5	32.9	1 499	1 031.5	467.5	1 752.2	1 027.4	724.8
72–83	Base metal and metal articles	4 670.4	16 540	–11 870	6 831.7	13 264.1	–6 432.4	12 079.5	12 165.5	–86
84–85	Machinery and electrical appliances	13 906.9	35 847	–21 940	19 714.8	41 652.2	–21 937.4	27 667.2	46 996.5	–19 329.3
86–89	Vehicles	1 926.4	8 723	–6 797	2 823	9 702.9	–6 879.9	4 115.8	5 364.5	–1 248.7
90–92	Optical, precision & musical instruments	2 684.3	3 380	–696.1	3 568.7	3 670	–101.3	4 702.7	4 505.6	197.1
93	Arms	297.9	75.2	222.7	189.8	54	135.8	206.2	156.5	49.7
94–96	Miscellaneous manufactured articles	6 101.6	801.4	5 300	8 209.5	891.1	7 318.4	9 481.8	1 042.6	8 439.2
97–98	Antiques and works of art	42.9	2	40.9	46.7	2	44.7	43.9	11.9	32
other	Other	0.212	41.6	–41.39	0.403	19	–18.597	0.002	1.6	–1.598
All	All	91 744.21	1E+05	–12 215	121 006.5	115 614.1	5 392.403	148 779.5	132 083.9	16 695.6

Notes: All figures are rounded up to the nearest decimal point. 1998 is the latest year for which trade data for China are available at the time of writing.

Source: *China Customs Statistics Yearbook* (1998).

Exports	1996 Imports	Net exports	Exports	1997 Imports	Net exports	Exports	1998 Imports	Net exports	Total Exports	% Share	Rank
4 183.4	953.3	3 230.1	4 203.2	917.1	3 286.1	3 842.4	1 054.5	2 787.9	22 896.1	2.604260475	
4 088.3	3 405.7	682.6	4 904.9	2 329.6	2 575.3	4 921.9	2 502	2 419.9	27 883.5	3.171539998	10
382.4	1 694.9	−1 312.5	680.8	1 678	−997.2	327.8	1 487.7	−1 159.9	2 558.2	0.290976155	
5 075	2 410.3	2 664.7	4 655.5	2 564	2 091.5	4 284.6	1 946.8	2 337.8	26 091.1	2.967667877	
7 374.7	9 234.1	−1 859.4	8 598.9	13 010.1	−4 411.2	6 508	9 337	−2 829	39 090.6	4.446263971	7
8 425	10 412.6	−1 987.6	9 393.2	10 302.4	−909.2	9 653.6	11 035.5	−1 381.9	46 060	5.2389812	6
4 421.1	10 251.2	−5 830.1	5 801.9	11 456.2	−5 654.3	6 174.4	11 574.5	−5 400.1	26 001.6	2.95748792	
5 387.9	2 563.3	2 824.6	6 267.7	2 681.8	3 585.9	5 913.9	2 429	3 484.9	31 467.8	3.579227369	8
2 053	1 571	482	2 204.1	1 989.1	215	1 831.5	1 981.8	−150.3	11 131.2	1.266090915	
1 025.1	4 236.7	−3 211.6	1 323.6	4 981.2	−3 657.6	1 344.6	5 010.7	−3 666.1	6 176.5	0.702530773	
34 965.2	16 684.2	18 281	43 224.2	17 214.9	26 009.3	40 476.5	14 390.3	26 086.2	214 823.7	24.43459239	1
8 545.5	456.1	8 089.4	10 187.6	454.4	9 733.2	10 270.1	377	9 893.1	50 841.6	5.78285251	5
2 638.2	1 012.1	1 626.1	3 239.6	1 046.1	2 193.5	3 182.9	1 148	2 034.9	15 045.6	1.711324697	
1 278.2	1 049.2	229	1 787.5	1 378.4	409.1	2 095.4	1 235.1	860.3	9 293.7	1.057089005	
10 395.5	12 670.7	−2 275.2	13 385.2	12 521.5	863.7	12 627.6	12 466.9	160.7	59 989.9	6.82340335	4
31 065.3	49 021.2	−17 955.9	38 270	46 758.3	−8 488.3	43 615.2	50 984.8	−7 369.6	174 239.4	19.8184312	2
4 178.5	5 350	−1 171.5	5 272.8	5 554.3	−281.5	6 392.5	5 591	801.5	24 709	2.810464318	
5 187.9	4 643.4	544.5	6 321.5	4 671.8	1 649.7	6 561.6	4 926.9	1 634.7	29 026.7	3.301570465	9
181.3	106	75.3	286.6	17.7	268.9	261.3	5.9	255.4	1 423.1	0.161867003	
10 145.8	1 103.2	9 042.6	12 708	820.7	11 887.3	13 468	741	12 727	60 114.7	6.837598419	3
50.4	3.4	47	74.8	22.9	51.9	55.2	10.5	44.7	313.9	0.035703782	
0.052	0.222	−0.17	0	0.102	−0.102	0.001	0.016	−0.015	0.67	7.62075E−05	
151 047.8	138 832.8	12 214.93	182 791.6	142 370.6	40 421	183 809	140 236.9	43 572.09	879 178.6	100	

electrical appliances. In contrast, the export performance of its mineral products, chemicals, plastics, pulp and paper, and wood and wood products sectors were poor due to domestic supply shortage, rising demand caused by population growth and lack of technology.

To explore further the extent of commodity overlaps between ASEAN countries and China in third country markets, Table 14.3 lists their respective top 10 major exports and their respective rankings. The top 10 exports account for a disproportionately large share of their total exports, that is 83.4 percent in the case of China, 82.1 percent in Indonesia, 84.7 percent in Thailand, 89.4 percent in the Philippines, 92.5 percent in Malaysia and 94.1 percent in Singapore. Singapore, Malaysia and the Philippines have relied most heavily on machinery and electrical appliances (electronics) exports, which accounted for more than 50 percent of their total exports, while Indonesia and Thailand's exports are relatively more diversified. It is evident from this table that there is a high degree of similarity between China and selected ASEAN countries in terms of their export structures. Textiles and apparel, which ranks first in China's top 10 exports, is also the second most important export sector for Indonesia, the Philippines and Thailand. Machinery and electrical appliances, which ranks second in China's top 10 exports, is also the most important export sector for Malaysia, the Philippines, Singapore and Thailand. These significant commodity overlaps point to the competitive nature of their respective exports.

There are also market overlaps. Table 14.4 shows the market distribution of China's exports. Hong Kong has remained the largest market. A significant portion of China's exports, however, which are destined for other markets pass through Hong Kong. If this portion is excluded, the US market is China's largest export market among its trading partners. China's exports are heavily concentrated with these three countries – Hong Kong, the US and Japan – accounting for more than 50 percent of China's total exports in 1998. It is, therefore, evident that China and the ASEAN countries are competing for similar markets. As in the case of the ASEAN countries, the US and Japan are China's top export destinations, accounting for about 36 percent of China's total exports in 1998.

14.3.2   ASEAN's Export Competitiveness

Whether the ASEAN countries will eventually experience trade and investment diversions as a result of China's WTO membership will depend mainly on their degree of export competitiveness *vis-à-vis* China in the production of the abovementioned commodities. Table 14.5 shows a comparison of unit labour costs among the ASEAN5 countries and China. It is quite clear that China has a lower unit labour cost compared to any of the ASEAN5 countries.

Table 14.3 China and ASEAN Top 10 exports

Country	% share	Country	% share
China		Indonesia	
Textiles and apparel	24.44	Mineral products	27.9
Machinery and electrical appliances	19.82	Textiles and apparel	12.6
Miscellaneous manufactured articles	6.84	Wood and wood articles	10.5
Base metal and metal articles	6.82	Machinery and electrical appliances	7.5
Footware	5.78	Antiques and works of art	4.9
Chemicals	5.24	Plastics	4.8
Mineral products	4.45	Footware	4.0
Hides and leather	3.58	Live animals	3.4
Optical, precision & musical instruments	3.3	Base metal and metal articles	3.3
Vegetable products	3.17	Fats and oils	3.2
	83.44		82.1
Malaysia		Philippines	
Machinery and electrical appliances	52.7	Machinery and electrical appliances	54.95
Mineral products	8.11	Textiles and apparel	13.08
Wood and wood articles	6.52	Fats and oils	3.34
Fats and oils	6.4	Prepared foodstuffs	3.32
Plastics	4.9	Base metal and metal articles	2.98
Textiles and apparel	3.65	Miscellaneous manufactured articles	2.97
Base metal and metal articles	2.93	Mineral products	2.77
Vehicles	2.74	Vegetable products	2.54

Table 14.3 continued

Country	% share	Country	% share
Chemicals	2.43	Optical, precision & musical instruments	1.83
Miscellaneous manufactured articles	2.16	Vehicles	1.66
	92.53		89.44
Singapore		Thailand	
Machinery and electrical appliances	63.09	Machinery and electrical appliances	32.55
Mineral products	7.49	Textiles and apparel	11.01
Chemicals	5.01	Prepared foodstuffs	8.21
Base metal and metal articles	3.01	Plastics	8.05
Optical, precision & musical instruments	2.9	Vegetable products	5.88
Antiques and works of art	2.81	Live Animals	5.7
Plastics	2.71	Gems	4.84
Textiles and apparel	2.59	Footware	2.96
Prepared foodstuffs	2.31	Base metal and metal articles	2.94
Vehicles	2.17	Vehicles	2.65
	94.09		84.79

Source: China Customs Statistics Yearbook (various issues).

Table 14.4 Market distribution of China's exports (%): 1986–98

	Hong Kong	Japan	US	Germany	S. Korea	Canada	Taiwan	ASEAN	Asia	Australia
1986	33.8	15.3	8.5	3.4	0.8	1.0	n.a.	5.9	60.9	0.7
1987	37.4	16.2	7.7	3.3	0.8	1.1	n.a.	5.9	61.8	0.8
1988	40.8	16.7	7.1	3.1	0.6	0.9	n.a.	5.6	64.1	0.9
1989	48.0	15.9	8.4	3.1	0.6	0.9	n.a.	5.8	64.5	0.9
1990	42.9	14.5	8.3	3.3	0.6	0.7	0.5	6.0	71.8	0.7
1991	44.7	14.2	8.6	3.3	0.7	0.8	0.8	5.8	74.2	0.8
1992	44.3	13.7	10.1	2.9	0.6	0.8	0.8	5.0	71.9	0.8
1993	24.0	17.2	18.5	4.3	0.7	1.3	1.6	5.1	57.3	1.2
1994	26.7	17.8	17.7	3.9	0.4	1.2	1.9	5.3	60.7	1.2
1995	24.7	19.1	16.8	3.8	0.3	1.0	n.a.	6.0	61.9	1.1
1997	24.0	17.4	17.9	3.6	5.0	1.0	1.9	6.9	59.6	1.3
1998	21.1	16.1	20.7	4.0	3.4	1.2	n.a.	6.0	53.4	1.5

Source: For 1986–1995, Lee (1996: 50); For 1997–1998, China Customs Statistics Yearbook (1998)

Table 14.5   China and the ASEAN5 countries: unit labour cost comparison

| | Unit labour cost in US dollars (cents) | | | | |
	1985	1986	1997	1998	1999
China	0.07	0.06	0.07	0.07	0.07
Indonesia	0.21	0.16	0.14	0.09	0.09
Malaysia	0.4	0.37	0.25	0.25	0.25
Philippines	0.29	0.3	n.a.	n.a.	n.a.
Singapore	0.46	0.41	0.68	0.71	0.59
Thailand	n.a.	n.a.	0.28	0.36	0.33

Notes: Unit labour costs figures show the labour cost in cents per 1 dollar worth of output.

Source: Lee and Abeysinghe (1999).

In 1998 and 1999 due to the crisis-induced massive depreciation of the *rupiah*, Indonesia's unit labour cost has significantly decreased to almost the same level as China. The overall pattern of unit labour costs is quite consistent with the relative factor endowments of these countries. China with the most abundant labour has the lowest unit labour cost while Singapore with scarce labour has the highest unit labour cost.

To further examine the ASEAN countries' export performance and competitiveness relative to China, a constant market share (CMS) analysis (Leamer and Stern, 1970) is applied to two sectors where China and the ASEAN countries are likely to compete intensively: textiles and clothing, and machinery and electrical appliances (electronics).

Although this approach has some limitations, it is a commonly used methodology in analysing a country's export competitiveness and is useful for this study because not only can it include multiple destinations, it can also take into account the major factors determining a country's export performance including competitiveness. Details of the CMS methodology are explained in Appendix 2. In brief, the CMS provides a set of summary statistics indicating whether a particular exporting country has maintained its share of all importers' markets for traded commodities over a specified time interval. Export performance can be attributed to four factors: the standard effect, which reflects the export growth performance of its competitors; the commodity composition effect, which reflects the contribution of the export structure to export growth; the market distribution effect, which measures the contribution of the market distribution structure to export growth and the competitive residual, which indicates the net gain or loss in export growth attributable to the exporting country's competitiveness.

Table 14.6 ASEAN textiles and clothing exports: constant market share analysis, 1993–96

	Export growth (%)	Standard growth (%)	Commodity composition effect (%)	Market distribution effect (%)	Competitive residual (%)
Textiles					
Indonesia	22.12	33.2	60.49	0.16	–49.57
Malaysia	89.2	33.2	34.54	5.4	16.06
Philippines	84.9	33.2	30.64	–10.0	31.06
Singapore	0.8	33.2	28.3	1.78	–62.48
Thailand	50.6	33.2	30.63	–2.9	–10.33
Clothing					
Indonesia	9.18	34.56	0.64	0.21	–38.83
Malaysia	–0.2	34.56	4.37	–61.3	22.17
Philippines	9.4	34.56	1.8	–29.4	2.44
Singapore	–11.4	34.56	7.32	–33.5	–19.78
Thailand	–10.18	34.56	1.0	–18.2	–27.36

Source: Calculated based on trade data derived from China Customs Statistics (various issues) and from ASEAN Secretariat.

Textiles and clothing

The results of the CMS analysis on textiles and clothing are shown in Table 14.6. They compare the ASEAN5 export performance in textiles and clothing between 1993 and 1996. The choice of this period is appropriate because it is the period before the 1997 crisis and is, therefore, a normal set of years. The first column of the table shows that the ASEAN5 countries' exports of textiles increased by 22.12 percent for Indonesia, 89.2 percent for Malaysia, 84.9 percent for the Philippines, 0.8 percent for Singapore and 50.6 percent for Thailand. In comparison, China's export growth was 33.2 percent for the same period. Thus, except for Indonesia and Singapore, they have performed better than China. The reason for this better export performance was mainly due to the commodity composition effect. Despite apparent lack of competitiveness relative to China, Thailand's exports of textiles expanded as a result of its concentration in rapidly-growing commodity items The competitiveness factor was an extremely important contributor to Malaysia and the Philippines' faster export growth, while in the case of Indonesia, Singapore and Thailand, the competitiveness factor was negative. The importance of the commodity composition effect means that the ASEAN5 exports of textiles were concentrated in commodity groups, the import demand for which was growing relatively quickly. The positive competitive residual factor implies that Malaysia and the Philippines' exports of textiles can compete with China's.

In terms of clothing exports, it is evident that China has a far better export performance than any other ASEAN5 country mainly due to market distribution effects and the competitiveness factor. ASEAN5 exports of clothing were concentrated in the world's sluggish markets and, with the exception of Malaysia and the Philippines, were less competitive relative to China's.

A breakdown of ASEAN5 and Chinese textiles and clothing exports across commodity groups is given in Table 14.7. In textile exports, there are significant differences in commodity composition between the ASEAN5 countries and China. Cotton dominates China's exports of textiles, while man-made filaments and man-made staple fibres dominate in the case of Indonesia, Malaysia, Singapore and Thailand. Knitted fabrics dominate the Philippine export of textiles. Perhaps the most important difference is that cotton textiles and fabrics are much more important to China than to any ASEAN5 country. These data confirm the earlier results from the CMS analysis that commodity composition is one of the factors explaining the differences in export growth of textiles between the ASEAN countries and China.

In the case of clothing, except for Malaysia and Singapore, non-knitted apparel dominates China and ASEAN5 exports. It also confirms the earlier CMS results that commodity composition is a relatively unimportant explanatory variable of the difference in exports of clothing between China and the ASEAN5 countries. In contrast, the competitiveness factor has played a significant role in the performance of clothing exports. It is evident from the results that China has outperformed every ASEAN country. Although Malaysia and the Philippines have positive competitiveness residuals, the residuals are too marginal to exert any significant impact on their overall export performance. Further evidence that tends to indicate China's dominance in the export of clothing can be seen from China's ranking as the world's top clothing exporter. For the period 1995–97, not only did China retain its lead as the world's largest clothing exporter, but it also increased its world market share from 15.3 percent in 1995 to 18.0 percent in 1997 (United Nations Conference on Trade and Development, 1999, p. 329). This seems to imply that, with its entry into the WTO, China is more likely to further strengthen its dominance in the clothing export market.

Machinery and electrical appliances (electronics)
Table 14.8 presents the results of the constant market share analysis as applied to electronics exports. Due to availability of data, the time interval chosen is 1992 and 1999 on the assumption that 1999 is a normal year for which up-to-date data are available. The analysis only covers the export performance in the

Table 14.7 Composition of textiles and clothing exports: China and ASEAN5 countries, 1993–96

		China		Indonesia		Malaysia		Philippines		Singapore		Thailand	
		% Share	Rank	% Share	Rank	% Share	Rank	% Share	Rank	% Share	Rank	% Share	Rank
50	Silk	9.31286	5	0.164415	10	0.128423	10	0.643814	9	3.771765	5	1.970008	9
51	Wool	7.900524	3	0.174396	9	10.24551	5	0.214943	10	0.450599	10	4.944907	5
52	Cotton	32.90887	1	21.31231	3	14.79581	3	10.30952	6	17.1439	2	20.21268	2
53	Other vtfibre	4.03085	9	0.0422	11	0.051703	11	11.08845	4	0.323486	11	1.4442	11
54	Man-made filaments	4.456893	8	34.28945	1	33.20759	1	6.521209	7	12.31521	4	16.56501	3
55	Man-made staple fibres	20.97929	2	30.35292	2	24.65622	2	22.41848	2	39.41353	1	38.94775	1
56	Special yarns	1.843512	10	0.805742	8	1.654785	6	10.60104	5	2.972933	8	5.438845	4
57	Carpets, floor coverings	5.2158	6	1.018229	7	0.777627	9	2.366907	8	1.978113	9	2.096217	8
58	Woven fabrics	4.627208	7	7.402522	4	1.138216	8	12.40705	3	3.2774	7	4.01373	6
59	Laminated txt fabrics	1.361745	11	3.125731	5	1.63562	7	0.184657	11	3.70727	6	2.825407	7
60	Knitted fabrics	7.362451	4	1.312094	6	11.7085	4	23.24393	1	14.64579	3	1.641244	10
		100		100		100		100		100		100	
61	Knitted apparel	29.45662	2	31.67062	2	50.27101	1	38.16707	2	60.78925	1	39.18923	2
62	Not-knitted clothing	60.76244	1	62.81057	1	46.7115	2	58.91185	1	33.27267	2	56.3341	1
63	Other articles	9.78094	3	5.518817	3	3.017485	3	2.921074	3	5.938086	3	4.476671	3
		100		100		100		100		100		100	

Source: Calculated from data supplied by the ASEAN Secretariat and from China Customs Statistics Yearbook (various issues).

Table 14.8   Exports of electronics: constant market share analysis, 1992–99

Countries	% Growth	Standard growth (%)		Commodity composition effect (%)	Comparative residual (%)
Indonesia	508.17	NICs	123.67	–41.56	426.06
		China	519.12	–48.03	–37.08
		All	176.63	–49.72	381.26
Malaysia	196.88	NICs	123.67	–14.77	87.98
		China	519.12	29.44	–351.68
		All	176.63	–21.88	42.76
Philippines	433.65	NICs	123.67	12.48	297.5
		China	519.12	–12.07	–73.4
		All	176.63	–0.61	257.63
Singapore	69.42	NICs	123.67	–0.76	–53.49
		China	519.12	542.19	–991.89
		All	176.63	20.35	–127.56
Thailand	138.47	NICs	123.67	–15.49	30.29
		China	519.12	238.53	–619.18
		All	176.63	–10.25	–27.91
China	519.12	NICs	123.67	–20.88	416.33
		ASEAN5	156	–41.39	404.51
		All	176.63	–28.92	371.41

Notes: NICs = Taiwan, South Korea and Hong Kong; 'All' includes the ASEAN5, the NICs and China.

Source: Calculated based on data obtained from Development Bank of Singapore database.

US market due to data availability. However, the US has remained the largest market for Asian electronics. Hence, the overall export performance of ASEAN electronics sector hinges to a great extent on whether they can maintain their export competitiveness in the US market. Three different standard exporters are used to see if the results differ depending on the type of standards used.

Two observations are made on the results shown in Table 14.8. First, China always has positive competitiveness residuals regardless of which standard exporter is used. In contrast, all the ASEAN5 countries always have negative competitiveness residuals, when China is used as the standard exporter. Second, Singapore is the only ASEAN country which has negative competitiveness residuals regardless of which standard exporter is used. The impressive growth of China's electronics exports to the US can further be evidenced by the fact that China's share in the US electronics market has increased from

9.5 percent in 1992 to 21.2 percent in 1999. In contrast, Singapore's market share has plunged from 21.8 percent in 1992 to 13.4 percent in 1999. This is part of the overall trend in China's export orientation towards electronics and machinery exports as resources are diverted from quota-constrained textiles and clothing production towards other manufacturing activities, including electronics and machinery, aided by rapid capital accumulation and foreign capital.

The CMS results, however, are aggregative in nature and may hide differences in export performance for the various components of this sector. This sector is thus subdivided into three major components at the 2-digit HS level: office data and data processing machines, telecommunications and equipment and electrical machinery. It is highly possible that some ASEAN countries can be more competitive than China in certain sub-sectors particularly in higher value-added ones. It should be pointed out that China's export of electronics and machinery have a high import content and are low value-added with the labour-intensive portion of the production process being conducted in China. It is, therefore, not surprising that China dominates the telecommunications and equipment in the US market among the major Asian exporters, as Table 14.9 shows. China's remarkable export performance in these export items was mainly supported by its low labour and land costs relative to the ASEAN countries. In the export of office data and data processing machines, Singapore is the most competitive *vis-à-vis* China and its other regional rivals due to its large favourable industry mix effect reflecting the high concentration of office data and data processing machines, particularly disk drives, in its industrial output. However, China is catching up fast in the export of office machines and data processing machines, which could be largely attributed to China's lower production costs. For example, between 1992 and 1999 the share of office data and data processing machines in China's total exports of electronics to the US increased from 14.9 percent to 36.2 percent, which accounted for 17.0 percent of the total office data and data processing machines exports from Asia – an increase from 14.7 percent in 1998, as can be seen from Table 14.9.

14.3.3 Overall Trade Implications Based on Previous Studies

A number of empirical studies have been conducted to assess the overall economic implications of China's membership in the WTO, using simulation exercises based on computable general equilibrium framework. See, for example, Gilbert and Wahl (2000) for a comprehensive survey of empirical studies using this approach. The general equilibrium approach can complement the partial equilibrium results presented above in two important ways. First, since it is a multi-regional model of world production and trade, it can take into account the overall trade implications (exports to third country markets as well

Table 14.9 *US Electronics imports from Asia: market share (%)*

	Office data and data processing machines		Telecommunications and equipment		Electrical machinery and appliances		Total	
	1998	1999	1998	1999	1998	1999	1998	1999
China	14.7	17.0	38.9	37.8	17.3	18.0	19.8	21.2
Indonesia	1.0	1.3	5.9	5.1	1.4	1.2	2.0	2.0
Malaysia	14.3	15.5	19.1	18.5	15.0	14.6	15.4	15.7
Philippines	5.5	5.2	3.4	2.2	13.6	13.3	8.0	7.6
Singapore	27.5	23.3	2.7	3.0	7.5	6.3	15.9	13.4
Thailand	6.6	5.7	7.2	6.5	5.1	5.0	6.2	5.6
Hong Kong	0.9	0.6	1.5	0.9	5.3	4.5	2.6	2.1
South Korea	7.9	11.4	9.7	14.7	19.3	20.7	12.2	15.4
Taiwan	21.9	19.9	11.5	11.3	16.3	16.5	18	17.1
	100.3	99.9	99.9	100.0	100.8	100.1	100.1	100.1

Note: Figures may not add up due to rounding.

Source: Development Bank of Singapore.

248

as to China) of China's WTO membership. Second, it contains a database for all other sectors not explored in the preceding analysis and, thus, can explore the overall trade implications for other sectors.

Two trade scenarios are usually compared. Scenario 1 (base scenario) captures the trade impact of WTO trade liberalization without China, and Scenario 2 (alternative scenario) captures the trade impact of WTO trade liberalization with China. For each trade scenario the simulation generates results regarding the effects on exports and imports, terms of trade and so forth. The differences between the two scenarios represent the estimates of the impact of China joining the WTO on the other developing countries. The estimates should, however, be regarded as results from controlled experiments, which can provide an indication of the directions of exports, rather than as forecasts.

So far empirical studies examining the likely economic implications of China's accession to the WTO for developing countries based on the computable general equilibrium framework include Bach et al. (1996), Yang (1996, 1999), Wang and Tuan (1996), Wang (1997, 1999), Fan and Zheng (2000), Li and Lejour (2000), Walmsley and Hertel (2000) and Tongzon (2001). Bach et al. (1996) and the two papers by Yang (1996, 1999) used a static model projected to 2005. Wang and Tuan (1996) and Wang (1997) used a 1992 base for their static simulations while Tongzon (2001) used the 1996 database for static simulations. Wang (1999), and Walmsley and Hertel (2000) used recursive dynamic simulation techniques. The remaining two studies used more detailed single-economy models of China.

Three of these recent studies related to the estimation of the trade impact of China joining the WTO are worth noting because some of their findings are directly relevant to the current investigation. A study by Wang (1997) on the impact of China and Taiwan joining the WTO on US and world agricultural trade, using a 12-region and 14-sector computable general equilibrium model for world production and trade, revealed that net exports of labour-intensive products from China could increase dramatically, by about US$40 billion a year. Competition for the world labour-intensive goods market would stiffen, demand for capital and technology-intensive products would go up, causing prices for textiles and apparel to decline and prices for capital- and technology-intensive products to increase worldwide, thus improving industrial countries' terms of trade. On the other hand, since China is a net importer of food and agricultural products, the US would benefit in terms of increased volume and price for US food and agricultural exports. A WTO with China and Taiwan would expand US food and agricultural market shares in Asia, including China, Taiwan, Hong Kong, Korea, and the ASEAN countries, but would reduce exports of labour-intensive products from the ASEAN5 countries. The main focus of this study is its impact on the US economy and particularly in relation to agricultural trade. The study lumped the ASEAN5 countries into one region or grouping and thus failed to indicate the impact on individual ASEAN5 countries.

Another study by Wang (1999), which analysed the impact of China's accession to the WTO on world labour-intensive export markets, has certain findings which address some of the concerns of the ASEAN countries. Breaking ASEAN into four regions (Indonesia, Malaysia and Singapore, the Philippines and Thailand), the study showed a differentiated trade impact on individual ASEAN5 countries of China's WTO membership. Overall, it showed that the impact of China's accession to the WTO on Malaysia and Singapore's exports would be neutral, while the impact for Indonesia, the Philippines and Thailand would be negative. The results of this study provided useful insights in understanding the impact of China's entry to the WTO, particularly in relation to the concerns of the ASEAN countries. However, one could not differentiate the impacts on Malaysia and Singapore separately due to the treatment of Malaysia and Singapore as one region in the simulation exercises. Although there are many trade similarities between Singapore and Malaysia, they are not certainly identical and therefore, the impact of China's accession to the WTO should differ between these two countries.

To address these concerns, Tongzon (2001) adopted similar simulations using the multi-region computable general equilibrium version 4 of GTAP, which includes Vietnam, an important member of ASEAN. Apart from being a flexible model in terms of commodity and country aggregation, this version also allows one to consider Malaysia and Singapore as separate entities. Based on the tariff reductions agreed in the Uruguay Round and China's unilateral tariff reductions consistent with the recently-signed US–China Trade Agreement, the simulation exercises produced for the ASEAN6 countries (Indonesia, Malaysia, the Philippines, Singapore, Thailand and Vietnam) the following results:[2]

- The implementation of the WTO trade liberalization measures would benefit all member countries in terms of overall exports, whether China is in or out of the WTO, mainly due to the greater market opportunities presented by a more liberal world market. However, what China's accession to the WTO does is to reduce the overall export growth for some ASEAN countries as China competes for market access with ASEAN countries.

- In volume terms, total exports for the Philippines and Singapore are expected to decline relative to a liberalized trading regime without China, while the other ASEAN countries' performances such as Indonesia, Malaysia, Thailand and Vietnam are expected to improve.

- For Indonesia, the greatest expansion in exports would be found in paper products, metal and metal products and vegetable oils and fats. Malaysia would experience the largest increase in exports of beverages and tobacco, and vegetable oils while Thailand in vegetable oils, metal and metal products and paper products, the bulk of which would go to China, which is a net importer of these products. With China's WTO membership, ASEAN countries rich in natural resources like wood, rubber, tin, petroleum and palm oil, would take advantage of China's more liberalized market.

- Vietnam's overall volume of exports is expected to increase moderately due to the good export performance of their agricultural and mineral products. The sector whose exports would grow the fastest as a result of China's WTO membership is Vietnam's beverages and tobacco sector, but this sector has a very low base. Vietnam, being a major producer of petroleum, coal, rubber, rice and other agricultural products, would benefit from an expected rise in demand for these products in China. The expected expansion in exports for these products to China would be enough to compensate for the reduction in Vietnam's labour-intensive exports (wearing apparel and transport).

- The Philippines would experience an overall decline in export volume mainly due to a substantial decrease in exports from its leather products and wearing apparel, while Singapore's overall decline could be attributed to a large reduction in leather products, wearing apparel and electronics exports. The expected decline in its main export item, electronics, could be a result of losing to China's electronics sector without any compensating increase in exports from its other sectors. Singapore is getting too expensive to remain competitive as it tries to move up the high-technology ladder. With China's WTO membership, more technology-based industries, such as circuit board manufacturing and assembly are likely to shift their operations over to China where production costs are relatively cheaper. Singapore's services sector would gain from China's entry to the WTO, but its gain would not be enough to compensate for the reduced growth in the electronics sectors on which Singapore's exports are heavily concentrated.

- Unlike in the wearing apparel exports, all the ASEAN6 countries would gain from China's entry in terms of higher export growth for its textile sector, with the exception of Singapore. Thailand would have the highest export gain mainly due to the favourable commodity composition effect as referred to in the previous section.

- Except for Singapore, ASEAN6 countries would experience a terms of trade deterioration. Trade liberalization under the WTO would intensify competition in the market for labour-intensive products – major exports of developing countries – and the inclusion of China in the WTO would further expand production and exports of labour-intensive products in the world market, further reducing export prices for these products. On the other hand, increased production and trade would induce higher demand for capital and skill-intensive products from developed countries. Since the ASEAN countries, except Singapore, are major exporters of labour-intensive products (such as textiles, clothing and miscellaneous manufactures) and major importers of capital and skill-intensive products, they would experience a terms of trade deterioration, as a result of China's entry into the WTO. Singapore would experience a favourable terms of trade appreciation as it is a major producer of capital-intensive manufactures relative to other ASEAN countries. Malaysia's terms of trade are also expected to deteriorate but not as much as other ASEAN countries.

• Using nominal values, instead of volumes, the simulations results generated point to a more optimistic scenario in which all ASEAN6 countries, with the exception of Vietnam, would gain with Malaysia gaining most in exports. However, the trade gains are relatively small in magnitude. It also indicated that ASEAN6 countries with the exception of Vietnam would experience an increase in the value of exports to China at the expense of their exports to the rest of the world, suggesting a change in their trade patterns away from their traditional trading partners towards China.

The above studies have revealed different estimates on trade impacts and welfare implications of China's WTO accession due partly to their differences in tariff reduction assumptions and different levels of aggregation. Further, the magnitudes of trade and welfare estimates associated with China's WTO accession are generally small due to the exclusion of some non-tariff barriers in the estimation in the absence of data and due to the fact that the models can not capture the dynamic implications of trade liberalization. However, they are helpful in giving us at least some indication of the likely direction of the impacts, as well as providing us with common findings, which give us an insight into the probable economic implications of China's WTO accession for the ASEAN countries.

One common finding coming out from all these studies is that China is expected to be the biggest beneficiary from its WTO accession, while the impacts on other developing countries including ASEAN are varied. In terms of the likely effects on production and trade patterns, the results of these studies are also broadly similar. Removal of tariff barriers allows China and the world economy to align their production more closely to the pattern of comparative advantage. Hence, trade liberalization tends to lead to expansion of labour-intensive production in China (textiles, clothing and other light manufactures) and declines in agricultural production. The resulting trade patterns would reflect the internal changes to the Chinese economy – expansion of exports of light manufactures and expansion of imports of agricultural products, the former being destined mostly for the developed world (US, Europe and Japan) at the expense of Southeast Asia. Further, other countries would win or lose depending on whether they are producers of products that China expands its imports of (agriculture and capital-intensive manufactures), or expands its exports of (textiles, clothing and labour-intensive electronics).

It should be reiterated that the results generated here are based on stylized simplification of the world economy and are based on certain *ceteris paribus* assumptions. For example, the model assumes that the projected tariff reductions under the WTO would bring about greater market access while other factors would remain constant. Therefore, the actual numbers reported here need to be interpreted as indicative rather than as precise forecasts.

14.3.4 Impact on Foreign Direct Investment

In the area of attracting foreign direct investment (FDI), China commands an overwhelming advantage over ASEAN. China by itself is a huge market and is endowed with a low-cost and highly-educable workforce. Coupled with economic reforms and the opening up of its market, doing business there has been getting less difficult. Moreover, its political leaders are committed to provide the political will to sustain the wave of reforms and the policy of economic deregulation. As a result, China has matured from 'one nation, two systems' to 'one system, ten nations' – a commonwealth of semi-autonomous self-governing economic regions, which augurs well in generating investors' confidence and in turn attracting the inflow of capital (*The Straits Times*, 2 August 2001, p. 14).

With the return of Hong Kong and Macau to China and under increasing economic integration between Taiwan and China, a *de facto* non-institutional regional grouping has evolved. This trinity has provided investors with a massive market and elevated the attractiveness of China in engendering capital inflows. Trade and investment links between Taiwan and China have been increasing over time, despite the lack of official encouragement from both sides. Attracted by cheaper labour costs in China, the sharing of language and culture and its huge potential market, a large number of Taiwanese manufacturers have relocated their operations to the mainland. In 2000 China absorbed 40 percent of Taiwan's total outward investment and 74 percent of Taiwanese firms had invested in China, an increase over the previous year. Taiwanese investment in China has evolved from the traditional labour-intensive industries to the high-tech and modern sectors such as semi-conductors. In 2000 the electronics industry has accounted for 56 percent of total Taiwanese investment in China, followed by plastics, basic metals and metal products.

China's WTO membership will only reinforce the growing economic integration between Taiwan and China which, with more access to capital, technology and management know-how, could further strengthen its position as a fiercest competitor to ASEAN not only in low-end but also in high-end electronics production.[3] Already, Taiwan's investments in China have hit US$100 billion in the past two decades – attracted to the mainland's cheap land and labour and the ease of communication (*The Straits Times*, 11 August 2001, p. S12).

In stark contrast, ASEAN is an institutional regional grouping with diverse members, cultures and jurisdiction. The onslaught of the recent economic crisis and the resulting political and social instability, particularly in Indonesia and the Philippines – two large members of ASEAN – have further eroded the confidence of investors. The loss of credibility in the ability of ASEAN as an institution to rally the member countries towards a unified approach to deal with external shocks, like the recent Asian crisis, has also made the ASEAN a less attractive destination for foreign investment. All these point to an intensified competition for FDI between China and ASEAN.

It has been argued that an inadequate institutional framework, high inflation and the pervasiveness of bureaucratic red tape and corruption have worked against China. But China enjoys political stability, an effective system of semi-autonomous and self-governing economic regions (such as Shenzen, Shanghai, Dalian, Tianjin, Shenyang and Suzhou) and a stable currency. Further, foreign investors are looking at the long-term benefits of investing in China more than its short-run problems. As a result, FDI has been steadily flowing into China at the expense of ASEAN. As shown in Table 2.5b, the overall ASEAN5 share in total FDI inflows to developing countries has been on a continuous decline since 1987–92 while the share of China has been rising. Specifically, between 1996 and 1997 while the ASEAN share declined from 17.0 percent to 14.2 percent, the share of China increased from 29.7 percent to 39.3 percent. Further, in absolute terms FDI inflows into China have grown consistently for the period 1993–98, averaging 10.8 percent. In contrast, FDI inflows into the ASEAN5 countries declined by 21 percent in 1998 during the Asian crisis. This significant drop in 1998 could largely be attributed to the political uncertainty-induced capital flight in Indonesia, significant FDI reductions in Malaysia and Singapore due to the Asian crisis and the growing investment diversion in favour of China. China was also slightly affected by the Asian crisis in 1998 as manifested in China's share in total FDI inflows to developing countries declining from 39.3 percent in 1997 to 27.4 percent in 1998. However, China's overall share in FDI continued to grow so that from 1988 to 2000 realized FDI in China grew at an average annual rate of 23 percent to reach a cumulative total of US$339 billion, capturing about 70 percent of all FDI in Asia.

Japan Exim Bank survey of Japanese investors has confirmed the trend. China in 1997 retained the top rank as the 'most promising FDI destination' whereas most ASEAN economies had slipped in their ranking. Thailand dropped from second to fourth place, Malaysia from sixth place to eighth place, Vietnam from fifth place to sixth place and Singapore from ninth place off the top 10 list. Only the Philippines has bucked the downward trend with a rise from eighth to seventh place (*Business Times,* 28 December 1997).

The above studies investigating the implications of China's WTO accession have also indicated that the rapid accumulation of capital in China will result in further expansion of Chinese manufactured exports and heavier reliance on agricultural imports as China's comparative advantage increasingly shifts further away from agriculture towards light and heavy manufactures. This change in China's trade patterns is likely to hurt those economies supplying those goods in which China has a strong comparative advantage. Expanding investment into China in response to rapid growth may also raise the price of capital thus adversely affecting net-debtor countries (Gilbert and Wahl, 2000, p. 9).

14.4   CONCLUSION

The trade implications of China's entry to the WTO for ASEAN countries are varied depending on whether or not they continue to rely heavily on clothing and other labour-intensive manufactured exports and on lower-end electronics exports without sufficient agricultural and mineral resource-based exports to depend on. Given China's large pool of educable labour force and with more firms of higher-end electronics continuing to relocate to China for its potentially large domestic market, even the more developed members of ASEAN, such as Singapore and Malaysia, are likely to face increasing competition from China as the latter's high-end sector (that is office data and data processing machines sector) continues to develop aided by continued inflows of foreign capital into China. In the case of those ASEAN countries that are relatively well endowed with agricultural and mineral resources, China's admission to the WTO may not pose a threat to their overall export performance in the short run, but in the long run these countries cannot depend on non-renewable resources like minerals nor can they count on agricultural exports as a reliable source of foreign exchange earnings.

Although the expected static impacts on the ASEAN countries based on simulation exercises may not sound alarming due to the small magnitudes of trade gains/loss estimates, one should not underestimate the potentially significant implications of China's WTO accession for the ASEAN countries' economic future. The dynamic implications of foreign investment diversion may not augur well for the ASEAN region's long-term export growth prospects.[4] ASEAN countries should, therefore, try to maximize the opportunities offered by a more liberalized trading environment and the enormous market potential provided by China. They should also adopt counteractive measures to deal with the growing competition and maintain their attractiveness for foreign investment. These policy recommendations are further discussed in greater detail in Tongzon (2001).

SUGGESTIONS FOR FURTHER READINGS

For a survey of empirical studies using a computable general equilibrium approach relating to trade liberalization in China and their policy implications, Gilbert and Wahl (2000) is recommended. For an empirical study on export competitiveness of China and ASEAN in the US market, see Voon (1998).

NOTES

1. The focus of this analysis will be on ASEAN5 (Indonesia, Malaysia, the Philippines, Singapore and Thailand) due to data unavailability for the other members of ASEAN.
2. The average tariff reductions applied for other regions are 31.7 percent for the US, 41.7 percent for Canada, 25.7 percent for the EU, 30.7 percent for Australia and New Zealand, 35.6 percent for Japan, 30.0 percent for the NICs (minus Singapore), 37 percent for Malaysia and Singapore, 8.6 percent for Indonesia, 12.6 percent for the Philippines, 25.2 percent for Thailand, 10.0 percent for Vietnam, 10 percent for South America, and 10 percent for the rest of the world. Due to incomplete data for the less-developed countries, tariff equivalents of the non-tariff barriers such as quotas and subsidies could not be calculated and the trade implications of removing these non-tariff barriers could not be estimated.
3. Taiwan's high-powered presidential advisory group has recommended dropping a decade-long policy of restrictions on investments in China and lifting a half-century ban on direct economic exchanges across the Taiwan Strait (*The Straits Times*, 13 August 2001, p. 4). Taiwan's Ministry of Finance has already raised the ceiling for China-bound investment from 20 percent of funds raised overseas to 50 percent in May 2001.
4. Singapore and Malaysia in particular are likely to be hurt most given their relatively high dependence on foreign direct investment as an engine of growth.

15. Economic recovery and growth prospects

Chapter 10 described the 1997 Asian crisis and its economic implications for the ASEAN countries. It was shown that the crisis has significantly stalled the economic progress experienced by these countries and set back the economic and social gains they have achieved in the past decades. After two turbulent and devastating years, their economies seemed to have turned the corner. During the years 1999 and 2000, their currencies started to stabilize (except for the June 2000 slide of the Indonesian rupiah), interest rates were much lower compared to their crisis levels, exports were up, and most economic pundits expected another year of positive growth. But the first eight months of 2001 have seen some signs of economic slowdown with weaker export growth for the ASEAN countries. The tragic terrorist attacks of 11 September 2001 have only further dampened the short-term economic outlook for the ASEAN countries.[1] Will the ASEAN countries be able to recover and get back to their pre-crisis growth path? What are the key external and internal obstacles that may threaten their economic recovery and long-term growth prospects? This chapter will try to address these questions as the ASEAN countries are trying to cope with the aftermath of the 1997 economic crisis and the current global slowdown.

15.1 SIGNS OF ECONOMIC RECOVERY IN 1999 AND 2000

Strong signs of economic recovery in the region have emerged for two consecutive years after the end of the crisis. As Table 10.3 indicated, the ASEAN economies, after experiencing negative or low growth rates in 1997 and 1998, started to bounce back to experience positive or higher growth rates in 1999 and 2000, underpinned by robust growth in exports and a restored level of consumer confidence fuelled by lower interest rates and relatively stable currencies. Indonesia and the Philippines, despite the enormous political and social difficulties faced, managed to achieve positive growths. Singapore, which has managed the crisis quite well, enjoyed a remarkable growth performance in 2000, growing by almost 10 percent The transitional economies of

Table 15.1   ASEAN exports of electronics, 1993–99 (US$million)

Exports	1993	1994	1995	1996	1997
Brunei	0.0000	21.97	31.93	32.50	0.00
Growth %			45.29	1.81	(99.99)
Indonesia	1 779.4	2 643.0	3 397.8	4 775.3	4 079.1
Growth %		48.53	28.56	40.54	(14.58)
Malaysia	21 534.3	28 125.6	35 231.3	40 350.4	40 956.3
Growth %		30.61	25.26	14.53	1.50
Philippines	3 814.6	5 324.9	8 074.6	10 264.5	15 702.7
Growth %		39.59	51.64	27.12	52.98
Singapore	41 499.1	57 134.7	67 119.6	74 857.9	82 507.9
Growth %		37.68	17.48	11.53	10.22
Thailand	10 269.2	13 662.5	17 029.2	19 443.5	20 411.6
Growth %		33.04	24.64	14.18	4.98

Sources: IMF, *International Financial Statistics* (2000); ASEAN Secretariat.

ASEAN also saw a continuation of their economic recovery, as their exports and inward investments are linked closely with their Asian neighbours.

15.2   GROWTH PROSPECTS FOR THE ASEAN REGION

After posting an encouraging economic recovery in 1999 and 2000, the region, however, has experienced a marked slowdown at the turn of this new century. Singapore has suffered the largest downturn with an expected negative growth of 1.5 to 2.5 percent in 2001. Despite the announcements by policymakers and multilateral lenders that there will be no repeat of the 1997 Asian crisis, it raises some concern about the sustainability of the 1999 and 2000 economic recovery and about the possibility of another crisis. It is argued that whether the ASEAN countries will have a sustainable economic recovery or experience another crisis would depend on the ASEAN countries' ability to overcome the following key external and internal constraints facing them.

15.2.1   Key External Constraints

The economic pick up in 1999 and 2000 after the 1997 crisis was mainly underpinned by a buoyant electronics market and the continued strength of

1998	1999	1999 US Share (%)	Japan Share (%)	EU Share (%)	ASEAN Share (%)
0.01	0.0035				
177.78	(30.00)	0	0	0	100
3 962.4	4 782.0				
(2.86)	20.68	14.4	14.6	9.6	47.7
43 418.8	51 477.1				
6.01	18.56	26.6	6.1	21.6	25.1
20 817.3	26 586.1				
32.57	27.71	26.4	12.4	20.5	16.2
75 605.7	81 049.3				
(8.37)	7.20	22.6	7.1	15.7	22.8
18 627.2	21 168.8				
(8.74)	13.64	24.8	10.9	18.3	22.8

the US economy. As can be gleaned from Table 15.1, all the hardest-hit countries in ASEAN have shown remarkable export performances in their respective electronics sectors after the crisis years of 1997 and 1998. With the exception of Brunei, which relies heavily on the exports of oil and gas, and Indonesia with its rich natural resources, the electronics sector has remained the largest item in the ASEAN6 countries' export structures and one of the fastest-growing exports for the period 1993–98. The main bulk of Malaysia, the Philippines, Singapore and Thailand's exports are in this category. More than 50 percent of Malaysia, the Philippines and Singapore's exports are accounted for by these exports, as previously illustrated in Table 14.3. Trade in this group of commodity items largely occurs under the umbrella of US-based multinational corporations (MNCs), which explains the bulk of transactions attributed to intra-industry and intra-firm trade between the ASEAN branches of MNCs and associated companies in various parts of the world. Thus, the ASEAN countries' heavy reliance on electronics exports and on the US market has made them highly vulnerable to changes in market conditions in the electronics sectors and in the US economy. The current economic hardships felt in the ASEAN region mainly due to the worldwide slowdown in the electronics market and the US and aggravated by the recent terrorist attacks have illustrated the ASEAN countries' vulnerability in this regard.

The dominance and continued growth of this sector in most ASEAN countries could be mainly attributed to the relocation of lower-end electronics production by export-oriented MNCs taking advantage of the ASEAN countries' relatively low labour costs, available skilled labour and other pro-foreign investment incentives. The attractiveness of these markets in terms of having an abundant supply of educated workforce (the Philippines and Singapore), lower land and labour costs (the Philippines and Thailand) and adequate infrastructure (Malaysia and Singapore) has encouraged MNCs to set up their headquarters and manufacturing operations in this region. On the demand side, continued strong global demand for electronics products, underpinned by the growing services sector and improved living standards, have further stimulated the production of electronic products.

The relocation of these foreign-controlled firms has boosted not only the ASEAN exports of electronics but also the ASEAN imports of electronics because of the sourcing of their raw materials and intermediate inputs from their branches or parent companies. It is, however, important to note that each country specializes in different products within the electronics category. Singapore produces more of office and data processing equipment, while Malaysia and Thailand specialize in telecommunications and sound recording equipment, and the Philippines in the electrical machinery and appliances subcategory.

Second, there is the issue of growing competition in the age of globalization. As capital becomes more mobile and as other newly emerging economies are opening up and getting their houses in order, the ASEAN6 countries are finding the world market and the market for foreign capital increasingly competitive. China in particular and its membership in the WTO will increasingly present opportunities as well as challenges for the ASEAN countries. This issue was already discussed in more detail in the preceding chapter.

Third, the recent economic crisis has put further into question the effectiveness of ASEAN as a regional organization. There was an expectation during the crisis that the ASEAN countries could come up with a concerted approach to deal effectively with the crisis. As seen during the crisis, there were instead different approaches and stands of individual members, which were more concerned about their own domestic economies. In the early stages of the crisis Malaysia resorted to the use of capital controls. In Indonesia the former President Suharto toyed with the idea of a currency board before accepting the IMF programme. In Thailand there were serious disagreements within the cabinet of the then Prime Minister Chavalit Yongchaiyudh on how to handle the Thai economic meltdown. Four months into the crisis, ASEAN finally made a simple announcement that the countries affected should deal with their own problems with help of the International Monetary Fund (IMF) and other donor countries. This lack of concerted approach and ineffectiveness of ASEAN to respond immediately and collectively to the crisis has greatly undermined its international reputation and standing.

In the political sphere ASEAN was accused of being ineffective in preventing the political upheavals in Cambodia that culminated in a coup, and was blamed for the failure to persuade Myanmar to improve on its human rights record, which has seriously affected the grouping's external relations, especially with the European Union. The slow coordinated response to the occasional haze coming from the forest fires in Indonesia with transnational implications has often been cited as a manifestation of the ineffectiveness of ASEAN as a rallying point.

Its ineffectiveness has emanated from its decentralized structure and traditional mode of cooperation. Its highly decentralized structure with no supranational body in charge of enforcing decisions and its adherence to the principle of non-interference in domestic affairs of member countries have slowed its response to certain events that require quick actions. It was, therefore, understandable that no other ASEAN country had voiced any comments on Thailand's precarious economic conditions before the 1997 crisis, or criticized the policies implemented. Any comments would have been interpreted as a violation of this cardinal principle on which the mode of ASEAN cooperation has been based since its existence. Although this principle had served ASEAN well in the past decades, the non-interference principle has not been well equipped or adequate to meet the demands of greater regional integration and to effectively address the new challenges in the twenty-first century.

Thus, whether or not ASEAN as an organization will become relevant and effective in rallying the member countries towards a common purpose in dealing with the challenges facing them would greatly depend on their ability to adopt a mode of cooperation that is appropriate to deal with the changing economic environment. The principle of active engagement, as previously advocated by Thailand and supported by the Philippines, allows member countries to comment on each other's domestic affairs. This is particularly relevant in relation to economic issues with regional implications.

The further expansion of ASEAN with the admission of the transitional countries of Southeast Asia into the grouping, which have different political orientations and levels of economic development, is another major development that might constrain ASEAN to function effectively. The ASEAN countries should find ways to narrow the gaps between the older members and the new members so that the issue of division of gains and costs in the process of trade liberalization can be more easily resolved. Unless this significant divide is narrowed, it would be difficult for ASEAN to move forward in terms of economic cooperation and integration.

The absence of a catalyst to provide a leadership role within the grouping may reduce the pace of economic cooperation in ASEAN. Indonesia, the biggest member of ASEAN, had provided leadership to the organization before the 1997 crisis by providing directions to many activities of the organization. With the enormous internal difficulties facing Indonesia today, it would be unreasonable to expect it to provide the same leadership role. Whether or not one of the other members of ASEAN can provide a leadership role in the post-crisis period will partly determine the future of ASEAN as an effective organization.

There are also key internal constraints specific to the respective countries of ASEAN, in addition to the above key external constraints, which may threaten their continued economic recovery and long-term growth prospects.

15.2.2   Key Internal Constraints

ASEAN6

Thailand   The banking system remains reluctant to provide liquidity to the economic system in the presence of high NPLs and high levels of provisioning. Although there has been a 22 percent decline in Thailand's NPLs from a high of 48 percent in 1999, this decline was attributed to successful loan restructuring by Thai banks through debt rescheduling and transferring of the problem loans to Asset Management Companies – a mechanism used by banks to separate the bad loans from their good assets so as to bring down NPLs on their books (estimated at US$50 billion for the entire financial system).[2] Thailand is also said to be lagging behind South Korea and Malaysia in implementing much-needed financial and legal reforms. The recently revised bankruptcy law needs to be further improved to effectively tilt the resolution process in favour of creditors. The high costs of pursuing bankruptcy actions needs to be brought down. Much has to be done to deal with the problem of politicians having vested interests blocking the reforms to the legal framework. Unless this can be overcome, Thailand's future economic prospects may be severely affected.

Thailand's commitment to privatization seems to be wavering. The sale of key state enterprises in the financial, energy and aviation sectors to private firms is still to be completed. It is important that the new government under Thaksin should press on with the required reforms and ensure that these reforms are effectively implemented, notwithstanding the presence of intra-coalition politics and fiscal constraints.[3]

Temptations to defer further reforms until growth is more firmly rooted should be resisted. Thailand should also start dealing with issues related to its long-term export competitiveness. Although the new government's inward-looking policy has rightly recognized the important role of domestic demand stimulation in its long-term economic recovery and sustainability, it cannot afford to overlook the importance of external trade to its economy.

Indonesia The outlook for a sustainable economic recovery in Indonesia is still highly uncertain, although the political leadership issue has been resolved with the recent installation of Megawati Sukarnoputri as Indonesia's next president. An unstable political and social climate in the country, engendered by ongoing internal political rivalry and strife, longstanding ethnic tensions and the growing unrest in the neighbouring islands of Aceh and Irian Jaya over claims for political independence from Indonesia, are the main reasons behind the country lagging behind the rest of the region in the economic recovery process. Much of Indonesia's recovery prospects lie in the settlement of the current political and social uncertainties and the government's ability to press through with the reforms and resolve the raging demands for political independence from certain parts of the country. Unless these conflicts are resolved, Indonesia's political and social stability will remain in question and this could further slow down the pace of economic recovery from the recent Asian crisis. Apart from these political and social problems, its economic recovery is severely constrained by a huge foreign debt (standing at US$262 billion), which now accounts for roughly 170 percent of its GDP (estimated at US$154 billion for the year 2000). Servicing its debt could become a real headache and limit the government's ability to pursue an expansionary fiscal policy to stimulate growth (as the public sector debt accounts for 58 percent of the total debt).

Indonesia has not substantially benefited from improved international competitiveness gained through the depreciation of the rupiah. This could be accounted for by the almost dysfunctional banking situation that still prevails in the country. Thus, it is crucial that NPLs are reduced and banks are re-capitalized quickly. But the slow asset sales and the high cost of bank recapitalization will further pose a major burden to the government already saddled with significant foreign debt obligations. Due to the massive funds and expertise required, it is important that the country attract sufficient foreign investors. The first step towards this will be to restore confidence in the Bank Indonesia and IBRA.

In corporate restructuring, though new bankruptcy laws are in place and further legal reforms are in the pipeline, weak enforcement has slowed progress significantly. The challenge for Indonesia is to match the new legal framework with a dispassionate and effective enforcement. Moreover, unemployment and poverty escalated in Indonesia during the crisis. This has taken its toll in undermining social security to a certain extent. More formal social safety net arrangements need to be worked out in the long term to ensure minimal disruption caused by social problems to the sustained recovery of the country. But over a quarter of the total budget spending has been allocated to debt repayment so that after allowances are made for investment infrastructure, state salaries and military expenditures, very little is left for social safety nets and other social expenditures.

Malaysia   While signs of export recovery are quite promising for Malaysia, a few outstanding issues remain to be resolved in regards to the future economic prospects of the country after the crisis. First, the future of the capital controls needs to be reevaluated. It was widely accepted that the ringgit was grossly undervalued in real terms. To a large extent, this had helped Malaysia chalk up a trade surplus in 1999 and 2000. However, the benefits of an artificially depreciated real exchange rate are likely to be temporary, as vindicated by this year's trend pointing to an overvaluation of the ringgit in the context of the weaker regional currencies and its marked slowdown in exports. With various other factors to consider, the Malaysian authorities will soon have to choose between a more flexible exchange rate regime, or consider an adjustment of the ringgit. The restriction on outflows of short-term capital by way of a levy imposition has created more administrative hassle and costs to investing in Malaysia and may turn investors away. Further, the imposition of control and the uncertainty of its duration have reduced the predictability of the government's policy.

The second outstanding issue that needs to be resolved is that of long-run competitiveness and productivity growth. Issues related to industrial policy and organization as well as ownership structure needs to be addressed. Currently, internationally competitive firms are largely foreign owned and controlled. To strengthen the local firms to become internationally competitive, changes to allow market forces to play a bigger role in determining ownership and control of wealth are likely to be needed. These, however, do not come easily due to the various underlying social factors.

There is the perennial problem of labour shortage both in the skilled and unskilled categories. As Malaysia tries to move up the production ladder to produce more capital-intensive and knowledge-intensive products for exports, it is constrained by the shortage of skilled manpower. It is crucial that Malaysia can diversify its manufactured exports so that it can reduce its high reliance on labour-intensive electronic exports. Similarly, its recent policy of developing the export potential of their agricultural sector is constrained by the apparent shortage of available labour to work in the agricultural sector. Its current reliance on foreign labour cannot be a long-run solution to Malaysia's skilled and unskilled labour shortage problem.

Although Malaysia was more successful in implementing financial reforms than Thailand and Indonesia, the pace of corporate governance and restructuring has been slow, hampered by nationalist sentiments and political interference.[4]

Singapore   As an open economy, Singapore's economic recovery after the 1997 crisis has been quite phenomenal. After growing by only 1.0 percent in 1998, it bounced back in 1999 and registered a growth of 9.9 percent in 2000 by riding on the wave of electronics boom and the upswing of the US market. But Singapore's ability to sustain its exports and economic growth depends mainly on how it can successfully maintain its shift towards more capital-intensive and knowledge-intensive manufacturing and services in light of its relatively high labour and land costs caused by domestic skilled labour and land shortage. Singapore has been looking out for foreign talents to come and work in Singapore. But in this age of globalization other countries have also been doing the same as they continually face labour supply constraints in their knowledge-intensive sectors. In the increasingly competitive world where knowledge becomes the most important resource, Singapore needs to produce a more creative and entrepreneurial workforce.

Philippines   The Philippines' long-term growth prospects largely hinge on how successfully it can regain investors' confidence after it has been rocked by a number of demoralizing incidents under the previous Estrada administration. The scandal at the stock exchange which led to the fall of the share market, the lack of peace and order in Mindanao and the recent allegations of cronyism, favouritism and graft and corruption under the Estrada administration have driven away a number of existing and potential foreign investors. The peaceful change of government on 9 January 2001, dubbed as People's Power 2, which saw the ousting of Estrada from the reins of power and the installation of Gloria Macapagal-Arroyo as the next President, has restored to some extent the level of investors' confidence in the Philippine economy, as manifested in the recent recovery of the stock market and the stabilization of the Philippine peso after the assumption of the new government under Arroyo. But there are still concerns about a potential destabilization threat from the ousted Estrada and his loyalists, and the ability of the present administration to strengthen the quality of governance and to solve the inherited economic problems including the huge budgetary deficit.[5] The past history has seen how its export performance was tied to the political climate of the day. Although economic factors (such as inadequate infrastructure, inefficient bureaucracy and low level of economic policy effectiveness) will continue to play a significant role as in the past in its development process, political and social stability will continue to emerge as the most important variable.

Brunei   Brunei's long-term growth prospects will hinge mainly on whether or not it can succeed in promoting its services industry particularly in the area of tourism and financial services and its small and medium enterprises (SMEs) in order to reduce its heavy reliance on oil and gas. As discussed in Chapter 2, the government in Brunei has been the main driver of its economy in terms of output and employment generation, and the need to foster the growth of its private sector has long been recognized for its long-term economic recovery and sustainability. The recent financial debacle, which led to massive losses for the government of Brunei, and the increasingly tight financial situation facing the monarchy have but heightened the need for economic diversification. It is, therefore, essential for Brunei to ensure the success of its economic diversification policy by implementing quickly and effectively the necessary measures.[6]

Transitional economies of ASEAN

The economic prospects for the ASEAN transitional economies will hinge mainly on whether they can overcome the basic economic constraints relating to the absence of sufficient capital and human resources, inadequate infrastructure, limited private sector and weak institutions. Because of their similarity in factor endowments and levels of economic development, there is a significant overlapping of constraints among them, although they differ in relative importance.

Myanmar Like other least developed countries, Myanmar's economic performance is constrained by the fact that they are heavily reliant on agricultural products (such as rice, teak, hardwood and pulses) for their exports, which are highly income and price inelastic. Export diversification has been identified as the long-term solution for a sustainable economic growth but this requires foreign capital injections and adequate skilled manpower, which Myanmar is short of. Its private sector is small and weak as Myanmar has a long history of socialism.

It is crucial for Myanmar to attract more foreign capital to assist in its industrialization and export diversification drive in the context of its low domestic savings and growing current account deficit. The current government has been offering generous fiscal incentives for foreign investment ranging from tax holidays for a specific period of time (one year) to accelerated tax depreciation schemes to import tax exemptions for imports required for production. But given the political climate and the current anti-government campaign to boycott and impose economic sanctions on Myanmar for its alleged human rights violations, many prospective investors from industrialized countries have been reluctant to invest to take advantage of Myanmar's abundant natural resources. The continued grip by the military has often been justified on the basis that political stability is needed in the context of existing ethnic rebellion and growing demands for autonomy among various ethnic groups. The current military regime has always maintained that it is determined not to allow a disintegration of Myanmar and thus sees the military control as the only option. However, failure to attract more foreign investment under these circumstances is likely to result in a lower growth path.

Vietnam   The significant pick up in export growth experienced in 1999 is not likely to be sustainable in the long run (in the context of a declining foreign investment and inefficient SOEs) unless Vietnam's domestic private sector can grow sufficiently in size and export orientation. Despite some progress made to develop the domestic private sector, this sector continues to face major constraints affecting their development and expansion, as discussed in Chapter 12.

Laos   Export and market diversification no doubt is the long-term key to achieving a sustainable export growth. A recovery in foreign investment is, therefore, an important element in this strategy. Apart from liberalizing and integrating its economy into the global trading environment, Laos should also achieve and maintain political and social stability and improve its weak and inefficient administrative system.

Currently, flights between Laos and other ASEAN countries are very limited. Direct air services exist only between Thailand and Laos served by only two airlines: Thai airways and Laos national airlines. Flight frequency is limited: only twice a week for Laos national airlines and once a day for Thai Airways. Air fares between these two countries are also rather exorbitant, despite their geographical proximity. These limitations have contributed to making Laos less attractive as a tourist destination.

Cambodia   With the political situation stabilizing, Cambodia can now hope to build its economy by linking it with other economies through trade. Although Cambodia's overall exports may remain robust in the short and medium term as their garment exports continue to enjoy a preferential market access to other industrialized countries, its long-run economic future will depend on how much they can diversify and improve on the quality of their exports. Cambodia's export structure is similar to those of Vietnam, Laos and Myanmar due to their similar factor endowments and similar levels of economic development. It is, therefore, bound to compete with these countries. But in the pursuit of export diversification and product quality improvement, it faces basic constraints. Its infrastructure and distribution networks (especially irrigation system, roads in the countryside and ports) have been ravaged by a long civil war. This makes it extremely difficult to collect and transport the agricultural goods produced in the countryside for export. There is a significant lack of an educated and skilled workforce and apparent absence of local entrepreneurs (capitalists) as many of them were tragically exterminated during the terror years of the *Pol Pot* regime, constraining their ability to move up the production ladder. They are now embarking on a massive infrastructure development programme to rebuild roads and upgrade their ports to allow more ship visits. There is a growing demand for more skills and higher education, but this demand growth is not matched with a sufficient supply of qualified teachers.

15.3   CONCLUSION

Whether or not the ASEAN countries will attain a sustainable economic recovery and enjoy long-term growth prospects will depend on the ASEAN countries' ability to deal with the key external and internal obstacles facing them in the aftermath of the 1997 Asian crisis.

Apart from heavy reliance on electronics exports and the US market, they are facing increasing competition from newly emerging economies. Further, there are major structural weaknesses facing ASEAN as an organization, which need to be addressed to make ASEAN an effective and relevant organization. In particular, ASEAN as an organization has not been quite effective in rallying them towards a coordinated approach in dealing with economic challenges.

Although their currencies are now generally stable and interest rates lower than during the crisis, the structural reforms in the financial sector are still far from over. The task of strengthening their banking sector and improving corporate governance remains unfinished. Although mergers and re-capitalization of banks have proceeded well and non-performing loans (NPLs) have been reduced, the NPLs are still quite high particularly in Indonesia and Thailand. This problem continues to restrict the ability of their financial institutions to provide loans to business enterprises. Indonesia and the Philippines continue to face political and social instability leading to a loss of investors' confidence. While Malaysia's economic fundamentals are getting stronger, she still has to deal with the issue of exchange rate controls, the choice between more flexible and fixed exchange rate regimes and labour shortage. Singapore's long-term economic future largely hinges on its ability to shift its export structure towards more capital and knowledge-intensive manufacturing and towards services. Brunei's limited private sector and heavy dependence on oil and gas exports remain her major source of internal constraints. Moreover, the task of building the necessary institutional framework and improving the corporate governance is a long process.

On the other hand, the main obstacle faced by the transitional economies of ASEAN is its low level of diversification in production and its inability to take advantage of the liberalized markets given their insufficient capital and human resource development, inadequate infrastructure (social and physical), under-developed private sector and weak institutions.

SUGGESTIONS FOR FURTHER READING

For a good analysis of the challenges and prospects facing the ASEAN economies after the 1997 Asian crisis, read Mya, Than (ed.) (2001) and Lim Chong Yah (2001).

NOTES

1. The long-term impact of this tragic event on the ASEAN economies cannot yet be assessed at the time of writing. But its short-term adverse economic implications are already evident. Since the incident, their stock markets have suffered massive losses engendered by a climate of uncertainties while their exports of goods and services, particularly tourism, have further declined. Despite the tight security measures implemented and the assurances made by the governments of Indonesia, Malaysia and the Philippines, the fear that Muslim extremists would retaliate against the Americans and their supporters in these respective countries, as the war against terrorism unfolds, has further deterred to some extent incoming foreign investments and tourists. To avoid their economies sliding further into recession, the governments of Singapore and Malaysia have recently announced a stimulus package to pump-prime their respective economies by lowering interest rates, increasing public spending and providing financial assistance to those hardest-hit business sectors. On the other hand, the US government is seriously designing a stimulus plan to rescue the economy from a steep recession.
2. Thailand's financial sector carried around US$20 billion worth of NPLs at the end of 2000, around half the level seen in mid-1999. Thaksin's new government will set up a new body to remove the remaining bad loans by buying the bad debts from Thai banks financed by way of issuance of 10-year bonds (*The Straits Times*, 16 February 2001, p. S10).
3. Thailand's use of fiscal policy stimulus is constrained by its high public debt (which is currently valued at US$80 billion, accounting for 60 percent of Thailand's GDP).
4. It was reported that the Malaysian government has bailed out several large firms close to the ruling party, which has discouraged foreign investors from doing business in Malaysia (*The Economist*, 9–15 June 2001).
5. The Arroyo administration has inherited a huge budget deficit from the Estrada administration, which was financed by government borrowings. It was estimated that the total public debt upon the assumption of Arroyo amounted to 760 billion pesos (S$29 billion) which translates to an additional 10, 133 pesos per capita debt to every Filipino, to finance the budget deficit arising from declining tax collections and depreciation of the peso (*The Straits Times*, 13 February 2001, p. A5).
6. The most recent measure was the decision to make Brunei an international financial centre to rival existing financial centres in the region such as Singapore, Hong Kong, Sydney and Labuan by capitalizing on its comparative advantages: political stability, lower land costs compared to Hong Kong and Singapore, superior infrastructure, and absence of income tax.

Appendices

APPENDIX 1   ESTIMATION EQUATIONS FOR TRADE CREATION AND DIVERSION

Equations for measuring trade creation and trade diversion effects under the aforementioned assumptions are as follows:

$$dQ_p = \%PX_p\,(1 + Ep)\,Q_p$$

$$dQ_f = \%PM_p\,(1 + Ef)\,Q_f \qquad (A.1)$$

The rate of changes of PXp is measured by:

$$\%PX_p = \frac{n_m + (1-a)E_f \cdot RP}{aE_p(1+RP) + n_m + (1-a)E_f}$$
$$\approx \frac{n_m + (1-a)E_f}{aE_p + n_m + (1-a)E_f} \cdot \frac{RP}{1+RP} \qquad (A.2)$$

The rate of change of *PMp* is:

$$\%PM_p = \frac{aE_p \cdot RP}{n_m + (1-a)E_f(1+RP) + aE_p}$$
$$\approx \frac{aE_p}{n_m + (1-a)E_f + aE_p} \cdot \frac{RP}{1+RP} \qquad (A.3)$$

where

dQ_p = change in the volume/value of imports from the preference-receiving country;

dQ_f = change in the volume/value of imports from the nonpreferred countries;

$\%PX_p$ = proportional change in the preference-receiving country's export price;

$\%PM_p$ = proportional change in the importer's price;

Q_p, Q_f = original volume/value of imports from preferred and nonpreferred countries, respectively;

a = market share of the preference-receiving countries as a group;

RP = rate of preference, that is preference margin as a proportion of c.i.f. value plus preferential tariff;

n_m = price elasticity of the preference-granting country's import demand;

E_p = price elasticity of the preference-receiving country's export supply to the preference-granting country;

E_f = price elasticity of nonpreferred country's export supply to the preference-granting country;

The above equation (A.2) is derived from Figure 3.1, drawn from Kojima (1969) as follows:

$$RP = (P_2 - P_4)/P_4 = AD/P_4 = AE + ED/P_4 \tag{A.5}$$

$$RP = \frac{AE}{ED}\frac{ED}{P_4} + \frac{ED}{P_4}1 \tag{A.6}$$

But,

$$\frac{AE}{ED} = \frac{aE_p}{n_m + (1-a)E_f}(1+RP) \tag{A.7}$$

Substituting (A.7) into (A.6), and solving for ED/P_4, we have

$$RP = \frac{aE_p}{n_m + (1-a)E_f}(1+RP) \cdot \frac{ED}{P_4} + \frac{ED}{P_4}$$

$$= \frac{ED}{P_4}\left[\frac{aE_p}{n_m + (1-a)E_f}(1+RP)+1\right] \tag{A.8}$$

$$ED/P_4 = \frac{RP/aE_p(1+RP)+n_m + (1-a)E_f}{n_m + (1-a)E_f}$$

$$= \frac{[n_m + (1-a)E_f]\cdot RP}{aE_p(1+RP)+n_m + (1-a)E_f} \tag{A.9}$$

The equation (A.3) is derived from the same diagram as follows:

$$RP = [P_2 - P_4]/P_2 = AD/P_4 = ED + AE/P_2 \tag{A.10}$$

$$RP = \frac{ED}{AE} \cdot \frac{AE}{P_2} + \frac{AE}{P_2} \tag{A.11}$$

But,

$$ED/AE = \frac{n_m + (1-a)E_f}{aE_p}(1+RP) \tag{A.12}$$

Substituting (A.12) into (A.11), and solving or AE/P_2, we have

$$RP = \frac{n_m + (1-a)E_f(1+RP)}{aE_p} \cdot \frac{AE}{P_2} + \frac{AE}{P_2} \tag{A.13}$$

$$AE/P_2 = \frac{RP/n_m + (1-a)E_f(1+RP)}{aE_p} + 1 \tag{A.14}$$

$$AE/P_2 = \frac{aE_p \cdot RP}{n_m + (1-a)E_f(1+RP) + aE_p} + 1 \tag{A.15}$$

APPENDIX 2   CONSTANT MARKET SHARE ANALYSIS (CMS)

Constant market share analysis is a means of assessing a country's export competitiveness relative to its competitors. It provides a set of summary statistics indicating whether an exporting country has maintained its market share for all markets or certain markets for all traded commodities or for certain traded commodities over a specified time interval. The method has been frequently applied in the literature on international trade (see, for example, Leamer and Stern, 1970; Richardson, 1971; Van Dijk and Verbruggen, 1981 and Tyres et al., 1986). The essential result is the following identity, which links the change over time in a country's exports, X, to four components, each with its own distinct meaning:

$$(X' - X)/X = r + \Sigma (r_i - r) X_i/X + \Sigma (r_{ij} - r_i) X_{ij}/X$$
$$+ \Sigma (X'_{ij} - X_{ij} - r_{ij})/X$$

where

r = standard growth; $\Sigma \, (r_i - r) \, X_i/X$ = commodity composition effect; $\Sigma \, (r_{ij} - r_i) \, X_{ij}/X$ = market distribution effect and $\Sigma \, (X'_{ij} - X_{ij} - r_{ij})/X$ = competitiveness residual.

X = focus country's exports in the first year;

X' = focus country's exports in the last year of the interval;

X_i = total value of the focus country's exports of commodity i;

X_{ij} = total value of the focus country's exports of commodity i to destination j;

r = rate of growth of standard exporter's total exports;

r_i = rate of growth of standard exporter's exports of commodity i;

r_{ij} = rate of growth of standard exporters' exports of commodity i to destination j;

X'_{ij} = focus country's exports of commodity i to destination j in the last year of the time interval.

The standard growth indicates the general growth of world exports or world exports to the focus destination. It reflects the export growth performance of the focus exporter's competitors.

The commodity composition effect is positive when the focus country's exports are concentrated in commodities the demand for which has been strongest in the focus destination.

The market distribution effect is positive where the focus exporter has distributed its exports to the most rapidly growing centres of demand. Both the market distribution and commodity composition effects depend on the distribution of focus exports in the base year and hence do not take account of change during the interval period.

The competitiveness residual indicates the net gain or loss in export growth of the focus exporter, relative to the standard, after changes in commodity composition and market distribution have been accounted for. The assumption on which the word 'competitiveness' effect is based is that changes in the focus country's share of a particular country's market for a particular commodity take place over time in response to changes in the relative competitiveness of the focus exporter's product. Thus, if this term is positive, the focus exporter is considered to be a strong competitor, out-competing its rivals.

Bibliography

BOOKS AND ARTICLES

Abimanyu, Anggito (1995), 'Source of Indonesian Economic Growth and its Total Factor Productivity', Presented at the 20th Federation of ASEAN Economic Association Conference, 7–8 December, Singapore.

Abonyi, George (1994), 'Challenges of Growth Triangles in SEA for Regional Institutions', Paper presented during the 4th SEA Roundtable on Economic Development, Kuala Lumpur, June.

Ahmed, H. and J.L. Tongzon (1997), 'An investigation of economic linkages among ASEAN group of countries', *ASEAN Economic Bulletin*, **15**(2), 121–36.

Ahmed, S. and J.H. Park (1994), 'Sources of macroeconomic fluctuations in small open economies', *Journal of Macroeconomics*, **16** (Winter), 1–36.

Alburo, F.A., C.C. Bautista and M.S.H. Gochoco (1992), 'Pacific direct investment flows into ASEAN', *ASEAN Economic Bulletin*, **8**(3), pp. 284–320.

Alten, F. (1995), *The Role of Government in the Singapore Economy*, New York: P. Lang Press.

Amsden, Alice (1989), *Asia's Next Giant: South Korea and Late Industrialization*, London: Oxford University Press.

Anderson, K. and R. Blackhurst (eds) (1993), *Regional Integration and the Global Trading System*, New York: Harvester Wheatsheaf.

Ariff, Mohamed (1994a), 'APEC and ASEAN: Complementing or Competing?' in S.Y. Chia (ed.), *APEC: Challenges and Opportunities*, Singapore: Institute of Southeast Asian Studies, Chapter 7.

Ariff, Mohamed (1994b), 'Structural Change, Economic Development and the Role of the State; The Malaysian Experience', in Vu Than Anh (ed.), *The Role of the State in Economic Development: Experiences of the Asian Countries*, Hanoi: Social Science Publishing House.

Ariff, M. and L.H. Tan (eds) (1988), *ASEAN Trade Policy Options*, Singapore: Oxford University Press and ISEAS, pp. 1–37.

Armington, P.S. (1969), 'A theory of demand for products distinguished by place of production', *IMF Staff Papers* **16**, 159–78.

Arndt, H. (1993), 'Anatomy of regionalism', *Journal of Asian Economics*, **4**(2), 271–82.

Arndt, H.W. and Hal Hill (eds) 1999), *Southeast Asia's Economic Crisis*, Singapore: Institute of Southeast Asian Studies.

ASEAN Secretariat (1978), *Ten Years of ASEAN*, Jakarta.

ASEAN Secretariat (1995), *An Overview*, Jakarta.

ASEAN Secretariat (1997), *ASEAN Economic Cooperation: Transition and Transformation*, Singapore: Institute of Southeast Asian Studies.

ASEAN Secretariat (1998), *Hanoi Declaration 1998*, 16th December 1998, *http://www.aseansec.org/summit/6th/prg_hdec.htm*).

Asian Development Bank (1998), 'The financial crisis in Asia', *Asian Development Outlook*, pp. 19–37.

Athukorala, Prema-Chandra and J. Menon (1996), 'Foreign Direct Investment in ASEAN; Can AFTA Make a Difference?', in Joseph Tan (ed.), *AFTA in the Changing International Economy,* Singapore: Institute of Southeast Asian Studies, pp. 76–92.

Austria, Myrna and Will Martin (1995), 'Macroeconomic Instability and Growth in the Philippines: A Dynamic Approach', Presented at the 20th FAEA Conference,7–8 December, Singapore.

Bach, C.F., W. Martin and J.A. Stevens (1996), 'China and the WTO: tariff offers, exemptions and welfare implications', *Weltwirtschaftliches Archiv*, **132**, 409–31.

Bach, C., B. Dimaranan, T. Hertel, and W. Martin (forthcoming), 'Market growth, structural change and the gains from the Uruguay Round', *Review of International Economics*.

Balassa, B. (1978), 'Exports and economic growth: further evidence', *Journal of Development Economics*, **5**,181–9.

Balassa, B. (1985), *Adjustment to External Shocks in Developing Countries*, World Bank Staff Working Paper No. 472, Washington, DC.

Balassa, B. (1991), *Economic Policies in the Pacific Area Developing Countries,* New York: New York University Press.

Balisacan, Arsenio M. (1989), 'Philippine Agricultural Development in Historical Perspective', in M.F. Montes and H. Sakai (eds), *Philippine Macroeconomic Perspective: Developments and Policies,* Tokyo: Institute of Developing Economies.

Balisacan, Arsenio M. (1996), 'Rural Poverty and Access to Land Resources in the Philippines', in M.G. Quibria (ed.), *Rural Poverty in Developing Asia*, Manila: Asian Development Bank, vol. 2, pp. 465–99.

Bandara, J. (1991), 'Computable general equilibrium models for development policy analysis in LDCs', *Journal of Economic Survey*, **5**(1), 3–69.

Bautista, R.M. (1992), *Development Policy in East Asia: Economic Growth and Poverty Alleviation*, Singapore: Institute of Southeast Asian Studies, pp. 1–53.

Baxter, M. and A. Stockman (1989), 'Business cycles and the exchange rate regime: some international evidence', *Journal of Monetary Economics*, **23**, 377–400.

Beason, Richard and David Weinstein (1993), *Growth, Economies of Scale and Targeting in Japan (1955–90)*, Harvard Institute of Economic Research Discussion Paper 1644, October.

Bergsten, C. Fred (1996), 'A New Vision for the World Trading System', Paper presented at the World Trade Congress, 24 April, Singapore.

Beveridge, S. and C.R. Nelson (1981), 'A new approach to decomposition of economic time series into permanent and transitory components with particular attention to measurement of the business cycle', *Journal of Monetary Economics*, **7**, 151–74.

Bhagwati, Jagdish (1968), 'Trade Liberalization Among LDCs, Trade Theory and GATT Rules', in J.N. Wolf (ed.), *Value, Capital and Growth: Papers in Honour of J.R. Hicks*, Oxford: Oxford University Press.

Bhagwati, Jagdish (1991), *The World Trading System at Risk*, Princeton: Princeton University and Harvester Wheatsheaf.

Bhagwati, Jagdish (1996), 'Preferential Trading Areas and Multilateralism: Strangers, Friends or Foes?', Paper Presented at the Staff Seminar, 19 September, National University of Singapore.

Blackhurst, Richard et al. (1995), 'The Uruguay Round and Market Access: Opportunities and Challenges for Developing Countries', in W. Martin and L. Winters (eds), *The Uruguay Round and the Developing Countries*, Washington, DC: The World Bank, pp. 97–115.

Brittan, Sir Leon (1996), 'Expanding World Trade: Challenges for the WTO', Paper presented at the World Trade Congress, 24 April, Singapore.

Brockmeier, M. (1996), *A Graphical Exposition of the GTAP Model*, GTAP Technical Paper, Center for Global Trade Analysis, Purdue University, West Lafayette, IN.

Cabanilla, L.S. (1988), 'ASEAN Cooperation in Food, Agriculture and Forestry: Past and Future Directions', in H. Esmara (ed.), *ASEAN Economic Cooperation: A New Perspective*, Singapore: Chopmen Publishers, pp. 55–68.

Carling, R.G. (1995), 'Fiscal and Monetary Policies', in K. Bercuson (ed.), *Singapore: A Case Study in Rapid Development*, IMF Occasional Paper No. 119, Washington DC.

Chambers, V. (1993), 'ASEAN-EC relations: the intersection of two regional groupings or the rise of economic rivals?', *Journal of Asian Business*, **9**, 55–76.

Chee Peng Lim (1987), 'ASEAN Cooperation in Industry: Looking Back and Looking Forward', in Sopiee Noordin et al. (eds), *ASEAN at the Crossroads*, Malaysia: Institute of Strategic and International Studies, pp. 91–138.

Chee Peng Lim and Jang-Won Suh (eds) (1988), *ASEAN Industrial Cooperation: Future Perspectives and an Alternative Scheme*, Kuala Lumpur: Asian and Pacific Development Centre.

Chee, S. and R.V. Navaratnam (1992), 'The Role of the Public Sector in Economic Growth', in H.Y. Teh and K.L. Goh (eds), *Malaysia's Economic Vision: Issues and Challenges*, Selangor: Pelanduk Publications.

Chenery, H. (1979), *Structural Change and Development Policy*, New York: Oxford University Press.

Cheetham, R. (1998), 'Asia Crisis', Paper presented at the Conference on U.S.–ASEAN–Japan Policy Dialogue. School of Advanced International Studies of Johns Hopkins University, 7–9 June, Washington, DC.

Chia, Siow Yue (1985), 'The Role of Foreign Trade and Investment in the Development of Singapore', in W. Galenson (ed.), *Trade, Foreign Investment and Economic Growth in the Newly Industrializing Countries*, Madison: University of Wisconsin Press.

Chia, Siow Yue (1986), 'Direct Foreign Investment and the Industrialization Process in Singapore', in Lim Chong-Yah and Peter Lloyd (eds), *Resources and Growth in Singapore*, Singapore: Oxford University Press.

Chia, Siow Yue (1992), 'China's Economic Relations with ASEAN Countries', in S.K. Sandhu et al. (eds), *The ASEAN Reader*, Singapore: Institute of Southeast Asian Studies, pp. 340–44.

Chia, Siow Yue (1993), 'Foreign Direct Investment in ASEAN Economies', *Asian Development Review*, **11**(1), 60–102.

Chia, Siow Yue (1995), 'Singapore and Regional Economic Groupings', *Seminar on Singapore Economy in the Asia Pacific*, 31 March, National University of Singapore, Singapore.

Chiew, Eddie (1987), 'ASEAN Cooperation in Food and Agriculture: Looking Back and Looking Forward', in S. Noordin et al. (eds), *ASEAN at the Crossroads*, Malaysia: Institute of Strategic and International Studies, pp. 303–22.

Chin, T.H. and H.G. Ng (eds) (1995), *Economic Management and Transition Towards a Market Economy: An Asian Perspective*, Singapore: World Scientific.

Chinwanno Chulacheeb and Somsak Tambunlertchai (1983), 'Japanese Investment in Thailand and its Prospects in the 1980s', in Sueo Sekiguchi (ed.), *ASEAN–Japan Investment Relations*, Singapore: Institute of Southeast Asian Studies.

Chng, Meng Kng (1985), 'ASEAN Economic Cooperation: The Current Status', *Southeast Asian Affairs*, Singapore: ISEAS.

Chng, Meng Kng (1991), 'A Comparative Study of the Industrialization Experience of ASEAN Countries', in Edward K.Y. Chen et al. (eds),

Industrial and Trade Development in Hong Kong, Centre of Asian Studies, University of Hong Kong.

Chng, Meng Kng (1992), 'Institutional Structure for Enhanced Economic Cooperation', in *ASEAN Economic Cooperation for the 1990s*, A report prepared for the ASEAN Standing Committee, the Philippine Institute for Development Studies and ASEAN Secretariat, pp. 91–105.

Chng, Meng Kng and R. Hirono (1992), 'ASEAN–Japan Economic Cooperation', in K.S. Sandhu et al. (eds), *The ASEAN Reader*, Singapore: Institute of Southeast Asian Studies, pp. 329–34.

Coase, R. (1960), 'The problem of social cost', *Journal of Law and Economics*, **3**, 1–44.

Cooper, C.A. and B.F. Massell (1965), 'Towards a General Theory of Customs Union for Developing Countries', *Journal of Political Economy*, **73**(5), 461–76.

Cooper, R.N. (1985), 'Economic Interdependence and Coordination of Economic Policies', in R.W. Jones and P.B. Kenen (eds), *Handbook of International Economics* vol. 2, New York: North Holland, pp. 1195–234.

Dellas, H. (1986), 'A real model of the world business cycle', *Journal of International Money and Finance*, **5**, 381–94.

Department of Labour and Employment (1995), *The Overseas Employment Programme*, Manila: DOLE.

Development Bank of Singapore (2000), 'Competition among Asian economies' electronics exports: winners and losers', *Asia Economic Briefing*, 1–4 March.

Dewatripont, M. and G. Michel (1987), 'On closure rules, homogeneity and dynamics in applied general equilibrium models', *Journal of Development Economics*, **26**, 65–76.

Dollar, D. (1996), 'Economic reform, openness and Vietnam's entry into ASEAN', *ASEAN Economic Bulletin*, **13**(2), 169–84.

Economic and Social Commission for Asia and the Pacific (ESCAP) (1994), Steering Group of the Committee for Regional Economic Cooperation, Fifth Meeting, 29 August–1 September, Kunming, China.

Economic and Social Commission for Asia and the Pacific (ESCAP) (1995), *Trade Prospects for the Year 2000 and Beyond for the Asian and Pacific Region*, New York: United Nations.

Edwards, Sebastian (1992), 'Trade orientation, distortions and growth in developing countries', *Journal of Development Economics*, **39**, July, 31–57.

Edwards, Sebastian (1993), 'Openness, trade liberalization and growth in developing countries', *Journal of Economic Literature*, **31**, September, 1358–93.

Engle, R.F. and C.W. Granger (1987), 'Cointegration and error correction: representation, estimation and testing', *Econometrica*, **55**, 251–76.

Esfahani, H.S. (1991), 'Exports, imports and economic growth in semi–industrialized countries', *Journal of Development Economics*, **35**, 93–116.

Esmara, H. (1988), *ASEAN Economic Cooperation: A New Perspective*, Singapore: Chopmen Publishers, Ch. 7.

Evers, Hans-Dieter (1995), *The Growth of an Industrial Labour Force and the Decline of Poverty in Indonesia*, Indonesia: Southeast Asian Affairs.

Ezaki, Mitsuo and Sun Lin (2000), 'Trade Liberalization and the Economy of China: A Dynamic CGE Analysis (1997–2010)', Paper presented at the 7th Convention of the East Asian Economic Association, 17–18 November, Singapore.

Fan, M. and Y. Zheng (2000), 'The Impact of China's Trade Liberalization for WTO Accession: A Computable General Equilibrium Analysis', mimeo, Institute of Quantitative and Technical Economics, Chinese Academy of Social Sciences.

Feder, G. (1983), 'On exports and economic growth', *Journal of Development Economics*, **12**, 59–73.

Feder, G., R.E. Just and D. Zilberman (1985), 'Adoption of agricultural innovations in developing countries: a survey', *Economic Development and Cultural Change*, **83**, 255–98.

Feder, G. et al. (1988), *Land Policies and Farm Productivity in Thailand*, John Hopkins Press for the World Bank.

Feldstein, M.S. (1986), *International Debt Service and Economic Growth: Some Simple Analytics*, NBER Working Paper No.2138.

Foundation for International Human Resource Development (1999), 'From Miracle to Crisis: A Summary of the Effects of the Asian Economic Crisis for ASEAN and Indo-China Countries', Paper presented at the Inaugural Leadership Forum, 24–26 February, Imperial Queen's Park Hotel, Bangkok, Thailand.

Fukase, Emiko and Will Martin (1999), 'Evaluating the Implications of Cambodia's Accession to AFTA: A General Equilibrium Model (CGE) Approach', Paper prepared as part of the AFTA Expansion Project, World Bank.

Ghaffar, F. (1996), 'The Southern Growth Triangle: A Recent Form of Malaysia–Singapore Economic Cooperation', Paper presented at the Sixth Malaysia-Singapore Forum, Petaling Jaya, 6–8 December.

Gilbert, J. and T. Wahl (2000), 'Applied General Equilibrium Assessment of Trade Liberalization in China', Paper presented at the Workshop on China's Accession to the WTO: An Overview of Recent Analyses, Beijing, 19–20 October.

Gillis, Malcolm et al. (1996), *Economics of Development*, New York: W.W. Norton & Company.

Godinez, Z.F. (1989), 'Privatization and deregulation in the Philippines: an option package worth pursuing?', *ASEAN Economic Bulletin*, **5**(3), 259–89.

Goh Keng Swee (1977), 'Government Owned Enterprises', Speech given at the Income Annual General Meeting, 20 June, Singapore.

Gonzalez, Joaquin L. III (1995), 'The Philippines Labor Diaspora: Patterns and Trends', Paper presented at the 1995 ASEAN Inter-University Seminar on Social Development, Cebu, Philippines.

Granger, C. (1969), 'Investigating causal relations by econometric models and cross-spectral methods', *Econometrica*, **37**, 428–38.

Granger, C. (1986), 'Developments in the study of cointegrated economic variables', *Oxford Bulletin of Economics and Statistics*, **48**, 213–28.

Greenaway, D. (1993), 'Liberalizing foreign trade through rose tinted glasses', *Economic Journal*, **103**, 208–23.

Greenaway, D. and D. Sapsford (1994), 'What does liberalization do for exports and growth?', *Weltwirtschaftliches Archiv*, Band 130, 153–73.

Greenwood, J.G. (1993), 'Portfolio investment in Asian and Pacific economies: trends and prospects', *Asian Development Review*, **11**(1).

Guilkey, D.K. and M.K. Salemi (1982), 'Small sample properties of three tests for Granger causal ordering in a bivariate stochastic system', *Review of Economics and Statistics*, **64**, 668–80.

Habir, Ahmad D. (1990), 'State Enterprises: Reform and Policy Issues', in Hall Hill and Terry Hull (eds), *Indonesia Assessment 1990*, Political and Social Change Monograph 11, Canberra: Australian National University, pp. 91–107.

Han, Soo Kim and Ann Weston (1993), 'A North American Free Trade Agreement and East Asian developing countries', *ASEAN Economic Bulletin*, **9**(3), March.

Harris, Stuart and Brian Bridges (1983), *European Interest in ASEAN*, London: Royal Institute of International Affairs.

Hashim, Abd Amin Bin Haji (1996), *Foreign Direct Investment and Spillover Effects in Brunei Darussalam*, Masters Thesis. Department of Economics, National University of Singapore.

Hayami, Yujiro, M. Agnes, R. Quisumbing, and L.S. Adriano. (1990), *Towards an Alternative Land Reform Paradigm: A Philippine Perspective*, Manila: Ateneo de Manila University Press.

Herdt, R.W. and C. Capule (1983), *Adoption, Spread and Production Impact of Modern Rice Varieties in Asia*, Los Banos: International Rice Research Institute.

Hertel, T. (ed.) (1997), *Global Trade Analysis: Modelling and Applications*, New York: Cambridge University Press.

Hertel, T. and M. Tsigas (1997), 'Structure of GTAP', in T. Hertel (ed.), *Global*

Trade Analysis: Modelling and Applications, New York: Cambridge University Press.

Hertel, T., E. Ianchovichina and B. McDonald (1998), 'Multi-Region General Equilibrium Modelling', in J. Francois and K. Reinert (eds), *Applied Methods for Trade Policy Analysis: A Handbook*, New York: Cambridge University Press.

Hill, Hall (1988), *Foreign Investment and Industrialization in Indonesia*, Singapore: Oxford University Press.

Hill, Hall (1990), 'Foreign investment and East Asian economic development', *Asian-Pacific Economic Literature*, **4**(2), September.

Hill, Hall (1992), 'Manufacturing Industry', in A. Booth (ed.), *The Oil Boom and After: Indonesian Economic Policy and Performance in the Soeharto Era*, Oxford: Oxford University Press.

Hill, Hall (1994), 'ASEAN economic development: an analytical survey (The State of the Field)', *The Journal of Asian Studies*, **53**(3), August, 832–66.

Hooper, P. and C.L. Mann (1989), *The Emergence and Persistence of the US external imbalance, 1980–87*, Princeton Studies in International Finance.

Huff, K., K. Hanslow, T. Hertel and M. Tsigas (1997), 'GTAP Behavioral Parameters', in T. Hertel (ed.), *Global Trade Analysis: Modelling and Applications*, New York: Cambridge University Press.

Huq, Ataul (1994), *Malaysia's Economic Success*, Malaysia: Pelanduk Publications.

Idem (1974), 'Determinants of DFI', *Philippine Economic Journal*, Third Trimester.

Imada, P., M. Montes and S. Naya (1991), 'A Free Trade Area: Implications for ASEAN', ISEAS Current Economic Affairs Series, ASEAN Economic Research Unit, Institute of Southeast Asian Studies, Singapore.

Ingavata, P. (1989), 'Privatization in Thailand: slow progress amidst much opposition', *ASEAN Economic Bulletin*, **5**(23), 319–35.

Inkeles, A. and D.H. Smith (1974), *On Becoming Modern*, London: Heinemann.

Institute of Developing Economies (1988), *Business Cycles in Five ASEAN Countries, India and Korea*, Tokyo: Insatsu Co.

International Country Risk Guide (1996), **27**(5), May.

Ito, Takatosshi (1998), 'The Asian Financial Turmoil: What went wrong and what have we learnt', Paper presented at the Workshop on the Financial Crisis and Asian Economies, 6 March, Singapore.

Jacobs, R., E. Leamer and M. Ward (1979), 'Difficulties with testing for causation', *Economic Inquiry*, **17**, 401–13.

James, William E. (1983), 'Asian agriculture in transition: key policy issues', *Asian Development Bank*, September.

James, W.E., S. Naya and G.M. Meier (1989), *Asian Economic Development:*

Economic Success and Policy Lessons, Madison, WI: University of Wisconsin Press, Chapter 1.

Johnson, B.F. and T.P. Tomich (1985), 'Agricultural strategies and agrarian structure', *Asian Development Review*, **3**(2), 1–37.

Johnson, Chalmers (1982), *MITI and the Japanese Miracle*, Stanford University Press.

Johnson, Harry G. (1958), *International Trade and Economic Growth: Studies in Pure Theory*, London: Allen & Unwin.

Johnson, Harry G. (1965), 'An economic theory of protectionism, tariff bargaining and the formation of customs unions', *Journal of Political Economy*, **73** (June), 256–83.

Jomo, K.S. (1991), 'Whither Malaysia's new economic policy?', *Pacific Affairs*, **63**(4), 469–99.

Jomo, K.S. (1994), 'Privatization' in K.S. Jomo (ed.), *Malaysia's Economy in the Nineties*, Malaysia: Pelanduk Publications.

Jomo, K.S. and C. Edwards (1993), 'Malaysian Industrialization in Historical Perspective', in K.S. Jomo (ed.), *Industrializing Malaysia: Policy, Performance and Prospects*, London: Routledge.

Jung, W.S. and P.J. Marshall (1985), 'Exports, growth and causality in developing countries', *Journal of Development Economics*, **18**, 1–13.

Kavoussi, R. (1984), 'Export expansion and economic growth: further empirical evidence', *Journal of Development Economics*, **14**, 241–50.

Kawai, H. (1994), 'International comparative analysis of economic growth: trade liberalization and productivity', *The Developing Economies*, **32**(4), 373–97.

Keefer, P. and S. Knack (1993), 'Why Don't Poor Countries Catch Up? A Cross-National Test of An Institutional Explanation', Center for Institutional Reform and the Informal Sector, University of Maryland at College Park.

Kemp, M.C. (1962), 'The gain from international trade', *Economic Journal*, **72** (December), 803–19.

Khin Khin Myint Jensen (1956), 'The Chinese in the Philippines During the American Regime: 1896–1946', Ph.D. Thesis, University of Wisconsin.

Knetsch, J.L. (1990), 'Environmental policy implications of disparities between willingness to pay and compensation demanded measures of values', *Journal of Environmental Economics and Management*, **18**, 227–37.

Kojima, K. (1969), 'Trade preferences for developing countries: a Japanese assessment', *Hitotsubashi Journal of Economics*, **20**, February, 1–12.

Kreinin, M. and M. Plummer (1992), 'Effects of economic integration in industrial countries on ASEAN and the Asian NIEs', *World Development*, **20**(9), 1345–66.

Kreinin, M. and M. Plummer (1998), 'Ex-post estimates of the European Single Market Programme on the exports of developing countries', *ASEAN Economic Bulletin*, **15**(2), 206–14.

Krishna, Pravin and Jagdish Bhagwati (1994), 'Necessarily Welfare-enhancing Customs Unions with Industrialization Constraints: A Proof of the Cooper–Massell–Johnson–Bhagwati Conjecture', Columbia University Working Papers, April.

Krongkaew, M. (1994), 'Income distribution in East Asian developing countries: an update', *Asian Pacific Economic Literature*, **8**(2), November, 58–70.

Krugman, Paul (1979), 'A model of balance of payments crises', *Journal of Money, Credit and Banking*, **11**, 311–25.

Krugman, Paul (1998), 'What Happened to Asia?', Manuscript, MIT, January, (http://web.mit.edu/krugman/www/).

Kumar, Sree (1992), 'Assessing AFTA', in K.S. Sandhu et al. (eds), *The ASEAN Reader*, Singapore: Institute of Southeast Asian Studies, pp. 516–18.

Kuyly, Keo (1998), 'The Impact of the Asian Economic Crisis on Cambodia's Economy', Paper presented at the Regional Workshop on The Impact of the Asian Economic Crisis on the GMS Economies, 23–27 November 1998, Thammasat University, Bangkok, Thailand.

Le, Vu Khanh (1995), 'Vietnam Opens Up the Economy, Joins ASEAN and International Trade', Paper presented at the Seminar on Regional Economic Integration: AFTA and APEC Perspective-Implications for Vietnam, Hanoi (4–5 December) and Ho Chi Minh (7–8 December).

Leamer, E.E. and R.M. Stern (1970), *Quantitative International Economics*, Boston: Allyn and Bacon.

Ledesma, A.J. (1982), *Landless Workers and Rice Farmers: Peasant Subclasses Under Agrarian Reform in Two Philippine Villages*, Los Banos: International Rice Research Institute.

Lee, Hwee Chen and Tilak Abeysinghe (1999), *Singapore's Cost Competitiveness in the Region Before and After the Crisis* (unpublished), Department of Economics, National University of Singapore.

Lee, Tsao Yuan (1990), 'An overview of the ASEAN economies', *Singapore Economic Review*, **35**(1), 16–37.

Lee, Tsao Yuan (ed.) (1991), *Growth Triangle*, Singapore: Institute of Southeast Asian Studies.

Leightner, Jonathan E. (1999), 'Globalization and Thailand's Financial Crisis', *Journal of Economic Issues*, **33**(2), 367–73.

Levine, Ross and David Renelt (1992), 'A sensitivity analysis of cross-country growth regressions', *American Economic Review*, **82**, September, 942–63.

Lewis, W.A. (1955), *The Theory of Economic Growth*, London: Allen and Unwin.

Li, X. and A. Lejour (2000), 'The Sectoral Impact of China's Access to the WTO: A Dynamic CGE Analysis', mimeo, Netherlands Bureau for Economic Policy Analysis and Institute for Quantitative and Technical Economics.

Lim Chong Yah and Associates (1988), *Policy Options for the Singapore Economy*, Singapore: McGraw-Hill.

Lim Chong Yah (1991), *Development and Underdevelopment*, Singapore: Longman Publications, pp. 197–214.

Lim Chong Yah (2001), *Southeast Asia: The Long Road Ahead*, Singapore: World Scientific Publishing Co.

Lim, David (1996), *Explaining Economic Growth: A New Analytical Framework*, Aldershot, UK: Edward Elgar.

Limskul, Kitti (1995), 'Sources of Economic Growth and Development in Thailand', Paper presented at the 20th Federation of ASEAN Economic Associations Conference, 7–8 December, Singapore.

Lipsey, Richard (1957), 'The theory of customs unions: trade diversion and welfare', *Economica*, **24**, 40–46.

Lipsey, Richard (1960), 'The theory of customs unions: a general survey', *Economic Journal*, **70**, 498–513.

Lopez-Mejia, A. (1999), 'Large Capital Flows: A Survey of the Causes, Consequences and Policy Responses', Working Paper No. 99/17, IMF.

Low, L. (1991), *The Political Economy of Privatization in Singapore*, Singapore: McGraw-Hill.

Low, L. and M.H. Toh (1989), 'Economic Outlook: ASEAN 1993/94', in H. Osada and D. Hiratsuka (eds), *Business Cycles in Five ASEAN Countries, India and Korea*, Tokyo: Institute of Developing Economies.

MacKinnon, J. (1990), 'Critical Values For Cointegration Tests', Working paper, University of California, San Diego.

Maddison, A. (1970), *Economic Progress and Policy in Developing Countries*, London: Allen and Unwin.

Mahathir, Mohamad (1970), *The Malay Dilemma*, Kuala Lumpur: Federal Publications.

Mangahas, M. (1985), 'Rural Poverty and Operation Land Transfer in the Philippines', in R. Islam (ed.), *Strategies for Alleviating Poverty in Rural Asia*, Dhaka and Bangkok: Bangladesh Institute for Development Studies and International Labour Organization.

Martin, Will and L. Alan Winters (eds) (1995), *The Uruguay Round and the Developing Economies*, World Bank Discussion Papers, Washington, DC: The World Bank.

McClelland, D.C. (1961), *The Achieving Society*, New York: Van Nostrand.

McVey, Ruth (ed.)(1992), *Southeast Asian Capitalists*, New York: Southeast Asia Programme, Cornell University.

Meade, Edward James (1955), *The Theory of Customs Union*, Amsterdam: North-Holland.

Meade, Edward James (1956), *A Geometry of International Trade*, London: G. Allen & Unwin.

Menon, J. (1997), *Lao PDR in the ASEAN Free Trade Area: Trade, Revenue and Investment Implications*, Research Monograph No. 97–101. Melbourne: Centre for Policy Studies, Monash University.

Meyanathan, S. and I. Haron (1987), 'ASEAN Trade Cooperation: A Survey of the Issues', in Sopiee Noordin et al. (eds), *ASEAN at the Crossroads*, Malaysia: Institute of Strategic and International Studies, pp. 13–38.

Michaely, M. (1977), 'Exports and growth: an empirical investigation', *Journal of Development Economics*, **4**, 49–53.

Michalopolous, C. and K. Jay (1973), 'Growth of Exports and Income in the Developing World', AID Discussion Paper 28, Washington, DC.

Min Tang and Myo Thant (1993), 'Growth Triangles: Conceptual Issues and Operational Problems', Paper presented at the Workshop on Growth Triangles in Asia, ADB, Manila, February.

Mohamed, Rugayah (1994), 'Public Enterprises', in K.S. Jomo (ed.), *Malaysia's Economy in the Nineties*, Malaysia: Pelanduk Publications.

Montes, Manuel F. (1998), *The Currency Crisis in Southeast Asia* (updated edition), Singapore: Institute of Southeast Asian Studies.

Mookerjee, R. and J. Tongzon (1997), 'Small open economies and business cycles: evidence from the ASEAN group of countries', *Journal of Asia Pacific Economy*, **2**(1), 58–81.

Moreno, R. (1995), 'Macro-economic behaviour during periods of speculative pressure or realignment: evidence from Pacific Basin economies', *Federal Reserve Bank of San Francisco Economic Review*, pp. 3–15.

Mya, Than (1992), 'ASEAN, IndoChina and Myanmar', in S.K. Sandhu et al. (eds), *The ASEAN Reader*, Singapore: Institute of Southeast Asian Studies, pp. 344–51.

Mya, Than (ed.) (2001), *ASEAN Beyond the Regional Crisis: Challenges and Initiatives*, Singapore: Institute of Southeast Asian Studies.

Myers, Norman (1988), 'Tropical deforestation and climatic change', *Environmental Conservation*, **15**(4), 293–8.

Myo Thant (1998), 'Regionalization Drive in Asia: Government Initiatives, Private Sector Participation and Foreign Direct Investment', Paper presented at the Joint International Conference on The New Role of Government in a Market Economy, 5–6 February, Singapore.

Myo Thant and Min Tang (eds)(1996), *Indonesia–Malaysia–Thailand Growth Triangle: Theory to Practice*, Manila: Asian Development Bank.

Nadal De Simone, F. (1995), 'Macroeconomic perspective of AFTA's problems and prospects', *Contemporary Economic Policy*, April, 49–62.

Nadal De Simone, F. and Jose Tongzon (1997), 'Is there a business cycle in Singapore? Is there a Singaporean business cycle?', *Atlantic Economic Journal*, **25**(1), 60–79.

Naidu, G. (1988), 'ASEAN Cooperation in Transport', in H. Esmara (ed.), *ASEAN Economic Cooperation: A New Perspective*, Singapore: Chopmen Publishers, pp. 191–227.

Navaratnam, R.V. (1987), 'ASEAN Cooperation in Transportation: Looking Back and Looking Forward', in S. Noordin et al.(eds), *ASEAN at the Crossroads*, Malaysia: Institute of Strategic and International Studies, pp. 357–69.

Naya, Seiji (1987), 'Economic Performance and Growth Factors of the ASEAN Countries', in Linda G. Martin. (ed.), *ASEAN Success Story: Social, Economic and Political Dimensions*, Honolulu: East-West Centre, pp. 47–87.

Naya, S. and C. Barretto (1994), 'Future Prospects for the ASEAN Free Trade Area', Paper presented at the WEA International Conference, 8–13 January.

Naya, Seiji and P. Imada (1990), 'Trade and Investment Linkage in ASEAN Countries', in Soon Lee Ying (ed.), *Foreign Direct Investment in ASEAN*, Honolulu: East-West Centre.

Naya, Seiji and P. Imada (1992), 'Implementing AFTA', in K.S. Sandhu et al. (eds), *The ASEAN Reader*, Singapore: Institute of Southeast Asian Studies, pp. 513-15.

Naya, Seiji, K.S. Sandhu, M. Plummer and N. Akrasanee (1992), 'ASEAN–US Initiative', in K.S. Sandhu et al. (eds), *The ASEAN Reader*, Singapore: Institute of Southeast Asian Studies, pp. 321–8.

Nelson, C.R. and C.I. Plosser (1982), 'Trends and random walks in macroeconomic time series', *Journal of Monetary Economics*, **10**, 139–62.

Ng, Chee Yuan and K.W. Toh (1992), 'Privatization in the Asian Pacific region', *Asian Pacific Economic Literature*, **6**(2), 42–68.

Ng, Chee Yuan and Norbert Wagner (eds) (1991), *Marketization in ASEAN*, Singapore: Institute of Southeast Asian Studies.

Ng, Sai Cheong (1994/95), 'Vietnam as a Transitional Economy: Problems and Opportunities', Honours Thesis, Department of Economics, National University of Singapore.

Nijathaworn, B. (1993), 'Managing Foreign Capital in a Rapidly Growing Economy: Thailand's Recent Experience and Issues', Paper presented at the International Conference on the Asia Pacific Economy, 25–28 August, Cairns, Australia, pp. 18–19.

Obstfeld, M. (1986), 'Rational and self-fulfilling balance of payments crises', *American Economic Review*, March.

Okamoto, Yumiko and Fredrik Sjoholm (1999), 'Protection and the Dynamics of Productivity Growth: The Case of Automotive Industries in Indonesia', Working Paper No. 324, Working Paper Series in Economics and Finance, Stockholm School of Economics, Sweden.

Ooi Guat Tin (1987), 'ASEAN Preferential Trading Arrangements: An Assessment', in Sopiee Noordin et al. (eds), *ASEAN at the Crossroads*, Malaysia: Institute of Strategic and International Studies, pp. 55–61.

Osada, H. and D. Hiratsuka (eds)(1989), *Business Cycles in Five ASEAN Countries, India and Korea*, Tokyo: Institute of Developing Economies.

Oshima, H. (1993), *Strategic Processes in Monsoon Asia's Economic Development*, London: John Hopkins University Press.

Osman-Rani, H. (1985), 'New Directions in Industrialization: Some Strategic Issues', in K.S. Jomo (ed.), *Malaysia's New Economic Policies*, Kuala Lumpur: Malaysian Economic Association.

Otsuka, K. (1991), 'Determinants and consequences of land reform implementation in the Philippines', *Journal of Development Economics*, **35**, 339–55.

Pangestu, Mari (1996), 'The Role of the State and Economic Development in Indonesia', in M. Pangestu (ed.), *Economic Reform, Deregulation and Privatization*, Jakarta: Centre for Strategic and International Studies, pp. 96–132.

Pasadilla, Gloria and Cid Terosa (1999), 'Social Impact of the Asian Crisis in the Philippines', Paper presented at the 74th Annual Western Economics Association International Conference, 6–10 July, Sheraton Harbor Island, San Diego, California.

Parsonage, James (1994), 'The State and Globalisation: Singapore's Growth Triangle Strategy', Working Paper No.23, Asia Research Centre on Social, Political and Economic Change, Murdoch University, Western Australia, February, pp. 5–7.

Pearce, D. and R. Turner (1990), *Economics of Natural Resources and the Environment*, Baltimore: Johns Hopkins Press, Chapters 4–7.

Peebles, Gavin and Peter Wilson (1996), *The Singapore Economy*, Aldershot, UK: Edward Elgar, pp. 200–210.

Perkins, D.H. (1994), 'There are at least three models of East Asian development', *World Development*, **22**(4), 655–61.

Perry, M. and C. Grundy-Warr (1996), 'Growth Triangles, International Economic Integration and the Singapore-Indonesian Border Zone', in D. Rumley (ed.), *Global Geopolitical Change and the Asia Pacific: A Regional Perspective*, London: Avebury.

Phang Sock Yong (1993), 'Singapore's motor vehicle policy: review of recent changes and a suggested alternative', *Transportation Research* (A), July, 329–36.

Piei, Mohd. Haflah and Noor Aini Khalifah (1996), 'Vietnam in ASEAN: trade, investment and other effects', *ASEAN Economic Bulletin*, **13**(2), 200–211.

Pomfret, Richard (1994), 'Strategic Trade and Industrial Policy as an Approach to Locational Competitiveness: What Lessons for Asia?', Paper presented at the 1994 Kiel Week Conference on Locational Competition in the World Economy, Institut fur Weltwirtschaft, Kiel, Germany, 22–23 June.

Puntasen, Apichai (1988), 'ASEAN Cooperation in Tourism', in H. Esmara (ed.), *ASEAN Economic Cooperation: A New Perspective*, Singapore: Chopmen Publishers, pp. 205–27.

Pupphavesa, W. and M. Geeve (1994), 'AFTA and NAFTA: Complementing or Competing?', in S.Y. Chia (ed.), *APEC: Challenges and Opportunities*, Singapore: Institute of Southeast Asian Studies, Chapter 8.

Pussarangsri, B. and S. Chamnivickorn (1995), 'Trade Liberalization and FDI Policies of ASEAN Countries', Paper presented at the 20th Federation of ASEAN Economic Associations Conference, Singapore, 7–8 December.

Quibria, M.G. (ed.) (1996), *Rural Poverty in Developing Asia*, vol.2, Manila: Asian Development Bank.

Radelet, Steven and Jeffrey Sachs (1998), 'The Onset of the East Asian Financial Crisis', Manuscript, Harvard Institute for International Development, March, (http://www.hiid.harvard.edu/pub/other/).

Ramstetter, E.D. (1993), 'Prospects for foreign firms in developing economies of the Asia and Pacific region', *Asian Development Review*, **11**(1), 151–85.

Rao, Bhanoji (1998), 'East Asian economies: the crisis of 1997–98,' *Economic and Political Weekly*, **33**(23), 397–1416.

Rao, B. and C. Lee (1995), 'Sources of Growth in the Singapore Economy and its Manufacturing and Service Sectors', Paper presented at the 20th Federation of ASEAN Economic Associations Conference, Singapore, 7–8 December.

Richardson, J.D. (1971), 'A constant market share analysis of export growth', *Journal of International Economics*, **1**, 227–39.

Riedel, James (1988), 'Economic Development in East Asia: Doing What Comes Naturally?', in Helen Hughes (ed.), *Achieving Industrialization in East Asia*, Cambridge, UK: Cambridge University Press, pp. 1–38.

Rieger, H.C. (1985), *ASEAN Cooperation and intra-ASEAN Trade*, Singapore: Institute of Southeast Asian Studies.

Rieger, H.C. (1992), 'ASEAN–EC Economic Cooperation', in S.K. Sandhu et al. (eds) (1992), *The ASEAN Reader*, Singapore: Institute of Southeast Asian Studies, pp. 335–39.

Romer, Paul R. (1994), 'New goods, old theory and the welfare costs of trade restrictions', *Journal of Development Economics*, **43**, 5–38.

Ronnas, P. (1992), *Employment Generation Through Private Entrepreneurship in Vietnam*, Asian Regional Team for Employment Promotion (ARTEP), International Labour Organization.

Rostow, W.W. (1952), *The Process of Economic Growth*, New York: Norton.

Samuelson, P.A. (1939), 'Gains from international trade', *Canadian Journal of Economics and Political Science*, **5** (May), 195–205.

Sandhu, K. et al. (eds) (1992), *The ASEAN Reader*, Singapore: ISEAS, pp. xxvii–xxii, 3–49, 50–82, 242–53, 260–64.

Sathiendrakumar, R. (1993), 'Economic Evaluation of Alternative Policy Options Available to Control Fund Pollutants', Paper presented at the Staff Seminar, Department of Economics and Statistics, January 28 (mimeo).

Saw Swee-Hock (1980), 'ASEAN Economic Cooperation', in Saw Swee-Hock (ed.), *ASEAN Economies in Transition*, Singapore University Press, pp. 322–36.

Schultz, Siegfried (1996), 'Regionalism of World Trade: Dead End or Way Out?', in M.P. Van Dijk and S. Sideri (eds), *Multilateralism versus Regionalism: Trade Issues After the Uruguay Round*, London: Frank Cass & Co. Ltd.

Schulze, David (1988), 'ASEAN Cooperation in Banking and Finance', in H. Esmara (ed.), *ASEAN Economic Cooperation: A New Perspective*, Singapore: Chopmen Publishers, pp. 157–89.

Seda, Maria (ed.) (1993), *Environmental Management in ASEAN: Perspectives on Critical Regional Issues*, Singapore: Institute of Southeast Asian Studies.

Senhadji, A.S. (1997), 'Two common problems related to the use of the Armington aggregator in computable equilibrium models', *Applied Economics Letters*, **4**(1), 23–5.

Shaikh, A.H. (1992), 'Malaysia's public enterprises: a performance evaluation', *ASEAN Economic Bulletin*, **9**(2), 207–18.

Shoven, J. and J. Whalley. (1992), *Applying General Equilibrium*, New York: Cambridge University Press.

Snodgrass, D.R. (1980), *Inequality and Economic Development in Malaysia*, Petaling Jaya: Oxford University Press.

Srinivasan, T. and J. Whalley (eds) (1986), *General Equilibrium Trade Policy Modelling*, Cambridge, MA: MIT Press.

Tambunlertchai, Somsak (1993), 'Manufacturing' in P. Warr (ed.), *The Thai Economy in Transition*, Cambridge: Cambridge University Press.

Tan, Gerald (1987), 'ASEAN Preferential Trading Arrangements: An Overview', in Sopiee Noordin et al. (eds), *ASEAN at the Crossroads*, Malaysia: Institute of Strategic and International Studies, pp. 63–9.

Tan, Gerald (1996), *ASEAN Economic Development and Cooperation*, Singapore: Times Academic Press.

Tan Kong Yam, M.H. Toh and L. Low (1992) 'ASEAN and Pacific Economic Cooperation', in K.S. Sandhu et al. (eds), *The ASEAN Reader*, Singapore: Institute of Southeast Asian Studies, pp. 311–20.

Teh, Robert R. (1999), 'Completing the CEPT Scheme for AFTA', Paper submitted for seminar-workshop on *Beyond AFTA and Towards an ASEAN Common Market*, 18–20 October, Manila.

Tham Siew Yean (1995), 'Productivity, Growth and Development in Malaysia', 20th Federation of ASEAN Economic Association (FAEA) Conference, Singapore, 7–8 December.

Thambipillai, Pushpa (1995), 'The East ASEAN Growth Area: Political and Economic Environment', Presented at the EAGA Forum in conjunction with the EAGA EXPO, Bandar Seri Begawan, 2–3 November.

Thee Kian Wie (1991), 'The surge of Asian NIC investment into Indonesia', *Bulletin of Indonesian Economic Studies*, **27**(3), 55–88.

Todaro, Michael P. (1997), *Economic Development in the Third World*, Sixth edition, New York: Addison-Wesley Publishing Company, Chapter 10.

Toh Mun Heng and Linda Low (eds) (1993), *Regional Cooperation and Growth Triangles in ASEAN*, Singapore: Times Academic Press.

Toh Mun Heng and Linda Low (1994), 'Capital Stock, Latent Resource and Total Factor Productivity in Singapore', Paper presented at the Workshop on Measuring Productivity and Technological Progress, Faculty of Business Administration, National University of Singapore, August.

Tongzon, Jose (1986), 'Australian trade preferences for developing countries: are quotas necessary?', *Economic Papers*, **5**(3), pp. 53–64.

Tongzon, J.L. (1999), 'The challenge of regional economic integration: the Vietnamese perspective', *The Developing Economies*, **3** (2), 137–61.

Tongzon, J.L.(2001), 'China's membership in the WTO and the exports of the developing economies of East Asia: a computable general equilibrium approach', *Applied Economics* **33**(15), 1943–59.

Tongzon, J.L. and S. Ganesalingam (1994), 'An evaluation of ASEAN port performance and efficiency', *Asian Economic Journal*, **8**(3), 317–30.

Tongzon, J.L. and T.K. Loh (1995), 'Trade Liberalizaton and Growth: The ASEAN4 Experience', Singapore (unpublished typescript).

Triandis, H.C. (1971), 'Some Psychological Dimensions of Modernization', Proceedings of the 17th International Congress of Applied Psychology, Brussels, vol. 2, 56–75.

Triandis, H.C. (1973), 'Subjected Culture and Economic Development', *International Journal of Psychology*, **8**,163–80.

Tsao, Yuan (1986), 'Sources of Growth Accounting for the Singapore Economy', in Lim Chong-Yah and Peter Lloyd (eds), *Resources and Growth in Singapore*, Singapore: Oxford University Press.

Tyler, W. (1981), 'Growth and Export Expansion in Developing Countries:

Some Empirical Evidence', *Journal of Development Economics*, **9**, 121–30.

Tyres, R., P. Phillips and C. Findlay (1986), 'ASEAN and China exports of labour-intensive manufactures: performance and prospects', *ASEAN Economic Bulletin*, **3**(3), 339–66.

United Nations Economic and Social Commission for Asia and the Pacific (1994), *Review and Analysis of Intraregional Trade Flows in Asia and the Pacific*. Note by the Secretariat. Steering Group of the Committee for Regional Economic Cooperation, Fifth Meeting, 29 August–1 September, Kunming, China.

Van Dijk, P. and H. Verbruggen (1981), 'A Constant Market Shares Analysis of ASEAN Manufactured Exports to the EEC', Paper presented to the Conference on ASEAN–EEC Relations, Institute of Southeast Asian Studies, Singapore, 6–8 August.

Viner, Jacob (1950), *The Customs Union Issue*, New York: Carnegie Endowment for International Peace.

Voon, J. (1998), 'Export competitiveness of China and ASEAN in the US market', *ASEAN Economic Bulletin*, **14**(3), 273–91.

Vyas, V.S. (1983), 'Asian agriculture: achievements and challenges', *Asian Development Review*, **1**(2), 27–44.

Wade, Robert (1990), *Governing the Market: Economic Theory and Taiwan's Industrial Policies*, New Jersey: Princeton University Press.

Walmsley, T. and T. Hertel (2000), 'China's Accession to the WTO: Timing is Everything', Paper presented at the International Conference on Global Economic Transformation After the Asian Economic Crisis, Hong Kong.

Wang, Zhi (1997), 'China and Taiwan access to the World Trade Organization: implications for US agriculture and trade', *Agricultural Economics*, **17**, 239–64.

Wang, Zhi (1999), 'Impact of China's WTO entry on world labour intensive export market – a recursive dynamic CGE analysis', *World Economy*, **22**, 379–405.

Wang, Z. and F. Tuan (1996), 'The impact of China and Taiwan's WTO membership on world trade: a computable general equilibrium analysis', *American Journal of Chinese Studies*, **3**, 177–204.

Weber, M. (1904), *The Protestant Ethic and the Spirit of Capitalism*, translated by T. Parsons, 1930, London: Allen and Unwin.

Willenbockel, D. (1999), 'On apparent problems with the use of the Armington Aggregator in computable general equilibrium models', *Applied Economics Letters*, **6**(9), 589–91.

Wolfensohn, James D. (1996), 'Emerging Trends in East Asia: New Directions in the World Bank's Partnership', Paper delivered at a meeting organized by the Institute of Policy Studies, Singapore, 10 May.

Wong Fot-chyi and Gan Wee-beng (1994), 'Total factor productivity growth in the Singapore manufacturing industries during the 1980s', *Journal of Asian Economics*, **5**(2), 180–81.

Wong, J. (1979), *ASEAN Economies in Perspective*, Singapore: The Macmillan Press, Chapter 4.

Wong, C.M. (1987), 'ASEAN Cooperation in Tourism: Looking Back and Looking Forward', in S. Noordin et al. (eds), *ASEAN at the Crossroads*, Malaysia: Institute of Strategic and International Studies, pp. 372–93.

World Bank (1992), *Vietnam Restructuring Public Finance and Public Enterprises: An Economic Report*, 15 April, Country Operations Division, Country Department I, East Asia and Pacific Region.

World Bank (1993a), *Historically Planned Economies: A Guide to the Data*, Washington, DC.

World Bank (1993b), *The East Asian Miracle: Economic Growth and Public Policy*, New York: Oxford University Press, Chapter 1.

World Bank (1994), *Vietnam Public Sector Management and Private Sector Incentives: An Economic Report*, 26 September, Country Operations Division, Country Department I, East Asia Pacific Region.

World Bank (1997), *Private Capital Flows to Developing Countries: The Road to Financial Integration*, New York: Oxford University Press.

World Resources Institute (1990), *World Resources 1990–91*, New York: Basic Books.

Yang, Y. (1996), 'China's WTO membership: what's at stake?', *World Economy*, **19**, 681–2.

Yang, Y. (1999), 'Completing the WTO accession negotiations: issues and challenges', *World Economy*, **22**, 513–34.

Yeung, Wai-chung (1997), 'The Globalisation of Ethnic Chinese Business Firms From Southeast Asia: Strategies, Processes and Competitive Advantage', Paper presented at the Chinese Business in Southeast Asia Conference, Kuala Lumpur, 23–25 June.

Yoshihara, K. (1988), *The Rise of Ersatz Capitalism in Southeast Asia*, New York: Oxford University Press, pp. 1–131.

Young, Alwyn (1992), 'A Tale of Two Cities: Factor Accumulation and Technical Change in Hong Kong and Singapore', in NBER *Macroeconomics Annual 1992*, no. 7, Stanley Fischer and Olivier Blanchard, Cambridge: MIT Press.

Young, Alwyn (1994a), 'The Tyranny of Numbers: Confronting the Statistical Realities of the East Asian Growth Experience', National Bureau of Economic Research Working Paper No. 4680, March.

Young, Alwyn (1994b), 'Lessons from the East Asian NICs: a contrarian view', *European Economic Review*, **38**.

Yun-Peng Chu and Hal Hill (eds) (2001), *The Social Impact of the Asian Financial Crisis*, Cheltenham, UK: Edward Elgar.

Zhang, Xiaoguang and Peter G. Warr (1995), 'China's Re-entry to GATT: A General Equilibrium Analysis of Tariff Reduction', China and East Asia Trade Policy, Pacific Economic Papers No.250, Australia–Japan Research Centre, Canberra.

MAGAZINES AND NEWSPAPERS

Asiaweek, 12 January 1996, 'Future in Review', pp. 46–7.
Asiaweek, 19 January 1996, 'Vital Signs', p. 60.
Asiaweek, 12 July 1996, 'Bottom Line', p. 53.
Asiaweek, 4 October 1996, 'No Pain, No Gain', pp. 25–7.
Asiaweek, 24 January 1997, 'Class Struggle', pp. 22–3.
The Business Times Shipping Times, 6 January 1997, 'Manila Sets Up 6 Direct Shipping Routes in EAGA', p. 1.
Business Times, 28 Dec 1997, 'ASEAN and China as Destinations for Foreign Direct Investment', p. 1.
Dow Jones International News, 2 January 1999, 'Vietnam Prime Minister: 1999 is Pivotal Year for Nation'.
The Economist, 11–17 February 1995, 'Asia at your Service', pp. 59–60.
The Economist, 14–20 November 1998, 'Hands to the Plough', pp. 29–30.
The Economist, 20–26 November 1999, 'China Opens Up'.
The Economist, 8–14 January 2000, 'Goodnight, Vietnam', p. 62.
The Economist, 9–15 June 2001, 'Dr. Mahathir's One-Man Show', p. 81.
Far Eastern Economic Review, **153**(38), September 1991, 'Focus: Environment in Asia 1991', pp. 37–57.
Far Eastern Economic Review, 16 June 1994, 'Rewards of Liberalization', pp. 48–50.
Myan View, 'Will Myanmar benefit from joining ASEAN', July 1997, pp. 1–3.
The Straits Times, 20 October 1990, 'Razaleigh Hits Out at Federal Gov't Over GT Plan', p. 23.
The Straits Times, 27 August 1992, 'ASEAN Will Remain Attractive Despite NAFTA, Says Nomura', p. 36.
The Straits Times, 1 October 1992, 'Republic's Trade Likely to Face Threat From Mexico, Says UOB', p. 44.
The Straits Times, 4 November 1992, 'Regional Trade Groupings: Building or Stumbling Blocks'.
The Straits Times, 9 December 1993, 'ASEAN Adopts Index to Monitor Air Pollution', p. 22.
The Straits Times, 11 December 1993, 'Ethnic Chinese Conglomerates Own 30 Per Cent of Indonesian Economy', p. 12.
The Straits Times, 12 December 1993, 'GATT Fever', pp. 7–8.

The Straits Times, 9 August 1994, 'Crucial 12 Months for ASEAN as it Embarks on New Phase of Diplomacy', p. 23.

The Straits Times, 4 September 1994, 'Open Regionalism: Framework for Asia-Pacific Economic Ties', p. 34.

The Straits Times, 23 October 1994, 'ASEAN Agreement on Environment Protection', p. 22.

The Straits Times, 7 March 1995, 'ADB Takes Steps to Preserve Region's Forests', p. 15.

The Straits Times, 25 March 1995, 'PM: Singapore Must Nurture New Breed of MNCs', p. 1.

The Straits Times, 4 August 1995, 'Growth Triangle Boosts Investments in Johor to S$8.5b', p. 21.

The Straits Times, 9 September 1995, 'ASEAN Ministers Give Pledge On Services' (Tan Kim Song), p. 1.

The Straits Times, 23 September 1995, 'Europe, Asia Can Become True Partners', p. 1

The Straits Times, 5 March 1996, 'Jakarta Announces Package Aimed at Boosting Exports'.

The Straits Times, 1 August 1996, 'The $850m Traffic Snarls', p. 10.

The Straits Times, 16 August 1996, 'TDB Office in KL will Provide New Push for Economic Ties', p. 46.

The Straits Times, 31 August 1996, 'Could Asian Economies Go the Way of Mexico?', p. 37.

The Straits Times, 12 September 1996, 'Philippine Economy Moving Towards Path of Sustainable Growth', p. 41.

The Straits Times, 5 October 1996, 'Vietnam Mulls Over Changes to Tax, Foreign Investment Laws', p. 45.

The Straits Times, 9 October 1996, 'New Balance in World Order with Maturing of East Asian Economies', p. 38.

The Straits Times, 7 January 1997, 'Indonesia Considers Tax Breaks for Strategic Industries', p. 38.

The Straits Times, 24 January 1997, 'Singapore is KL's Top Foreign Investor', p. 80.

The Straits Times, 18 March 1997, 'Karimun Launch Reaffirms Pledge to Work for Mutual Benefits', p. 20.

The Straits Times, 30 June 1998, 'Gov't Acts to Boost Economy. Dr. Hu's Announcement on Off-budget Measure,' pp. 28–9.

The Straits Times, 12 June 1999, 'Cambodians Turned to Begging in Thailand', p. 38.

The Straits Times, 19 January 2000, 'Indonesia Projects 4% Growth this year', p. 63.

The Straits Times, 19 January 2000, 'Unemployment may Hit 40 Million', p. 34.

The Straits Times, 21 February 2000, 'China and EU Start Talks on WTO Deal', p. 28.

The Straits Times, 25 March 2000, 'Region Agrees to Set Up Asian Support Fund', p. 49.

The Straits Times, 24 June 2000, 'Little Cheer as Thailand Graduates from IMF Scheme', p. 74.

The Straits Times, 13 February 2001, 'Estrada Left a $29b Debt Headache for Filipinos', p. A5.

The Straits Times, 16 February 2001, 'Firm to Buy Thai Banks' Bad Debts', p. S10.

The Straits Times, 2 August 2001, 'Asia's Next Crisis: Made in China,' Kenichi Ohmae, p. 14.

The Straits Times, 11 August 2001, 'Taiwan's Investments in China Hit $177b Mark,' p. S12.

The Straits Times, 13 August 2001, 'Revamp of Taiwan–China Economic Ties,' p. 4.

The Sunday Times, 23 August 1992, 'The Role of State-owned Enterprises', p. 6.

The Sunday Times, 17 September 1995, 'Spreading the Gains of Growth'.

The Sunday Times, 24 September 1995, 'The Role of Government in the East Asian Miracle', pp. 4–5.

The Sunday Times, 31 March 1996, 'How Fair Are the Country's Trade Practices: An Interview with Trade and Industry Minister Ariwibowo', p. 4.

The Sunday Times, 5 January 1997, 'Philippine Economy Likely to Continue Surge', p. 15.

The Sunday Times, 25 February 2001, 'Batam Remains Attractive for Foreign Investments', p. 18.

Time, 17 January 1994, 'Growing by Leaps-Triangle', pp. 26–8.

Tribune Business News, 18 March 1999, 'Rocked by Asian Crisis,Vietnam Facing Economic Meltdown'.

STATISTICAL SOURCES

AFTA Reader, Jakarta: ASEAN Secretariat (various issues).

ASEAN Agricultural Development Planning Centre (1991), *ASEAN Statistical Yearbook on Food, Agriculture and Forestry: 1980–1990*, Bangkok, Thailand.

Asian Development Bank (ADB) (1995 and 1996), *Key Indicators of Developing and Pacific Countries*.

Asian Development Bank, *Asian Development Outlook* (various issues).

Brunei Ministry of Finance (1993), *Brunei Darussalam Statistical Yearbook*.

Brunei Statistics Division, *Brunei Darussalam Key Indicators* (various issues).

China and the World Trade Organization, Web page address, http://www.geocities.com./SoHo/Lofts?6168/wto_china.html

China Customs Statistics Yearbook (various issues), Hong Kong: Economic Information and Agency.

ICEF-MIF Merger Congress, *World Industry Trends*, 22 November 1995, Washington DC, USA.

International Monetary Fund, *Direction of Trade Yearbook* (various issues).

International Monetary Fund, *Direction of Trade Statistics* (various issues).

International Monetary Fund, *International Financial Statistics* (various issues).

Malaysian Ministry of International Trade and Industry, *International Trade and Industry Report* (1994).

National Development Planning Agency (2001), *Strategic Plan for Poverty Alleviation: 2001–2005* (unpublished).

National Statistics Office of Thailand (1998), *Labour Force Survey: October 1998*. Bangkok.

Singapore Department of Statistics, *Economic Survey of Singapore* (various issues).

United Nations Conference on Trade and Development, *Handbook of International Trade and Development Statistics* (various issues).

United Nations Conference on Trade and Development (1999), *World Commodity Survey 1999–2000. Market Trends and the World Economic Environment.*

United Nations Conference on Trade and Development, *World Investment Report* (various issues).

Vietnam Jewel of Asia (1993).

Vietnam's General Statistical Office, *Statistical Yearbook* (various issues).

World Bank, *World Development Report* (various issues).

World Bank (2000), *Country Brief*, September.

World Economic Forum, *The World Competitiveness Report* (1992, 1994 and 1995).

World Trade Organization, *Regionalism and the World Trading System* (1995).

Index